The
Gallup
Poll

Public Opinion 1980

GEORGE H. GALLUP, founder and chairman of
The Gallup Poll, received a Ph.D. in psychology from
the University of Iowa in 1928. From his undergraduate
days he has had three prime interests: survey research,
public opinion, and politics.
Dr. Gallup is the author of many articles on public
opinion and advertising research and he has published
the following books: *The Pulse of Democracy* (1940);
A Guide Book to Public Opinion Polls (1944); *The Gallup
Political Almanac* (1952); *Secrets of Long Life* (1960);
The Miracle Ahead (1964); *The Sophisticated Poll
Watcher's Guide* (Rev. 1976); *The Gallup Poll,
1935–1971* (1972); *The Gallup Poll: Public Opinion, 1972–1977* (1978);
1978 (1979); *1979* (1980); and *1980* (1981).

Other Gallup Poll Publications Available from Scholarly Resources

The Gallup Poll: Public Opinion, 1979
ISBN 0-8420-2170-1 (1980)

The Gallup Poll: Public Opinion, 1978
ISBN 0-8420-2159-0 (1979)

The Gallup Poll: Public Opinion, 1972–1977
2 volumes ISBN 0-8420-2129-9 (1978)

The International Gallup Polls: Public Opinion, 1979
ISBN 0-8420-2180-9 (1981)

The International Gallup Polls: Public Opinion, 1978
ISBN 0-8420-2162-0 (1980)

The
Gallup
Poll

Public Opinion 1980

Dr. George H. Gallup
Founder and Chairman

SR Scholarly Resources Inc.
Wilmington, Delaware

ACKNOWLEDGMENTS

The preparation of this volume has involved the entire staff of the Gallup Poll and their contributions are gratefully acknowledged. I particularly wish to thank James Shriver, III, managing editor of the Gallup Poll, and Professor Fred L. Israel of the City College of New York, who has been the principal coordinator of this volume and of the seven volumes that preceded it.

G. H. G.

Scholarly Resources Inc.
104 Greenhill Avenue
Wilmington, DE 19805

Library of Congress Catalog Card Number: 79-56557
International Standard Serial Number: 0195–962X
International Standard Book Number: 0-8420-2181-7

CONTENTS

FOREWORD

The 1980 presidential election dominated the nation's attention and occupied most of the Gallup Poll's efforts throughout the year. Although the Gallup Poll has been involved in every presidential and off-year congressional election since 1936, the 1980 election was different in many respects.

Probably most unique was the fact that neither major-party candidate possessed much personal appeal for the voters. In no election since 1952, when the Gallup Poll first used the Stapel Scalometer to measure personal popularity, have both candidates scored in the lower levels of this attitude scale.

This lack of personal appeal of the leading candidates, perhaps more than anything else, induced John Anderson to enter the presidential race. Anderson is the only third-party candidate in the history of the Gallup Poll who had no ready-made constituency and no strong political ideology. His main appeal to voters, therefore, had to be the inadequacies of the two major-party candidates. He suffered the fate of most third-party or independent candidates, receiving only 7% of the popular vote.

The difficulty experienced by the electorate in trying to decide which major-party candidate would make the better president was evidenced in the volatility of the candidates' polling strength during the campaign. In April, President Carter led Ronald Reagan by 8 percentage points in a head-to-head Gallup Poll contest. Following the GOP convention in July, however, Reagan gained the lead by a wide 16 percentage-point margin. After the Democratic convention in August the two men were exactly even.

Ten days before election day the Gallup Poll results showed Carter in the lead by 3 points, but this was before the presidential debate between Carter and Reagan. The debate turned out to be disastrous to President Carter. Virtually all polls and telephone call-ins showed that television viewers were of the opinion that Reagan had won the debate.

The final blow to President Carter's chances was dealt by a new twist in the Iranian crisis two days before the election. Hopes for the release of the hostages before election day were dashed as White House efforts proved unavailing.

In its final election report the Gallup Poll reported Governor Reagan in the lead by a margin of 47% to 44% for Carter. Anderson won 8% of the votes in the final survey, while other candidates won 1%. In comparison, the official election figures showed Reagan winning 50.8% of the popular vote, Carter 41.0%, Anderson 6.6%, and others 1.6%.

The Gallup Poll underestimated the full voter strength of Reagan, as did other national surveys. The poll's margin of error over the last three decades has been 1.6 percentage points. In this election it was 3.8. And the obvious lesson is that a polling organization must be prepared to conduct a nationwide poll on the Monday before election day, particularly when domestic or foreign events are changing election choices.

During the course of the election significant facts about the American electorate were brought to light by the Gallup Poll:

One finding is that a remedy for the low participation in presidential elections has yet to be discovered. It is frequently pointed out that in no major democracy in the world do so few voters cast their ballots. Our preelection surveys on voter registration and voting intention led to the conclusion that turnout on November 4 would be no higher than it was in the 1976 election, when only 54% of the eligible voting population bothered to go to the polls. As it turned out this estimate was on the optimistic side. Only 52.3% actually voted in the presidential race, the lowest since 1948.

In winning the election and a majority of seats in the U.S. Senate, the Republican party showed greater signs of grass-roots strength than it had in any election since Dwight Eisenhower won in 1952.

In only two of the last fifty years has the Republican party won the presidency and both houses of Congress. In the election of 1980 the GOP failed to carry the House of Representatives, but the party did show greater strength in both the executive and legislative branches of government than in any previous election since 1952.

In the 1980 campaign voters voiced more criticism of the electoral process than in any previous election in Gallup Poll history. This criticism is aimed at the way the nation selects and elects its presidents. A majority of the public would eliminate the electoral college and change the present primary system, voting in favor of a nationwide primary to be held on a single day. The majority also would shorten campaigns; and, perhaps most important, the public favors government funding of presidential campaigns, thereby lessening the power of pressure groups. Although the majority rejects the proposal to limit the presidency to one six-year term, this proposal is developing increasing support.

Apart from politics the dominant foreign issue of the year was the Iranian hostage crisis. At no time did a majority of the public demand that we rescue the captives with our military forces, and the abortive attempt to do so did not redound to Carter's credit.

The dominant domestic issue was inflation. Perhaps no other single issue played a more important part in the defeat of President Carter for reelection.

George H. Gallup

Princeton, NJ
April 1981

PREFACE

[This introductory essay by Dr. George Gallup is excerpted from a section entitled "How Polls Operate" from his book *The Sophisticated Poll Watcher's Guide.*]

THE CROSS-SECTION

The most puzzling aspect of modern polls to the layman is the cross-section or sample. How, for example, is it possible to interview 1,000 or 2,000 persons out of a present electorate of about 150 million and be sure that the relatively few selected will reflect accurately the attitudes, interests, and behavior of the entire population of voting age?

Unless the poll watcher understands the nature of sampling and the steps that must be taken to assure its representativeness, the whole operation of scientific polling is likely to have little meaning, and even less significance, to him.

With the goal in mind of making the process understandable, and at the risk of being too elementary, I have decided to start with some simple facts about the nature of sampling—a procedure, I might add, that is as old as man himself.

When a housewife wants to test the quality of the soup she is making, she tastes only a teaspoonful or two. She knows that if the soup is thoroughly stirred, one teaspoonful is enough to tell her whether she has the right mixture of ingredients.

In somewhat the same manner, a bacteriologist tests the quality of water in a reservoir by taking a few samples, maybe not more than a few drops from a half-dozen different points. He knows that pollutants of a chemical or bacteriological nature will disperse widely and evenly throughout a body of water. He can be certain that his tiny sample will accurately reflect the presence of harmful bacteria or other pollutants in the whole body of water.

Perhaps a more dramatic example is to be found in the blood tests given routinely in clinics and hospitals. The medical technician requires only a few drops of blood to discover abnormal conditions. He does not have to draw a quart of blood to be sure that his sample is representative.

These examples, of course, deal with the physical world. People are not as much alike as drops of water, or of blood. If they were, then the world of individuals could be sampled by selecting only a half-dozen persons anywhere. People are widely different because their experiences are widely different.

Interestingly, this in itself comes about largely through a sampling process. Every human being gathers his views about people and about life by his own sampling. And, it should be added, he almost invariably ends with a distorted picture because his experience is unique. For example, he draws conclusions about "California" by looking out of his car or airplane window, by observing the people he meets at the airport or on the streets, and by his treatment in restaurants, hotels, and other places. This individual has no hesitancy in telling his friends back home what California is really like—although his views, obviously, are based upon very limited sampling.

The Black man, living his life in the ghetto, working under conditions that are often unpleasant and for wages that are likely to be less than those of the white man who lives in the suburban community, arrives at his own views about racial equality. His sample, likewise, is unrepresentative even though it may be typical of fellow Blacks living under the same conditions. By the same token, well-to-do whites living in the suburbs with the advantages of a college education and travel have equally distorted views of equality. These distortions come about because their sampling, likewise, is based upon atypical experiences.

Although every individual on the face of the earth is completely unique, in the mass he does conform to certain patterns of behavior. No one has expressed this better than A. Conan Doyle, author of the Sherlock Holmes series. He has one of his characters make this observation:

> While the individual man is an insoluble puzzle, in the aggregate he becomes a mathematical certainty. You can never foretell what any one man will do, but you can say with precision what an average number will be up to. Individuals vary, but averages remain constant.

Whenever the range of differences is great—either in nature or man—the sampling process must be conducted with great care to make certain that all major variations or departures from the norm are embraced.

Since some differences that exist may be unknown to the researcher, his best procedure to be sure of representativeness is to select samples from the population by a chance or random process. Only if he follows this procedure can he be reasonably certain that he has covered all major variations that exist.

This principle can be illustrated in the following manner. Suppose that a government agency, such as the Bureau of the Census, maintained an up-to-date alphabetical list of the names of all persons living in the United States eighteen years of age and older. Such a file, at the present time, would include approximately 148 million names.

Now suppose that a survey organization wished to draw a representative sample of this entire group, a sample, say of 10,000 persons. Such a representative sample could be selected by dividing 150,000,000 by 10,000—which produces a figure of 15,000. If the researcher goes systematically through the entire file and records the name of every 15,000th listed, he can be sure that his sample is representative.

The researcher will find that this chance selection, in the manner described, has produced almost the right percentage of Catholics and Protestants, the proper proportion of persons in each age and educational level. The distribution of persons by occupation, sex, race, and income should be broadly representative and consistent with the best available census data. It is important, however, to emphasize the words "broadly representative." The sample—even of 10,000—most likely would not include a single person belonging to the Fox Indian tribe or a single resident of Magnolia, Arkansas. It might not include a single citizen of Afghanistan heritage or a single Zoroastrian.

For the purposes served by polls, a sample normally needs to be only broadly representative. A study could be designed to discover the attitudes of American Indians, in which case the Fox Indians should be properly represented. And a specially designed study of Arkansas would likely embrace interviews with residents of Magnolia.

But for all practical purposes, individuals making up these groups constitute such a small part of the whole population of the United States that their inclusion, or exclusion, makes virtually no difference in reaching conclusions about the total population or even of important segments of the population.

Unfortunately, there is no master file in the United States of persons over the age of eighteen that is available to the researcher. Moreover, even a few weeks after the decennial census such a file would be out of date. Some citizens would have died, some would have moved, and still others would have reached the age of eighteen.

Unlike some European countries, no attempt is made in the United States to keep voter registration lists complete and up to date. Because of this failure to maintain accurate lists of citizens and of registered voters, survey organizations are forced to devise their own systems to select samples that are representative of the population to be surveyed.

Any number of sampling systems can be invented so long as one all-important goal is kept in mind. Whatever the system, the end result of its use must be to give every individual an equal opportunity of being selected. Actually, not every individual will have an equal chance, since some persons will be hospitalized, some in mental or penal institutions, and some in the armed forces in foreign lands. But while these individuals help make up the total United States citizenry, most are disenfranchised by the voting laws of the various states or find difficulty in implementing their opinions at election time. Typically, therefore, they are not included in survey cross-sections.

The Gallup Poll has designed its sample by choosing at random not individuals as described previously, but small districts such as census tracts, census enumeration districts, and townships. A random selection of these small geographical areas provides a good starting point for building a national sample.

The United States population is first arranged by states in geographical order and then within the individual states by districts, also in geographical order. A sampling interval number is determined by dividing the total population of the nation by the number of interviewing locations deemed adequate for a general purpose sample of the population eighteen years of age and older. In the case of the Gallup Poll sample, the number of locations, so selected, is approximately 300.

At the time of this writing, the population of the United States eighteen years and older is approximately 150,000,000. Dividing 150,000,000 by 300 yields a sampling interval of 500,000. A random starting number is then chosen between 1 and 500,000 in order to select the first location. The remaining 299 locations are determined by the simple process of adding 500,000 successively until all 300 locations are chosen throughout the nation.

A geographical sampling unit having been designated, the process of selection is continued by choosing at random a given number of individuals within each unit. Suppose that the sampling unit is a census tract in Scranton, Pennsylvania. Using block statistics, published by the Census Bureau for cities of this size, a block, or a group of blocks, within the tract is chosen by a random method analogous to the procedure used to select the location.

Within a block or groups of blocks so selected, the interviewer is given a random starting point. Proceeding from this point, the interviewer meets his assignment by taking every successive occupied dwelling. Or, as an alternative procedure, he can be instructed to take every third or every fifth or every tenth dwelling unit and to conduct interviews in these designated homes.

In this systematic selection plan, the choice of the dwelling is taken out of the hands of the interviewer. As a reminder to the reader, it should be pointed out that the area or district has been selected by a random procedure; next, the dwelling within the district has been chosen at random. All that now remains is to select, at random, the individual to be interviewed within the household.

This can be done in several ways. A list can be compiled by the interviewer of all persons of voting age residing within each home. From such a household list, he can then select individuals to be interviewed by a random method. Ingenious methods are employed to accomplish this end. One survey organization in Europe, for example, instructs the interviewer to talk to the person in the household whose birthday falls on the nearest date.

Now the process is complete. The district has been selected at random; the dwelling unit within the district has been selected at random; and the individual within the dwelling unit has been selected at random. The end result is that every individual in the nation of voting age has had an equal chance of being selected.

This is the theory. In actual practice, problems arise, particularly in respect to the last stage of the process. The dwelling unit chosen may be vacant, the individual selected within a household may not be at home when the interviewer calls. Of course, the interviewer can return the next day; in fact, he or she can make a half-dozen call backs without finding the person. Each call back adds that much to the cost of the survey and adds, likewise, to the time required to complete the study.

Even with a dozen call backs, some individuals are never found and are never interviewed. They may be in the hospital, visiting relatives, on vacation, on a business trip, not at home except at very late hours, too old or too ill to be interviewed—and a few may even refuse to be interviewed.

Since no nationwide survey has ever reached every person designated by any random selection procedure, special measures must be employed to deal with this situation. In the early 1950s, the Gallup Poll introduced a system called Time-Place interviewing. After an intensive study of the time of day when different members of a household are at home, an interviewing plan was devised that enabled interviewers to reach the highest proportion of persons at the time of their first call.

Since most persons are employed outside the home, interviewing normally must be done in the late afternoon and evening hours, and on weekends. These are the times when men, and especially younger men, are likely to be at home and therefore available to be interviewed.

In various nations, survey organizations are working out new ways to meet this problem of the individual selected for the sample who is not at home. These new procedures may meet more perfectly the ideal requirements of random sampling.

Many ardent advocates of the procedure described as "quota sampling" are still to be found. This, it should be pointed out, was the system generally employed by the leading survey organizations in the pre-1948 era.

The quota system is simplicity itself. If the state of New York has 10% of the total population of the United States, then 10% of all interviews must come from this state. In the case of a national sample of 10,000, this would mean 1,000 interviews.

Going one step further, since New York City contains roughly 40% of the population of the state, then 40% of the 1,000 interviews must be allocated to New York City, or 400. And since Brooklyn has roughly a third of the total population of New York City, a third of the 400 interviews, or 133, must be made in this borough. In similar fashion, all of the 1,000 interviews made in the state of New York can be distributed among the various cities, towns, and rural areas. Other states are dealt with in similar fashion.

Making still further use of census data, the interviews to be made in each city, town, or rural areas can be assigned on an occupational basis: so many white-collar workers, so many blue-collar workers, so many farmers, so many business and professional people, so many retired persons, and so many on the welfare rolls. The allocation can also be made on the basis of rents paid. The interviewer, for example, may be given a "quota" of calls to be made in residential areas with the highest rental values, in areas with medium priced rentals, and in low rental areas.

Typically, in the quota sampling system, the survey organization predetermines the number of men and women and the age, the income, the occupation, and the race of the individuals assigned to each interviewer.

In setting such quotas, however, important factors may be overlooked. In 1960, for example, a quota sample that failed to assign the right proportion of Catholic voters would have miscalculated John Kennedy's political strength. An individual's religious beliefs, obviously, cannot be ascertained by his appearance or by the place where he dwells; this applies to other factors as well.

Not only do theoretical considerations fault the quota system but so do the problems that face the interviewer. When the selection of individuals is left to him, he tends to seek out the easiest-to-interview respondents. He is prone to avoid the worst slum areas, and consequently he turns up with interviews that are likely to be skewed on the high income and educational side. Typically, a quick look at the results of quota sampling will reveal too many persons with a college education, too many persons with average and above average incomes, and in political polls, too many Republicans. Therefore, one of the many advantages of the random procedure is that the selection of respondents is taken out of the hands of the interviewer. In the random method, the interviewer is told exactly where to go and when to go.

Another consideration with cross-sections is keeping them up to date. Although America's population is highly mobile, fortunately for polltakers the basic structure of society changes little. Perhaps the greatest change in America in recent years has been the rising level of education. In 1935, when the Gallup Poll first published poll results, only 7.2% of the adult population had attended college for one year or more. Today that figure is 27%.

How does a research organization know that the sample it has designed meets proper standards? Normally, examination of the socioeconomic data gathered by the interviewer at the end of each interview provides the answer. As the completed interview forms are returned from the field to the Princeton office of the Gallup Poll, the facts from each are punched into IBM cards. In addition to the questions that have dealt with issues and other matters of interest, the interviewer has asked each person to state his occupation, age, how far he went in school, his religious preference, whether he owns or rents his dwelling, and many other questions of a factual nature.

Since the Census Bureau Current Population Surveys provide data on each one of these factors, even a hasty examination will tell whether the cross-section is fairly accurate—that is, whether the important factors line up properly with the known facts, specifically:

—the educational level of those interviewed
—the age level
—the income level
—the proportion of males to females
—the distribution by occupations

—the proportion of whites to nonwhites
—the geographical distribution of cases
—the city-size distribution.

Typically, when the educational level is correct (that is, when the sample has included the right proportion of those who have attended college, high school, grade school, or no school), when the geographical distribution is right and all areas of the nation have been covered in the correct proportion, when the right proportion of those in each income level has been reached, and the right percentages of whites and nonwhites and of men and women are included—then usually other factors tend to fall in line. These include such factors as religious preference, political party preference, and most other factors that bear upon voting behavior, buying behavior, tastes, interests, and the like.

After checking all of the above "controls," it would be unusual to find that every group making up the total population is represented in the sample in the exact percentage that it should be. Some groups may be slightly larger or smaller than they should be. The nonwhite population eighteen years and older, which makes up 11% of the total population, may be found to be less, or more, than this percentage of the returned interviews. Those who have attended high school in the obtained interviews may number 58%, when actually the true figure should be 54%.

Ways have been developed to correct situations such as these that arise out of the over-representation or under-representation of given groups. The sample can be balanced, that is, corrected so that each group is included in the proportion it represents in the total population. When this procedure is followed, the assumption is made that persons within each group who are interviewed are representative of the group in question. But there are obvious limitations to this. If only a few persons are found in a given category, then the danger is always present that they may not be typical or representative of the people who make up this particular group or cell.

On the whole, experience has shown that this process of weighting by the computer actually does produce more accurate samples. Normally, results are changed by only negligible amounts—seldom by more than 1 or 2 percentage points.

A persistent misconception about polling procedures is that a new sample must be designed for measuring each major issue. Actually, Gallup Poll cross-sections are always based upon samples of the entire voting age population. Every citizen has a right to voice his opinion on every issue and to have it recorded. For this reason, all surveys of public opinion seek to reach a representative cross-section of the entire population of voting age.

Some people ask if we go back to the same persons with different polls. The answer, in the case of the Gallup Poll, is "no"; the same person is not interviewed again. Some survey research is based upon fixed cross-sections or "panels." The same persons are reinterviewed from time to time to measure shifts in opinion.

There are certain advantages to this system—it is possible to determine to what extent overall changes cloak individual changes. But a practical disadvantage is that the size of the sample remains fixed. Unless the panel is very large, reliable information cannot be produced for smaller subgroups. In the case of the Gallup Poll, the same question can be placed on any number of surveys and the total sample expanded accordingly, since the same persons are not reinterviewed.

Panels have other limitations. One has to do with determining the level of knowledge. Having asked a citizen what he knows about a certain issue in the first interview, he may very well take the trouble to read about it when he sees an article later in his newspaper or magazine. There is, moreover, a widespread feeling among researchers that the repeated interviewing of the same person tends to make him a "pro" and to render him atypical for this reason. But the evidence is not clear-cut on this point. The greatest weakness, perhaps, is that panels tend to fall apart; persons change their place of residence and cannot be found for a second or subsequent measurement; some refuse to participate more than once and must be replaced by substitutes.

THE SIZE OF SAMPLES

When the subject of public-opinion polls comes up, many people are quick to say that they do not know of anyone who has ever been polled.

The likelihood of any single individual, eighteen years of age or older, being polled in a sample of 1,500 persons is about one chance in 90,000. With samples of this size, and with the frequency that surveys are scheduled by the Gallup Poll, the chance that any single individual will be interviewed—even during a period of two decades—is less than one in 200.

An early experience of mine illustrates dramatically the relative unimportance of numbers in achieving accuracy in polls and the vital importance of reaching a true cross-section of the population sampled.

In the decade preceding the 1936 presidential election, the *Literary Digest* conducted straw polls during elections, with a fair measure of success. The *Literary Digest*'s polling procedure consisted of mailing out millions of postcard ballots to persons whose names were found in telephone directories or on lists of automobile owners.

The system worked so long as voters in average and above-average income groups were as likely to vote Democratic as Republican; and conversely, those in the lower income brackets—the have-nots—were as likely to vote for either party's candidate for the presidency.

With the advent of the New Deal, however, the American electorate became sharply stratified, with many persons in the above average income groups who had been Democrats shifting to the Republican banner, and those below average to the Democratic.

Obviously, a polling system that reached telephone subscribers and automobile owners—the perquisites of the better-off in this era—was certain to overestimate Republican strength in the 1936 election. And that is precisely what did happen. The *Literary Digest*'s final preelection poll showed Landon winning by 57% and Franklin D. Roosevelt losing with 43% of the two-party popular vote.

Landon did not win, as everyone knows. In fact, Roosevelt won by a whopping majority—62.5% to Landon's 37.5%. The error, more than 19 percentage points, was one of the greatest in polling history.

The outcome of the election spelled disaster for the *Literary Digest*'s method of polling, and was a boon to the new type of scientific sampling that was introduced for the first time in that presidential election by my organization, Elmo Roper's, and Archibald Crossley's.

The *Literary Digest* had mailed out 10,000,000 postcard ballots—enough to reach approximately one family in every three at that point in history. A total of 2,376,523 persons took the trouble to mark their postcard ballots and return them.

Experiments with new sampling techniques had been undertaken by my organization as early as 1933. By 1935 the evidence was clear-cut that an important change had come about in the party orientation of voters—that the process of polarization had shifted higher income voters to the right, lower income voters to the left.

When the presidential campaign opened in 1936, it was apparent that the *Literary Digest*'s polling method would produce an inaccurate figure. Tests indicated that a large majority of individuals who were telephone subscribers preferred Landon to FDR, while only 18% of those persons on relief rolls favored Landon.

To warn the public of the likely failure of the *Literary Digest,* I prepared a special newspaper article that was widely printed on July 12, 1936—at the beginning of the campaign. The article stated that the *Literary Digest* would be wrong in its predictions and that it would probably show Landon winning with 56% of the popular vote to 44% for Roosevelt. The reasons why the poll would go wrong were spelled out in detail.

Outraged, the *Literary Digest* editor wrote: "Never before has anyone foretold what our poll was going to show even before it started . . . Our fine statistical friend (George Gallup) should be advised that the Digest would carry on with those old fashioned methods that have produced correct forecasts exactly one hundred percent of the time."

When the election had taken place, our early assessment of what the *Literary Digest* poll would find proved to be almost a perfect prediction of the *Digest*'s final results—actually within 1 percentage point. While this may seem to have been a foolhardy stunt, actually there was little risk. A sample of only 3,000 postcard ballots had been mailed by my office to the same lists of persons who received the

Literary Digest ballot. Because of the workings of the laws of probability, that 3,000 sample should have provided virtually the same result as the *Literary Digest*'s 2,376,523 which, in fact, it did.

Through its own polling, based upon modern sampling procedures, the Gallup Poll, in the 1936 election, reported that the only sure states for Landon were Maine, Vermont, and New Hampshire. The final results showed Roosevelt with 56% of the popular vote to 44% for Landon. The error was 6.8 percentage points, the largest ever made by the Gallup Poll. But because it was on the "right" side, the public gave us full credit, actually more than we deserved.

The *Literary Digest* is not the only poll that has found itself to be on the "wrong" side. All polls, at one time or another, find themselves in this awkward position, including the Gallup Poll in the election of 1948. Ironically, the error in 1936—a deviation of 6.8 percentage points from the true figure—was greater than the error in 1948—5.4 percentage points. But the public's reaction was vastly different.

The failure of polls to have the winning candidate ahead in final results is seldom due to the failure of the poll to include enough persons in its sample. Other factors are likely to prove to be far more important, as will be pointed out later.

Examination of probability tables quickly reveals why polling organizations can use relatively small samples. But first the reader should be reminded that sampling human beings can never produce findings that are *absolutely* accurate except by mere chance, or luck. The aim of the researcher is to come as close as possible to absolute accuracy.

Since money and time are always important considerations in survey operations, the goal is to arrive at sample sizes that will produce results within acceptable margins of error. Fortunately, reasonably accurate findings can be obtained with surprisingly small samples.

Again, it is essential to distinguish between theory and practice. Probability tables are based upon mathematical theory. In actual survey work, these tables provide an important guide, but they can't be applied too literally.

With this qualification in mind, the size of samples to be used in national surveys can now be described. Suppose, for example, that a sample comprises only 600 individuals. What is the theoretical margin of error? If the sample is a perfectly drawn random sample, then the chances are 95 in 100 that the results of a poll of 600 in which those interviewed divide 60% in favor, 40% opposed (or the reverse) will be within 4 percentage points of the true figure; that is, the division in the population is somewhere between 56% and 64% in favor. The odds are even that the error will be less than 2 percentage points—between 58% and 62% in favor, 42% to 38% opposed.

What this means, in the example cited above, is that the odds are 19 to 1 that in repeated samplings the figure for the issue would vary in the case of those favoring the issue from 56% to 64%; the percentage of those opposed would vary between 44% and 36% in repeated samples. So, on the basis of a national sample of only 600 cases, one could say that the odds are great that the addition of many cases—

even millions of cases—would not likely change the majority side to the minority side.

Now, if this sample is doubled in size—from 600 to 1,200—the error factor using the 95 in 100 criterion or confidence level is decreased from 4 percentage points to 2.8 percentage points; if it is doubled again—from 1,200 to 2,400—there is a further decrease—from 2.8 to 2.0, always assuming a mathematically random sample.

Even if a poll were to embrace a total of 2,000,000 individuals, there would still be a chance of error, although tiny. Most survey organizations try to operate within an error range of 4 percentage points at the 95 in 100 confidence level. Accuracy greater than this is not demanded on most issues, nor in most elections, except, of course, those that are extremely close.

Obviously, in many fields an error factor as large as 4 percentage points would be completely unacceptable. In fact, in measuring the rate of unemployment, the government and the press place significance on a change as small as 0.1%. At present, unemployment figures are based upon nationwide samples carried out by the U.S. Bureau of Labor Statistics in the same general manner as polls are conducted. The government bases its findings on samples of some 50,000 persons. But samples even of this size are not sufficient to warrant placing confidence in a change as small as 0.1%. And yet such a change is often headlined on the front pages as indicating a real and significant change in the employment status of the nation.

Even if one were totally unfamiliar with the laws of probability, empirical evidence would suffice to demonstrate that the amassing of thousands of cases does not change results except to a minor extent.

An experiment conducted early in the Gallup Poll's history will illustrate this point. At the time—in the middle 1930s—the National Recovery Act (N.R.A.) was a hotly debated issue. Survey results were tabulated as the ballots from all areas of the United States were returned. The figures below are those actually obtained as each lot of new ballots was tabulated.

NUMBER OF RETURNED BALLOTS	PERCENT VOTING IN FAVOR OF THE N.R.A.
First 500	54.9%
First 1,000	53.9
First 5,000	55.4
First 10,000	55.4
First 30,000	55.5

From these results it can be seen that if only 500 ballots had been received, the figure would have differed little from the final result. In fact the greatest difference found in the whole series is only 1.6 percentage points from the final result.

This example represents a typical experience of researchers in this field. But one precaution needs to be observed. The returns must come from a representative sample of the population being surveyed; otherwise they could be as misleading as trying to project the results of a national election from the vote registered late in the afternoon of election day in a New Hampshire village.

The theoretical error, as noted earlier, can be used only as a guide. The expected errors in most surveys are usually somewhat larger. In actual survey practice, some sample design elements tend to reduce the range of error, as stratification does; some tend to increase the range of error as, for example, clustering. But these are technical matters to be dealt with in textbooks on statistics.

Survey organizations should, on the basis of their intimate knowledge of their sampling procedures and the analysis of their data, draw up their own tables of suggested tolerances to enable laymen to interpret their survey findings intelligently.

The normal sampling unit of the Gallup Poll consists of 1,500 individuals of voting age, that is, eighteen years and over. A sample of this size gives reasonable assurance that the margin of error for results representing the entire country will be less than 3 percentage points based on the factor of size alone.

The margin for sampling error is obviously greater for subgroups. For example, the views of individuals who have attended college are frequently reported. Since about one-fourth of all persons over eighteen years have attended college, the margin of error must be computed on the basis of one-fourth the total sample of 1,500, or 375. Instead of a margin of error of 3 percentage points, the error factor increases to 6 or 7 percentage points in the typical cluster sample.

In dealing with some issues, interest focuses on the views of subgroups such as Blacks, labor union members, Catholics, or young voters—all representing rather small segments of the total population. Significant findings for these subgroups are possible only by building up the size of the total sample.

This can be done in the case of the Gallup Poll by including the same question or questions in successive surveys. Since different, but comparable, persons are interviewed in each study, subgroup samples can be enlarged accordingly. Thus, in a single survey approximately 165 Blacks and other nonwhites would be interviewed in a sample of 1,500, since they constitute 11% of the total voting-age population. On three successive surveys a total of 495 would be reached—enough to provide a reasonably stable base to indicate their views on important political and social issues.

Since much interest before and after elections is directed toward the way different groups in the population vote, it has been the practice of the Gallup Poll to increase the size of its samples during the final month before election day to be in a position to report the political preferences of the many groups that make up the total population—information that cannot be obtained by analyzing the actual election returns. Election results, for example, do not reveal how women voted as opposed to men, how the different age groups voted, how different religious groups voted, how different income levels voted. Many other facts about the public's voting habits can be obtained only through the survey method.

During the heat of election campaigns, critics have asserted on occasion that the Gallup Poll increases its sample size solely to make more certain of being "right." Examination of trend figures effectively answers this criticism. The results reported on the basis of the standard sampling unit have not varied, on the average, more than 1 or 2 percentage points from the first enlarged sample in all of the national elections of the last two decades, and this, of course, is within the margin of error expected.

Persons unfamiliar with the laws of probability invariably assume that the size of the sample must bear a fixed relationship to the size of the "universe" sampled. For example, such individuals are likely to assume that if a polling organization is sampling opinions of the whole United States, a far larger sample is necessary than if the same kind of survey is to be conducted in a single state, or in a single city. Or, to put this in another way, the assumption is that since the population of the United States is roughly ten times that of New York State, then the sample of the United States should be ten times as large.

The laws of probability, however, do not work in this fashion. Whenever the population to be surveyed is many times the size of the sample (which it typically is), the size of samples must be almost the same. If one were conducting a poll in Baton Rouge, Louisiana, on a mayoralty race, the size of the sample should be virtually the same as for the whole United States. The same principle applies to a state.

Two examples, drawn from everyday life, may help to explain this rather mystifying fact. Suppose that a hotel cook has two kinds of soup on the stove—one in a very large pot, another in a small pot. After thoroughly stirring the soup in both pots, the cook need not take a greater number of spoonsful from the large pot or fewer spoonsful from the small pot to taste the quality of the soup, since the quality should be the same.

The second example, taken from the statistician's world, may shed further light on this phenomenon. Assume that 100,000 black and white balls are placed in a large cask. The white balls number 70,000; the black balls, 30,000. Into another cask, a much smaller one, are placed 1,000 balls, divided in exactly the same proportion: 700 white balls, 300 black balls.

Now the balls in each cask are thoroughly mixed and a person, blindfolded, is asked to draw out of each cask exactly 100 balls. The likelihood of drawing 70 white balls and 30 black balls is virtually the same, despite the fact that one cask contains 100 times as many balls as the other.

If this principle were understood then hours of Senate floor time could have been saved in recent years. Senator Albert Gore, of Tennessee, a few years ago, had this to say about the Gallup Poll's sampling unit of 1,500—as reported in the *Congressional Record*:

As a layman I would question that a straw poll of less than 1 per cent of the people could under any reasonable circumstance be regarded as a fair and meaningful cross-section. This would be something more than 500 times as large a sample as Dr. Gallup takes.

In the same discussion on the Senate floor, Senator Russell Long of Lousiana added these remarks:

I believe one reason why the poll information could not be an accurate reflection of what the people are thinking is depicted in this example. Suppose we should try to find how many persons should be polled in a city the size of New Orleans in order to determine how an election should go. In a city that size, about 600,000 people, a number of 1,000 would be an appropriate number to sample to see how the election was likely to go. . . . In my home town of Baton Rouge, Lousiana, I might very well sample perhaps 300 or 400 people and come up with a fairly accurate guess as to how the city or the parish would go, especially if a scientific principle were used. But if I were to sample only a single person or two or three in that entire city, the chances are slim that I would come up with an accurate guess.

If the reader has followed the explanation of the workings of the laws of probability, and of earlier statements about the size of samples, he will be aware of two errors in the senator's reasoning. Since both cities, New Orleans and Baton Rouge, have populations many times the size of the sample he suggested, both require samples of the same size. The second is his assumption that any good researcher would possibly attempt to draw conclusions about either city on the basis of "a single person or two."

The size of the "universe" to be sampled is typically very great in the case of most surveys; in fact, it is usually many times the size of the samples to be obtained. A different principle applies when the "universe" is small. The size of a sample needed to assess opinions of the residents of a community of 1,000 voters is obviously different from that required for a city that is much larger. A sample of 1,000 in such a town would not be a sample; it would be a complete canvass.

DEVELOPING POLL QUESTIONS

Nothing is so difficult, nor so important, as the selection and wording of poll questions. In fact, most of my time and effort in the field of polling has been devoted to this problem.

The questions included in a national survey of public opinion should meet many tests: they must deal with the vital issues of the day, they must be worded in a way to get at the heart of these issues, they must be stated in language understandable to the least well educated, and finally, they must be strictly impartial in presenting the issue.

If any reader thinks this is easy, let him try to word questions on any present-day issue. It is a tough and trying mental task. And even years of experience do not make the problem less onerous.

One rule must always be followed. No question, no matter how simple, must reach the interviewing stage without first having gone through a thorough pretesting procedure. Many tests must be applied to see that each question meets required standards.

Every survey organization has its own methods of testing the wording of questions. Here it will suffice to describe in some detail how the Gallup Poll goes about this task.

Pretesting of questions dealing with complicated issues is carried on in the Interviewing Center maintained in Hopewell, New Jersey, by the Gallup organizations. Formerly, this center was a motion-picture theater. In the early 1950s it was converted into an interviewing center. The town of Hopewell is located in the middle of an area with a total population of 500,000—an area that includes the cities of Trenton and Princeton, suburban communities, small towns, and rural districts. Consequently, people from many walks of life are available for interviewing.

Pretesting procedures normally start with "in-depth" interviews with a dozen or more individuals invited to come to the center. The purpose of these interviews is to find out how much thought each participant has given to the issue under consideration, the level of his or her knowledge about the issue, and the important facets that must be probed. Most of the questions asked in these sessions are "open" questions—that is, questions which ask: "What do you know about the XX problem? What do you think about it? What should the government do about it?" and so forth.

In conversations evoked by questions of this type, it is possible, in an unhurried manner, to discover how much knowledge average persons have of a given issue, the range of views regarding it, and the special aspects of the issue that need to be probed if a series of questions is to be developed.

The next step is to try out the questions, devised at this first stage, on a new group of respondents, to see if the questions are understandable and convey the meaning intended. A simple test for this can be employed. After reading the question, the respondent is asked to "play back" what it says to him. The answer quickly reveals whether the person being interviewed understands the language used and whether he grasps the main point of the question. This approach can also reveal, to the trained interviewer, any unsuspected biases in the wording of the question. When the language in which a question is stated is not clear to the interviewee, his typical reaction is: "Will you read that question again?" If questions have to be repeated, this is unmistakable evidence that they should be worded in a simpler and more understandable manner.

Another procedure that has proved valuable in testing questions is the self-administered interview. The respondent, without the benefit of an interviewer, writes out the answers to the questions. The advantages of this procedure are many. Answers show whether the individual has given real thought to the issue and reveal, also, the degree of his interest. If he has no opinion, he will typically leave the question blank. If he has a keen interest in the issue, he will spell out his views in some detail. And if he is misinformed, this becomes apparent in what he writes.

Self-administered questionnaires can be filled out in one's own home, or privately in an interviewing center. Since the interviewer is not at hand, many issues, such as those dealing with sex, drug addiction, alcoholism, and other personal matters, can be covered in this manner. The interviewer's function is merely to drop off the questionnaire, and pick it up in a sealed envelope the next day—or the respondent can mail it directly to the Princeton office.

Even with all of these precautions, faulty question wordings do sometimes find their way onto the survey interviewing form. Checks for internal consistency, made when the ballots are returned and are tabulated, usually bring to light these shortcomings.

Most important, the reader himself must be the final judge. The Gallup Poll, from its establishment in 1935, has followed the practice of including the exact wording of questions, when this is important, in the report of the poll findings. The reader is thus in a position to decide whether the question is worded impartially and whether the interpretation of the results, based upon the question asked, is fair and objective.

A United States senator has brought up another point about questions:

> How do pollsters like yourself determine what questions to ask from time to time? It seems to me that pollsters can affect public opinion simply by asking the question. The results could be pro or anti the president depending upon the questions asked and the president's relation to it.

To be sure, a series of questions could be asked that would prove awkward to the administration, even though worded impartially, and interpreted objectively. But this would be self-defeating because it would soon become apparent to readers and commentators that the survey organization was not engaged solely in fact-finding but was trying to promote a cause.

One way to prevent unintentional biases from creeping into survey operations is to have a staff that is composed of persons representing the different shades of political belief—from right to left. If not only the questions but also the written reports dealing with the results have to run this gamut—as is the practice in the Gallup office—the dangers of unintentional bias are decreased accordingly.

Still one more safeguard in dealing with biases of any type comes about through the financial support of a poll. If sponsors represent all shades of political belief, then economic pressures alone help to keep a poll on the straight and narrow path.

So much for bias in the wording and selection of questions. This still does not answer the question posed by some who wish to know what standards or practices are followed in deciding what issues to present to the public.

Since the chief aim of a modern public opinion poll is to assess public opinion on the important issues of the day and to chart the trend of sentiment, it follows that most subjects chosen for investigation must deal with current national and international issues, and particularly those that have an immediate concern for the typical citizen. Newspapers, magazine, and the broadcast media are all useful sources of ideas for polls. Suggestions for poll subjects come from individuals and institutions—from members of Congress, editors, public officials, and foundations. Every few weeks the public itself is questioned about the most important problems facing the nation, as they see them. Their answers to this question establish priorities, and provide an up-to-date list of areas to explore through polling.

A widely held assumption is that questions can be twisted to get any answer you want. In the words of one publisher: "If you word a question one way you get a result which may differ substantially from the result you get if you word the question in a different way."

It's not that easy. Questions can be worded in a manner to bring confusing and misleading results. But the loaded question is usually self-defeating because it is obvious that it is biased.

Hundreds of experiments with a research procedure known as the split-ballot technique (one-half the cross-section gets Question A, the other half Question B) have proved that even a wide variation in question wordings did not bring substantially different results if the basic meaning or substance of the question remained the same.

Change the basic meaning of the question, add or leave out an essential part, and the results will change accordingly, as they should. Were people insensitive to words—if they were unable to distinguish between one concept and another—then the whole *raison d'être* of polling would vanish.

Often the interpreters of poll findings draw inferences that are not warranted or make assumptions that a close reading of the question does not support. Consider, for example, these two questions:

"Do you feel the United States should have gotten involved in Vietnam in the first place?"

"Do you feel the United States should have helped South Vietnam to defend itself?"

While at first glance these questions seem to deal with the same point— America's involvement—actually they are probing widely different aspects of involvement. In the first case, the respondent can read in that we helped Vietnam "with our own troops"; in the second question, that our help would have been limited to materials. Many polls have shown that the American people are willing to give military supplies to almost any nation in the world that is endangered by the communists, but they are unwilling to send troops.

If the two questions cited above did not bring substantially different results, then all the other poll results dealing with this issue would be misleading.

Questions must be stated in words that everyone understands, and results are likely to be misleading to the extent that the words are not fully understood. Ask people whether they are disturbed about the amount of pornography in their magazines and newspapers and you will get one answer; if you talk about the amount of smut you will get another.

Word specialists may insist that every word in the language conveys a slightly different connotation to every individual. While this may be true, the world (and polls) must operate on the principle that commonly used words convey approximately the same meaning to the vast majority. And this fact can easily be established in the pretesting of questions. When a question is read to a respondent and he is then asked to "play it back" in his own words, it becomes quickly evident whether he has understood the words, and in fact, what they mean to him.

Some questions that pass this test can still be faulty. The sophisticated poll watcher should be on the alert for the "desirable goal" question. This type of question ties together a desirable goal with a proposal for reaching this end. The respondent typically reacts to the goal as well as to the means. Here are some examples of desirable goal questions:

"To win the war quickly in Vietnam, would you favor all-out bombing of North Vietnam?"

"To reduce crime in the cities, would you favor increasing jail and prison sentences?"

"In order to improve the quality of education in the United States, should teachers be paid higher salaries?"

These questions, which present widely accepted goals accompanied by the tacit assumption that the means suggested will bring about the desired end, produce results biased on the favorable side.

The more specific questions are, the better. One of the classic arguments between newspapers and television has centered around a question that asks the public: "Where do you get most of your news about what's going on in the world today—from the newspaper, or radio, or television, or magazines, or talking to people, or where?" The answers show TV ahead of daily newspapers. But when this question is asked in a way to differentiate between international news, and local and state news, TV wins on international news, but the daily newspaper has a big lead on local news. A simple explanation is that the phrase, "What is going on in the *world?*" is interpreted by the average citizen to mean in the faraway places—not his home city.

People are extremely literal minded. A farmer in Ontario, interviewed by the Canadian Gallup Poll, was asked at the close of the interview how long he had lived in the same house; specifically, the length of his residence there. The answer that came back was "Twenty-six feet and six inches."

Whenever it is possible, the questions asked should state both sides of the issue. Realistic alternatives should be offered, or implied.

Looking back through more than four decades of polling, this aspect of question wording warrants the greatest criticism. There is probably little need to state the other side, or offer an alternative, in a question such as this: "Should the voting age be lowered to include those eighteen years of age?" The alternative implied is to leave the situation as it is.

An excellent observation has been made by a political scientist on the faculty of a New England college:

> Somehow more realism must be introduced into polls. . . . People often affirm abstract principles but will not be willing to pay the price of their concrete application. For example, would you be willing to pay more for each box of soap you buy in order to reduce ground pollution—or $200 more for your next car in order to reduce air pollution, etc.?

This type of question is similar to the desirable goal question. The public wants to clear the slums, wants better medical care, improved racial relations, better schools, better housing. The real issue is one of priorities and costs. The role of the public opinion poll in this situation is to shed light on the public's concern about each major problem, establish priorities, and then discover whether the people are willing to foot the bill.

The well-informed person is likely to think of the costs involved by legislation that proposes to deal with these social problems. But to the typical citizen there is no immediate or direct relationship between legislation and the amount he has to pay in taxes. Congress usually tries to disguise costs by failing to tie taxes or costs to large appropriations, leaving John Doe with the impression that someone else will pay the bill.

Still another type of question that is suspect has to do with good intentions. Questions of this type have meaning only when controls are used and when the results are interpreted with a full understanding of their shortcomings.

Examples of questions that fall into this category are those asking people if they "plan to go to church," "read a book," "listen to good music," "vote in the coming election," and so forth.

To the typical American the word "intend" or "plan" connotes many things, such as "Do I think this is a good idea?" "Would I like to do it?" "Would it be good for me?" "Would it be good for other people?" These and similar questions of a prestige nature reveal attitudes, but they are a poor guide to action.

Behavior is always the best guide. The person who attended church last Sunday is likely to go next Sunday, if he says he plans to. The citizen who voted in the last election and whose name is now on the registration books is far more likely to vote than the person who hasn't bothered to vote or to register, even though he insists that he "plans" to do both.

Probably the most difficult of all questions to word is the type that offers the respondent several alternatives. Not only is it hard to find alternatives that are mutually exclusive; it is equally difficult to find a series that covers the entire range of opinions. Added to this is the problem of wording each alternative in a way that doesn't give it a special advantage. And finally, in any series of alternatives that ranges from one extreme of opinion to the other, the typical citizen has a strong inclination to choose one in the middle.

As a working principle it can be stated that the more words included in a question, either by way of explanation or in stating alternatives, the greater the possibilities that the question wording itself will influence answers.

A member of the editorial staff of a newsmagazine voiced a common reaction when he observed:

> On more than a few occasions I have found that I could not, were I asked, answer a poll with a "yes" or "no." More likely my answer would be "yes, but" or "yes, if." I wonder whether pollsters can't or just don't want to measure nuances of feeling.

Obviously it is the desire of a polling organization to produce a full and accurate account of the public's views on any given issue, nuances and all.

First, however, it should be pointed out that there are two main categories of questions serving two different purposes—one to *measure* public opinion, the other to *describe* public opinion. The first category has to do with the "referendum" type of question. Since the early years of polling, heavy emphasis has been placed upon this type of question, which serves in effect as an unofficial national referendum on a given issue, actually providing the same results, within a small margin of error, that an official nationwide referendum would if it were held at the same time and on the same issue.

At some point in the decision process, whether it be concerned with an important issue before Congress, a new law before the state legislature, or a school bond issue in Central City, the time comes for a simple "yes" or "no" vote. Fortunately, or unfortunately, there is no lever on a voting machine that permits the voter to register a "yes, if" or a "yes, but" vote. While discussion can and should proceed at length, the only way to determine majority opinion is by a simple count of noses.

If polling organizations limited themselves to the referendum type of question they would severely restrict their usefulness. They can and should use their machinery to reveal the many facets of public opinion of any issue, and to shed light on the reasons why the people hold the views they do; in short, to explore the "why" behind public opinion.

More and more attention is being paid to this diagnostic approach and the greatest improvements in the field of public opinion research in the future are likely to deal with this aspect of polling.

One of the important developments in question technique was the development in the late 1940s of a new kind of question design that permits the investigation of views on any issue of a complex nature.

This design, developed by the Gallup Poll, has been described as the "quintamensional approach" since it probes five aspects of opinion:

1. the respondent's awareness and general knowledge about it,
2. his overall opinions,
3. the reasons why he holds his views,
4. his specific views on specific aspects of the problem,
5. the intensity with which he hold his opinions.

This question design quickly sorts out those who have no knowledge of a given issue—an important function in successful public opinion polling. And it can even reveal the extent or level of knowledge of the interviewee about the issue.

This is how the system works. The first question put to the person being interviewed (on any problem or issue no matter how complex) is this: "Have you heard or read about the XXX problem (proposal or issue)?"

The person being interviewed can answer either "yes" or "no" to this question, or he can add, "I'm not sure." If he answers in the negative, experience covering many years indicates that he is being entirely truthful. If he answers "yes" or "I'm not sure" he is then asked: "Please tell me in your own words what the debate (or the proposal or issue) is about." At this point the person interviewed must produce evidence that reveals whether he has some knowledge of the problem or issue.

The reader might imagine himself in this interviewing situation. You are called upon by an interviewer and in the course of the interview are asked if you have "heard or read about the Bronson proposal to reorganize the Security Council of the United Nations." The answer is likely to be "no." Possibly you might say: "I seem to have heard about it somewhere." Or suppose that, just to impress the interviewer (something that rarely happens) you fall into the trap of saying "yes."

The next question puts you neatly and delicately on the spot. It asks you to describe in your own words what the Bronson proposal is. You have to admit at this point that you do not know, or come up with an answer that immediately indicates you do not know what it is.

At this stage the questioning can be expanded to discover just how well informed you are. If it is an issue or proposal, then you can be asked to give the main arguments for and the main arguments against the plan or issue. In short, by adding questions at this stage, the *level* of knowledge of the respondent can be determined.

The next question in the design is an "open" question that asks simply: "What do you think should be done about this proposal?" or "How do you think this issue should be resolved?" This type of question permits the person being interviewed to give his views without any specifics being mentioned. Answers, of course, are recorded by the interviewer as nearly as possible in the exact words of the respondent.

The third category of questions seeks to find out the "why" behind the respondent's views. This can be done with a simple question asking: "Why do you feel that way?" or variations of this, along with "nondirective" probes such as "What else?" or "Can you explain that in greater detail?"

The fourth category in the design poses specific issues that can be answered in "yes" or "no" fashion. At this fourth stage it is possible to go back to those who were excluded by the first two questions: those who said they had not heard or read about the issue in question or proved, after the second question, that they were uninformed.

By explaining in neutral language to this group what the problem or issue is and the specific proposals that have been made for dealing with it, the uninformed can voice their opinions, which later can be compared with those of the already informed group.

The fifth category attempts to get at the intensity with which opinions are held. How strongly does each side hold to its views? What action is each individual willing to take to see that his opinion prevails? What chance is there that he may change his mind?

This, then, is the quintamensional approach. And its special merit is that it can quickly sort out the informed from the uninformed. The views of the well informed can be compared not only with the less well informed but with those who are learning about the issue for the first time. Moreover, through cross-tabulations, it is possible to show how special kinds of knowledge are related to certain opinions.

The filtering process may screen out nearly all individuals in the sample because they are uninformed, but it is often of interest and importance to know how the few informed individuals divide on a complex issue. When the best informed individuals favor a proposal or issue, experience indicates that their view tends to be accepted by lower echelons as information and knowledge become more widespread.

But this is not the invariable pattern. In the case of Vietnam, it was the best educated and the best informed who reversed their views as the war went on. The least well educated were always more against the war in Vietnam.

It is now proper to ask why, with all of its obvious merits, this question design is not used more often. The answer is that polling organizations generally avoid technical and complex issues, preferring to deal with those on which the vast majority of Americans have knowledge and opinions. Often the design is shortened to embrace only the filter question that seeks to find out if the individual has read or heard about a given issue, and omits the other questions.

In the field of public opinion research, one finds two schools of thought: one is made up largely of those in academic circles who believe that research on public attitudes should be almost entirely descriptive or diagnostic; the other, made up largely of persons in political life or in journalism or allied fields, who want to know the "score." It is the task of the polling organization to satisfy both groups. And to do this, both categories of questions must be included in the surveys conducted at regular intervals.

The long experience of the Gallup Poll points to the importance of reporting trends of opinion on all the continuing problems, the beliefs, the wishes of the people.

In fact, about four out of every ten questions included in a typical survey are for the purpose of measuring trends. Simple "yes" and "no" questions are far better suited to this purpose than "open-ended" questions, and this accounts chiefly for the high percentage of this type of question in the field of polling.

INTERVIEWERS AND INTERVIEWING PROBLEMS

Since the reliability of poll results depends so much on the integrity of interviewers, polling organizations must go to great lengths to see that interviewers follow instructions conscientiously.

A professor at an Ivy League college sums up the problems that have to do with interviewers in this question: "How do you insure quality control over your interviewers, preventing them from either influencing the answers, mis-recording them, or filling in the forms themselves?"

Before these specific points are dealt with, the reader may wish to know who the interviewers are and how they are selected and trained.

Women make the best interviewers, not only in the United States but in virtually every nation where public opinion survey organizations are established. Generally, they are more conscientious and more likely to follow instructions than men. Perhaps the nature of the work makes interviewing more appealing to them. The fact that the work is part-time is another reason why women prefer it.

Most interviewers are women of middle age, with high-school or college education. Most are married and have children.

Very few interviewers devote full time to this work. In fact, this is not recommended. Interviewing is mentally exhausting and the interviewer who works day after day at this task is likely to lose her zeal, with a consequent drop in the quality of her work.

When an area is drawn for the national cross-section, the interviewing department of the polling organization finds a suitable person to serve as the interviewer in this particular district. All the usual methods of seeking individuals who can meet the requirements are utilized, including such sources as school superintendents, newspaper editors, members of the clergy, and the classified columns of the local press.

Training for this kind of work can be accomplished by means of an instruction manual, by a supervisor, or by training sessions. The best training consists of a kind of trial-by-fire process. The interviewer is given test interviews to do after she has completed her study of the instruction manual. The trial interviews prove whether she can do the work in a satisfactory manner; more important, making these interviews enables the interviewer to discover if she really likes this kind of work. Her interviews are carefully inspected and investigated. Telephone conversations often straighten out procedures and clear up any misunderstandings about them.

Special questions added to the interviewing form and internal checks on consistency can be used to detect dishonesty. Also, a regular program of contacting persons who have been interviewed—to see if they in fact have been interviewed—is commonly employed by the best survey organizations.

It would be foolhardy to insist that every case of dishonesty can be detected in this manner, but awareness of the existence of these many ways of checking honesty removes most if not all of the temptation for the interviewers to fill in the answers themselves.

Experience of many years indicates that the temptation to "fudge" answers is related to the size of the work load given to the interviewer. If too many interviews are required in too short a time, the interviewer may hurry through the assignment, being less careful than she otherwise would be and, on occasion, not above the temptation to fill in a last few details.

To lessen this pressure, the assignment of interviews given to Gallup Poll interviewers has been constantly reduced through the years. At the present time, an assignment consists of only five or six interviews, and assignments come at least a week apart. This policy increases the cost per interview but it also keeps the interviewer from being subjected to too great pressure.

In the case of open questions that require the interviewer to record the exact words of the respondent, the difficulties mount. The interviewer must attempt to record the main thought of the respondent as the respondent is talking, and usually without benefit of shorthand. The addition of "probe" questions to the original open-end questions helps to organize the response in a more meaningful way. In certain circumstances, the use of small tape recorders, carried by the interviewer, is highly recommended.

So much for the interviewer's side of this situation. What about the person being interviewed? How honest is he?

While there is no certain way of telling whether a given individual is answering truthfully, the evidence from thousands of surveys is that people are remarkably honest and frank when asked their views in a situation that is properly structured—that is, when the respondent knows the purpose of the interview and is told that his name will not be attached to any of the things he says, and when the questions are properly worded.

It is important to point out that persons reached in a public opinion survey normally do not know the interviewer personally. For this reason, there is little or no reason to try to impress her. And, contrary to a widely held view, people are not inclined to "sound off" on subjects they know little about. In fact, many persons entitled, on the basis of their knowledge, to hold an opinion about a given problem or issue often hesitate to do so. In the development of the quintamensional procedure, described earlier, it was discovered that the opening question could not be stated: "Have you *followed* the discussion about the XX issue?" Far too many said they hadn't. And for this reason the approach had to be changed to ask: "Have you *heard or read* about the XX issue?"

The interviewer is instructed to read the question exactly as it is worded, and not try to explain it or amplify it. If the interviewee says, "Would you repeat that?" (incidentally, this is always the mark of a bad question), the interviewer repeats the question, and if on the second reading the person does not understand or get the point of the question, the interviewer checks the "no opinion" box and goes on to the next question.

But don't people often change their minds? This is a question often asked of poll-takers. The answer is, "Of course." Interviewed on Saturday, some persons may have a different opinion on Sunday. But this is another instance when the law of averages comes to the rescue. Those who shift their views in one direction will almost certainly be counterbalanced by those who change in the opposite direction. The net result is to show no change in the overall results.

Polls can only reflect people as they are—sometimes inconsistent, often uninformed. Democracy, however, does not require that every individual, every voter, be a philosopher. Democracy requires only that the sum total of individual views—the collective judgment—add up to something that makes sense. Fortunately, there now exists some forty years of polling evidence to prove the soundness of the collective judgment of the people.

How many persons refuse to be interviewed? The percentage is very small, seldom more than 10% of all those contacted. Interestingly, this same figure is found in all the nations where public opinion polls are conducted. Refusals are chiefly a function of lack of interviewing skill. Top interviewers are rarely turned down. This does not mean that a man who must get back to work immediately or a woman who has a cake in the oven will take thirty to forty-five minutes to discuss issues of the day. These situations are to be avoided. And that is why the Time-Place interviewing plan was developed by the Gallup Poll.

Readers may wonder how polls allow for the possible embarrassment or guilty conscience factor that might figure in an interviewee's answers to some questions. For example, while a voter might be prepared to vote for a third-party candidate like George Wallace, he might be uneasy about saying so to a stranger sitting in his living room.

When interviews and the interviewing situation are properly structured, however, this does not happen. In the 1968 election campaign, to follow the same example, the Gallup Poll found Wallace receiving at one point as much as 19% of the total vote. Later his popularity declined. The final poll result showed him with 15% of the vote; he actually received 14%. If there had been any embarrassment about admitting being for Wallace, his vote would obviously have been under-estimated by a sizable amount.

Properly approached, people are not reluctant to discuss even personal matters—their private problems, their religion, sex. By using an interesting technique developed in Sweden, even the most revealing facts about the sex life of an individual can be obtained. And the same type of approach is found to be highly successful in finding out the extent of drug use by college students. Many studies about the religious beliefs of individuals have been conducted by the Gallup Poll without meeting interviewing difficulties.

The desire to have one's voice heard on issues of the day is almost universal. An interviewer called upon an elderly man and found him working in his garden. After he had offered his views on many subjects included in the poll, he called to the interviewer who had started for her car, and said: "You know, two of the most important things in my life have happened this week. First, I was asked to serve on a jury, and now I have been asked to give my views in a public opinion poll."

MEASURING INTENSITY

To the legislator or administrator the intensity with which certain voters or groups of voters hold their opinions has special significance. If people feel strongly enough about a given issue they will likely do something about it—write letters, work for a candidate who holds a contrary view, contribute money to a campaign, try to win other voters to their candidate. To cite an example: Citizens who oppose any kind of gun control laws, though constituting a minority of the public, feel so strongly about this issue that they will do anything they can to defeat such legislation. As a result, they have succeeded in keeping strict gun laws from being adopted in most states and by the federal government.

Since most legislation calls for more money, a practical measure of the intensity of feeling about a given piece of legislation is the willingness to have taxes increased to meet the costs.

One politician made this criticism of polling efforts: "Issue polling often fails to differentiate between hard and soft opinion. If the issue is national health insurance, then the real test is not whether the individual favors it but how much more per year he is willing to pay in taxes for such a program."

This is a merited criticism of polls and, as stated earlier, one that points to the need for greater attention on the part of polling organizations. The action that an individual is willing to take—the sacrifice he is willing to undergo—to see that his side of an issue prevails is one of the best ways of sorting out hard from soft opinion.

Questions put to respondents about "how strongly" they feel, "how important it is to them," and "how much they care" all yield added insights into the intensity of opinions held by the public. The fact, however, that they are used as seldom as they are in the regular polls, here and abroad, indicates that the added information gained does not compensate for the time and the difficulties encountered by the survey interviewer. Most attitude scales are, in fact, better suited to the classroom with students as captive subjects than to the face-to-face interviews undertaken by most survey organizations.

The best hope, in my opinion, lies in the development of new questions that are behavior- or action-oriented. Here, then, is an important area where both academicians and practitioners can work together in the improvement of present research procedures.

The specific complaint mentioned above—that of providing a more realistic presentation of an issue—can probably be dealt with best in the question wording, as noted earlier.

While verbal scales to measure intensity can be usefully employed in many situations, two nonverbal scales have gained wide acceptance and use throughout the world. Since they do not depend upon words, language is no barrier to their use in any nation. Moreover, they can be employed in normal interviewing situations, and on a host of problems.

The scales were devised by Jan Stapel of the Netherlands Institute of Public Opinion and by Hadley Cantril and a colleague, F. P. Kilpatrick. While the scales seem to be similar, each has its own special merits.

The Stapel scale consists of a column of ten boxes. The five at the top are white, the five at the bottom black.

The boxes are numbered from +5 to −5. The interviewer carries a reproduction of this scale and at the appropriate time in the interview hands it to the respondent. The interviewer explains the scale in these or similar words: "You will notice that the boxes on this card go from the highest position of plus 5—something you like very much—all the way down to the lowest position of minus 5—or something you dislike very much. Now, how far up the scale, or how far down the scale, would you rate the following?"

After this explanation, the interviewer asks the respondent how far up or down the scale he would rate an individual, political party, product, company, proposal, or almost anything at issue. The person is told "put your finger on the box" that best represents his point of view; or, in other situations, to call off the number opposite the box. The interviewer duly records this number on his interviewing form.

One of the merits of the Stapel Scalometer is that it permits the person being interviewed to answer two questions with one response: whether he has a positive or a negative feeling toward the person or party or institution being rated, and at the same time the degree of his liking or disliking. By simply calling off a number he indicates that he has a favorable or unfavorable opinion of the F.B.I., of Jimmy Carter, or of the Equal Rights Amendment, and how much he likes or dislikes each. In actual use, researchers have found the extreme positions on the scale are most indicative and most sensitive to change. These are the $+4$ and $+5$ positions on the favorable side and the -4 and -5 positions on the negative side. Normally these two positions are combined to provide a "highly favorable" or a "highly unfavorable" rating.

Scale ratings thus obtained are remarkably consistent and remarkably reliable in ranking candidates and parties. In fact, the ratings given to the two major-party candidates have paralleled the relative standings of the candidates in elections, especially when the party ratings are averaged with the candidate ratings.

Cantril and Kilpatrick devised the "Self-Anchoring Scale."* Cantril and his associate, Lloyd Free, used this scale to measure the aspirations and fears of people in different nations of the world—both those living in highly developed countries and those in the least developed. They sought "to get an overall picture of the reality worlds in which people lived, a picture expressed by individuals in their own terms and to do this in such a way . . . as to enable meaningful comparisons to be made between different individuals, groups of individuals, and societies."

The Self-Anchoring scale is so simple that it can be used with illiterates and with people without any kind of formal education. A multination survey in which this measuring instrument was employed included nations as diverse in their educational and living standards as Nigeria, India, the United States, West Germany, Cuba, Israel, Japan, Poland, Panama, Yugoslavia, Philippines, Brazil, and the Dominican Republic.

---

*F. P. Kilpatrick and Hadley Cantril, "Self-Anchoring Scale." *Journal of Individual Psychology,* November 1960.

The scale makes use of a ladder device.

———— 10 ————
———— 9 ————
———— 8 ————
———— 7 ————
———— 6 ————
———— 5 ————
———— 4 ————
———— 3 ————
———— 2 ————
———— 1 ————
———— 0 ————

The person being interviewed describes his own wishes and hopes, the realization of which would constitute the best possible life. This is the top anchoring point of the scale. At the other extreme, the same individual describes his worries and fears embodied in the worst possible life he can imagine. With the use of this device, he is asked where he thinks he stands on the ladder today. Then he is asked where he thinks he stood in the past, and where he thinks he will stand in the future.

This same procedure was used by Albert Cantril and Charles Roll in a survey called *Hopes and Fears of the American People*—a revealing study of the mood of the American people in the spring of 1971.

Use of this scale would be extremely helpful in pursuing the goal set forth by Alvin Toffler in his book *Future Shock*. He writes:

The time has come for a dramatic reassessment of the directions of change, a reassessment made not by the politicians or the sociologists or the clergy or the elitist revolutionaries, not by technicians or college presidents, but by the people themselves. We need, quite literally, to "go to the people" with a question that is almost never asked of them: "*What kind of a world do you want 10, 20, or 30 years from now?*" We need to initiate, in short, a continuing plebiscite on the future. Toffler points out that "the voter may be polled about specific issues, but not about the general shape of the preferable future."

This is true to a great extent. With the exception of the Cantril-Free studies, this area has been largely overlooked by polling organizations. Toffler advocates a continuing plebiscite in which millions of persons would participate. From a practical point of view, however, sampling offers the best opportunity to discover just what the public's ideas of the future are—and more particularly, the kind of world they want ten years, twenty years, or thirty years from now.

REPORTING AND INTERPRETING POLL FINDINGS

Public opinion polls throughout the world have been sponsored by the media of communication—newspapers, magazines, television, and radio. It is quite proper, therefore, to answer this question: "How well do the various media report and evaluate the results of a given poll?"

Since October 1935, Gallup Poll reports have appeared weekly in American newspapers in virtually all of the major cities. During this period, I am happy to report, no newspaper has changed the wording of poll releases sent to them to make the findings fit the newspaper's editorial or political views. Editors, however, are permitted to write their own headlines because of their own special type and format policies; they can shorten articles or, in fact, omit them if news columns are filled by other and more pressing material.

Since the funds for the Gallup Poll come from this source and since the sponsoring newspapers represent all shades of political belief, the need for strict objectivity in the writing and interpretation of poll results becomes an economic as well as a scientific necessity.

At various stages in the history of the Gallup Poll, charges have been made that the poll has a Republican bias, and at other times, a Democratic bias, largely dependent upon whether the political tide is swinging toward one side or the other. Even a cursory examination of the findings dealing with issues of the day, and of election survey results, will disprove this.

The Gallup Poll is a fact-finding organization, or looked at in another way, a kind of scorekeeper in the political world.

When poll findings are not to the liking of critics there is always a great temptation to try to discredit the poll by claiming that it is "biased," that it makes "secret adjustments" and that it manipulates the figures to suit its fancy, and that it is interfering with "democratic dialogue." Such charges were heard often in earlier years, but time has largely stilled this kind of attack on the poll's integrity.

Limitations of space, in the case of newspapers, and of time in the case of television and radio, impose restrictions on the amount of detail and analysis that can be included in any one report. The news media have a strong preference for "hard" news, the kind that reports the most recent score on candidate or party strength, or the division of opinion on highly controversial subjects. This type of news, it should be added, makes up the bulk of their news budgets.

These space and time requirements do require a different kind of poll report form from one that would be written to satisfy those who prefer a full and detailed description of public opinion.

A political writer for a large metropolitan newspaper has raised this point: "Is it not more accurate to report a point spread instead of a simple single figure? . . . If so, would it not be more responsible to state it that way, even though it would take away some of the sharpness in published reports?"

A degree of error is inherent in all sampling and it is important that this fact be understood by those who follow poll findings. The question is how best to achieve this end. One way, of course, is to educate the public to look at all survey results not as fixed realities or absolutes but as reliable estimates only.

The best examples, as noted earlier, are the monthly figures on unemployment and the cost of living. Should these be published showing a point spread or the margin of error? If they were, then the monthly index of unemployment, based as it is on a sample of 50,000, would read, at a given point in time, not 8.8%, but 8.5% to 9.1%. Reporting the cost of living index in such fashion would almost certainly cause trouble, since many labor contracts are based upon changes as small as 0.1%.

In reporting the trend of opinion, especially on issues, the inclusion of a point spread would make poll reports rather meaningless, particularly if the trend were not a sharp one. The character of the trend curve itself normally offers evidence of the variations due to sample size.

In the case of elections, the reporting of the margin of error can, on occasion, be misleading to the reader. The reason is that polling errors come from many sources, and often the least of these in importance is the size of the sample. Yet, the statistical margin of error relates solely to this one factor.

An example may help to shed light on this point. A telephone poll taken in a mayoralty race in a large eastern city, reported the standings of the candidates and added that they were accurate within "a possible error margin of 3.8%." In short, the newspaper in which the results were published and the polling organization assured readers that the results perforce had to be right within this margin, based upon the laws or probability. Actually, the poll figure was 14 percentage points short on the winning candidate. Factors other than the size of the sample were responsible for this wide deviation.

The best guide to a poll's accuracy is its record. If allowance is to be made for variation in the poll's reported figures, then perhaps the best suggestion, to be reasonably certain that the error will not exceed a stated amount in a national election, is to multiply by 2.5 the average deviation of the poll in its last three or four elections.

Still another way to remind readers and viewers of the presence of some degree of error in all survey findings is to find a word or words that convey this fact. A growing practice among statisticians in dealing with sampling data is to refer to results as "estimates." Unfortunately, this word conveys to some the impression that subjective judgments have entered into the process. A better word needs to be found that removes some of the certainty that is too often attached to poll percentages without, at the same time, erring in the opposite direction. The word "assessment" has been adopted by some survey researchers and it is hoped that it will come into general use in the future.

DESIGN OF THE SAMPLE

The design of the sample used in the Gallup Poll is that of a replicated probability sample down to the block level in the case of urban areas and to segments of townships in the case of rural areas.

After stratifying the nation geographically and by size of community in order to insure conformity of the sample with the latest available estimates by the Census Bureau of the distribution of the adult population, about 350 different sampling locations or areas are selected on a strictly random basis. The interviewers have no choice whatsoever concerning the part of the city or county in which they conduct their interviews.

Interviewers are given maps of the area to which they are assigned, with a starting point indicated, and are required to follow a specified direction. At each occupied dwelling unit, interviewers are instructed to select respondents by following a prescribed systematic method. This procedure is followed until the assigned number of interviews is completed. The standard sample size for most Gallup Polls is 1500 interviews. This is augmented in specific instances where greater survey accuracy is considered desirable.

Since this sampling procedure is designed to produce a sample that approximates the adult civilian population (18 and older) living in private households in the United States (that is, excluding those in prisons and hospitals, hotels, religious institutions, and on military reservations), the survey results can be applied to this population for the purpose of projecting percentages into numbers of people. The manner in which the sample is drawn also produces a sample that approximates the population of private households in the United States. Therefore, survey results also can be projected in terms of numbers of households when appropriate.

SAMPLING TOLERANCES

It should be remembered that all sample surveys are subject to sampling error; that is, the extent to which the results may differ from what would be obtained if the whole population surveyed had been interviewed. The size of such a sampling error depends largely on the number of interviews. Increasing the sample size lessens the magnitude of possible error and vice versa.

The following tables may be used in estimating sampling error. The computed allowances (the standard deviation) have taken into account the effect of the sample design upon sampling error. They may be interpreted as indicating the range (plus or minus the figure shown) within which the results of repeated samplings in the same time period could be expected to vary, 95 percent of the time (or at a confidence level of .5), assuming the same sampling procedure, the same interviewers, and the same questionnaire.

Table A shows how much allowance should be made for the sampling error of a percentage. The table would be used in the following manner: Say a reported percentage is 33 for a group that includes 1500 respondents. Go to the row "percentage near 30" in the table and then to the column headed "1500." The number at this point is three, which means that the 33 percent obtained in the sample is subject to a sampling error of plus or minus 3 points. Another way of saying it is that very probably (95 chances out of 100) the average of repeated samplings would be somewhere between 30 and 36, with the most likely figure being the 33 obtained.

In comparing survey results in two subsamples, such as men and woman, the question arises as to how large must a difference between them be before one can be reasonably sure that it reflects a statistically significant difference. In Table B and C, the number of points that must be allowed for, in such comparisons, is indicated.

For percentages near 20 or 80, use Table B; for those near 50, Table C. For percentages in between, the error to be allowed for is between that shown in the two tables.

Here is an example of how the tables should be used: Say 50 percent of men and 40 percent of women respond the same way to a question—a difference of 10 percentage points. Can it be said with any assurance that the ten-point difference reflects a significant difference between men and women on the question? (Samples, unless otherwise noted, contain approximately 750 men and 750 women.)

Because the percentages are near 50, consult Table C. Since the two samples are about 750 persons each, look for the place in the table where the column and row labeled "750" converge. The number six appears there. This means the allowance for error should be 6 points, and the conclusion that the percentage among men is somewhere between 4 and 16 points higher than the percentage among women would be wrong only about 5 percent of the time. In other words, there is a considerable likelihood that a difference exists in the direction observed and that it amounts to at least 4 percentage points.

If, in another case, male responses amount to 22 percent, and female to 24 percent, consult Table B because these percentages are near 20. The column and row labeled "750" converge on the number five. Obviously, then, the two-point difference is inconclusive.

TABLE A

Recommended Allowance for Sampling Error of a Percentage

In Percentage Points
(at 95 in 100 confidence level)*
Size of the Sample

	3000	1500	1000	750	600	400	200	100
Percentages near 10	2	2	2	3	4	4	5	7
Percentages near 20	2	3	3	4	4	5	7	9
Percentages near 30	2	3	4	4	4	6	8	10
Percentages near 40	3	3	4	4	5	6	9	11
Percentages near 50	3	3	4	4	5	6	9	11
Percentages near 60	3	3	4	4	5	6	9	11
Percentages near 70	2	3	4	4	4	6	8	10
Percentages near 80	2	3	3	4	4	5	7	9
Percentages near 90	2	2	2	3	4	4	5	7

*The chances are 95 in 100 that the sampling error is not larger than the figures shown.

TABLE B

Recommended Allowance for Sampling Error of the Difference Between Two Subsamples

In Percentage Points
(at 95 in 100 confidence level)*

Percentages near 20 or percentages near 80

Size of the Sample	1500	750	600	400	200
1500	3				
750	4	5			
600	5	6	6		
400	6	7	7	7	
200	8	8	8	9	10

TABLE C

Percentages near 50

Size of the Sample	1500	750	600	400	200
1500	4				
750	5	6			
600	6	8	8		
400	7	8	8	9	
200	10	10	11	11	13

*The chances are 95 in 100 that the sampling error is not larger than the figures shown.

RECORD OF
GALLUP POLL ACCURACY

Year	Gallup Final Survey*		Election Result*	
1980	47.0%	Reagan	50.8%	Reagan
1978	55.0	Democratic	54.0	Democratic
1976	48.0	Carter	50.0	Carter
1974	60.0	Democratic	58.9	Democratic
1972	62.0	Nixon	61.8	Nixon
1970	53.0	Democratic	54.3	Democratic
1968	43.0	Nixon	43.5	Nixon
1966	52.5	Democratic	51.9	Democratic
1964	64.0	Johnson	61.3	Johnson
1962	55.5	Democratic	52.7	Democratic
1960	51.0	Kennedy	50.1	Kennedy
1958	57.0	Democratic	56.5	Democratic
1956	59.5	Eisenhower	57.8	Eisenhower
1954	51.5	Democratic	52.7	Democratic
1952	51.0	Eisenhower	55.4	Eisenhower
1950	51.0	Democratic	50.3	Democratic
1948	44.5	Truman	49.9	Truman
1946	58.0	Republican	54.3	Republican
1944	51.5	Roosevelt	53.3[2]	Roosevelt
1942	52.0	Democratic	48.0[1]	Democratic
1940	52.0	Roosevelt	55.0	Roosevelt
1938	54.0	Democratic	50.8	Democratic
1936	55.7	Roosevelt	62.5	Roosevelt

*The figure shown is the winner's percentage of the Democratic-Republican vote except in the elections of 1948, 1968, and 1976. Because the Thurmond and Wallace voters in 1948 were largely split-offs from the normally Democratic vote, they were made a part of the final Gallup Poll preelection

[1]Final report said Democrats would win control of the House, which they did even though the Republicans won a majority of the popular vote.
[2]Civilian vote 53.3, Roosevelt soldier vote 0.5 = 53.8% Roosevelt. Gallup final survey based on civilian vote.

estimate of the division of the vote. In 1968 Wallace's candidacy was supported by such a large minority that he was clearly a major candidate, and the 1968 percents are based on the total Nixon-Humphrey-Wallace vote. In 1976, because of interest in McCarthy's candidacy and its potential effect on the Carter vote, the final Gallup Poll estimate included Carter, Ford, McCarthy, and all other candidates as a group.

Average Deviation for 23
    National Elections . . . . 2.3 percentage points

Average Deviation for 16
    National Elections
    Since 1950, inclusive . . . . 1.6 percentage points

Trend in Deviation Reduction

Elections	Average Error
1936–48	4.0
1950–58	1.7
1960–68	1.5
1970–78	1.1
1970–80	1.5
1966–80	1.2

CHRONOLOGY

This chronology is provided to enable the reader to relate poll results to specific events or series of events that may have influenced public opinion.

1979

December 4   President Carter officially declares himself a candidate for reelection.

December 13   Saudi Arabia, Venezuela, United Arab Emirates, and Qatar raise their oil prices by 33%.

December 15   Former Shah Mohammed Reza Pahlavi leaves the United States for Panama.

The International Court of Justice unanimously demands the release of the American hostages and rejects the Iranian position that the issue cannot be considered in isolation from U.S. activities in Iran since 1953.

December 21   President Carter announces that he will ask the UN Security Council to impose economic sanctions against Iran.

December 24–25   Three U.S. clergymen visit the hostages, now in their fiftieth day of confinement.

December 27   The Soviet Union invades Afghanistan.

December 31   UN Secretary General Kurt Waldheim leaves for Tehran in an effort to negotiate the release of the hostages.

1980

January 4   The United States embargoes grain exports to the Soviet Union.

January 11   The Labor Department reports that the rate of unemployment remained virtually the same during December, rising only 0.1% to 5.9%.

January 12   The United States offers Pakistan economic and military assistance to help strengthen Pakistan's security after the Soviet invasion of Afghanistan. On January 17, President Zia refuses the offer saying that his country needs much more aid than the United States proposed.

January 18   Former Supreme Court Justice William Douglas dies.

              Gold bullion prices soar to $835 an ounce on the London market.

              The government reveals the economy grew a moderate 1.4% during the last quarter of 1979, making the growth rate 2.3% for the year.

January 21   Precinct caucuses in Iowa give President Carter 59% of the Democratic vote to Senator Edward Kennedy's 31%. In the Republican party, George Bush wins with 32% of the votes, Ronald Reagan gains 29%, and Senator Howard Baker receives 16%.

January 23   President Carter delivers his third State of the Union message. He warns that the United States is prepared to go to war to protect the oil supply routes of the Persian Gulf region.

January 25   The Labor Department reports that consumer prices rose 13.3% in 1979, the largest annual increase in thirty-three years.

              Finance and Foreign Minister Abolhassan Bani-Sadr is elected president of Iran. Hope for the resolution of the hostage crisis emerges, as Bani-Sadr had been the only revolutionary leader to openly criticize the militants who seized the U.S. embassy.

January 29   Canada helps six American diplomats escape from Iran.

1980

February 1   The Labor Department announces that the unemployment rate jumped to 6.2% in January, the highest level in eighteen months.

February 3   As part of an inquiry into suspected political corruption, thirty-one public officials, including a U.S. senator and seven representatives, were subjects of a two-year FBI undercover operation called Abscam. During Operation Abscam, investigators videotaped and recorded meetings between undercover agents, who posed as businessmen and Arab sheiks willing to pay bribes, and public officials who were paid hundreds of thousands of dollars for political favors.

February 7   Chrysler Corporation discloses a 1979 loss of $1.1 billion, the largest yearly loss in American corporate history.

February 13   President Carter, as a step toward freeing the hostages, gives public approval to a "carefully defined" international commission of inquiry into Iranian grievances.

February 15   The producer price index, the measure of wholesale goods ready to be sold to retailers and manufacturers, increased 1.6% in January. This was the largest monthly rise in five years and led the Federal Reserve System to tighten credit by increasing the discount rate to a record 13%.

February 22   The Labor Department reports that the consumer price index increased 1.4% in January.

February 23   A five-member UN commission goes to Tehran to investigate the rule of the deposed shah. When the commission arrives Ayatollah Khomeini says that the hostages can be released only by a parliament that is to be elected in March.

February 25   President Carter admits that inflation has "reached a crisis stage."

February 26   Ronald Reagan wins a large victory over his Republican opponents in the New Hampshire primary. In the Democratic primary, Carter defeats Kennedy.

March 1   Former President Gerald Ford declares that Reagan cannot win the general election and invites the Republican party to ask him to run again for president.

1980

March 3	President Carter disavows an American vote in favor of a UN Security Council resolution that calls on Israel to dismantle its settlements in the West Bank and Gaza Strip.
March 4	Carter and Reagan win the Vermont primaries.
	Kennedy and Representative John Anderson win the Massachusetts primaries.
March 7	The producer price index soared 1.5% in February. Energy prices rose 7.5% during the month.
March 8	Reagan wins the South Carolina primary.
March 11	Carter and Reagan win primaries in Florida, Georgia, and Alabama.
March 14	President Carter introduces a new five-point anti-inflation program.
March 23	The shah leaves Panama for Egypt.
March 25	Kennedy wins the New York and Connecticut primaries.
	The government announces that the average American worker lost 1.4% of his purchasing power in February. This means that for the first two months of 1980 the quantity of goods and services the worker could buy declined at an annual rate of 17.3%.
March 31	President Carter sends Congress a revised budget for fiscal 1981, which contains $15 billion in proposed spending cuts.
April 1	Reagan and Carter win the Wisconsin primaries.
April 3	The prime lending rate increases to 20%.
April 4	The March unemployment rate reached 6.2%.
April 7	The United States severs diplomatic relations with Iran, imposes an embargo on its exports to that country, and orders the ouster of more than fifty Iranian diplomats.
April 17	President Carter initiates a ban on all imports from Iran, financial transfers to Iran, and travel to Iran by Americans.

1

President Carter states that a "short" recession has begun.

April 22   Kennedy and Bush win the Pennsylvania primaries.

The Labor Department reports that consumer prices rose 1.4% in March.

The foreign ministers of the nine-member European Community vote unanimously to impose economic and diplomatic sanctions against Iran on May 17 unless "decisive progress" is made toward the release of the American hostages.

The U.S. Olympic Committee decides to boycott the 1980 summer Olympics in Moscow.

April 24   More than 600 Cuban-American boats begin to evacuate thousands of Cubans to Key West.

The United States attempts to rescue the Americans held hostage in Tehran, but the mission is canceled due to equipment failure. Eight Americans are killed and five injured during the pullout in a collision between a helicopter and a transport plane.

Anderson announces that he will run for the presidency as an independent candidate.

April 26   Iran says the American hostages have been removed from the U.S. embassy in Tehran to other cities in the country to prevent further rescue attempts.

April 28   Secretary of State Cyrus Vance resigns because he cannot support President Carter's decision to undertake a military mission to rescue the hostages.

April 29   President Carter names Senator Edmund Muskie to be secretary of state.

May 2   The Labor Department reveals that unemployment rose to 7% in April, the highest level since August 1977.

May 4   Reagan and Carter win the Texas primaries.

1980

May 14   Just nine days after he had welcomed the illegal Cuban refugees streaming into Key West with "open heart and open arms," President Carter changes his policy and opposes the private flotilla that had transported an estimated 46,000 Cubans into the United States.

May 16   The government reports that industrial output declined 1.9% in April, the largest drop in more than five years.

May 17–19   Racial rioting in Miami, Florida, leaves 18 people dead, over 350 injured, and causes an estimated $100 million in property damage.

May 18   Mount St. Helens, a volcano located in southwestern Washington state, erupts. Scientists estimate that the explosion released energy more than 500 times greater than the atomic bomb that destroyed Hiroshima in World War II.

May 24   The World Court orders the immediate release of all American hostages held in Iran.

May 27   As a result of several state primaries, Reagan and Carter each seem assured of the necessary delegates to win their party's presidential nomination.

May 29   Vernon Jordan, president of the National Urban League, is shot and seriously wounded by a sniper in Fort Wayne, Indiana.

June 3   On the final day of the presidential primaries, Carter wins three of the eight primaries and gains 321 delegates, giving him the clear majority needed for renomination. Kennedy, however, wins the other five contests, and he continues to argue that Carter cannot win the November election.

June 6   The Labor Department announces that the unemployment rate increased to 7.8% in May.

June 10   The Organization of Petroleum Exporting Countries increases the price of crude oil.

June 18   The Commerce Department estimates that the gross national product plunged at an annual rate of 8.5% in the second quarter of 1980.

1980

June 19   President Carter authorizes the sale of thirty-eight tons of enriched uranium to India, overruling a decision of the Nuclear Regulatory Commission.

June 24   The Labor Department projects that the 1980 inflation rate will be approximately 11%.

June 27   President Carter approves a peacetime draft registration funding bill.

July 8   The Department of Labor reveals that the producer price index rose 0.8% in June.

July 14   Billy Carter, brother of the president, registers with the Justice Department as an agent of the government of Libya.

July 14–17   The Republican National Convention, meeting in Detroit, nominates Reagan as its presidential candidate and Bush as its vice-presidential candidate.

July 24   General Motors discloses a record $412 million loss for the second quarter of 1980.

July 27   Deposed Shah Mohammed Reza Pahlavi dies in Cairo.

July 31   Chrysler Corporation reports the largest loss by a U.S. automobile maker—$536.1 million in the second quarter of 1980.

August 4   A Senate panel begins a month-long investigation into the White House's role in the Billy Carter–Libya financial arrangements.

August 5   The United States adopts a new strategy for nuclear war that would give priority to attacking military and political targets in the Soviet Union rather than destroying cities and industrial complexes.

August 11–14   The Democratic National Convention in New York City nominates President Carter and Vice-President Walter Mondale as its candidates.

August 25   Independent presidential candidate Anderson selects Patrick Lucey as his running mate.

1980

September 9   When the League of Women Voters includes Anderson in its first presidential debate, Carter refuses to participate. He insists that the first debate should be between himself and Republican candidate Reagan.

September 21   The Reagan–Anderson debate takes place in Baltimore before a television audience estimated at 50 million. The two candidates disagree on almost all issues.

September 23   The Department of Labor announces that the consumer price index rose by 0.7% in August. From January through August the index increased at an annual rate of 12.1%.

October 2   For the first time since 1861 the House of Representatives expels a member. Representative Michael Myers was convicted of bribery and conspiracy as a result of the Abscam investigation.

After a nine-week inquiry into Billy Carter's relationship with Libya, the Senate Judiciary panel finds no evidence of illegal actions.

October 28   The League of Women Voters in Cleveland, Ohio, sponsors a ninety-minute televised debate between Carter and Reagan.

November 2   The Iranian parliament (Majlis) approves U.S. demands and announces they will release hostages as conditions are fulfilled.

November 3   Following a meeting with Ayatollah Ruhollah Khomeini, Iranian militants give Tehran responsibility for the U.S. hostages.

November 4   Reagan is elected president, receiving 50.75% of the vote compared to 41.02% for Carter. Anderson receives 6.61%. While more than 86 million people voted, that figure represents only 53.9% of the eligible voters in the country. This is the lowest turnout since the 1948 presidential election.

November 21   By a 73 to 1 vote the Senate passes the largest ($161 billion) peace or wartime defense money bill.

December 16   Alexander M. Haig, Jr., is named secretary of state designate.

December 19   The prime interest rate reaches a record 21.5%.

Grade School

Better 26%
Worse 55
Don't know 19

By Age
18–24 Years

Better 39%
Worse 50
Don't know 11

25–29 Years

Better 34%
Worse 55
Don't know 11

30–49 Years

Better 31%
Worse 59
Don't know 10

50 Years and Over

Better 28%
Worse 56
Don't know 16

JANUARY 3
PREDICTIONS FOR 1980

Interviewing Date: 11/30–12/3/79
Survey #144-G

As far as you're concerned, do you expect next year—1980—will be better or worse than 1979?

Better 31%
Worse 56
Don't know 13

By Race
White

Better 31%
Worse 57
Don't know 12

Nonwhite

Better 35%
Worse 49
Don't know 16

By Education
College

Better 34%
Worse 56
Don't know 10

High School

Better 32%
Worse 56
Don't know 12

As far as you're concerned, do you expect next year—1980—will be a year of economic prosperity or a year of economic difficulty?

Prosperity 13%
Difficulty 79
Don't know 8

By Race
White

Prosperity 13%
Difficulty 80
Don't know 7

Nonwhite

Prosperity 20%
Difficulty 67
Don't know 13

By Education
College
Prosperity 12%
Difficulty 82
Don't know 6

High School
Prosperity 13%
Difficulty 79
Don't know 8

Grade School
Prosperity 17%
Difficulty 70
Don't know 13

By Age
18–24 Years
Prosperity 18%
Difficulty 77
Don't know 5

25–29 Years
Prosperity 16%
Difficulty 75
Don't know 9

30–49 Years
Prosperity 12%
Difficulty 82
Don't know 6

50 Years and Over
Prosperity 12%
Difficulty 77
Don't know 11

Note: The mood of major industrialized nations of the world is somber as the 1980s begin, but it is more optimistic among the less developed nations of the Third World.

In a major international survey involving twenty-two nations, which was conducted by Gallup International Research Institutes at the end of 1979, pessimism concerning the overall prospects for 1980 outweighed optimism. Pessimism runs strongest in Great Britain, Austria, India, Italy, the United States, and Canada. However, exceptions found among the developed nations are the Scandinavian countries of Finland, Sweden, and Norway, where the majority of opinion is that 1980 will be a better year than 1979.

In sharp contrast to the pessimistic views in many of the developed nations is the overall world outlook. In Korea, for example, optimism outweighs pessimism nearly 5 to 1. Optimism also runs high in Mexico and in the South American nations of Uruguay, Chile, Brazil, and the oil-exporting nation of Venezuela.

In a previous sixty-nation survey, conducted by the Gallup International Research Institutes for the Charles F. Kettering Foundation, results showed expectations for a better life during the next five years to be highest in Latin America and Africa.

JANUARY 7
REPUBLICAN PRESIDENTIAL CANDIDATES

Interviewing Date: 12/7–10/79
Survey #145-G

Would you please look over this list and tell me which of these persons, if any, you have heard something about?

Gerald Ford 93%
Ronald Reagan 92
John Connally 78
Howard Baker 65
Robert Dole 61
George Bush 53
Charles Percy 50
Harold Stassen 41
Elliot Richardson 36
William Simon 30
Jesse Helms 26
John Anderson 24
Philip Crane 20
Jack Kemp 19
James Thompson 13

Robert Ray 9
Larry Pressler..................... 9
Benjamin Fernandez 8

Here is a list of people who have been mentioned as possible presidential candidates for the Republican party in 1980. [Respondents were handed a card with eighteen names listed.] Which one would you like to see nominated as the Republican candidate for president in 1980?

Republicans

	First choices	With Ford's vote redistributed
Reagan	40%	47%
Ford	18	—
Connally	10	12
Baker	9	12
Bush	7	8
Dole	4	6
All others	6	6
Don't know	6	9

Independents

	First choices	With Ford's vote redistributed
Reagan	28%	35%
Ford	22	—
Baker	9	13
Connally	9	12
Bush	4	4
Percy	4	4
All others	8	13
Don't know	16	19

Note: Ronald Reagan has increased his lead over the field of Republican presidential hopefuls and now wins 40% of the Republican vote nationwide. And in second place with 18% is Gerald Ford, who although not an active candidate has not completely ruled himself out of contention.

Showing gains over other Republican contenders, since the last measurement in November 1979, is George Bush who is fifth in the current rankings, the choice of 7% compared to 2% in the earlier survey. A key factor in Bush's increased popularity is better recognition among the electorate. While little change in name awareness is found in the case of the other seventeen candidates tested since the previous measurement in August 1979, Bush has registered sharp gains. In August, 38% of the total sample recognized his name—today the figure is 53%.

JANUARY 7
PRESIDENT CARTER

Interviewing Date: 1/4–6/80
Survey #146-G

Do you approve or disapprove of the way Carter is handling his job as president?

Approve............................56%
Disapprove 33
No opinion......................... 11

By Sex
Male

Approve............................56%
Disapprove 36
No opinion......................... 8

Female

Approve............................56%
Disapprove 31
No opinion......................... 13

By Race
White

Approve............................56%
Disapprove 34
No opinion......................... 10

Nonwhite

Approve............................61%
Disapprove 27
No opinion......................... 12

By Education
College
Approve.............................56%
Disapprove 38
No opinion......................... 6

High School
Approve.............................56%
Disapprove 33
No opinion.........................11

Grade School
Approve.............................57%
Disapprove 25
No opinion.........................18

By Region
East
Approve.............................57%
Disapprove 32
No opinion.........................11

Midwest
Approve.............................54%
Disapprove 34
No opinion.........................12

South
Approve.............................62%
Disapprove 28
No opinion.........................10

West
Approve.............................51%
Disapprove 42
No opinion......................... 7

By Politics
Republicans
Approve.............................40%
Disapprove 51
No opinion......................... 9

Democrats
Approve.............................65%
Disapprove 26
No opinion......................... 9

Independents
Approve.............................53%
Disapprove 36
No opinion.........................11

By Religion
Protestants
Approve.............................57%
Disapprove 33
No opinion.........................10

Catholics
Approve.............................54%
Disapprove 36
No opinion.........................10

By Community Size
One Million and Over
Approve.............................51%
Disapprove 38
No opinion.........................11

500,000–999,999
Approve.............................54%
Disapprove 36
No opinion.........................10

50,000–499,999
Approve.............................59%
Disapprove 31
No opinion.........................10

2,500–49,999
Approve.............................62%
Disapprove 27
No opinion.........................11

Under 2,500; Rural

Approve...............................56%
Disapprove 34
No opinion............................10

Interviewing Date: 11/4–6/80
Survey #146-G

Suppose the choice for president in the Democratic convention in 1980 narrows down to Jimmy Carter and Edward Kennedy. Which one would you prefer to have the Democratic convention select?

Choice of Democrats

Carter...............................51%
Kennedy 37
Undecided............................12

Choice of Independents

Carter...............................52%
Kennedy 37
Undecided............................11

Note: President Jimmy Carter's popularity remains at a high level, with 56% of Americans expressing approval of his performance in office, as determined by a national in-person survey completed on January 6. In an early December 1979 survey, his rating was 61%.

The 61%, recorded in a telephone survey for *Newsweek* by the Gallup Organization Inc., represented the largest increase in presidential popularity in the four decades that the Gallup Poll has made these measurements, exceeding those that accompanied Pearl Harbor and the signing of the Vietnamese peace treaty.

The current survey also shows Carter continuing to lead Senator Edward Kennedy as the choice of Democratic voters nationwide for the 1980 presidential nomination. Carter's 51% to 37% margin represents his best showing to date. In the previous survey, the president led Kennedy 48% to 40%.

JANUARY 8
PRESIDENTIAL TRIAL HEATS

Interviewing Date: 1/4–6/80
Survey #146-G

Asked of registered voters: Suppose the presidential election were being held today. If Jimmy Carter were the Democratic candidate and Ronald Reagan were the Republican candidate, which would you like to see win? [Those who named another person or who were undecided were asked: As of today, do you lean more to Carter, the Democrat, or to Reagan, the Republican?]

Carter...............................62%
Reagan...............................33
Other 1
Undecided............................ 4

By Sex
Male

Carter...............................59%
Reagan...............................36
Other 2
Undecided............................ 3

Female

Carter...............................64%
Reagan...............................30
Other 1
Undecided............................ 5

By Race
White

Carter...............................60%
Reagan...............................35
Other 1
Undecided............................ 4

Nonwhite

Carter...............................76%
Reagan...............................16
Other 2
Undecided............................ 6

By Education

College

Carter..............................60%
Reagan.............................36
Other 1
Undecided.........................3

High School

Carter..............................63%
Reagan.............................32
Other 1
Undecided.........................4

Grade School

Carter..............................60%
Reagan.............................31
Other 1
Undecided.........................8

By Region

East

Carter..............................67%
Reagan.............................27
Other 1
Undecided.........................5

Midwest

Carter..............................63%
Reagan.............................32
Other 2
Undecided.........................3

South

Carter..............................58%
Reagan.............................37
Other 2
Undecided.........................3

West

Carter..............................56%
Reagan.............................41
Other ....*
Undecided.........................3

By Age

18–24 Years

Carter..............................66%
Reagan.............................30
Other 1
Undecided.........................3

25–29 Years

Carter..............................70%
Reagan.............................28
Other 1
Undecided.........................1

30–49 Years

Carter..............................60%
Reagan.............................34
Other 3
Undecided.........................3

50 Years and Over

Carter..............................60%
Reagan.............................35
Other ....*
Undecided.........................5

Labor Union Families Only

Carter..............................66%
Reagan.............................31
Other ....*
Undecided.........................3

Non-Labor Union Families Only

Carter..............................60%
Reagan.............................34
Other 1
Undecided.........................5

*Less than 1%

Asked of registered voters: Suppose the presidential election were being held today. If Jimmy Carter were the Democratic candidate and Gerald Ford were the Republican candidate, which would you like to see win? [Those who named another person or who were undecided were asked: As of today, do you lean more to Carter, the Democrat, or to Ford, the Republican?]

Carter.............................58%
Ford...............................37
Other..............................1
Undecided..........................4

By Sex
Male

Carter.............................55%
Ford...............................40
Other..............................1
Undecided..........................4

Female

Carter.............................61%
Ford...............................34
Other..............................1
Undecided..........................4

By Race
White

Carter.............................56%
Ford...............................39
Other..............................1
Undecided..........................4

Nonwhite

Carter.............................74%
Ford...............................18
Other..............................3
Undecided..........................5

By Education
College

Carter.............................55%
Ford...............................42
Other..............................1
Undecided..........................2

High School

Carter.............................58%
Ford...............................36

Other..............................2
Undecided..........................4

Grade School

Carter.............................64%
Ford...............................27
Other..............................1
Undecided..........................8

By Region
East

Carter.............................56%
Ford...............................36
Other..............................*
Undecided..........................8

Midwest

Carter.............................58%
Ford...............................39
Other..............................1
Undecided..........................2

South

Carter.............................65%
Ford...............................31
Other..............................1
Undecided..........................3

West

Carter.............................53%
Ford...............................41
Other..............................3
Undecided..........................3

By Age
18–24 Years

Carter.............................57%
Ford...............................41
Other..............................*
Undecided..........................2

25–29 Years

Carter.............................56%
Ford...............................41
Other..............................2
Undecided..........................1

30–49 Years

Carter.............................59%
Ford.............................34
Other 2
Undecided.........................5

50 Years and Over

Carter.............................58%
Ford.............................37
Other 1
Undecided.........................4

Labor Union Families Only

Carter.............................65%
Ford.............................32
Other 1
Undecided.........................2

Non-Labor Union Families Only

Carter.............................56%
Ford.............................38
Other 1
Undecided.........................5

*Less than 1%

Asked of registered voters: Suppose the presidential election were being held today. If Edward Kennedy were the Democratic candidate and Ronald Reagan were the Republican candidate, which would you like to see win? [Those who named another person or who were undecided were asked: As of today, do you lean more to Kennedy, the Democrat, or to Reagan, the Republican?]

Kennedy 50%
Reagan............................42
Other 2
Undecided.........................6

By Sex
Male

Kennedy 49%
Reagan............................43
Other 2
Undecided.........................6

Female

Kennedy 52%
Reagan............................40
Other 2
Undecided.........................6

By Race
White

Kennedy 47%
Reagan............................45
Other 2
Undecided.........................6

Nonwhite

Kennedy 81%
Reagan............................11
Other ....*
Undecided.........................8

By Education
College

Kennedy 48%
Reagan............................45
Other 3
Undecided.........................4

High School

Kennedy 51%
Reagan............................42
Other 1
Undecided.........................6

Grade School

Kennedy 55%
Reagan............................33
Other 1
Undecided.........................11

By Region
East

Kennedy 56%
Reagan............................35
Other 2
Undecided.........................7

Midwest

Kennedy 47%
Reagan 45
Other 3
Undecided 5

South

Kennedy 48%
Reagan 45
Other 1
Undecided 6

West

Kennedy 50%
Reagan 43
Other 1
Undecided 6

By Age
18–24 Years

Kennedy 69%
Reagan 27
Other 1
Undecided 3

25–29 Years

Kennedy 58%
Reagan 34
Other 5
Undecided 3

30–49 Years

Kennedy 52%
Reagan 40
Other 1
Undecided 7

50 Years and Over

Kennedy 43%
Reagan 49
Other 2
Undecided 6

Labor Union Families Only

Kennedy 60%
Reagan 34
Other 2
Undecided 4

Non-Labor Union Families Only

Kennedy 47%
Reagan 44
Other 2
Undecided 7

*Less than 1%

Asked of registered voters: Suppose the presidential election were being held today. If Edward Kennedy were the Democratic candidate and Gerald Ford were the Republican candidate, which would you like to see win? [Those who named another person or who were undecided were asked: As of today, do you lean more to Kennedy, the Democrat, or to Ford, the Republican?]

Kennedy 45%
Ford 49
Other 1
Undecided 5

By Sex
Male

Kennedy 43%
Ford 51
Other 1
Undecided 5

Female

Kennedy 47%
Ford 46
Other 1
Undecided 6

By Race
White

Kennedy 41%
Ford 53
Other 1
Undecided 5

Nonwhite

Kennedy 76%
Ford 16
Other .... *
Undecided 8

By Education
College

Kennedy 39%
Ford 54
Other 1
Undecided 6

High School

Kennedy 47%
Ford 48
Other 1
Undecided 4

Grade School

Kennedy 51%
Ford 38
Other 1
Undecided 10

By Region
East

Kennedy 47%
Ford 47
Other .... *
Undecided 6

Midwest

Kennedy 40%
Ford 54

Other 2
Undecided 4

South

Kennedy 45%
Ford 48
Other 1
Undecided 6

West

Kennedy 49%
Ford 43
Other 2
Undecided 6

By Age
18–24 Years

Kennedy 58%
Ford 40
Other .... *
Undecided 2

25–29 Years

Kennedy 46%
Ford 49
Other 1
Undecided 4

30–49 Years

Kennedy 48%
Ford 45
Other 1
Undecided 6

50 Years and Over

Kennedy 39%
Ford 53
Other 2
Undecided 6

Labor Union Families Only

Kennedy 57%
Ford 39
Other 1
Undecided 3

Non-Labor Union Families Only

Kennedy 41%
Ford 52
Other 1
Undecided 6

*Less than 1%

Note: President Jimmy Carter has consolidated his advantage over top Republicans Ronald Reagan and Gerald Ford and now leads Reagan 62% to 33%, and Ford 58% to 37%. His Democratic rival, Senator Edward Kennedy, trails Ford 45% to 49%, and leads Reagan by only a small margin of 50% to 42%.

The latest trial heat results show little change from the previous tests taken in December. These results, however, represented the most dramatic turn-about in the four decades since the Gallup Poll began conducting test elections.

The magnitude of the changes in the political fortunes of the candidates tested is evident in the fact that Carter climbed from a near tie with Reagan in September to a 6-point edge in mid-October and moved out to a 24-point advantage in the December survey. Against Ford, Carter progressed from a 9-point deficit in September to an 18-point lead in December.

On the other hand, Kennedy's lead over Reagan declined sharply, from 28 points in September to 5 points in December. His margin over Ford shrank from 20 points in September to 9 points in October, and in the December survey he trailed Ford by 8 points.

JANUARY 9
IRANIAN SITUATION

Interviewing Date: 1/4–7/80
Survey #146-G

Do you approve or disapprove of the way Jimmy Carter is handling the crisis in Iran?

Approve 61%
Disapprove 30
No opinion 9

By Sex
Male

Approve 61%
Disapprove 32
No opinion 7

Female

Approve 61%
Disapprove 29
No opinion 10

By Race
White

Approve 62%
Disapprove 30
No opinion 8

Nonwhite

Approve 54%
Disapprove 35
No opinion 11

By Education
College

Approve 69%
Disapprove 26
No opinion 5

High School

Approve 59%
Disapprove 32
No opinion 9

Grade School

Approve 55%
Disapprove 29
No opinion 16

By Region
East

Approve 65%
Disapprove 27
No opinion 8

Midwest

Approve.............................63%
Disapprove 28
No opinion.......................... 9

South

Approve.............................59%
Disapprove 31
No opinion..........................10

West

Approve.............................57%
Disapprove 35
No opinion.......................... 8

By Age
18–24 Years

Approve.............................57%
Disapprove 38
No opinion.......................... 5

25–29 Years

Approve.............................59%
Disapprove 36
No opinion.......................... 5

30–49 Years

Approve.............................60%
Disapprove 31
No opinion.......................... 9

50 Years and Over

Approve.............................65%
Disapprove 24
No opinion..........................11

By Politics
Republicans

Approve.............................55%
Disapprove 37
No opinion.......................... 8

Democrats

Approve.............................66%
Disapprove 25
No opinion.......................... 9

Independents

Approve.............................59%
Disapprove 34
No opinion.......................... 7

If the hostages are released unharmed, which one of the following do you think the United States should do with respect to Iran?

Punish Iran diplomatically and
    economically.....................61%
Use military force against Iran.......... 6
Do nothing..........................25
Don't know 8

By Sex
Male

Punish Iran diplomatically and
    economically.....................65%
Use military force against Iran.......... 7
Do nothing..........................23
Don't know 5

Female

Punish Iran diplomatically and
    economically.....................59%
Use military force against Iran.......... 4
Do nothing..........................27
Don't know 10

By Race
White

Punish Iran diplomatically and
    economically.....................63%
Use military force against Iran.......... 6
Do nothing..........................24
Don't know 7

Nonwhite

Punish Iran diplomatically and
    economically 50%
Use military force against Iran 7
Do nothing. 33
Don't know 10

By Education
College

Punish Iran diplomatically and
    economically 68%
Use military force against Iran 3
Do nothing. 26
Don't know 3

High School

Punish Iran diplomatically and
    economically 61%
Use military force against Iran 6
Do nothing. 24
Don't know 9

Grade School

Punish Iran diplomatically and
    economically 49%
Use military force against Iran 9
Do nothing. 28
Don't know 14

By Region
East

Punish Iran diplomatically and
    economically 60%
Use military force against Iran 6
Do nothing. 27
Don't know 7

Midwest

Punish Iran diplomatically and
    economically 64%
Use military force against Iran 4
Do nothing. 25
Don't know 7

South

Punish Iran diplomatically and
    economically 59%
Use military force against Iran 8
Do nothing. 24
Don't know 9

West

Punish Iran diplomatically and
    economically 64%
Use military force against Iran 4
Do nothing. 24
Don't know 8

By Age
18–24 Years

Punish Iran diplomatically and
    economically 62%
Use military force against Iran 5
Do nothing. 27
Don't know 6

25–29 Years

Punish Iran diplomatically and
    economically 63%
Use military force against Iran 7
Do nothing. 23
Don't know 7

30–49 Years

Punish Iran diplomatically and
    economically 61%
Use military force against Iran 7
Do nothing. 26
Don't know 6

50 Years and Over

Punish Iran diplomatically and
    economically 61%
Use military force against Iran 5
Do nothing. 24
Don't know 10

By Politics

Republicans

Punish Iran diplomatically and
  economically 66%
Use military force against Iran 3
Do nothing. 25
Don't know 6

Democrats

Punish Iran diplomatically and
  economically 61%
Use military force against Iran 7
Do nothing. 26
Don't know 6

Independents

Punish Iran diplomatically and
  economically 62%
Use military force against Iran 6
Do nothing. 23
Don't know 9

*If one or more of the hostages is harmed,
which one of the following do you think
the United States should do with respect to
Iran?*

Punish Iran diplomatically and
  economically 52%
Use military force against Iran 36
Do nothing. 2
Don't know 10

By Sex

Male

Punish Iran diplomatically and
  economically 48%
Use military force against Iran 43
Do nothing. 2
Don't know 7

Female

Punish Iran diplomatically and
  economically 55%
Use military force against Iran 30

Do nothing. 3
Don't know 12

By Race

White

Punish Iran diplomatically and
  economically 52%
Use military force against Iran 37
Do nothing. 2
Don't know 9

Nonwhite

Punish Iran diplomatically and
  economically 52%
Use military force against Iran 30
Do nothing. 2
Don't know 16

By Education

College

Punish Iran diplomatically and
  economically 57%
Use military force against Iran 34
Do nothing. 3
Don't know 6

High School

Punish Iran diplomatically and
  economically 50%
Use military force against Iran 39
Do nothing. 2
Don't know 9

Grade School

Punish Iran diplomatically and
  economically 48%
Use military force against Iran 28
Do nothing. 2
Don't know 22

By Region

East

Punish Iran diplomatically and
  economically 54%
Use military force against Iran 34

Do nothing. 2
Don't know 10

Midwest

Punish Iran diplomatically and
  economically 55%
Use military force against Iran 34
Do nothing. 2
Don't know 9

South

Punish Iran diplomatically and
  economically 46%
Use military force against Iran. 39
Do nothing 3
Don't know 12

West

Punish Iran diplomatically and
  economically 52%
Use military force against Iran. 38
Do nothing 2
Don't know 8

By Age
18–24 Years

Punish Iran diplomatically and
  economically 46%
Use military force against Iran. 41
Do nothing 4
Don't know 9

25–29 Years

Punish Iran diplomatically and
  economically 49%
Use military force against Iran. 42
Do nothing 2
Don't know 7

30–49 Years

Punish Iran diplomatically and
  economically 49%
Use military force against Iran. 42
Do nothing 2
Don't know 7

50 Years and Over

Punish Iran diplomatically and
  economically 58%
Use military force against Iran. 26
Do nothing 2
Don't know 14

By Politics
Republicans

Punish Iran diplomatically and
  economically 56%
Use military force against Iran. 35
Do nothing 1
Don't know 8

Democrats

Punish Iran diplomatically and
  economically 54%
Use military force against Iran. 35
Do nothing 2
Don't know 9

Independents

Punish Iran diplomatically and
  economically 46%
Use military force against Iran. 40
Do nothing 4
Don't know 10

*How do you feel the Iranian situation will
end up—do you think the hostages will be
released or not?*

Yes, will. 51%
No, will not. 34
No opinion 15

By Sex
Male

Yes, will. 55%
No, will not. 32
No opinion 13

Female

Yes, will...........................47%
No, will not.......................36
No opinion 17

By Race
White

Yes, will...........................51%
No, will not.......................35
No opinion 14

Nonwhite

Yes, will...........................52%
No, will not.......................28
No opinion 20

By Education
College

Yes, will...........................59%
No, will not.......................28
No opinion 13

High School

Yes, will...........................50%
No, will not.......................37
No opinion 13

Grade School

Yes, will...........................40%
No, will not.......................33
No opinion 27

By Region
East

Yes, will...........................55%
No, will not.......................32
No opinion 13

Midwest

Yes, will...........................55%
No, will not.......................33
No opinion 12

South

Yes, will...........................44%
No, will not.......................38
No opinion 18

West

Yes, will...........................50%
No, will not.......................32
No opinion 18

By Age
18–24 Years

Yes, will...........................52%
No, will not.......................37
No opinion 11

25–29 Years

Yes, will...........................44%
No, will not.......................44
No opinion 12

30–49 Years

Yes, will...........................52%
No, will not.......................34
No opinion 14

50 Years and Over

Yés, will...........................51%
No, will not.......................30
No opinion 19

By Politics
Republicans

Yes, will...........................51%
No, will not.......................33
No opinion 16

Democrats

Yes, will...........................52%
No, will not.......................34
No opinion 14

Yes, will. 51%
No, will not. 35
No opinion 14

Note: Approval of President Jimmy Carter's handling of the Iranian crisis declined during December, reflecting growing public impatience over the unresolved fate of the U.S. hostages. However, in early January approval still outweighed disapproval by a 2-to-1 margin.

In the latest survey, 61% approve while 30% disapprove. In December approval outweighed disapproval by a 4-to-1 ratio, 77% to 19%.

While a smaller percentage of the electorate approves of Carter's handling of Iran, little change has been noted in the proportion of Americans approving of the president's overall performance in office. Thus, it would appear that disapproval on Iran results more from growing impatience over the failure to resolve the crisis rather than from disapproval of Carter's specific actions regarding the Iranian situation.

Supporting this thesis are additional survey findings that show no increase since December in the percentages of Americans who think we should use military force against Iran. If the hostages are released unharmed, only 6% say we should use military force to punish Iran. Yet even if the hostages are harmed, punitive diplomatic and economic measures (52%) are favored over military action (36%).

In addition, expectations run as high as they did earlier that the U.S. hostages eventually will be released. About half (51%) of the public predict the hostages will be released, while 34% hold the opposite view.

JANUARY 15
AFGHANISTAN SITUATION

Interviewing Date: 1/11–12/80
Special Telephone Survey

Have you heard or read about the Soviet intervention in Afghanistan?

Yes. 92%
No. 8

Asked of those who responded in the affirmative: Do you approve or disapprove of the way President Carter is handling this situation?

Approve. 57%
Disapprove 25
No opinion 18

Which of the following do you favor in respect to the situation in Afghanistan— send U.S. troops to help the Afghans who are fighting the Soviets; send U.S. arms to help the Afghans who are fighting the Soviets; put only economic and diplomatic pressure on the Soviet Union; do nothing; or have no opinion?

Send troops. 9%
Send arms 21
Economic and diplomatic pressure 52
Do nothing 5
No opinion 13

Do you approve or disapprove of President Carter's decision to halt grain sales to the Soviet Union?

Approve. 76%
Disapprove 13
No opinion 11

As you know, present plans call for holding the 1980 summer Olympics in Moscow. It has been proposed that the 1980 Olympics be moved to another nation as a protest to the Soviet intervention in Afghanistan. Do you favor or oppose this proposal?

Favor. 72%
Oppose. 17
No opinion 11

Some people feel the Soviets intervened in Afghanistan because U.S. foreign policy has not been tough enough. Others feel the Soviets would have intervened in Afghanistan no matter what U.S. policy was. Which position comes closest to your view?

Policy not tough enough 32%
Would have intervened regardless of
    policy 53
No opinion 15

Note: In a nationwide telephone survey completed prior to President Jimmy Carter's State of the Union Address, a majority (57%) of Americans approved of Carter's response to the Soviet invasion of Afghanistan.

Direct Soviet intervention in Afghanistan began on December 27, when President Hafizullah Amin was overthrown in a Soviet-backed coup and replaced by Babrak Karmal, regarded as little more than a puppet of the Soviet Union. Since Karmal's takeover, the Soviets have built up their military presence in Afghanistan and are thought to have eighty to one hundred thousand troops there.

The use of Soviet troops in this volatile and strategically important region of Southwest Asia has greatly increased apprehension over Soviet expansionism in the Middle East and prompted President Carter to take measures to punish the Soviets for their actions.

Carter's first moves against the Soviet Union received overwhelming support from the public. About three out of four Americans (76%) approved of Carter's decision to halt grain shipments to the Soviet Union, while only 13% disapproved of the embargo.

A proposal to move the 1980 summer Olympics out of Moscow was favored by 72% of Americans, with only 17% opposing the relocation. According to an earlier survey, conducted for *Newsweek* by the Gallup Organization, 56% of the public would want the United States to boycott the summer Olympics if they are not moved from Moscow.

Americans generally felt that the present foreign policy of the United States had little effect on the Soviet's decision to invade Afghanistan. The opinion of the majority (53%) was that the Soviets would have intervened in Afghanistan regardless of U.S. policy, while about one out of three (32%) felt that the Russian intervention was prompted by a lack of toughness in U.S. foreign policy.

JANUARY 20
NATIONWIDE PRIMARY ELECTION

Interviewing Date: 11/30–12/3/79
Survey #144-G

It has been suggested that presidential candidates be chosen by the voters in a nationwide primary election instead of by political party conventions as at present. Would you favor or oppose this?

Favor 66%
Oppose 24
No opinion 10

By Education
College

Favor 63%
Oppose 32
No opinion 5

High School

Favor 68%
Oppose 22
No opinion 10

Grade School

Favor 63%
Oppose 18
No opinion 19

By Region
East

Favor 66%
Oppose 25
No opinion 9

Midwest

Favor............................65%
Oppose...........................23
No opinion 12

South

Favor............................68%
Oppose...........................23
No opinion 9

West

Favor............................65%
Oppose...........................27
No opinion 8

By Politics

Republicans

Favor............................62%
Oppose...........................31
No opinion 7

Democrats

Favor............................64%
Oppose...........................25
No opinion 11

Independents

Favor............................72%
Oppose...........................21
No opinion 7

Note: With the number of presidential primaries more than doubling over the past twelve years, from seventeen in 1968 to thirty-five today, the American people continue to overwhelmingly favor a plan to replace the many state races with a single national primary, allowing voters in all fifty states to choose the nominees by direct popular vote.

The proposal for a nationwide primary election has had the support of the American public for nearly three decades. As early as February 1952, Americans gave their approval to such a plan by an overwhelming 6-to-1 margin. Each of seven national Gallup surveys conducted since that time has shown a heavy majority in favor of the plan. In all these surveys, including the latest, the plan also has had strong bipartisan backing.

Here is the trend since the series began:

	Favor	Oppose	No opinion
1976	68%	21%	11%
1968	76	13	11
1964	62	25	13
1956	58	27	15
1955	58	27	15
Sept. 1952	73	16	11
Feb. 1952	73	12	15

This year about three-fourths of the delegates to the Democratic and Republican national conventions will be chosen in the presidential primaries. In 1968 only about 40% of convention delegates were the products of state primaries.

The chief arguments given by students of the American political process who favor the idea of a nationwide presidential primary are:

1. Under the present system, many Americans are denied the opportunity to vote directly for their candidate.

2. Primaries frequently do not give a true measure of a party's strongest candidate because not all candidates enter each state primary.

3. The American people become jaded with presidential campaigns, which now stretch over the better part of a year. Surveys have found the public to favor shorter campaigns, such as those conducted in England.

4. Primaries are a grueling process, leaving the candidates physically exhausted and their funds depleted.

5. Crossover voting confuses the true support for candidates. In certain states Republican voters are able to vote in Democratic primaries and Democratic voters in Republican primaries.

Those opposed to the idea of a nationwide presidential primary offer these arguments:

1. Under the present system a candidate has to confront many trying situations, allowing the public to better judge for themselves.

2. The generally low voter turnout for the state primaries suggests that if there were a run-off in a nationwide primary, voter participation would be lower than it is now—voters would resist going to the polls a second time, resulting in an even smaller proportion of the electorate selecting the candidates than is presently the case.

3. A nationwide primary virtually would eliminate any opportunity for voters to hear candidates' views on regional issues or to see the candidates in person. Presumably, although traditional whistle-stopping tours would continue, the great majority of voters would receive most of their exposure to the candidates through the national media, principally television.

4. A nationwide primary would tend to favor nominees who are well known to voters and have large financial resources, excluding "dark horses" who gradually can work their way into public familiarity under the state primary system and thus gain financial support.

JANUARY 24
NUCLEAR POWER PLANTS

Interviewing Date: 1/4–7/80
Survey #146-G

> Do you feel that nuclear power plants operating today are safe enough with the present safety regulations, or do you feel that their operations should be cut back until more strict regulations can be put into practice?

Safe enough 30%
Cut back 55
No opinion 15

By Sex
Male

Safe enough 39%
Cut back 50
No opinion 11

Female

Safe enough 22%
Cut back 60
No opinion 18

By Race
White

Safe enough 32%
Cut back 55
No opinion 13

Nonwhite

Safe enough 17%
Cut back 55
No opinion 28

By Education
College

Safe enough 32%
Cut back 61
No opinion 7

High School

Safe enough 31%
Cut back 54
No opinion 15

Grade School

Safe enough 21%
Cut back 49
No opinion 30

By Region
East

Safe enough 25%
Cut back 63
No opinion 12

Midwest

Safe enough 33%
Cut back 53
No opinion 14

South

Safe enough.........................28%
Cut back 50
No opinion 22

West

Safe enough.........................36%
Cut back 55
No opinion 9

By Age
18–24 Years

Safe enough.........................25%
Cut back 63
No opinion 12

25–29 Years

Safe enough.........................23%
Cut back 68
No opinion 9

30–49 Years

Safe enough.........................34%
Cut back 51
No opinion 15

50 Years and Over

Safe enough.........................31%
Cut back 51
No opinion 18

By Income
$25,000 and Over

Safe enough.........................45%
Cut back 51
No opinion 4

$20,000–$24,999

Safe enough.........................30%
Cut back 56
No opinion 14

$15,000–$19,999

Safe enough.........................30%
Cut back 57
No opinion 13

$10,000–$14,999

Safe enough.........................30%
Cut back 59
No opinion 11

$5,000–$9,999

Safe enough.........................25%
Cut back 53
No opinion 22

Under $5,000

Safe enough.........................19%
Cut back 54
No opinion 27

By Community Size
One Million and Over

Safe enough.........................23%
Cut back 61
No opinion 16

500,000–999,999

Safe enough.........................25%
Cut back 61
No opinion 14

50,000–499,999

Safe enough.........................35%
Cut back 52
No opinion 13

2,500–49,999

Safe enough.........................27%
Cut back 57
No opinion 16

Under 2,500; Rural

Safe enough.........................36%
Cut back 48
No opinion 16

Note: Despite the protests of antinuclear demonstrators in recent months, the proportion of Americans who feel that the nuclear power plants operating today are safe enough with the present safety regulations has increased since last April, from 24% to 30%.

At the same time, however, a majority (55%) continues to feel that nuclear operations should be cut back until stricter regulations can be put into effect. In April 1979, 66% favored more stringent operational policies.

Public sentiment for a cut-back jumped sharply following the nuclear accident at the Three-Mile Island plant near Harrisburg, Pennsylvania, last March—from 40% in a 1976 survey to the 66% figure in April.

Although a majority of Americans favor caution in the operation of nuclear power plants, Gallup surveys have shown that most Americans feel it is important that more nuclear plants be built in order to meet the future power needs of the nation.

Public opinion regarding the safety of current nuclear plant operations divides sharply along political lines, with Democrats far more likely than Republicans to favor a cut-back until stricter regulations can be put into practice.

Easterners are more likely to favor a slower approach than are persons living in other geographical regions. Young persons lean more toward this view than do those over thirty, and persons with a college background favor caution to a greater extent than do those with less formal education.

Last fall a presidential commission named to study the accident at Three-Mile Island listed among its conclusions that:

1. The accident was due primarily to human error, not to malfunctioning equipment.

2. The amount of radiation released during the accident was so small that it did not pose a serious health problem to area residents.

3. There was never a danger of the nuclear reactor exploding.

4. Because of the way in which nuclear power plants were then built, operated, and regulated, such an accident was "eventually inevitable."

5. Future commercial reactors should be built in remote areas; existing plants near population centers should be required to pass tougher safety standards.

6. The training of plant operators must be upgraded by sending all atomic workers to government-certified training centers.

7. Future plants should not be given operating licenses until the federal government approves local and state emergency evacuation plans.

The report concludes that nuclear power will be eliminated as an important energy source unless there are major changes in the industry to effect more stringent safety regulations.

JANUARY 27
CARTER VS. KENNEDY

Interviewing Date: 1/4–7/80
Survey #146-G

Here is a list of terms—shown as pairs of opposites—that have been used to describe President Jimmy Carter. [Respondents were handed a card with terms listed.] From each pair of opposites, would you select the term which you feel best describes Carter?

Positive Terms

Bright, intelligent	71%
A person of exceptional abilities	29
Decisive, sure of himself	39
A religious person.	78
Says what he believes even if unpopular	57
Puts country's interests ahead of politics	58
You know where he stands on issues	33
A man of high moral principles.	78
A man you can believe in.	50
Displays good judgment in a crisis	74
Sympathetic to problems of the poor	58
Offers imaginative, innovative solutions to national problems	41
Has strong leadership qualities	34

Sides with the average citizen 49
A likable person 71
Takes moderate, middle-of-the-road
    positions 77
Has a well-defined program for
    moving the country ahead 31

Negative Terms

Not too bright 18%
A person of average abilities 59
Uncertain, indecisive, unsure 48
Not particularly religious 11
Tells people what they want to hear 31
Too much of a politician 29
Hard to know where he stands 55
Not particularly moral 10
A man you can't be sure of 37
Panics, loses control in a crisis 11
Not particularly sympathetic
    to problems of the poor 28
Offers unimaginative solutions
    to national problems 43
Lacks strong leadership qualities 54
Sides with special interests 36
Not particularly likable 17
An extremist; takes extreme positions 9
Has no clear-cut program for
    moving the country ahead 56

Here is a list of terms—shown as pairs of opposites—that have been used to describe Senator Edward Kennedy. [Respondents were handed a card with terms listed.] From each pair of opposites, would you select the term which you feel best describes Kennedy?

Positive Terms

Bright, intelligent 72%
A person of exceptional abilities 48
Decisive, sure of himself 57
A religious person 41
Says what he believes even
    if unpopular 44
Puts country's interests ahead
    of politics 31
You know where he stands on issues 45

A man of high moral principles 33
A man you can believe in 35
Displays good judgment in a crisis 50
Sympathetic to problems of the poor 56
Offers imaginative, innovative
    solutions to national problems 50
Has strong leadership qualities 58
Sides with the average citizen 42
A likable person 62
Takes moderate, middle-of-the-road
    positions 44
Has a well-defined program for
    moving the country ahead 40

Negative Terms

Not too bright 16%
A person of average abilities 39
Uncertain, indecisive, unsure 30
Not particularly religious 45
Tells people what they want to hear 44
Too much of a politician 56
Hard to know where he stands 42
Not particularly moral 53
A man you·can't be sure of 51
Panics, loses control in a crisis 33
Not particularly sympathetic
    to problems of the poor 29
Offers unimaginative solutions
    to national problems 33
Lacks strong leadership qualities 28
Sides with special interests 43
Not particularly likable 25
An extremist; takes extreme positions 41
Has no clear-cut program for
    moving the country ahead 44

Note: In a Gallup Poll conducted in early January, prior to the Iowa caucuses, President Jimmy Carter lagged behind Edward Kennedy with respect to possessing strong leadership qualities, but the Massachusetts senator's advantage was not nearly as great as it was last summer. Specifically, 58% of Americans ascribed this trait to Kennedy in January, while 34% did so to Carter. In surveys conducted last July and August the comparable figures were 76% and 27%. Even those who chose Carter over Kennedy for the Democratic presidential nomination were more likely to perceive Kennedy than Carter as having strong leadership qualities, 50% to 40%.

Not only were Carter supporters more apt to ascribe strong leadership qualities to Kennedy than to the president but also they were more inclined to say that Kennedy is a person of exceptional abilities (41% to 37%).

Carter, however, continues to be viewed by the electorate as a man of high moral principles to a substantially greater degree than was Kennedy. This perception was found among Kennedy supporters as well, among whom 73% ascribed this trait to Carter and 49% to Kennedy. Carter also led among Kennedy supporters as a religious person, 73% to 55%.

When all the attributes for both men were scored, it was found that Carter held an edge over Kennedy on eight of the seventeen items, while Kennedy led on five, and four were considered a draw. In contrast in the earlier surveys, Kennedy led on eleven of the attributes, Carter on four, and on two there was a standoff.

FEBRUARY 3
GUN CONTROL

Interviewing Date: 11/2–5/79
Survey #142-G

Do you think there should or should not be a law which would forbid the possession of pistols and revolvers except by the police and other authorized persons?

Yes, should 31%
No, should not. 65
No opinion. 4

By Sex
Male

Yes, should 25%
No, should not. 71
No opinion. 4

Female

Yes, should 36%
No, should not. 59
No opinion. 5

By Race
White

Yes, should 32%
No, should not. 65
No opinion. 3

Nonwhite

Yes, should 22%
No, should not. 67
No opinion. 11

By Education
College

Yes, should 33%
No, should not. 64
No opinion. 3

High School

Yes, should 29%
No, should not. 66
No opinion. 5

Grade School

Yes, should 32%
No, should not. 63
No opinion. 5

By Region
East

Yes, should 46%
No, should not. 50
No opinion. 4

Midwest

Yes, should 32%
No, should not. 62
No opinion. 6

South

Yes, should 20%
No, should not. .77
No opinion. 3

West

Yes, should 23%
No, should not. .73
No opinion. 4

By Age
18–24 Years

Yes, should 28%
No, should not. .66
No opinion. 6

25–29 Years

Yes, should 33%
No, should not 65
No opinion 2

30–49 Years

Yes, should 29%
No, should not 67
No opinion 4

50 Years and Over

Yes, should 33%
No, should not 63
No opinion 4

By Community Size
One Million and Over

Yes, should 46%
No, should not 47
No opinion 7

500,000–999,999

Yes, should 35%
No, should not 58
No opinion 7

50,000–499,999

Yes, should 37%
No, should not 61
No opinion 2

2,500–49,999

Yes, should 22%
No, should not 76
No opinion 2

Under 2,500; Rural

Yes, should 18%
No, should not 78
No opinion 4

Interviewing Date: 1/4–7/80
Survey #146-G

In general, do you feel that the laws covering the sale of handguns should be made more strict, less strict, or kept as they are now?

More strict 59%
Less strict 6
Same 29
No opinion 6

By Sex
Male

More strict 52%
Less strict 8
Same 35
No opinion 5

Female

More strict 64%
Less strict 5
Same 23
No opinion 8

By Race
White

More strict 58%
Less strict 6
Same 30
No opinion 6

Nonwhite

More strict 61%
Less strict 8
Same 20
No opinion 11

By Education
College

More strict 65%
Less strict 4
Same 26
No opinion 5

High School

More strict 56%
Less strict 8
Same 30
No opinion 6

Grade School

More strict 56%
Less strict 6
Same 27
No opinion 11

By Region
East

More strict 71%
Less strict 5
Same 20
No opinion 4

Midwest

More strict 54%
Less strict 7
Same 31
No opinion 8

South

More strict 50%
Less strict 8
Same 34
No opinion 8

West

More strict 59%
Less strict 5
Same 29
No opinion 7

By Age
18–24 Years

More strict 58%
Less strict 7
Same 27
No opinion 8

25–29 Years

More strict 58%
Less strict 6
Same 29
No opinion 7

30–49 Years

More strict 59%
Less strict 7
Same 29
No opinion 5

50 Years and Over

More strict 58%
Less strict 5
Same 29
No opinion 8

By Community Size
One Million and Over

More strict 70%
Less strict 6
Same 19
No opinion 5

500,000–999,999

More strict 61%
Less strict 7
Same 27
No opinion 5

50,000–499,999

More strict 57%
Less strict 6
Same 30
No opinion 7

2,500–49,999

More strict 55%
Less strict 7
Same 31
No opinion 7

Under 2,500; Rural

More strict 52%
Less strict 6
Same 35
No opinion 7

Gun Owners Only

More strict 48%
Less strict 7
Same 39
No opinion 6

Nongun Owners Only

More strict 68%
Less strict 5
Same 21
No opinion 6

In Massachusetts a law requires that a person who carries a gun outside his home must have a license to do so. Would you approve or disapprove of having such a law in your state?

Approve............................ 75%
Disapprove 2
No opinion 5

By Sex
Male

Approve............................ 69%
Disapprove 27
No opinion 4

Female

Approve............................ 81%
Disapprove 13
No opinion 6

By Race
White

Approve............................ 75%
Disapprove 21
No opinion 4

Nonwhite

Approve............................ 77%
Disapprove 12
No opinion 11

By Education
College

Approve............................ 80%
Disapprove 17
No opinion 3

High School

Approve............................ 72%
Disapprove 23
No opinion 5

Grade School

Approve............................ 76%
Disapprove 13
No opinion 11

By Region
East

Approve............................ 85%
Disapprove 11
No opinion 4

Midwest

Approve............................ 72%
Disapprove 23
No opinion 5

South

Approve............................69%
Disapprove 25
No opinion 6

West

Approve............................73%
Disapprove 21
No opinion 6

By Age
18–24 Years

Approve............................78%
Disapprove 19
No opinion 3

25–29 Years

Approve............................82%
Disapprove 18
No opinion........................ *

30–49 Years

Approve............................72%
Disapprove 24
No opinion 4

50 Years and Over

Approve............................75%
Disapprove 17
No opinion 8

By Community Size
One Million and Over

Approve............................86%
Disapprove 10
No opinion 4

500,000–999,999

Approve............................74%
Disapprove 18
No opinion 8

50,000–499,999

Approve............................76%
Disapprove 20
No opinion 4

2,500–49,999

Approve............................70%
Disapprove 25
No opinion 5

Under 2,500; Rural

Approve............................68%
Disapprove 26
No opinion 6

Gun Owners Only

Approve............................65%
Disapprove 30
No opinion 5

Nongun Owners Only

Approve............................83%
Disapprove 12
No opinion 5

*Less than 1%

Asked of those who said they approved of the Massachusetts licensing law: Under the Massachusetts law, anyone who is convicted of carrying a gun outside his home without having obtained a license is sentence to a mandatory year in jail. Would you approve or disapprove of this?

Approve............................50%
Disapprove 21
No opinion 4
                                  ───
                                  75%*

By Sex
Male

Approve............................44%
Disapprove 21
No opinion 4
                                  ───
                                  69%*

Female

Approve	56%
Disapprove	20
No opinion	5
	81%*

By Race
White

Approve	50%
Disapprove	21
No opinion	4
	75%*

Nonwhite

Approve	51%
Disapprove	20
No opinion	7
	78%*

By Education
College

Approve	55%
Disapprove	22
No opinion	3
	80%*

High School

Approve	45%
Disapprove	22
No opinion	5
	72%*

Grade School

Approve	57%
Disapprove	12
No opinion	7
	76%*

By Region
East

Approve	65%
Disapprove	14
No opinion	6
	85%*

Midwest

Approve	49%
Disapprove	19
No opinion	4
	72%*

South

Approve	39%
Disapprove	27
No opinion	4
	70%*

West

Approve	46%
Disapprove	24
No opinion	3
	73%*

By Age
18–24 Years

Approve	45%
Disapprove	25
No opinion	8
	78%*

25–29 Years

Approve	53%
Disapprove	25
No opinion	4
	82%*

30–49 Years

Approve	48%
Disapprove	19
No opinion	5
	72%*

50 Years and Over

Approve	53%
Disapprove	19
No opinion	3
	75%*

By Community Size

One Million and Over

Approve	66%
Disapprove	15
No opinion	5
	86%*

500,000–999,999

Approve	51%
Disapprove	18
No opinion	6
	75%*

50,000–499,999

Approve	47%
Disapprove	24
No opinion	5
	76%*

2,500–49,999

Approve	48%
Disapprove	19
No opinion	3
	70%*

Under 2,500; Rural

Approve	40%
Disapprove	25
No opinion	4
	69%*

Gun Owners Only

Approve	38%
Disapprove	24
No opinion	4
	66%*

Nongun Owners Only

Approve	60%
Disapprove	18
No opinion	5
	83%*

*Percentage of total sample.

Note: Much of the current debate over gun legislation focuses on the handgun, with public opinion overwhelmingly in favor (59%) of stricter laws covering the sale of handguns. As early as 1938 Americans favored more stringent controls on handguns.

Not only do Americans approve of stricter gun controls in general but also of the specific provisions of the Bartley-Fox Act. This law was recorded on the Massachusetts books in April 1975 and provides that a person carrying a gun outside his home must have a license and anyone convicted of carrying a gun without a license receives a mandatory one-year jail sentence. Since the Bartley-Fox law went into effect, gun-related crimes have declined proportionately more in Massachusetts than in the nation as a whole. According to an article by Donald C. McKay, Jr., in the *Christian Science Monitor,* gun-related armed robberies in Massachusetts declined 35.1%, while armed robberies declined 11.7% nationally.

Retired Judge J. John Fox, who coauthored the law with former Speaker David Bartley of the Massachusetts House of Representatives, contends that the secret of the law's success in preventing gun-related crimes is attributed to three factors: (1) widespread knowledge of the law; (2) speedy trials required by the law; and (3) the certainty of punishment under the law's mandatory sentence if one is caught carrying a gun illegally.

The desire for stricter curbs, however, falls short of support for an outright ban, with 65% of the public voting against a law that would forbid the possession of handguns except by the police and other authorized persons.

Among the factors contributing to the public's opinion on the stricter sale of handguns are the growing fear of crime and the widespread concern over the number of deaths caused by handguns. It is estimated that nearly half of the 20,000 murders in America in 1978 were committed with pistols or revolvers. The latest Gallup audit on the incidence of crime shows that one in five U.S. households has been hit by crime at least once in the last twelve months, with either property stolen or a member of the household the victim of a physical assault.

Three persons in ten (31%) favor a law forbidding the possession of handguns, while 65% are opposed. Sharp differences are noted by the background characteristics of survey respondents, including region and size of community. In the East and in the nation's largest cities, for example, opinion is almost evenly divided.

While there is a great deal of controversy surrounding the entire subject of gun control and what steps, if any, should be taken to combat gun-related accidents and crimes, there is one aspect of the problem that is beyond dispute—there are plenty of guns in the hands of Americans. Almost every other home (45%) has at least one gun, with the incidence of ownership reaching 53% in the South and 70% in the smaller communities and rural areas.

Rifles and shotguns are more popular with the public than are pistols and revolvers, with three households in ten having either a shotgun or rifle. About two in every ten have a pistol or revolver.

FEBRUARY 5
REPUBLICAN PRESIDENTIAL CANDIDATES

Interviewing Date: 2/1–4/80
Survey #148-G

Asked of Republicans: Suppose the choice for president in the Republican convention this year narrows down to Gerald Ford and Ronald Reagan. Which one would you prefer to have the Republican convention select?

Ford............................56%
Reagan...........................40
Undecided........................ 4

By Sex
Male

Ford............................54%
Reagan...........................44
Undecided........................ 2

Female

Ford............................57%
Reagan...........................37
Undecided........................ 6

By Education
College

Ford............................56%
Reagan...........................41
Undecided........................ 3

High School

Ford............................52%
Reagan...........................43
Undecided........................ 5

Grade School

Ford............................68%
Reagan...........................29
Undecided........................ 3

By Region
East

Ford............................65%
Reagan...........................27
Undecided........................ 8

Midwest

Ford............................65%
Reagan...........................32
Undecided........................ 3

South

Ford............................50%
Reagan...........................47
Undecided........................ 3

West

Ford............................33%
Reagan...........................66
Undecided........................ 1

By Age
18–24 Years

Ford..................................69%
Reagan...............................31
Undecided............................ *

25–29 Years

Ford..................................40%
Reagan...............................60
Undecided............................ *

30–49 Years

Ford..................................61%
Reagan...............................37
Undecided............................ 2

50 Years and Over

Ford..................................50%
Reagan...............................43
Undecided............................ 7

By Income
$25,000 and Over

Ford..................................63%
Reagan...............................34
Undecided............................ 3

$20,000–$24,999

Ford..................................57%
Reagan...............................38
Undecided............................ 5

$15,000–$19,999

Ford..................................56%
Reagan...............................42
Undecided............................ 2

$10,000–$14,999

Ford..................................51%
Reagan...............................47
Undecided............................ 2

$5,000–$9,999

Ford..................................58%
Reagan...............................36
Undecided............................ 6

Under $5,000

Ford..................................48%
Reagan...............................44
Undecided............................ 8

*Less than 1%

Asked of Republicans: Suppose the choice for president in the Republican convention this year narrows down to Ronald Reagan and George Bush. Which one would you prefer to have the Republican convention select?

Reagan...............................51%
Bush.................................40
Undecided............................ 9

By Sex
Male

Reagan...............................51%
Bush.................................43
Undecided............................ 6

Female

Reagan...............................52%
Bush.................................36
Undecided............................12

By Education
College

Reagan...............................41%
Bush.................................50
Undecided............................ 9

High School

Reagan...............................58%
Bush.................................33
Undecided............................ 9

Grade School

Reagan...............................52%
Bush.................................37
Undecided............................11

By Region
East

Reagan......................................39%
Bush..46
Undecided...............................15

Midwest

Reagan......................................48%
Bush..44
Undecided............................... 8

South

Reagan......................................57%
Bush..36
Undecided............................... 7

West

Reagan......................................67%
Bush..27
Undecided............................... 6

By Age
18–24 Years

Reagan......................................60%
Bush..26
Undecided...............................14

25–29 Years

Reagan......................................68%
Bush..30
Undecided............................... 2

30–49 Years

Reagan......................................44%
Bush..47
Undecided............................... 9

50 Years and Over

Reagan......................................51%
Bush..39
Undecided...............................10

By Income
$25,000 and Over

Reagan......................................49%
Bush..43
Undecided............................... 8

$20,000–$24,999

Reagan......................................43%
Bush..50
Undecided............................... 7

$15,000–$19,999

Reagan......................................53%
Bush..37
Undecided...............................10

$10,000–$14,999

Reagan......................................57%
Bush..35
Undecided............................... 8

$5,000–$9,999

Reagan......................................51%
Bush..39
Undecided...............................10

Under $5,000

Reagan......................................58%
Bush..24
Undecided...............................18

Asked of Republicans: Suppose the choice for president in the Republican convention this year narrows down to Gerald Ford and George Bush. Which one would you prefer to have the Republican convention select?

Ford..57%
Bush..37
Undecided............................... 6

By Sex
Male

Ford..49%
Bush..44
Undecided............................... 7

Female

Ford..65%
Bush..29
Undecided............................... 6

By Education
College
```
Ford..............................43%
Bush..............................50
Undecided......................... 7
```

High School
```
Ford..............................67%
Bush..............................28
Undecided......................... 5
```

Grade School
```
Ford..............................61%
Bush..............................29
Undecided.........................10
```

By Region
East
```
Ford..............................67%
Bush..............................22
Undecided.........................11
```

Midwest
```
Ford..............................59%
Bush..............................37
Undecided......................... 4
```

South
```
Ford..............................56%
Bush..............................42
Undecided......................... 2
```

West
```
Ford..............................42%
Bush..............................51
Undecided......................... 7
```

By Age
18–24 Years
```
Ford..............................78%
Bush..............................12
Undecided.........................10
```

25–29 Years
```
Ford..............................55%
Bush..............................38
Undecided......................... 7
```

30–49 Years
```
Ford..............................56%
Bush..............................38
Undecided......................... 6
```

50 Years and Over
```
Ford..............................53%
Bush..............................41
Undecided......................... 6
```

By Income
$25,000 and Over
```
Ford..............................53%
Bush..............................39
Undecided......................... 8
```

$20,000–$24,999
```
Ford..............................62%
Bush..............................34
Undecided......................... 4
```

$15,000–$19,999
```
Ford..............................60%
Bush..............................34
Undecided......................... 6
```

$10,000–$14,999
```
Ford..............................63%
Bush..............................36
Undecided......................... 1
```

$5,000–$9,999
```
Ford..............................68%
Bush..............................27
Undecided......................... 5
```

Under $5,000
```
Ford..............................34%
Bush..............................48
Undecided.........................18
```

Note: Former President Gerald Ford, although not an active candidate, now holds a wide 56% to 40% lead over Ronald Reagan in the latest showdown test among Republican voters nationwide. Support for Ford has grown from a virtual tie with Reagan in July to the 16-point margin in the current survey.

Ford also leads George Bush 57% to 37%, but Bush has made strong gains in recent weeks in his standing among all Republican presidential contenders. Reagan fares less well than Ford against Bush but leads him 51% to 40%.

In a survey conducted during the same time in 1976, Ford moved into a clear 55% to 35% lead over Reagan after he had tied with his rival in a January survey. Ford maintained a lead over Reagan in seven subsequent tests that year and led Reagan in the final preconvention survey, 50% to 43%.

After the Iowa caucuses but before the February 26 New Hampshire primary, three men dominated the choices of the nation's Republican and independent voters: Reagan, Ford, and Bush.

Since the previous January survey, Reagan's strength among Republicans has remained about the same, while both Ford and Bush have gained—in Bush's case, dramatically. Ford has moved up 4 points, while Bush's vote has increased 8 points.

When the vote given Ford is allocated to the active candidates (on the basis of second choices), Reagan is first with 48%, while Bush holds second place with 25%.

FEBRUARY 10
PRESIDENTIAL TRIAL HEATS

Interviewing Date: 2/1–4/80
Survey #148-G

Asked of registered voters: Suppose the presidential election were being held today. If President Jimmy Carter were the Democratic candidate and Ronald Reagan were the Republican candidate, which would you like to see win? [Those who named another person or who were undecided were asked: As of today, do you lean more to Carter, the Democrat, or to Reagan, the Republican?]

Carter............................ 60%
Reagan........................... 31
Other 3
Undecided........................ 6

By Sex
Male

Carter............................ 58%
Reagan........................... 34
Other 3
Undecided........................ 5

Female

Carter............................ 63%
Reagan........................... 28
Other 2
Undecided........................ 7

By Race
White

Carter............................ 58%
Reagan........................... 34
Other 3
Undecided........................ 5

Nonwhite

Carter............................ 77%
Reagan........................... 13
Other .... *
Undecided........................ 10

By Education
College

Carter............................ 61%
Reagan........................... 31
Other 3
Undecided........................ 5

High School

Carter.............................59%
Reagan............................32
Other 3
Undecided......................... 6

Grade School

Carter.............................63%
Reagan............................31
Other 1
Undecided......................... 5

By Region
East

Carter.............................58%
Reagan............................30
Other 3
Undecided......................... 9

Midwest

Carter.............................65%
Reagan............................27
Other 4
Undecided......................... 4

South

Carter.............................64%
Reagan............................30
Other 1
Undecided......................... 5

West

Carter.............................48%
Reagan............................44
Other 2
Undecided......................... 6

By Age
18–24 Years

Carter.............................70%
Reagan............................26
Other 1
Undecided......................... 3

25–29 Years

Carter.............................62%
Reagan............................27
Other 4
Undecided......................... 7

30–49 Years

Carter.............................61%
Reagan............................29
Other 4
Undecided......................... 6

50 Years and Over

Carter.............................57%
Reagan............................35
Other 2
Undecided......................... 6

Labor Union Families Only

Carter.............................65%
Reagan............................27
Other 4
Undecided......................... 4

Non-Labor Union Families Only

Carter.............................59%
Reagan............................33
Other 2
Undecided......................... 6

*Less than 1%

Asked of registered voters: Suppose the presidential election were being held today. If Jimmy Carter were the Democratic candidate and Gerald Ford were the Republican candidate, which would you like to see win? [Those who named another person or who were undecided were asked: As of today, do you lean more to Carter, the Democrat, or to Ford, the Republican?]

Carter.............................53%
Ford 40
Other 2
Undecided......................... 5

By Sex
Male
Carter	49%
Ford	45
Other	2
Undecided	4

Female
Carter	57%
Ford	36
Other	1
Undecided	6

By Race
White
Carter	51%
Ford	42
Other	2
Undecided	5

Nonwhite
Carter	70%
Ford	21
Other	*
Undecided	9

By Education
College
Carter	52%
Ford	42
Other	3
Undecided	3

High School
Carter	53%
Ford	40
Other	1
Undecided	6

Grade School
Carter	58%
Ford	36
Other	*
Undecided	6

By Region
East
Carter	51%
Ford	39
Other	3
Undecided	7

Midwest
Carter	55%
Ford	42
Other	1
Undecided	2

South
Carter	57%
Ford	37
Other	1
Undecided	5

West
Carter	48%
Ford	44
Other	1
Undecided	7

By Age
18–24 Years
Carter	55%
Ford	42
Other	1
Undecided	2

25–29 Years
Carter	49%
Ford	43
Other	2
Undecided	6

30–49 Years
Carter	53%
Ford	40
Other	2
Undecided	5

50 Years and Over

Carter................................54%
Ford...................................39
Other...................................1
Undecided..............................6

Labor Union Families Only

Carter................................54%
Ford...................................39
Other...................................3
Undecided..............................4

Non-Labor Union Families Only

Carter................................53%
Ford...................................40
Other...................................1
Undecided..............................6

*Less than 1%

Asked of registered voters: Suppose the presidential election were being held today. If President Jimmy Carter were the Democratic candidate and George Bush were the Republican candidate, which would you like to see win? [Those who named another person or who were undecided were asked: As of today, do you lean more to Carter, the Democrat, or to Bush, the Republican?]

Carter................................56%
Bush...................................34
Other...................................2
Undecided..............................8

By Sex
Male

Carter................................53%
Bush...................................38
Other...................................2
Undecided..............................7

Female

Carter................................59%
Bush...................................30
Other...................................1
Undecided.............................10

By Race
White

Carter................................54%
Bush...................................36
Other...................................2
Undecided..............................8

Nonwhite

Carter................................75%
Bush...................................10
Other...................................3
Undecided.............................12

By Education
College

Carter................................47%
Bush...................................44
Other...................................2
Undecided..............................7

High School

Carter................................59%
Bush...................................31
Other...................................1
Undecided..............................9

Grade School

Carter................................63%
Bush...................................25
Other...................................3
Undecided..............................9

By Region
East

Carter................................53%
Bush...................................34
Other...................................2
Undecided.............................11

Midwest

Carter............................57%
Bush..............................34
Other 3
Undecided........................ 6

South

Carter............................62%
Bush..............................29
Other 1
Undecided........................ 8

West

Carter............................50%
Bush..............................40
Other .... *
Undecided........................10

By Age
18–24 Years

Carter............................68%
Bush..............................29
Other 1
Undecided........................ 2

25–29 Years

Carter............................50%
Bush..............................36
Other 3
Undecided........................11

30–49 Years

Carter............................54%
Bush..............................34
Other 2
Undecided........................10

50 Years and Over

Carter............................56%
Bush..............................35
Other 1
Undecided........................ 8

Labor Union Families Only

Carter............................57%
Bush..............................33
Other 1
Undecided........................ 9

Non-Labor Union Families Only

Carter............................56%
Bush..............................34
Other 2
Undecided........................ 8

*Less than 1%

Asked of registered voters: Suppose the presidential election were being held today. If Senator Edward Kennedy were the Democratic candidate and Ronald Reagan were the Republican candidate, which would you like to see win? [Those who named another person or who were undecided were asked: As of today, do you lean more to Kennedy, the Democrat, or to Reagan, the Republican?]

Kennedy 40%
Reagan.............................48
Other 5
Undecided........................ 7

By Sex
Male

Kennedy 39%
Reagan.............................49
Other 4
Undecided........................ 8

Female

Kennedy 40%
Reagan.............................47
Other 5
Undecided........................ 8

By Race
White
Kennedy 34%
Reagan...........................53
Other 5
Undecided........................8

Nonwhite
Kennedy 83%
Reagan...........................4
Other 5
Undecided........................8

By Education
College
Kennedy 34%
Reagan...........................51
Other 7
Undecided........................8

High School
Kennedy 42%
Reagan...........................47
Other 5
Undecided........................6

Grade School
Kennedy 45%
Reagan...........................42
Other 2
Undecided........................11

By Region
East
Kennedy 43%
Reagan...........................40
Other 7
Undecided........................10

Midwest
Kennedy 36%
Reagan...........................52
Other 7
Undecided........................5

South
Kennedy 35%
Reagan...........................55
Other 3
Undecided........................7

West
Kennedy 48%
Reagan...........................41
Other 2
Undecided........................9

By Age
18–24 Years
Kennedy 54%
Reagan...........................37
Other 6
Undecided........................3

25–29 Years
Kennedy 50%
Reagan...........................34
Other 2
Undecided........................14

30–49 Years
Kennedy 39%
Reagan...........................50
Other 5
Undecided........................6

50 Years and Over
Kennedy 35%
Reagan...........................51
Other 5
Undecided........................9

Labor Union Families Only
Kennedy 47%
Reagan...........................39
Other 6
Undecided........................8

Non-Labor Union Families Only

Kennedy 37%
Reagan............................. 50
Other 5
Undecided.......................... 8

Asked of registered voters: Suppose the presidential election were being held today. If Edward Kennedy were the Democratic candidate and Gerald Ford were the Republican candidate, which would you like to see win? [Those who named another person or who were undecided were asked: As of today, do you lean more to Kennedy, the Democrat, or to Ford, the Republican?]

Kennedy 35%
Ford 57
Other 3
Undecided.......................... 5

By Sex
Male

Kennedy 34%
Ford 58
Other 3
Undecided.......................... 5

Female

Kennedy 36%
Ford 56
Other 2
Undecided.......................... 6

By Race
White

Kennedy 30%
Ford 63
Other 2
Undecided.......................... 5

Nonwhite

Kennedy 81%
Ford 9
Other 3
Undecided.......................... 7

By Education
College

Kennedy 28%
Ford 65
Other 3
Undecided.......................... 4

High School

Kennedy 38%
Ford 55
Other 2
Undecided.......................... 5

Grade School

Kennedy 42%
Ford 46
Other 3
Undecided.......................... 9

By Region
East

Kennedy 37%
Ford 53
Other 4
Undecided.......................... 6

Midwest

Kennedy 32%
Ford 62
Other 2
Undecided.......................... 4

South

Kennedy 34%
Ford 60
Other 2
Undecided.......................... 4

West

Kennedy 41%
Ford 50
Other 2
Undecided.......................... 7

By Age
18–24 Years

Kennedy 46%
Ford 52
Other 1
Undecided 1

25–29 Years

Kennedy 39%
Ford 53
Other 1
Undecided 7

30–49 Years

Kennedy 33%
Ford 62
Other 1
Undecided 4

50 Years and Over

Kennedy 34%
Ford 55
Other 4
Undecided 7

Labor Union Families Only

Kennedy 40%
Ford 53
Other 3
Undecided 4

Non-Labor Union Families Only

Kennedy 34%
Ford 58
Other 2
Undecided 6

Asked of registered voters: Suppose the presidential election were being held today. If Senator Edward Kennedy were the Democratic candidate and George Bush were the Republican candidate, which would you like to see win? [Those who named another person or who were undecided were asked: As of today, do you lean more to Kennedy, the Democrat, or to Bush, the Republican?]

Kennedy 38%
Bush 51
Other 3
Undecided 8

By Sex
Male

Kennedy 38%
Bush 51
Other 3
Undecided 8

Female

Kennedy 38%
Bush 50
Other 3
Undecided 9

By Race
White

Kennedy 33%
Bush 56
Other 3
Undecided 8

Nonwhite

Kennedy 79%
Bush 8
Other 4
Undecided 9

By Education
College

Kennedy 28%
Bush 62
Other 2
Undecided 8

High School

Kennedy 41%
Bush 47
Other 3
Undecided 9

Grade School

Kennedy 47%
Bush..............................41
Other 4
Undecided......................... 8

By Region
East

Kennedy 40%
Bush..............................45
Other 3
Undecided.........................12

Midwest

Kennedy 34%
Bush..............................53
Other 5
Undecided......................... 8

South

Kennedy 37%
Bush..............................52
Other 1
Undecided.........................10

West

Kennedy 40%
Bush..............................55
Other 1
Undecided......................... 4

By Age
18–24 Years

Kennedy 51%
Bush..............................41
Other 4
Undecided......................... 4

25–29 Years

Kennedy 45%
Bush..............................43
Other 2
Undecided.........................10

30–49 Years

Kennedy 34%
Bush..............................52
Other 3
Undecided.........................11

50 Years and Over

Kennedy 36%
Bush..............................53
Other 3
Undecided......................... 8

Labor Union Families Only

Kennedy 45%
Bush..............................42
Other 4
Undecided......................... 9

Non-Labor Union Families Only

Kennedy 36%
Bush..............................53
Other 2
Undecided......................... 9

Note: President Jimmy Carter holds wide leads over Gerald Ford, Ronald Reagan, and George Bush in the latest test elections, but Senator Edward Kennedy trails each of these potential GOP nominees. Of the three Republicans tested, Ford currently shows the greatest strength in these trial heats, followed by Bush and Reagan.

Carter has maintained roughly the same margin over Ford and Reagan that has been the recent pattern. (Bush was tested against Carter and Kennedy for the first time in the current survey.) On the other hand, Kennedy has slipped badly against both Ford and Reagan. Although Kennedy trailed Ford by only a narrow margin in early January, the gap between the two has widened considerably since then. Kennedy led Reagan in the earlier survey but now runs behind the former California governor.

FEBRUARY 11
WAGE-PRICE CONTROLS—
GAS RATIONING

Interviewing Date: 2/1–4/80
Survey #148-G

Would you favor or oppose having the government bring back wage and price controls?

Favor........................57%
Oppose........................34
No opinion.....................9

By Education
College

Favor........................50%
Oppose........................42
No opinion.....................8

High School

Favor........................59%
Oppose........................32
No opinion.....................9

Grade School

Favor........................66%
Oppose........................23
No opinion....................11

By Region
East

Favor........................62%
Oppose........................31
No opinion.....................7

Midwest

Favor........................61%
Oppose........................31
No opinion.....................8

South

Favor........................54%
Oppose........................34
No opinion....................12

West

Favor........................50%
Oppose........................42
No opinion.....................8

By Income
$25,000 and Over

Favor........................49%
Oppose........................44
No opinion.....................7

$20,000–$24,999

Favor........................58%
Oppose........................36
No opinion.....................6

$15,000–$19,999

Favor........................54%
Oppose........................40
No opinion.....................6

$10,000–$14,999

Favor........................62%
Oppose........................30
No opinion.....................8

$5,000–$9,999

Favor........................67%
Oppose........................21
No opinion....................12

Under $5,000

Favor........................61%
Oppose........................25
No opinion....................14

By Politics
Republicans

Favor........................52%
Oppose........................41
No opinion.....................7

Democrats

Favor.............................62%
Oppose............................28
No opinion........................10

Independents

Favor.............................55%
Oppose............................36
No opinion........................ 9

Labor Union Families Only

Favor.............................65%
Oppose............................27
No opinion........................ 8

Non-Labor Union Families Only

Favor.............................55%
Oppose............................36
No opinion........................ 9

Do you favor or oppose a law requiring gas rationing?

Favor.............................45%
Oppose............................47
No opinion........................ 8

By Education
College

Favor.............................54%
Oppose............................38
No opinion........................ 8

High School

Favor.............................42%
Oppose............................50
No opinion........................ 8

Grade School

Favor.............................40%
Oppose............................51
No opinion........................ 9

By Region
East

Favor.............................48%
Oppose............................42
No opinion........................10

Midwest

Favor.............................43%
Oppose............................49
No opinion........................ 8

South

Favor.............................42%
Oppose............................49
No opinion........................ 9

West

Favor.............................48%
Oppose............................46
No opinion........................ 6

By Income
$25,000 and Over

Favor.............................45%
Oppose............................49
No opinion........................ 6

$20,000–$24,999

Favor.............................47%
Oppose............................47
No opinion........................ 6

$15,000–$19,999

Favor.............................48%
Oppose............................44
No opinion........................ 8

$10,000–$14,999

Favor.............................42%
Oppose............................50
No opinion........................ 8

$5,000–$9,999

Favor.............................. 46%
Oppose............................ 45
No opinion......................... 9

Under $5,000

Favor.............................. 38%
Oppose............................ 45
No opinion......................... 17

By Politics
Republicans

Favor.............................. 42%
Oppose............................ 48
No opinion......................... 10

Democrats

Favor.............................. 47%
Oppose............................ 44
No opinion......................... 9

Independents

Favor.............................. 45%
Oppose............................ 49
No opinion......................... 6

Labor Union Families Only

Favor.............................. 45%
Oppose............................ 46
No opinion......................... 9

Non-Labor Union Families Only

Favor.............................. 45%
Oppose............................ 47
No opinion......................... 8

Note: The American electorate favors a return to wage/price controls—one of two key proposals advocated by Senator Edward Kennedy—but is evenly divided on the proposal for a law requiring gas rationing.

The two issues were highlighted in Kennedy—but is evenly divided on the proposal for of his loss to President Carter in the Iowa caucuses and as a response to the President's State of the Union Message. President Carter has consistently opposed both wage/price controls and gasoline rationing, despite mounting pressure from various quarters.

A majority (57%) of Americans surveyed would favor having the government bring back wage/price controls, while 34% oppose such a move. This is the highest percentage in favor of controls since President Richard Nixon removed them in April 1974.

Business and labor leaders also continue to oppose controls. Labor leaders believe wage controls unfairly penalize union workers, while business people fear that controls will cause shortages in some commodities.

While President Carter opposes gas rationing at this time, Senator Kennedy recently called for immediate gasoline rationing designed, in his words, to save 1.7 million barrels of oil daily over a three-year period. Kennedy believes rationing should be based on drivers' licenses, not on car registrations, as in the Carter administration's standby rationing plan.

FEBRUARY 17
DEFENSE SPENDING—MOST IMPORTANT NATIONAL PROBLEM

Interviewing Date: 1/25–28/80
Survey #147-G

There is much discussion as to the amount of money the government in Washington should spend for national defense and military purposes. How do you feel about this? Do you think we are spending too little, too much, or about the right amount?

Too little 49%
Too much 14
About right 24
Don't know 13

By Politics
Republicans

Too little 60%
Too much 7
About right 23
Don't know 10

Democrats

Too little 45%
Too much 17
About right 26
Don't know 12

Independents

Too little 52%
Too much 12
About right 23
Don't know 13

What do you think is the most important problem facing this country today?

International problems; foreign policy* . . . 44%
Inflation; high cost of living 39
Energy problems 12
Unemployment 4
Dissatisfaction with government 3
Moral decline; lack of religious
   commitment 2
Crime and lawlessness 1
Other 7
Don't know 2
                                      114%**

*Although it has been standard practice to report responses to this question without regard to duplication, the 44% cited above is a net, unduplicated figure, representing the percentage of respondents who named one or more problems relating to foreign affairs or energy problems. Some respondents named both the Iranian and Afghanistan crises, and on a gross, duplicated basis, the obtained figure for this category of responses is 51%.

**Total adds to more than 100% due to multiple responses.

Note: Reflecting widespread and growing concern over Soviet military actions in Afghanistan, public support for increased defense spending soared to the highest point recorded in Gallup surveys in more than a decade.

In the most recent survey, 49% say too little money is being allocated for defense, 14% say too much is being spent for this purpose, and 24% say the amount is about right. In a December survey, conducted prior to the Soviet invasion of Afghanistan, only 34% said too little was being spent, 21% said too much, and 33% about right.

Sharp differences are noted in terms of political party affiliation, with Republicans far more likely than Democrats to say that too little is being spent for national defense and military purposes.

The public's views on defense spending are recorded at a time when concern over international problems has risen dramatically. In the current survey, 44% of persons interviewed named an international problem as the most important problem facing the nation, while only 6% did so in the previous October survey. The proportion currently naming international problems is the highest since the Vietnam War in 1972.

Confronted by the Soviet threat abroad, President Carter recently sent Congress a budget for fiscal 1981 that increases defense spending substantially. To meet anticipated defense needs, Carter is requesting $157 billion for military expenditures in 1981, nearly $20 billion more than the 1980 figure. In addition, he pledged to add $90 billion to the defense budget in the next five years.

American military officials are reportedly encouraged by the Carter administration's plans to increase defense spending but see a shift in the military balance between the United States and the Soviet Union that probably cannot be redressed before the end of the 1980s.

FEBRUARY 21
RATING OF NATIONS

Interviewing Date: 1/25–28/80
Survey #147-G

You will notice that the ten boxes on this card go from the highest position of +5 for a country you have a very favorable opinion of all the way down to the lowest position of −5 for a country you have a very unfavorable opinion of. How far up the scale or how far down the scale would you rate the Soviet Union?

Plus 5	1%
Plus 4	1
Plus 3	2
Plus 2	4
Plus 1	5
Minus 1	7
Minus 2	6
Minus 3	9
Minus 4	9
Minus 5	53
Don't know	3

How far up the scale or how far down the scale would you rate mainland China?

Plus 5	2%
Plus 4	4
Plus 3	9
Plus 2	10
Plus 1	17
Minus 1	10
Minus 2	9
Minus 3	11
Minus 4	7
Minus 5	17
Don't know	4

How far up the scale or how far down the scale would you rate Taiwan?

Plus 5	3%
Plus 4	6
Plus 3	12
Plus 2	16
Plus 1	22
Minus 1	12
Minus 2	6
Minus 3	6
Minus 4	3
Minus 5	6
Don't know	8

How far up the scale or how far down the scale would you rate Egypt?

Plus 5	5%
Plus 4	7

Plus 3	22
Plus 2	18
Plus 1	19
Minus 1	9
Minus 2	5
Minus 3	4
Minus 4	1
Minus 5	4
Don't know	6

How far up the scale or how far down the scale would you rate Israel?

Plus 5	10%
Plus 4	10
Plus 3	21
Plus 2	16
Plus 1	17
Minus 1	7
Minus 2	4
Minus 3	4
Minus 4	1
Minus 5	5
Don't know	5

How far up the scale or how far down the scale would you rate Iran?

Plus 5	1%
Plus 4	*
Plus 3	1
Plus 2	2
Plus 1	3
Minus 1	7
Minus 2	5
Minus 3	9
Minus 4	9
Minus 5	60
Don't know	3

How far up the scale or how far down the scale would you rate Cuba?

Plus 5	1%
Plus 4	1
Plus 3	2
Plus 2	3
Plus 1	6

Minus 1	13
Minus 2	8
Minus 3	13
Minus 4	12
Minus 5	37
Don't know	4

How far up the scale or how far down the scale would you rate the United States?

Plus 5	66%
Plus 4	15
Plus 3	10
Plus 2	3
Plus 1	3
Minus 1	*
Minus 2	*
Minus 3	*
Minus 4	*
Minus 5	1
Don't know	2

*Less than 1%

Note: When Soviet troops marched into Afghanistan, much of the goodwill Americans held for the Soviet Union evaporated. Favorable attitudes toward the Soviet Union are lower today than at any other time in the last two decades. In the latest Gallup survey only 13% hold a favorable opinion of the Soviet Union, while one year ago 34% were favorably inclined toward that nation.

Prior to the Afghanistan invasion, the American public's goodwill toward the Soviet Union had been steadily increasing—21% in 1976, 26% in 1978, and 34% in 1979. Then came a sharp plunge following the Soviet invasion on December 27.

The recent increase in disillusionment with the Soviet Union is far more pronounced among Americans under fifty years old, possibly reflecting the fact that many younger people are not familiar with or did not live through the Cold War of the 1950s.

While far fewer hold a favorable opinion of the Soviet Union today than in 1979, an opposite trend is seen in views toward mainland China. One year ago 29% expressed positive attitudes toward mainland China; today 42% do so.

The findings reported here are based on a rating device called the Stapel Scalometer. This scale not only determines whether an opinion is a favorable or unfavorable one but also registers the intensity with which that opinion is held. Values on the scale run from a high of +5 to a low of −5.

In August 1953, during the Cold War, only 1% of Americans held a favorable opinion of the Soviet Union. By a ratio of 8 to 1, the public at that time believed the Soviet Union was determined to rule or dominate the world— a view that has persisted since the end of World War II.

By 1966, Americans had become far less antagonistic toward the Soviet Union, due in part to a shift in attitudes toward mainland China. The ideological split between the Soviet Union and the People's Republic had led many Americans to believe that Red China was a greater menace to world peace and that the Soviet Union would be our ally in the event of trouble between China and the United States.

By April 1973, one person in three (34%) held a favorable opinion of the Soviet Union, marking the highest vote of confidence in that nation since the days of the Cold War. And at the time of Soviet leader Leonid Brezhnev's visit to the United States in June 1973, favorable ratings had climbed to 45%, the highest favorable vote recorded for the Soviet Union since World War II.

Those expressing greatest disillusionment with the Soviet Union are adults under fifty years of age, the college educated, Democrats, and independents.

FEBRUARY 24
PRESIDENT CARTER

Interviewing Date: 2/1–4/80
Survey #148-G

Do you approve or disapprove of the way Carter is handling his job as president?

Approve............................55%
Disapprove 36
No opinion......................... 9

By Region
East

Approve............................54%
Disapprove 38
No opinion......................... 8

Midwest

Approve............................55%
Disapprove 35
No opinion.........................10

South

Approve............................64%
Disapprove 29
No opinion......................... 7

West

Approve............................44%
Disapprove 45
No opinion.........................11

By Politics
Republicans

Approve............................43%
Disapprove 50
No opinion......................... 7

Democrats

Approve............................65%
Disapprove 26
No opinion......................... 9

Independents

Approve............................48%
Disapprove 43
No opinion......................... 9

President Carter has two main jobs. One concerns the problems outside the country; the other concerns problems here in

the United States. Do you approve or disapprove of the way Carter is handling our foreign policy—that is, our relations with other nations?

Approve............................53%
Disapprove 40
No opinion......................... 7

By Sex
Male

Approve............................51%
Disapprove 43
No opinion......................... 6

Female

Approve............................54%
Disapprove 37
No opinion......................... 9

By Race
White

Approve............................53%
Disapprove 41
No opinion......................... 6

Nonwhite

Approve............................56%
Disapprove 31
No opinion.........................13

By Education
College

Approve............................56%
Disapprove 39
No opinion......................... 5

High School

Approve............................51%
Disapprove 43
No opinion......................... 6

Grade School

Approve............................56%
Disapprove 31
No opinion.........................13

By Region
East
Approve. 52%
Disapprove 38
No opinion. 10

Midwest
Approve. 56%
Disapprove 38
No opinion. 6

South
Approve. 58%
Disapprove 36
No opinion. 6

West
Approve. 42%
Disapprove 50
No opinion. 8

By Age
18–24 Years
Approve. 45%
Disapprove 49
No opinion. 6

25–29 Years
Approve. 46%
Disapprove 46
No opinion. 8

30–49 Years
Approve. 57%
Disapprove 36
No opinion. 7

50 Years and Over
Approve. 55%
Disapprove 37
No opinion. 8

By Politics
Republicans
Approve. 42%
Disapprove 51
No opinion. 7

Democrats
Approve. 61%
Disapprove 32
No opinion. 7

Independents
Approve. 48%
Disapprove 46
No opinion. 6

Do you approve or disapprove of the way Carter is handling our domestic problems—that is, our problems here at home?

Approve. 40%
Disapprove 52
No opinion. 8

By Sex
Male
Approve. 38%
Disapprove 56
No opinion. 6

Female
Approve. 42%
Disapprove 48
No opinion. 10

By Race
White
Approve. 38%
Disapprove 54
No opinion. 8

Nonwhite
Approve. 55%
Disapprove 34
No opinion. 11

By Education

College

Approve........................37%
Disapprove 57
No opinion.....................6

High School

Approve........................40%
Disapprove 52
No opinion.....................8

Grade School

Approve........................48%
Disapprove 41
No opinion.....................11

By Region

East

Approve........................38%
Disapprove 53
No opinion.....................9

Midwest

Approve........................40%
Disapprove 53
No opinion.....................7

South

Approve........................44%
Disapprove 48
No opinion.....................8

West

Approve........................37%
Disapprove 55
No opinion.....................8

By Age

18–24 Years

Approve........................37%
Disapprove 50
No opinion.....................13

25–29 Years

Approve........................35%
Disapprove 58
No opinion.....................7

30–49 Years

Approve........................40%
Disapprove 54
No opinion.....................6

50 Years and Over

Approve........................43%
Disapprove 49
No opinion.....................8

By Politics

Republicans

Approve........................29%
Disapprove 65
No opinion.....................6

Democrats

Approve........................50%
Disapprove 42
No opinion.....................8

Independents

Approve........................33%
Disapprove 59
No opinion.....................8

Labor Union Families Only

Approve........................38%
Disapprove 54
No opinion.....................8

Non-Labor Union Families Only

Approve........................41%
Disapprove 51
No opinion.....................8

Do you think President Carter is too tough in his dealing with the Soviet Union, not tough enough, or about right?

Too tough 3%
Not tough enough 60
About right 33
Don't know 4

Those Who Approve of Carter's Handling of Foreign Policy

Too tough 2%
Not tough enough 50
About right 45
Don't know 3

Those Who Disapprove of Carter's Handling of Foreign Policy

Too tough 4%
Not tough enough 77
About right 16
Don't know 3

Note: President Jimmy Carter's popularity rating, while having slipped somewhat in recent weeks, remains high, with 55% of all persons interviewed saying they approve of the way he is handling his job as president, compared to 36% who disapprove.

At the same time, however, only 40% approve of his handling of the nation's domestic problems. If the attention of the U.S. electorate in the weeks ahead shifts from international to domestic problems, Carter could be far more politically vulnerable than he is today.

While public approval of Carter's handling of our domestic problems is outweighed by disapproval (40% to 52%), almost the opposite percentages are recorded for the president's ability to handle our foreign policy, with 53% approving and 40% disapproving.

The following shows recent trends in President Carter's popularity:

	Approve	Disapprove	No opinion
Jan. 25–28, 1980	58%	32%	10%
Jan. 4–7, 1980	56	33	11
Dec. 5–6, 1979	61	30	9
Nov. 30–Dec. 3, 1979	51	37	12
Nov. 16–19, 1979	38	49	13
Nov. 2–5, 1979	32	55	13
Oct. 12–15, 1979	31	55	14
Oct. 5–8, 1979	29	58	13

FEBRUARY 28
VOTER REGISTRATION

Interviewing Date: 1/4–7; 1/25–28; 2/1–4/80
Survey #146-G; #147-G; #148-G

Is your name now recorded in the registration book of the precinct or election district where you now live?

	Yes
National	70%

By Sex

Male	71%
Female	70

By Race

White	71%
Nonwhite	64

By Education

College	76%
High school	68
Grade school	70

By Region

East	72%
Midwest	74
South	68
West	70

By Age

18–24 years	44%
25–29 years	52
30–49 years	74
50 years and over	85

By Politics

Republicans	81%
Democrats	69
Independents	59

By Occupation

Professional and business	77%
Clerical and sales	70
Manual workers	63
Non-labor force	81

Note: The level of voter registration at this time suggests that voter turnout next November may be as low as it was in the 1976 presidential election, when only 54.4% of the electorate went to the polls.

In surveys taken since the beginning of the year, 70% of adults interviewed indicate they are registered to vote or that the state in which they live does not require registration. The percentage recorded in surveys in early 1976 was virtually the same, 69%.

Despite the attention that has been focused on the low turnout in elections in the United States, current survey evidence indicates that little progress is being made to induce adults to register in their local election district.

Least likely to have registered to vote are 18-to-24-year-olds, with only 44% saying their names are registered in the communities where they live. On the other hand, 85% of those who are fifty years of age or older say they are registered.

Survey findings indicate that the profile of persons most likely to vote are those fifty years and over, the college-educated, professional and business people, and those in the higher income brackets. Least likely to vote are blacks living in the south, younger adults, and those in lower income families.

Although Democrats now enjoy a 2½-to-1 margin over Republicans, it is politically significant that proportionately more Republicans (81%) than Democrats (69%) say they are registered to vote.

Based on past voting behavior, some 80% to 85% of those who are registered will actually cast their ballots, which means that if the 1980 presidential election were being held today, only about 55% of the electorate could be expected to vote.

MARCH 2
MILITARY REGISTRATION AND THE DRAFT

Interviewing Date: 2/1–4/80
Survey #148-G

Do you think we should return to the military draft at this time, or not?

Should 59%
Should not 36
No opinion. 5

By Sex
Male

Should 66%
Should not 31
No opinion. 3

Female

Should 53%
Should not 40
No opinion. 7

By Race
White

Should 60%
Should not 35
No opinion. 5

Nonwhite

Should 49%
Should not 45
No opinion. 6

By Education
College

Should 55%
Should not 42
No opinion. 3

High School

Should 60%
Should not 35
No opinion. 5

Grade School

Should 61%
Should not 28
No opinion. 11

By Region

East

Should 56%
Should not 37
No opinion. 7

Midwest

Should 61%
Should not 34
No opinion. 5

South

Should 60%
Should not 35
No opinion. 5

West

Should 58%
Should not 39
No opinion. 3

By Age

18–24 Years

Should 41%
Should not 57
No opinion. 2

25–29 Years

Should 46%
Should not 48
No opinion. 6

30–49 Years

Should 67%
Should not 28
No opinion. 5

50 Years and Over

Should 62%
Should not 31
No opinion. 7

By Politics

Republicans

Should 65%
Should not 29
No opinion. 6

Democrats

Should 60%
Should not 35
No opinion. 5

Independents

Should 55%
Should not 41
No opinion. 4

If a draft were to become necessary, should young women be required to participate as well as young men, or not?

Should 51%
Should not 45
No opinion. 4

By Sex

Male

Should 58%
Should not 39
No opinion. 3

Female

Should 45%
Should not 50
No opinion. 5

By Race

White

Should 53%
Should not 44
No opinion. 3

Nonwhite

Should 42%
Should not 54
No opinion. 4

By Education
College
Should 60%
Should not 36
No opinion. 4

High School
Should 50%
Should not 47
No opinion. 3

Grade School
Should 41%
Should not 53
No opinion. 6

By Region
East
Should 56%
Should not 40
No opinion. 4

Midwest
Should 53%
Should not 44
No opinion. 3

South
Should 41%
Should not 56
No opinion. 3

West
Should 59%
Should not 37
No opinion. 4

By Age
18–24 Years
Should 49%
Should not 50
No opinion. 1

25–29 Years
Should 53%
Should not 45
No opinion. 2

30–49 Years
Should 53%
Should not 43
No opinion. 4

50 Years and Over
Should 50%
Should not 45
No opinion. 5

By Politics
Republicans
Should 50%
Should not 45
No opinion. 5

Democrats
Should 50%
Should not 46
No opinion. 4

Independents
Should 56%
Should not 42
No opinion. 2

Asked of those who replied in the affirmative: Should women be eligible for combat roles, or not?

Should 21%
Should not 28
No opinion. 2
                                                    51%*

By Sex
Male
Should 25%
Should not 31
No opinion. 2
                                                    58%*

Female

Should 17%
Should not 25
No opinion. 3
                                                    45%*

By Race
White

Should 21%
Should not 29
No opinion 3
                                                    53%*

Nonwhite

Should 20%
Should not 20
No opinion. 2
                                                    42%*

By Education
College

Should 26%
Should not 32
No opinion. 2
                                                    60%*

High School

Should 20%
Should not 27
No opinion 3
                                                    50%*

Grade School

Should 14%
Should not 25
No opinion. 2
                                                    41%*

By Region
East

Should 24%
Should not 30
No opinion. 2
                                                    56%*

Midwest

Should 18%
Should not 30
No opinion 5
                                                    53%*

South

Should 17%
Should not 22
No opinion. 2
                                                    41%*

West

Should 27%
Should not 31
No opinion. 1
                                                    59%*

By Age
18–24 Years

Should 27%
Should not 20
No opinion. 2
                                                    49%*

25–29 Years

Should 29%
Should not 19
No opinion. 5
                                                    53%*

30–49 Years

Should 23%
Should not 28
No opinion 2
                                                    53%*

50 Years and Over

Should 14%
Should not 34
No opinion. 2
                                                    50%*

By Politics
Republicans

Should 16%
Should not 32
No opinion 2
_____
50%*

Democrats

Should 21%
Should not 26
No opinion 3
_____
50%*

Independents

Should 24%
Should not 29
No opinion 3
_____
56%*

*Percentage of total sample

Would you favor or oppose the registration of the names of all young men so that in the event of an emergency the time needed to call up men for a draft would be reduced?

Favor 83%
Oppose 13
No opinion 4

By Sex
Male

Favor 85%
Oppose 13
No opinion 2

Female

Favor 81%
Oppose 13
No opinion 6

By Age
18–24 Years

Favor 77%
Oppose 21
No opinion 2

25–29 Years

Favor 77%
Oppose 17
No opinion 6

30–49 Years

Favor 85%
Oppose 12
No opinion 3

50 Years and Over

Favor 86%
Oppose 9
No opinion 5

By Politics
Republicans

Favor 89%
Oppose 9
No opinion 2

Democrats

Favor 81%
Oppose 13
No opinion 6

Independents

Favor 84%
Oppose 14
No opinion 2

Would you favor or oppose the registration of all young women under these circumstances?

Favor 56%
Oppose 40
No opinion 4

By Sex
Male

Favor................................59%
Oppose...............................38
No opinion........................... 3

Female

Favor................................52%
Oppose...............................42
No opinion........................... 6

By Age
18–24 Years

Favor................................58%
Oppose...............................42
No opinion........................... *

25–29 Years

Favor................................52%
Oppose...............................41
No opinion........................... 7

30–49 Years

Favor................................57%
Oppose...............................39
No opinion........................... 4

50 Years and Over

Favor................................54%
Oppose...............................40
No opinion........................... 6

By Politics
Republicans

Favor................................57%
Oppose...............................39
No opinion........................... 4

Democrats

Favor................................53%
Oppose...............................42
No opinion........................... 5

Independents

Favor................................58%
Oppose...............................39
No opinion........................... 3

*Less than 1%

Note: If a nationwide referendum were being held at this time, the U.S. public would vote both in favor of registering the names of young men and women as well as a return to the military draft. The latest survey shows 59% voting for a return to the draft and 36% opposed. In a March 1979 survey, opinion was evenly divided, with 45% in favor and 46% opposed.

While the public leans heavily toward a return to the draft at this time, support for drafting women is less solid, but opinion has moved in this direction since the 1979 survey. Today, 51% favor drafting women, versus 45% who oppose the idea—a shift from the earlier survey when 43% said women should be required to serve and 50% said they should not.

Sharp differences are recorded on the basis of the sex and age of survey respondents. Young adults (18 to 24), for example, vote against a return to the draft at this time (57% to 41%), while those thirty years and older back the draft by a 2-to-1 ratio or better.

When survey respondents who feel women should participate in the draft are asked whether they should be eligible for combat roles, opposition outweighs support 54% to 41%. These results are similar to those found in the earlier survey, when 51% said women should not be eligible and 44% held the opposite viewpoint.

The latest survey also shows the public to be in favor of registration for young men by better than a 6-to-1 ratio (83% to 13%), representing an increase in those backing registration since the 1979 survey, when 76% supported the proposed system and 17% were opposed.

A smaller majority (56%) favors registration for young women, with 40% opposed, compared to last March when 50% favored registration for young women and 41% were opposed.

As part of his State of the Union Address, President Jimmy Carter proposed that men and women, aged nineteen and twenty, register for military service probably beginning this summer, and that eighteen-year-olds be included starting January 1, 1981. Carter also suggested draft registration for women. If approved by Congress, the president's program would affect 4.2 million women and 4 million men.

Under Carter's proposal, persons aged nineteen and twenty would complete a form at their local post office, giving their name, address, date of birth, and Social Security number.

The last man to be drafted entered military service on June 30, 1973, and registration ended on April 1, 1975. Under the present law, Selective Service may register only men. Congress would have to enact new legislation before women could be ordered to register.

Although the president's draft registration proposal met with broad congressional approval when it was first offered, substantial opposition subsequently has developed, particularly to the registration of young women for military service. Much of the opposition to the Carter proposal centers around the contention that the registration plan would not save much time or money in the event of a national emergency. In late February a congressional subcommittee refused to provide funds for the registration of either men or women.

MARCH 4
PRESIDENT CARTER

Interviewing Date: 2/29–3/2/80
Survey #149-G

Do you approve or disapprove of the way Carter is handling his job as president?

Approve. 52%
Disapprove 37
No opinion. 11

Note: In the latest survey, 52% say they approve of the way Carter is handling his job as

chief executive, representing a 9-point decline since early December when 61% approved.

President Jimmy Carter's popularity rating continues to decline due to widespread concern over the nation's economy—slow growth in incomes and escalating prices. A majority of survey respondents in a recent Gallup Organization Economic Service survey expected their income to go up less than prices during the next twelve months, while another one-third said their income would just keep pace with inflation.

The public is feeling the increasing financial pressure, which is reflected in their overwhelming support for a balanced federal budget as well as for an increase in those who back wage/price controls. The current percentage in favor of controls (58%) is the highest recorded since President Nixon removed them in 1974.

MARCH 7
GERALD FORD

Interviewing Date: 2/29–3/3/80
Survey #149-G

Would you like to see Gerald Ford become an active candidate for president in 1980, or not?

Would 43%
Would not 49
No opinion. 8

Republicans Only

Would 50%
Would not 45
No opinion 5

Independents Only

Would 49%
Would not 45
No opinion 6

Note: Former President Gerald Ford has asked publicly for an expression of broad-based support from leaders of his party before he enters the 1980 presidential race. Political observers speculate that if Ford plans to enter the race, he will have to do so shortly because a later entry virtually could rule out his chances for the GOP nomination.

Evidence of GOP support at the grass-roots level is seen in the results of a recently completed Gallup survey that shows Republicans 50% to 45% in favor of Ford becoming an active candidate. Among voters who describe themselves as independents—a crucial bloc of voters for Republican presidential hopefuls—opinion also favors a Ford candidacy, 49% to 45%.

The importance of the independent vote is seen in the fact that no Republican in recent decades has won the presidency without the support of a majority of independent voters.

Prior to New Hampshire, Ford was in a virtual tie with Ronald Reagan as the nomination choice of Republican voters asked to choose from a list of eight men. Reagan was the selection of 34% compared to 32% for Ford. In the latest survey, conducted a few days after the New Hampshire primary, Ford trailed Reagan, 24% to 44%.

MARCH 9
PRESIDENTIAL TRIAL HEATS

Interviewing Date: 2/29–3/3/80
Survey #149-G

Asked of registered voters: Suppose the presidential election were being held today. If Jimmy Carter were the Democratic candidate and Ronald Reagan were the Republican candidate, which would you like to see win? [Those who named another person or who were undecided were asked: As of today, do you lean more to Carter, the Democrat, or to Reagan, the Republican?]

Carter...............................58%
Reagan..............................33
Other 3
Undecided........................ 6

By Region
East

Carter...............................60%
Reagan..............................30
Other 3
Undecided........................ 7

Midwest

Carter...............................56%
Reagan..............................32
Other 5
Undecided........................ 7

South

Carter...............................59%
Reagan..............................33
Other 1
Undecided........................ 7

West

Carter...............................54%
Reagan..............................39
Other 3
Undecided........................ 4

By Politics
Republicans

Carter...............................28%
Reagan..............................66
Other 2
Undecided........................ 4

Democrats

Carter...............................76%
Reagan..............................16
Other 3
Undecided........................ 5

Independents

Carter...............................56%
Reagan..............................31
Other 4
Undecided........................ 9

Asked of registered voters: Suppose the presidential election were being held today. If Jimmy Carter were the Democratic candidate and George Bush were the Republican candidate, which would you like to see win? [Those who named another person or who were undecided were asked: As of today, do you lean more to Carter, the Democrat, or to Bush, the Republican?]

Carter.............................	59%
Bush................................	30
Other	3
Undecided..........................	8

By Region
East

Carter.............................	55%
Bush................................	32
Other	2
Undecided..........................	11

Midwest

Carter.............................	54%
Bush................................	31
Other	5
Undecided..........................	10

South

Carter.............................	67%
Bush................................	26
Other	1
Undecided..........................	6

West

Carter.............................	59%
Bush................................	32
Other	2
Undecided..........................	7

By Politics
Republicans

Carter.............................	32%
Bush................................	57
Other	3
Undecided..........................	8

Democrats

Carter.............................	77%
Bush................................	16
Other	1
Undecided..........................	4

Independents

Carter.............................	56%
Bush................................	28
Other	3
Undecided..........................	13

Note: Despite strong showings by Republicans Ronald Reagan and George Bush in the state primary elections to date, President Jimmy Carter continues to hold a wide margin over these two leading GOP contenders, as determined by a nationwide survey of registered voters.

Carter leads Reagan 58% to 33% and Bush 59% to 30%. The results indicate that while Bush is far overshadowed by Reagan (60% to 36%) in the latest Gallup Poll test of the nomination choices of Republican voters nationwide, Bush demonstrates almost equal national voters' strength with Reagan in trial heats against Carter.

Since the previous survey the margin between Carter and Reagan, although still wide, has narrowed slightly. Carter led 60% to 31% in an early February survey. Little change, however, has occurred in the relative standings of Carter and Bush. In the earlier survey Carter led 56% to 34%.

Analysis of these test election results shows Reagan to be stronger against Carter than Bush among persons who classify themselves as Republicans and among those with a college background.

MARCH 12
THE OLYMPICS

Interviewing Date: 2/29–3/2/80
Survey #149-G

Do you think the United States should or should not participate in the Olympic Games in Moscow this summer?

Should	....	30%
Should not	....	61
No opinion	....	9

Good idea	....	64%
Poor idea	....	23
No opinion	....	13

By Sex
Male

Should	....	34%
Should not	....	60
No opinion	....	6

By Sex
Male

Good idea	....	64%
Poor idea	....	26
No opinion	....	10

Female

Should	....	27%
Should not	....	62
No opinion	....	11

Female

Good idea	....	63%
Poor idea	....	21
No opinion	....	16

By Age
18–24 Years

Should	....	43%
Should not	....	51
No opinion	....	6

By Age
18–24 Years

Good idea	....	66%
Poor idea	....	25
No opinion	....	9

25–29 Years

Should	....	37%
Should not	....	57
No opinion	....	6

25–29 Years

Good idea	....	61%
Poor idea	....	30
No opinion	....	9

30–49 Years

Should	....	31%
Should not	....	63
No opinion	....	6

30–49 Years

Good idea	....	66%
Poor idea	....	24
No opinion	....	10

50 Years and Over

Should	....	22%
Should not	....	66
No opinion	....	12

50 Years and Over

Good idea	....	61%
Poor idea	....	21
No opinion	....	18

It has been proposed that a permanent Olympic site be established in Greece. Does this sound like a good idea or a poor idea to you?

Note: A solid majority of the American people (61%) supports President Jimmy Carter's proposed boycott of the summer Olympics in Moscow.

A similar majority (64%) also favors a related Carter proposal that the games be returned permanently to Greece where they began almost 3,000 years ago. The so-called "modern" Olympics were revived in 1896, when they were held in Athens. Since then the games have taken place in many locations around the world. Only twice have the Olympics been suspended—during World War I and II. President Carter believes that holding the Olympics on a permanent basis in Greece would "eliminate any future political competition among nations to serve as hosts."

A crucial question in the debate over the Olympics is whether or not other nations will join the United States in a boycott of the summer Olympics. In order to present the most effective expression of international disapproval of the Soviet Union's invasion of Afghanistan, the United States must persuade other nations to join in the boycott. And although many nations have condemned the Soviet invasion, few publicly have committed themselves to support the United States boycott.

Surveys by Gallup-affiliated organizations in Great Britain and the Netherlands show the British public to be evenly divided on the question of their country's participation in the Moscow Olympics, while the people of the Netherlands lean toward participating in the Olympic games even if the United States does not enter.

In his State of the Union Address on January 23, President Carter said he would urge an American boycott of the summer Olympic games in Moscow if invading Soviet troops are not withdrawn from Afghanistan by February 20. The president, however, does not have the statutory power to prevent an American team from participating in the Moscow games. The ultimate authority rests with the U.S. Olympic Committee, which so far has refused to commit itself on the issue, hoping to find a way around President Carter's State of the Union declaration that "with Soviet invading forces in Afghanistan, neither the American people nor I will support sending an Olympic team to Moscow."

MARCH 19
PRESIDENT CARTER

Interviewing Date: 2/14–22; 22–29; 2/29–3/10; 7–15/80
Special Telephone Survey*

Do you approve or disapprove of the way Carter is handling his job as president?

February 14–22

Approve...........................55%
Disapprove 32
No opinion........................13

February 22–29

Approve...........................50%
Disapprove 34
No opinion........................16

February 29–March 10

Approve...........................44%
Disapprove 38
No opinion........................18

March 7–15

Approve...........................41%
Disapprove 45
No opinion........................14

*The results are based on telephone interviews with 2,043 adults, eighteen years and older, during the period February 14–March 15, with approximately 500 persons interviewed in each of four surveys.

Note: In the period of just one month—from mid-February to mid-March—President Jimmy Carter's job approval rating has declined 14 percentage points over four successive surveys, from 55% to 41% in the latest survey.

Any further decline in the weeks ahead could put Carter in a vulnerable situation in terms of his election strength against Ronald Reagan, with the 1980 political race beginning to look increasingly like a two-way battle between Carter and Reagan.

In late September, when Carter's job approval rating was at 30%, Carter and Reagan were in a virtual tie in a trial heat. Still earlier, in July, when Carter's approval rating stood at 29%, Reagan led the president 51% to 44%.

MARCH 20
CONGRESSIONAL ETHICS

Interviewing Date: 2/29–3/3/80
Survey #149-G

Do you believe there are senators and representatives now serving in Congress who won election by using unethical and illegal methods in their campaigns?

Yes................................78%
No.................................. 9
No opinion.........................13

By Education
College

Yes................................86%
No.................................. 7
No opinion......................... 7

High School

Yes................................81%
No.................................. 8
No opinion.........................11

Grade School

Yes................................55%
No.................................17
No opinion.........................28

By Age
18–24 Years

Yes................................87%
No.................................. 6
No opinion......................... 7

25–29 Years

Yes................................84%
No.................................. 9
No opinion......................... 7

30–49 Years

Yes................................81%
No.................................. 9
No opinion.........................10

50 Years and Over

Yes................................70%
No.................................11
No opinion.........................19

By Politics
Republicans

Yes................................79%
No.................................10
No opinion.........................11

Democrats

Yes................................74%
No.................................11
No opinion.........................15

Independents

Yes................................87%
No.................................. 6
No opinion......................... 7

Just your best guess—of the 535 present members of Congress, how many got there by using unethical or illegal campaign methods?

One-fifth or more 40%
Fewer than one-fifth.................35
No opinion.........................25

By Education
College

One-fifth or more 40%
Fewer than one-fifth. 46
No opinion. 14

High School

One-fifth or more 43%
Fewer than one-fifth. 33
No opinion. 24

Grade School

One-fifth or more 26%
Fewer than one-fifth. 23
No opinion. 51

By Age
18–24 Years

One-fifth or more 49%
Fewer than one-fifth. 37
No opinion. 14

25–29 Years

One-fifth or more 45%
Fewer than one-fifth. 39
No opinion. 16

30–49 Years

One-fifth or more 42%
Fewer than one-fifth. 36
No opinion. 22

50 Years and Over

One-fifth or more 31%
Fewer than one-fifth. 33
No opinion. 36

By Politics
Republicans

One-fifth or more 38%
Fewer than one-fifth. 39
No opinion. 23

Democrats

One-fifth or more 37%
Fewer than one-fifth. 35
No opinion. 28

Independents

One-fifth or more 46%
Fewer than one-fifth. 35
No opinion. 19

Note: The Abscam affair, an undercover FBI operation originally designed to gather evidence about stolen securities and works of art, subsequently produced allegations of political corruption implicating members of Congress and their associates in cases involving hundreds of thousands of dollars in bribes.

The recent indictments of several congressmen resulting from the Abscam affair again have focused attention on congressional ethics. In a survey completed shortly after the initial disclosure of the Abscam scandal, 78% of the electorate expressed the belief that there are senators and representatives serving in Congress who won election by using unethical and illegal methods in their campaigns. This is 11 points higher than the 67% figure recorded in a 1973 survey. In addition, four out of ten persons surveyed believed that one-fifth or more of the 535 members of Congress employed questionable methods to get elected.

In light of the Democratic majorities in both houses of Congress, it is interesting to note that there is little difference between the views of Republican and Democratic survey respondents. Even less surprising is the fact that more independents (87%) than members of either of the two major parties believed that congressmen now in office had employed corrupt methods to attain their present political positions.

MARCH 23
SALT II

Interviewing Date: 2/29–3/3/80
Survey #149-G

Have you heard or read about SALT II, the proposed nuclear arms agreement between the United States and the Soviet Union?

Yes.................................. 76%
No.................................. 24

Asked of those who replied in the affirmative: Everything considered, would you like to see the U.S. Senate ratify (vote in favor of) this proposed treaty, or not?

Would 30%
Would not 27
No opinion......................... 19
                                    76%*

By Education
College

Would 39%
Would not 40
No opinion......................... 12
                                    91%*

High School

Would 28%
Would not 24
No opinion......................... 22
                                    74%*

Grade School

Would 18%
Would not 14
No opinion......................... 22
                                    54%*

By Region
East

Would 35%
Would not 26
No opinion......................... 18
                                    79%*

Midwest

Would 30%
Would not 27
No opinion......................... 23
                                    80%*

South

Would 27%
Would not 28
No opinion......................... 18
                                    73%*

West

Would 25%
Would not 31
No opinion......................... 16
                                    72%*

By Age
18–24 Years

Would 34%
Would not 23
No opinion......................... 16
                                    73%*

25–29 Years

Would 38%
Would not 27
No opinion......................... 13
                                    78%*

30–49 Years

Would 31%
Would not 28
No opinion......................... 20
                                    79%*

50 Years and Over

Would 25%
Would not 29
No opinion.......................... 20
                                      74%*

By Income
$25,000 and Over

Would 39%
Would not 38
No opinion.......................... 13
                                      90%*

$20,000–$24,999

Would 34%
Would not 32
No opinion.......................... 16
                                      82%*

$15,000–$19,999

Would 31%
Would not 31
No opinion.......................... 21
                                      83%*

$10,000–$14,999

Would 31%
Would not 24
No opinion.......................... 22
                                      77%*

$5,000–$9,999

Would 25%
Would not 22
No opinion.......................... 19
                                      66%*

Under $5,000

Would 16%
Would not 13
No opinion.......................... 24
                                      53%*

By Politics
Republicans

Would 27%
Would not 35
No opinion.......................... 19
                                      81%*

Democrats

Would 32%
Would not 21
No opinion.......................... 19
                                      72%*

Independents

Would 29%
Would not 34
No opinion.......................... 18
                                      81%*

*Percentage of total sample

Note: Despite the marked deterioration in Soviet-American relations brought about by the Soviet invasion of Afghanistan and demands for a stronger defense posture toward the Russians, the American public remains evenly divided on the desirability of Senate ratification of the SALT II agreement with the Soviet Union.

Among the informed portion of the U.S. public, 26% would like to see the Senate ratify the arms limitation pact, 26% are opposed, and 9% are uncommitted. These figures are virtually unchanged from those recorded in a late September Gallup survey, prior to the Soviet invasion of Afghanistan on December 27.

The present status of American public opinion on SALT II, while showing little change since last fall, represents a proportional decline in informed support since the question series was first asked one year ago. Last March the ratio in favor of ratification was 3 to 1; by June it had slipped to 5 to 3; and in September and in the current survey those in favor and those opposed to ratification are about equal.

The current public support for SALT II is surprising in view of recent survey findings showing many Americans sharply critical of America's military posture vis-à-vis the Soviets.

Because of the complexity of this issue, the Gallup Poll sought to separate informed from uninformed opinion. The following represents the trend in support for SALT II ratification among the informed public:

Informed Opinion on SALT II
March 1979

Would	27%
Would not	9
No opinion	9
	45%*

June 1979

Would	34%
Would not	19
No opinion	11
	64%*

September 1979

Would	24%
Would not	26
No opinion	11
	61%*

*Percentage of total sample

Although the SALT II agreement already has been signed by both President Jimmy Carter and Soviet President Leonid Brezhnev, in a news conference on March 14 Carter said: "Because of the Soviet invasion of Afghanistan, it is obvious that we would not be successful in ratifying the SALT II treaty at this time." The president further stated that he will not ask the Senate to ratify SALT II until he has a chance to consult very closely with the congressional leadership, but he intends to honor the terms of the treaty if the Soviet Union also complies.

MARCH 27
COST OF LIVING

Interviewing Date: 1/25–28; 2/1–4/80
Survey #147-G; #148-G

What is the smallest amount of money a family of four (husband, wife, and two children) needs each week to get along in this community?

	Median Average
National	$250*

By Education

College	$298
High school	$249
Grade school	$202

By Region

East	$252
Midwest	$249
South	$249
West	$252

By Community Size

One million and over	$300
500,000–999,999	$298
50,000–499,999	$250
2,500–49,999	$248
Under 2,500; rural	$223

By Income

$15,000 and over	$299
$10,000–$14,999	$225
$5,000–$9,999	$226
Under $5,000	$201

By Occupation

Professional and business	$299
Clerical and sales	$249
Manual workers	$249
Non-labor force	$202

*Farm families were excluded from the survey since many farmers raise their own food.

What is the smallest amount of money your family needs each week to get along in this community?

	Median Average
National	$203*

By Education

College	$252
High school	$201
Grade school	$149

By Region

East	$202
Midwest	$201
South	$200
West	$248

By Community Size

One million and over	$250
500,000–999,999	$225
50,000–499,999	$201
2,500–49,999	$199
Under 2,500; rural	$200

By Income

$15,000 and over	$252
$10,000–$14,999	$199
$5,000–$9,999	$150
Under $5,000	$102

By Occupation

Professional and business	$298
Clerical and sales	$200
Manual workers	$202
Non-labor force	$148

By Size of Household

Single person	$126
Two-person family	$199
Three-person family	$200
Four-person family	$250
Five-person-or-more family	$298

*Farm families were excluded from the survey since many farmers raise their own food.

On the average, about how much does your family spend on food, including milk, each week?

	Median Average
National	$59*

By Education

College	$61
High school	$61
Grade school	$49

By Region

East	$62
Midwest	$55
South	$58
West	$62

By Community Size

One million and over	$73
500,000–999,999	$61
50,000–499,999	$56
2,500–49,999	$52
Under 2,500; rural	$56

By Income

$15,000 and over	$69
$10,000–$14,999	$52
$5,000–$9,999	$49
Under $5,000	$41

By Occupation

Professional and business	$70
Clerical and sales	$51
Manual workers	$64
Non-labor force	$46

By Size of Household

Single person $32
Two-person family.................... $50
Three-person family $62
Four-person family $71
Five-person-or-more family $90

*Farm families were excluded from the survey since many farmers raise their own food.

Note: President Carter's March 14 announcement of his antiinflation package was timely in view of the public's perceptions of the cost of living. Across the country Americans now believe it takes $250 a week for a family of four to make ends meet, representing a record median estimate.

The 12% increase recorded this past year— up $27 from the 1979 median estimate of $223 per week—represents the largest single dollar increase and one of the largest percentage increases in the audit's forty-three-year history.

In 1937 when the Gallup Poll first surveyed the public's perceptions of living costs, the median response was $30. After World War II, in 1947, the figure climbed to $43, but it did not hit three-digit proportions until 1967, when the median was $101.

Only once in the history of the audit has the annual percentage rate of increase been higher than it is today. During the Korean War from 1951 to 1952, the median estimate went from $50 per week to $60 per week, a 20% increase. And only twice has the annual rate of increase been as high as that recorded this year. That was in the mid-1960s and in 1976, when 12% annual increases were also recorded.

Looking ahead to the next twelve months, more than one-half of the respondents in a recent Gallup Organization Economic Service survey believe that their income will not keep up with prices, one-third expect only to keep pace with inflation, and 8% feel their income will exceed the cost of living.

The current results indicate that inflation has hit equally hard in all regions of the country. In the Midwest and South, the median estimates are both $249, whereas easterners and westerners feel it takes almost the same amount of money—$252—to subsist from week to week.

Community size is also a considerable factor, with residents of the nation's largest cities saying it takes $300 a week to keep a family of four going. Those living in rural areas and small towns report that a family could exist on $223 weekly.

The amount of money American families are paying at the grocery store continues to rise sharply. The median amount currently cited by respondents across the nation is the highest recorded since 1937, when this figure was only $11 per week. Between 1949 and 1969 the figure grew slightly from $25 to $33 per week, an increase of 32%. However, during the last decade there has been a 74% increase—from $34 in 1970 to $59 today, making it the highest annual dollar increase in the survey's history.

Sharpest contrasts reported in weekly food expenditures are those recorded by geographical region and community size. Regionally, food costs take a bigger portion—$62 per week— of the family budget of easterners, but the West, previously a relatively inexpensive region, has caught up with the Eastern median with food bills skyrocketing from $51 per week in 1979 to $62 in 1980. In comparison, $58 a week is spent on food in the South and $55 in the Midwest.

Residents of the largest cities report a median expenditure of $73 per week, while those living in the smaller towns and rural areas spend $56.

The trend since the inception of the cost-of-living survey in 1937 is presented below:

Minimum Amount Needed for a Family of Four*

	Median Average
1980	$250
1979	$223
1978	$201
1977	$199
1976	$177
1975	$161

1974	$152
1973	$149
1971	$127
1969	$120
1967	$101
1964	$81
1959	$79
1957	$72
1954	$60
1951	$50
1947	$43
1937	$30

*Nonfarm families

Weekly Food Expenditures*

	Median Average
1980	$59
1979	$53
1978	$50
1977	$48
1976	$48
1975	$47
1974	$42
1973	$37
1971	$35
1970	$34
1969	$33
1959	$29
1949	$25
1937	$11

*Nonfarm families

MARCH 30
FEDERAL BUDGET

Interviewing Date: 3/7–10/80
Survey #150-G

Have you heard or read about the proposal for a constitutional amendment which would require the federal government to balance the national budget each year?

Yes..................................45%
No...................................55

All persons in the survey (both those informed and those not) were then given basic information about a specific proposal, as follows: A proposed amendment to the Constitution would require Congress to approve a balanced federal budget each year. Government spending would have to be limited to no more than expected revenues, unless a three-fifths majority of Congress voted to spend more than expected revenue. Would you favor or oppose this amendment to the Constitution?

Favor................................67%
Oppose..............................13
Don't know 20

By Education
College

Favor................................70%
Oppose..............................19
Don't know 11

High School

Favor................................68%
Oppose..............................11
Don't know 21

Grade School

Favor................................55%
Oppose..............................11
Don't know 34

By Income
$25,000 and Over

Favor................................78%
Oppose..............................15
Don't know 7

$20,000–$24,999

Favor................................78%
Oppose..............................10
Don't know 12

$15,000–$19,999

Favor 69%
Oppose 15
Don't know 16

$10,000–$14,999

Favor 70%
Oppose 11
Don't know 19

$5,000–$9,999

Favor 59%
Oppose 15
Don't know 26

Under $5,000

Favor 48%
Oppose 11
Don't know 41

By Politics
Republicans

Favor 77%
Oppose 12
Don't know 11

Democrats

Favor 60%
Oppose 15
Don't know 25

Independents

Favor 70%
Oppose 11
Don't know 19

Informed Group Only

Favor 75%
Oppose 16
Don't know 9

If the budget were balanced, what effect, if any, do you think this would have on the

rate of inflation—would inflation probably increase a lot, increase a little, stay the same, decrease a little, or decrease a lot?

Increase a lot 5%
Increase a little 7
Stay the same 18
Decrease a little 37
Decrease a lot 16
Don't know 17

By Education
College

Increase a lot 3%
Increase a little 7
Stay the same 17
Decrease a little 45
Decrease a lot 18
Don't know 10

High School

Increase a lot 6%
Increase a little 8
Stay the same 19
Decrease a little 33
Decrease a lot 17
Don't know 17

Grade School

Increase a lot 7%
Increase a little 6
Stay the same 12
Decrease a little 34
Decrease a lot 11
Don't know 30

By Income
$25,000 and Over

Increase a lot 4%
Increase a little 7
Stay the same 17
Decrease a little 42
Decrease a lot 23
Don't know 7

$20,000–$24,999

Increase a lot	4%
Increase a little	7
Stay the same	17
Decrease a little	47
Decrease a lot	17
Don't know	8

$15,000–$19,999

Increase a lot	5%
Increase a little	7
Stay the same	18
Decrease a little	37
Decrease a lot	15
Don't know	18

$10,000–$14,999

Increase a lot	4%
Increase a little	9
Stay the same	16
Decrease a little	38
Decrease a lot	17
Don't know	16

$5,000–$9,999

Increase a lot	8%
Increase a little	5
Stay the same	20
Decrease a little	31
Decrease a lot	16
Don't know	20

Under $5,000

Increase a lot	7%
Increase a little	8
Stay the same	14
Decrease a little	26
Decrease a lot	7
Don't know	38

By Politics
Republicans

Increase a lot	2%
Increase a little	6
Stay the same	19
Decrease a little	41
Decrease a lot	20
Don't know	12

Democrats

Increase a lot	7%
Increase a little	7
Stay the same	17
Decrease a little	35
Decrease a lot	15
Don't know	19

Independents

Increase a lot	5%
Increase a little	8
Stay the same	19
Decrease a little	37
Decrease a lot	16
Don't know	15

Informed Group Only

Increase a lot	4%
Increase a little	6
Stay the same	17
Decrease a little	45
Decrease a lot	20
Don't know	8

If the budget were balanced, what effect, if any, do you think this would have on the number of employees in the federal government—would the number of government employees probably increase a lot, increase a little, stay the same, decrease a little, or decrease a lot?

Increase a lot	2%
Increase a little	6
Stay the same	17
Decrease a little	40
Decrease a lot	23
Don't know	12

By Education
College

Increase a lot	1%
Increase a little	5

Stay the same 15
Decrease a little 47
Decrease a lot........................ 27
Don't know 5

High School

Increase a lot......................... 2%
Increase a little 6
Stay the same 18
Decrease a little 38
Decrease a lot........................ 23
Don't know 13

Grade School

Increase a lot......................... 4%
Increase a little 6
Stay the same 19
Decrease a little 31
Decrease a lot........................ 17
Don't know 23

By Income

$25,000 and Over

Increase a lot......................... 1%
Increase a little 5
Stay the same 15
Decrease a little 41
Decrease a lot........................ 36
Don't know 2

$20,000–$24,999

Increase a lot......................... 3%
Increase a little 5
Stay the same 11
Decrease a little 53
Decrease a lot........................ 22
Don't know 6

$15,000–$19,999

Increase a lot......................... 2%
Increase a little 8
Stay the same 17
Decrease a little 40
Decrease a lot........................ 22
Don't know 11

$10,000–$14,999

Increase a lot......................... 2%
Increase a little 7
Stay the same 20
Decrease a little 39
Decrease a lot........................ 20
Don't know 12

$5,000–$9,999

Increase a lot......................... 2%
Increase a little 3
Stay the same 21
Decrease a little 36
Decrease a lot........................ 22
Don't know 16

Under $5,000

Increase a lot......................... 3%
Increase a little 4
Stay the same 21
Decrease a little 29
Decrease a lot........................ 13
Don't know 30

By Politics

Republicans

Increase a lot......................... 1%
Increase a little 4
Stay the same 11
Decrease a little 47
Decrease a lot........................ 30
Don't know 7

Democrats

Increase a lot......................... 2%
Increase a little 6
Stay the same 22
Decrease a little 36
Decrease a lot........................ 19
Don't know 16

Independents

Increase a lot......................... 2%
Increase a little 5
Stay the same 15

Decrease a little 43
Decrease a lot 26
Don't know 9

Informed Group Only

Increase a lot 2%
Increase a little 5
Stay the same 16
Decrease a little 43
Decrease a lot 29
Don't know 5

If the budget were balanced, what effect, if any, do you think this would have on government programs for people with low incomes or people on welfare—would the amount of money and services they receive from the government probably increase a lot, increase a little, stay the same, decrease a little, or decrease a lot?

Increase a lot 2%
Increase a little 10
Stay the same 24
Decrease a little 32
Decrease a lot 18
Don't know 14

By Education
College

Increase a lot 1%
Increase a little 9
Stay the same 21
Decrease a little 37
Decrease a lot 26
Don't know 6

High School

Increase a lot 3%
Increase a little 10
Stay the same 24
Decrease a little 31
Decrease a lot 16
Don't know 16

Grade School

Increase a lot 2%
Increase a little 12
Stay the same 25
Decrease a little 26
Decrease a lot 11
Don't know 24

By Income
$25,000 and Over

Increase a lot 1%
Increase a little 6
Stay the same 24
Decrease a little 38
Decrease a lot 26
Don't know 5

$20,000–$24,999

Increase a lot 2%
Increase a little 8
Stay the same 22
Decrease a little 40
Decrease a lot 21
Don't know 7

$15,000–$19,999

Increase a lot 1%
Increase a little 10
Stay the same 22
Decrease a little 34
Decrease a lot 17
Don't know 16

$10,000–$14,999

Increase a lot 3%
Increase a little 14
Stay the same 21
Decrease a little 32
Decrease a lot 18
Don't know 12

$5,000–$9,999

Increase a lot 2%
Increase a little 9
Stay the same 30

Decrease a little 26
Decrease a lot 13
Don't know 20

Under $5,000

Increase a lot 4%
Increase a little 12
Stay the same 23
Decrease a little 20
Decrease a lot 12
Don't know 29

By Politics
Republicans

Increase a lot 1%
Increase a little 11
Stay the same 18
Decrease a little 37
Decrease a lot 22
Don't know 11

Democrats

Increase a lot 2%
Increase a little 10
Stay the same 24
Decrease a little 33
Decrease a lot 16
Don't know 15

Independents

Increase a lot 2%
Increase a little 10
Stay the same 27
Decrease a little 30
Decrease a lot 19
Don't know 12

Informed Group Only

Increase a lot 1%
Increase a little 9
Stay the same 24
Decrease a little 37
Decrease a lot 22
Don't know 7

If the budget were balanced, what effect, if any, do you think this would have on the amount of taxes people have to pay— would taxes probably increase a lot, increase a little, stay the same, decrease a little, or decrease a lot?

Increase a lot 12%
Increase a little 23
Stay the same 24
Decrease a little 21
Decrease a lot 7
Don't know 13

By Education
College

Increase a lot 12%
Increase a little 28
Stay the same 25
Decrease a little 24
Decrease a lot 7
Don't know 4

High School

Increase a lot 13%
Increase a little 22
Stay the same 24
Decrease a little 20
Decrease a lot 7
Don't know 14

Grade School

Increase a lot 12%
Increase a little 17
Stay the same 25
Decrease a little 18
Decrease a lot 4
Don't know 24

By Income
$25,000 and Over

Increase a lot 9%
Increase a little 25
Stay the same 31
Decrease a little 25
Decrease a lot 6
Don't know 4

$20,000–$24,999

Increase a lot........................10%
Increase a little......................29
Stay the same 25
Decrease a little 21
Decrease a lot........................ 7
Don't know 8

$15,000–$19,999

Increase a lot........................12%
Increase a little......................27
Stay the same 26
Decrease a little 19
Decrease a lot........................ 7
Don't know 9

$10,000–$14,999

Increase a lot........................14%
Increase a little......................21
Stay the same 20
Decrease a little 21
Decrease a lot........................ 8
Don't know 16

$5,000–$9,999

Increase a lot........................10%
Increase a little......................21
Stay the same 28
Decrease a little 20
Decrease a lot........................ 4
Don't know 17

Under $5,000

Increase a lot........................20%
Increase a little......................18
Stay the same 14
Decrease a little 16
Decrease a lot........................ 6
Don't know 26

By Politics

Republicans

Increase a lot........................10%
Increase a little......................24
Stay the same 25
Decrease a little 25
Decrease a lot........................ 7
Don't know 9

Democrats

Increase a lot........................12%
Increase a little......................23
Stay the same 22
Decrease a little 21
Decrease a lot........................ 7
Don't know 15

Independents

Increase a lot........................14%
Increase a little......................24
Stay the same 26
Decrease a little 19
Decrease a lot........................ 6
Don't know 11

Informed Group Only

Increase a lot........................10%
Increase a little......................26
Stay the same 28
Decrease a little 22
Decrease a lot........................ 8
Don't know 6

Note: By a two-thirds majority (67%) the American public favors a constitutional amendment to require Congress to balance the federal budget each year. An even higher percentage of those who have read or heard about it approve a constitutional amendment that would require a balanced budget. This "aware group" votes 75% to 16% in favor of a constitutional amendment, with 9% undecided.

The majority opinion among the aware group is that a balanced budget would decrease inflation, the number of federal government employees, and the amount of money and services persons on low incomes or welfare would receive from the government. However, relatively few are convinced that a balanced budget would have a major impact in these respects.

The survey also reveals that the segment of the population aware of the budget proposal is closely divided on whether balancing the budget would increase or decrease taxes.

A constitutional amendment requiring a balanced budget is one on which both Republican and Democratic voters can agree, with large majorities in each party in favor of the proposal.

Following are the arguments, listed in order of frequency of mention, given by survey respondents who either favor or oppose a constitutional amendment to balance the budget:

Arguments in Favor of Constitutional Amendment to Balance Budget

1. Will control/decrease government spending and waste.
2. Will help slow down inflation.
3. It is good for governments, families, and individuals to balance their respective budgets.
4. The national debt is too high.

Arguments Against Constitutional Amendment to Balance Budget

1. Impractical, cannot be done.
2. Would hurt national security.
3. Would have to cut needed programs.
4. Would cause loss of jobs.

MARCH 31
DEMOCRATIC PRESIDENTIAL CANDIDATES

Interviewing Date: 3/28–31/80
Survey #151-G

Asked of Democrats: Suppose the choice for president in the Democratic convention in 1980 narrows down to Jimmy Carter and Edward Kennedy. Which one would you prefer to have the Democratic convention select?

Carter............................59%
Kennedy 31
Undecided.........................10

Note: Senator Edward Kennedy's upset victories over President Jimmy Carter in the March 25 New York and Connecticut Demo-cratic primaries have not translated into significant gains for the Massachusetts senator nationwide.

In the Wisconsin and Kansas primaries, President Carter held a 59% to 31% lead over Kennedy as the choice of Democratic voters nationwide for the 1980 presidential nomination. The current figures represent only a marginal change in the standings since the previous survey (March 7–10), when Carter led Kennedy 60% to 28% among Democrats, with 12% undecided.

During this same period there also has been little change in the president's popularity rating, with 39% in the current survey saying they approve of his handling of the presidency and 52% expressing disapproval. In comparison, Carter's approval score was 43% in the previous survey.

APRIL 1
PRESIDENTIAL TRIAL HEATS

Interviewing Date: 3/28–31/80
Survey #151-G

Asked of registered voters: Suppose the presidential election were being held today. If Jimmy Carter were the Democratic candidate and Ronald Reagan were the Republican candidate, which would you like to see win? [Those who named another person or who were undecided were asked: As of today, do you lean more to Carter, the Democrat, or to Reagan, the Republican?]

Carter............................50%
Reagan............................42
Other 2
Undecided.........................6

By Region
East

Carter............................54%
Reagan............................38
Other 1
Undecided.........................7

Midwest

Carter..............................52%
Reagan............................39
Other 2
Undecided..........................7

South

Carter..............................53%
Reagan............................41
Other 1
Undecided..........................5

West

Carter..............................38%
Reagan............................55
Other 2
Undecided..........................5

By Politics
Republicans

Carter..............................15%
Reagan............................80
Other 2
Undecided..........................3

Democrats

Carter..............................74%
Reagan............................20
Other 1
Undecided..........................5

Independents

Carter..............................41%
Reagan............................46
Other 3
Undecided..........................10

Asked of those who named Carter: Do you strongly support him or do you only moderately support him?

Strongly............................30%
Moderately 68
Can't say..........................2

Asked of those who named Reagan: Do you strongly support him or do you only moderately support him?

Strongly............................34%
Moderately 63
Can't say..........................3

Also asked of those who named Carter: Do you strongly oppose Reagan or do you only moderately oppose him?

Strongly............................31%
Moderately 58
Can't say..........................11

Also asked of those who named Reagan: Do you strongly oppose Carter or do you only moderately oppose him?

Strongly............................41%
Moderately 55
Can't say..........................4

Also asked of those who named Carter: Do you support him mostly because of the kind of man he is or mostly because of the positions he takes on issues?

The kind of man he is 48%
His positions on issues 36
Can't say..........................16

Also asked of those who named Reagan: Do you support him mostly because of the kind of man he is or mostly because of the positions he takes on issues?

The kind of man he is 23%
His positions on issues 65
Can't say..........................12

Asked of registered voters: If President Jimmy Carter were the Democratic candidate, running against Ronald Reagan, the Republican candidate, and John Anderson, an independent candidate, which would you like to see win? [Those who named another person or who were undecided were asked: As of today, do you lean more to Carter, the Democrat, to Reagan, the Republican, or to Anderson, the independent candidate?]

Carter.............................40%
Reagan.............................34
Anderson...........................21
Other 1
Undecided.......................... 4

By Sex
Male

Carter.............................40%
Reagan.............................35
Anderson...........................21
Other 1
Undecided.......................... 3

Female

Carter.............................41%
Reagan.............................34
Anderson...........................20
Other 1
Undecided.......................... 4

By Race
White

Carter.............................38%
Reagan.............................37
Anderson...........................21
Other 1
Undecided.......................... 3

Nonwhite

Carter.............................61%
Reagan.............................14
Anderson...........................20
Other 1
Undecided.......................... 4

By Education
College

Carter.............................35%
Reagan.............................35
Anderson...........................25
Other 1
Undecided.......................... 4

High School

Carter.............................41%
Reagan.............................35
Anderson...........................19
Other 1
Undecided.......................... 4

Grade School

Carter.............................50%
Reagan.............................30
Anderson...........................16
Other 1
Undecided.......................... 3

By Region
East

Carter.............................40%
Reagan.............................30
Anderson...........................26
Other 1
Undecided.......................... 3

Midwest

Carter.............................41%
Reagan.............................32
Anderson...........................21
Other 1
Undecided.......................... 5

South

Carter.............................48%
Reagan.............................38
Anderson...........................10
Other 1
Undecided.......................... 3

West

Carter.............................28%
Reagan.............................40
Anderson...........................27
Other 1
Undecided.......................... 4

By Age
18–24 Years

Carter..............................34%
Reagan.............................34
Anderson...........................27
Other .... *
Undecided......................... 5

25–29 Years

Carter..............................36%
Reagan.............................39
Anderson...........................22
Other .... *
Undecided......................... 3

30–49 Years

Carter..............................43%
Reagan.............................31
Anderson...........................21
Other 1
Undecided......................... 4

50 Years and Over

Carter..............................41%
Reagan.............................36
Anderson...........................19
Other 1
Undecided......................... 3

By Income
$25,000 and Over

Carter..............................35%
Reagan.............................36
Anderson...........................26
Other 1
Undecided......................... 2

$20,000–$24,999

Carter..............................39%
Reagan.............................34
Anderson...........................24
Other 1
Undecided......................... 2

$15,000–$19,999

Carter..............................37%
Reagan.............................42
Anderson...........................16
Other 2
Undecided......................... 3

$10,000–$14,999

Carter..............................48%
Reagan.............................29
Anderson...........................19
Other .... *
Undecided......................... 4

$5,000–$9,999

Carter..............................40%
Reagan.............................33
Anderson...........................22
Other .... *
Undecided......................... 5

Under $5,000

Carter..............................49%
Reagan.............................36
Anderson...........................11
Other .... *
Undecided......................... 4

By Politics
Republicans

Carter..............................12%
Reagan.............................68
Anderson...........................16
Other 1
Undecided......................... 3

Democrats

Carter..............................63%
Reagan.............................16
Anderson...........................17
Other 1
Undecided......................... 3

Independents

Carter.............................26%
Reagan............................36
Anderson..........................31
Other............................. 1
Undecided......................... 6

*Less than 1%

Note: President Jimmy Carter has lost considerable ground to Ronald Reagan in recent weeks and now holds only a slim 50%–42% edge over his principal GOP challenger. However, in the previous test election between the two men (February 29–March 3), Carter held a sizable 58% to 33% lead.

Representative John Anderson of Illinois, tested as an independent candidate in a three-way race against Carter and Reagan, shows surprising strength. Anderson wins the support of 21% of registered voters to 40% for Carter and 34% for Reagan. Anderson draws as much support from registered Democrats as from registered Republicans. Among registered voters who classify themselves as political independents, Anderson is in second place with 31% of the independent vote compared to 36% for Reagan and 26% for Carter.

Anderson's current support among all registered voters is almost the same as the 22% vote George Wallace received in a May 1972 three-way test election against Richard Nixon and Hubert Humphrey. The Anderson vote in the latest survey and Wallace's standing in 1972 exceed any preconvention third-party support in the Gallup Poll's forty-five years of polling experience.

APRIL 8
IRANIAN SITUATION

Interviewing Date: 3/28–31/80
Survey #151-G

Do you approve or disapprove of the way Jimmy Carter is handling the crisis in Iran?

Approve............................40%
Disapprove........................50
Don't know....................... 10

By Sex
Male

Approve............................42%
Disapprove........................52
Don't know....................... 6

Female

Approve............................37%
Disapprove........................49
Don't know....................... 14

By Race
White

Approve............................39%
Disapprove........................50
Don't know....................... 11

Nonwhite

Approve............................39%
Disapprove........................52
Don't know....................... 9

By Education
College

Approve............................43%
Disapprove........................50
Don't know....................... 7

High School

Approve............................38%
Disapprove........................51
Don't know....................... 11

Grade School

Approve............................40%
Disapprove........................46
Don't know....................... 14

By Region

East

Approve	37%
Disapprove	51
Don't know	12

Midwest

Approve	41%
Disapprove	49
Don't know	10

South

Approve	45%
Disapprove	47
Don't know	8

West

Approve	32%
Disapprove	55
Don't know	13

By Age

18–24 Years

Approve	34%
Disapprove	53
Don't know	13

25–29 Years

Approve	38%
Disapprove	54
Don't know	8

30–49 Years

Approve	38%
Disapprove	54
Don't know	8

50 Years and Over

Approve	44%
Disapprove	44
Don't know	12

By Politics

Republicans

Approve	28%
Disapprove	61
Don't know	11

Democrats

Approve	47%
Disapprove	44
Don't know	9

Independents

Approve	38%
Disapprove	54
Don't know	8

If the hostages are released unharmed, which one of the following do you think the United States should do with respect to Iran?

Punish Iran diplomatically and economically	54%
Use military force against Iran	4
Do nothing	33
Don't know	9

By Sex

Male

Punish Iran diplomatically and economically	57%
Use military force against Iran	5
Do nothing	32
Don't know	6

Female

Punish Iran diplomatically and economically	51%
Use military force against Iran	2
Do nothing	34
Don't know	13

By Race

White

Punish Iran diplomatically and
economically 56%
Use military force against Iran 3
Do nothing 31
Don't know 10

Nonwhite

Punish Iran diplomatically and
economically 35%
Use military force against Iran 7
Do nothing 46
Don't know 12

By Education

College

Punish Iran diplomatically and
economically 59%
Use military force against Iran 3
Do nothing 32
Don't know 6

High School

Punish Iran diplomatically and
economically 56%
Use military force against Iran 4
Do nothing 31
Don't know 9

Grade School

Punish Iran diplomatically and
economically 35%
Use military force against Iran 4
Do nothing 42
Don't know 19

By Region

East

Punish Iran diplomatically and
economically 58%
Use military force against Iran 2
Do nothing 33
Don't know 7

Midwest

Punish Iran diplomatically and
economically 57%
Use military force against Iran 4
Do nothing 32
Don't know 7

South

Punish Iran diplomatically and
economically 51%
Use military force against Iran 4
Do nothing 32
Don't know 13

West

Punish Iran diplomatically and
economically 47%
Use military force against Iran 6
Do nothing 34
Don't know 13

By Age

18–24 Years

Punish Iran diplomatically and
economically 63%
Use military force against Iran 3
Do nothing 29
Don't know 5

25–29 Years

Punish Iran diplomatically and
economically 50%
Use military force against Iran 6
Do nothing 33
Don't know 11

30–49 Years

Punish Iran diplomatically and
economically 55%
Use military force against Iran 3
Do nothing 33
Don't know 9

50 Years and Over

Punish Iran diplomatically and
   economically 49%
Use military force against Iran. 4
Do nothing 34
Don't know 13

By Politics
Republicans

Punish Iran diplomatically and
   economically 57%
Use military force against Iran. 5
Do nothing 30
Don't know 8

Democrats

Punish Iran diplomatically and
   economically 51%
Use military force against Iran. 3
Do nothing 36
Don't know 10

Independents

Punish Iran diplomatically and
   economically 58%
Use military force against Iran. 4
Do nothing 29
Don't know 9

*If one or more of the hostages is harmed,
which one of the following do you think the
United States should do with respect to
Iran?*

Punish Iran diplomatically and
   economically 53%
Use military force against Iran. 32
Do nothing 3
Don't know 12

By Sex
Male

Punish Iran diplomatically and
   economically 53%
Use military force against Iran. 37
Do nothing 3
Don't know 7

Female

Punish Iran diplomatically and
   economically 53%
Use military force against Iran. 28
Do nothing 3
Don't know 16

By Race
White

Punish Iran diplomatically and
   economically 53%
Use military force against Iran. 37
Do nothing 3
Don't know 7

Nonwhite

Punish Iran diplomatically and
   economically 53%
Use military force against Iran. 28
Do nothing 3
Don't know 16

By Education
College

Punish Iran diplomatically and
   economically 63%
Use military force against Iran. 27
Do nothing 3
Don't know 7

High School

Punish Iran diplomatically and
   economically 52%
Use military force against Iran. 36
Do nothing 2
Don't know 10

Grade School

Punish Iran diplomatically and
   economically 38%
Use military force against Iran. 29
Do nothing 6
Don't know 27

By Region

East

Punish Iran diplomatically and
   economically 60%
Use military force against Iran 28
Do nothing 2
Don't know 10

Midwest

Punish Iran diplomatically and
   economically 56%
Use military force against Iran 33
Do nothing 3
Don't know 8

South

Punish Iran diplomatically and
   economically 43%
Use military force against Iran 36
Do nothing 4
Don't know 17

West

Punish Iran diplomatically and
   economically 54%
Use military force against Iran 32
Do nothing 3
Don't know 11

By Age

18–24 Years

Punish Iran diplomatically and
   economically 51%
Use military force against Iran 41
Do nothing 2
Don't know 6

25–29 Years

Punish Iran diplomatically and
   economically 55%
Use military force against Iran 36
Do nothing 3
Don't know 6

30–49 Years

Punish Iran diplomatically and
   economically 54%
Use military force against Iran 33
Do nothing 3
Don't know 10

50 Years and Over

Punish Iran diplomatically and
   economically 54%
Use military force against Iran 26
Do nothing 3
Don't know 17

By Politics

Republicans

Punish Iran diplomatically and
   economically 56%
Use military force against Iran 33
Do nothing 2
Don't know 9

Democrats

Punish Iran diplomatically and
   economically 54%
Use military force against Iran 30
Do nothing 3
Don't know 13

Independents

Punish Iran diplomatically and
   economically 52%
Use military force against Iran 36
Do nothing 3
Don't know 9

*How do you feel the Iranian situation will
end up—do you think the hostages will be
released or not?*

Released 56%
Not released 29
Don't know 15

By Sex
Male

Released	61%
Not released	27
Don't know	12

Female

Released	51%
Not released	31
Don't know	18

By Race
White

Released	56%
Not released	29
Don't know	15

Nonwhite

Released	56%
Not released	26
Don't know	18

By Education
College

Released	65%
Not released	24
Don't know	11

High School

Released	54%
Not released	32
Don't know	14

Grade School

Released	46%
Not released	27
Don't know	27

By Region
East

Released	58%
Not released	26
Don't know	16

Midwest

Released	62%
Not released	26
Don't know	12

South

Released	49%
Not released	33
Don't know	18

West

Released	57%
Not released	29
Don't know	14

By Age
18–24 Years

Released	54%
Not released	34
Don't know	12

25–29 Years

Released	57%
Not released	34
Don't know	9

30–49 Years

Released	59%
Not released	28
Don't know	13

50 Years and Over

Released	55%
Not released	26
Don't know	19

By Politics
Republicans

Released	57%
Not released	32
Don't know	11

Democrats

Released 59%
Not released 25
Don't know 16

Independents

Released 54%
Not released 31
Don't know 15

Note: Findings on the public's attitudes on the probable fate of the hostages show that prior to the aborted rescue mission in Iran (April 24) 56% of Americans were fairly optimistic about the eventual release of the hostages, and economic and diplomatic sanctions against Iran were favored over the use of armed force. Offered a hypothetical situation in which the hostages are harmed, the public, by a 53% to 32% margin, still preferred nonmilitary measures to military action.

APRIL 10
PRESIDENT CARTER'S ECONOMIC PROGRAM

Interviewing Date: 3/28–31/80
Survey #151-G

Have you heard or read about President Carter's economic program which he announced on March 14?

Yes 67%
No 32
No answer 1

By Education
College

Yes 80%
No 20
No answer . . . . *

High School

Yes 66%
No 33
No answer 1

Grade School

Yes 47%
No 53
No answer . . . . *

By Region
East

Yes 66%
No 33
No answer 1

Midwest

Yes 70%
No 29
No answer 1

South

Yes 66%
No 34
No answer . . . . *

West

Yes 68%
No 31
No answer 1

By Age
18–24 Years

Yes 58%
No 41
No answer 1

25–29 Years

Yes 71%
No 28
No answer 1

30–49 Years

Yes 72%
No 28
No answer . . . . *

50 Years and Over

Yes................................66%
No.................................33
No answer.........................1

By Income
$25,000 and Over

Yes................................76%
No.................................24
No answer.........................*

$20,000–$24,999

Yes................................85%
No.................................15
No answer.........................*

$15,000–$19,999

Yes................................71%
No.................................28
No answer.........................1

$10,000–$14,999

Yes................................70%
No.................................29
No answer.........................1

$5,000–$9,999

Yes................................53%
No.................................46
No answer.........................1

Under $5,000

Yes................................40%
No.................................60
No answer.........................*

By Politics
Republicans

Yes................................67%
No.................................33
No answer.........................*

Democrats

Yes................................70%
No.................................29
No answer.........................1

Independents

Yes................................67%
No.................................33
No answer.........................*

Labor Union Families Only

Yes................................77%
No.................................23
No answer.........................*

Non-Labor Union Families Only

Yes................................64%
No.................................35
No answer.........................1

*Less than 1%

Asked of the aware group: Do you think this program will increase or decrease inflation?

Increase............................38%
Decrease...........................31
Will have no effect (volunteered)........19
No opinion 12

By Education
College

Increase............................33%
Decrease...........................38
Will have no effect (volunteered)........19
No opinion 10

High School

Increase............................44%
Decrease...........................26
Will have no effect (volunteered)........18
No opinion 12

Grade School

Increase.............................27%
Decrease...........................32
Will have no effect (volunteered).......19
No opinion 22

By Region
East

Increase.............................41%
Decrease...........................27
Will have no effect (volunteered).......19
No opinion 13

Midwest

Increase.............................40%
Decrease...........................30
Will have no effect (volunteered).......21
No opinion 9

South

Increase.............................30%
Decrease...........................39
Will have no effect (volunteered).......17
No opinion 14

West

Increase.............................44%
Decrease...........................25
Will have no effect (volunteered).......17
No opinion 14

By Age
18–24 Years

Increase.............................46%
Decrease...........................33
Will have no effect (volunteered).......14
No opinion 7

25–29 Years

Increase.............................48%
Decrease...........................24
Will have no effect (volunteered).......14
No opinion 14

30–49 Years

Increase.............................38%
Decrease...........................32
Will have no effect (volunteered).......20
No opinion 10

50 Years and Over

Increase.............................32%
Decrease...........................31
Will have no effect (volunteered).......20
No opinion 17

By Income
$25,000 and Over

Increase.............................40%
Decrease...........................33
Will have no effect (volunteered).......18
No opinion 9

$20,000–$24,999

Increase.............................39%
Decrease...........................37
Will have no effect (volunteered).......18
No opinion 6

$15,000–$19,999

Increase.............................42%
Decrease...........................30
Will have no effect (volunteered).......19
No opinion 9

$10,000–$14,999

Increase.............................40%
Decrease...........................29
Will have no effect (volunteered).......16
No opinion 15

$5,000–$9,999

Increase.............................34%
Decrease...........................26
Will have no effect (volunteered).......19
No opinion 21

Under $5,000

Increase...........................30%
Decrease 31
Will have no effect (volunteered).......22
No opinion 17

By Politics
Republicans

Increase...........................47%
Decrease 23
Will have no effect (volunteered).......18
No opinion 12

Democrats

Increase...........................33%
Decrease 38
Will have no effect (volunteered).......17
No opinion 12

Independents

Increase...........................41%
Decrease 26
Will have no effect (volunteered).......21
No opinion 12

Labor Union Families Only

Increase...........................46%
Decrease 24
Will have no effect (volunteered).......19
No opinion 11

Non-Labor Union Families Only

Increase...........................36%
Decrease 33
Will have no effect (volunteered).......18
No opinion 13

Also asked of the aware group: Do you think this program will increase or decrease unemployment?

Increase...........................67%
Decrease 14
Will have no effect (volunteered).......8
No opinion 11

By Education
College

Increase...........................72%
Decrease 12
Will have no effect (volunteered).......7
No opinion 9

High School

Increase...........................66%
Decrease 15
Will have no effect (volunteered).......8
No opinion 11

Grade School

Increase...........................50%
Decrease 19
Will have no effect (volunteered).......13
No opinion 18

By Region
East

Increase...........................63%
Decrease 14
Will have no effect (volunteered).......12
No opinion 11

Midwest

Increase...........................69%
Decrease 15
Will have no effect (volunteered).......8
No opinion 8

South

Increase...........................65%
Decrease 18
Will have no effect (volunteered).......5
No opinion 12

West

Increase...........................70%
Decrease 10
Will have no effect (volunteered).......9
No opinion 11

By Age

18–24 Years

Increase...............................68%
Decrease 14
Will have no effect (volunteered).........8
No opinion 10

25–29 Years

Increase...............................71%
Decrease 12
Will have no effect (volunteered).........4
No opinion 13

30–49 Years

Increase...............................70%
Decrease 13
Will have no effect (volunteered).........8
No opinion 9

50 Years and Over

Increase...............................61%
Decrease 17
Will have no effect (volunteered).......11
No opinion 11

By Income

$25,000 and Over

Increase...............................76%
Decrease 11
Will have no effect (volunteered).........6
No opinion 7

$20,000–$24,999

Increase...............................71%
Decrease 15
Will have no effect (volunteered).........6
No opinion 8

$15,000–$19,999

Increase...............................69%
Decrease 13
Will have no effect (volunteered).........6
No opinion 12

$10,000–$14,999

Increase...............................67%
Decrease 15
Will have no effect (volunteered).........8
No opinion 10

$5,000–$9,999

Increase...............................58%
Decrease 16
Will have no effect (volunteered).......11
No opinion 15

Under $5,000

Increase...............................51%
Decrease 24
Will have no effect (volunteered).........9
No opinion 16

By Politics

Republicans

Increase...............................70%
Decrease 10
Will have no effect (volunteered).......10
No opinion 10

Democrats

Increase...............................64%
Decrease 19
Will have no effect (volunteered).........7
No opinion 10

Independents

Increase...............................70%
Decrease 10
Will have no effect (volunteered).........9
No opinion 11

Labor Union Families Only

Increase...............................72%
Decrease 12
Will have no effect (volunteered).........7
No opinion 9

Non-Labor Union Families Only

Increase...............................65%
Decrease 15

Will have no effect (volunteered)....... 9
No opinion 11

Also asked of the aware group: As part of the president's economic program, the government would make it more difficult for people to buy things on time or credit. Do you think this would be a good idea or a poor idea?

Good idea..........................67%
Poor idea........................... 28
No opinion 5

By Education
College

Good idea..........................75%
Poor idea........................... 22
No opinion 3

High School

Good idea..........................65%
Poor idea........................... 31
No opinion 4

Grade School

Good idea..........................54%
Poor idea........................... 33
No opinion 13

By Region
East

Good idea..........................64%
Poor idea........................... 32
No opinion 4

Midwest

Good idea..........................70%
Poor idea........................... 25
No opinion 5

South

Good idea..........................69%
Poor idea........................... 27
No opinion 4

West

Good idea..........................67%
Poor idea........................... 28
No opinion 5

By Age
18–24 Years

Good idea..........................62%
Poor idea........................... 36
No opinion 2

25–29 Years

Good idea..........................65%
Poor idea........................... 32
No opinion 3

30–49 Years

Good idea..........................70%
Poor idea........................... 26
No opinion 4

50 Years and Over

Good idea..........................69%
Poor idea........................... 25
No opinion 6

By Income
$25,000 and Over

Good idea..........................78%
Poor idea........................... 19
No opinion 3

$20,000–$24,999

Good idea..........................75%
Poor idea........................... 22
No opinion 3

$15,000–$19,999

Good idea..........................61%
Poor idea........................... 36
No opinion 3

$10,000–$14,999

Good idea 63%
Poor idea 32
No opinion 5

$5,000–$9,999

Good idea 58%
Poor idea 38
No opinion 4

Under $5,000

Good idea 62%
Poor idea 27
No opinion 11

By Politics
Republicans

Good idea 66%
Poor idea 30
No opinion 4

Democrats

Good idea 71%
Poor idea 25
No opinion 4

Independents

Good idea 73%
Poor idea 24
No opinion 3

Labor Union Families Only

Good idea 64%
Poor idea 31
No opinion 5

Non-Labor Union Families Only

Good idea 69%
Poor idea 27
No opinion 4

Note: While a majority of Americans believe that President Carter's new economic plan will either increase the nation's soaring inflation rate or have no effect on it, they give solid support to his proposal to tighten consumer credit.

Sharp differences are found on the basis of political affiliation, with Democrats leaning only slightly toward a pessimistic view. On the other hand, Republicans are more inclined (2 to 1) to believe that the president's program will not decrease inflation. And two out of three of those aware of the president's plan feel unemployment will increase, which in fact is an expected consequence of the program.

While the public tends to be skeptical about the effectiveness of Carter's program for dealing with inflation, there is considerable support for making it more difficult for people to buy on time or credit. Upscale groups such as the college educated tend to be more optimistic about the plan's potential effectiveness in fighting inflation.

President Carter's position, announced in a March 14 address to the nation, is that a slowdown in the economy is necessary at this time in order to reduce inflation, which can best be accomplished by imposing a policy of tight money, controlling credit, and balancing the federal budget.

Most of the spending reductions that Carter has proposed will not take effect until the start of fiscal 1981, in October, with the biggest impact not likely to be felt until the fiscal year is well under way.

APRIL 17
DEMOCRATIC PRESIDENTIAL CANDIDATES

Interviewing Date: 4/11–14/80
Survey #153-G

Suppose the choice for president in the Democratic convention in 1980 narrows down to Jimmy Carter and Edward Kennedy. Which one would you prefer to have the Democratic convention select?

Choice of Democrats

Carter 53%
Kennedy 33
Undecided 14

Choice of Independents

Carter............................54%
Kennedy 26
Undecided.........................20

Do you approve or disapprove of the way Carter is handling his job as president?

Approve...........................39%
Disapprove 50
No opinion 11

By Politics
Republicans

Approve...........................28%
Disapprove 64
No opinion 8

Democrats

Approve...........................48%
Disapprove 41
No opinion 11

Independents

Approve...........................36%
Disapprove 54
No opinion 10

Interviewing Date: 4/9–10/80
Special Telephone Survey

Do you approve or disapprove of the way Jimmy Carter is handling the crisis in Iran?

Approve...........................40%
Disapprove 49
No opinion 11

The following is the trend since the Iranian situation series was begun in early December:

	Approve	Disapprove	No opinion
Mar. 28–31, 1980	40%	50%	10%
Feb. 29–Mar. 3, 1980	58	35	7
Jan. 4–7, 1980	61	30	9
Dec. 7–10, 1979	76	16	8

Note: President Jimmy Carter's once commanding lead among Democrats nationwide

over Senator Edward Kennedy for the 1980 presidential nomination shows further signs of erosion in the latest Gallup Poll test of the relative strength of the two men. Carter now leads the Massachusetts senator by 20 percentage points, compared to the previous survey (March 28–31) when he enjoyed a 28-point margin over Kennedy (59% to 31%), with 10% undecided.

The president's greatest show of strength against Kennedy was recorded in a survey conducted February 29–March 3, when Carter was the choice of 66% of Democrats compared to 27% for Kennedy. It is interesting to note that between the February/March survey and the mid-April findings reported here Kennedy has been the beneficiary of only 7 percentage points of Carter's 14-point attrition. The balance of the vote between the two men goes into the undecided column. Despite the decline in the proportion of Democrats who choose Carter in a head-to-head contest against Kennedy for their party's nomination, the choices of political independents remain basically unchanged since the earlier survey.

Not only has there been a sharp decline since early March in his lead for the nomination but also Carter's recent initiatives to correct the nation's economic woes and his imposition of stricter sanctions against the Iranian government have had no appreciable effect in bolstering the president's declining popularity.

APRIL 20
PRESIDENTIAL TRIAL HEATS

Interviewing Date: 4/11–14/80
Survey #153-G

Asked of registered voters: Suppose the presidential election were being held today. If Jimmy Carter were the Democratic candidate and Ronald Reagan were the Republican candidate, which would you like to see win? [Those who named another person or who were undecided were asked: As of today, do you lean more to Carter, the Democrat, or to Reagan, the Republican?]

Carter............................49%
Reagan............................43
Other 2
Undecided......................... 6

By Region
East

Carter............................54%
Reagan............................37
Other 4
Undecided......................... 5

Midwest

Carter............................44%
Reagan............................45
Other 3
Undecided......................... 8

South

Carter............................51%
Reagan............................42
Other 1
Undecided......................... 6

West

Carter............................44%
Reagan............................49
Other 1
Undecided......................... 6

By Politics
Republicans

Carter............................17%
Reagan............................78
Other 1
Undecided......................... 7

Democrats

Carter............................69%
Reagan............................23
Other 1
Undecided......................... 7

Independents

Carter............................41%
Reagan............................45

Other 5
Undecided......................... 9

Note: The 2-to-1 advantage (60% to 31%) that President Jimmy Carter held in early February in a test election against GOP front-runner Ronald Reagan has now narrowed to only a 6 percentage point lead.

In a nationwide Gallup survey completed April 14, Carter was the choice of 49% of registered voters compared to 43% for Reagan. This is the narrowest margin between the two presidential contenders recorded since Carter's political fortunes improved dramatically after the Iranian crisis erupted last November.

Asked of registered voters: If President Jimmy Carter were the Democratic candidate, running against Ronald Reagan, the Republican candidate, and John Anderson, an independent candidate, which would you like to see win? [Those who named another person or who were undecided were asked: As of today, do you lean more to Carter, the Democrat, to Reagan, the Republican, or to Anderson, the independent candidate?]

Carter............................41%
Reagan............................34
Anderson..........................18
Other 1
Undecided......................... 6

By Region
East

Carter............................43%
Reagan............................25
Anderson..........................23
Other 3
Undecided......................... 6

Midwest

Carter............................41%
Reagan............................35
Anderson..........................19
Other 1
Undecided......................... 4

South

Carter............................50%
Reagan............................36
Anderson.......................... 8
Other .... *
Undecided.......................... 5

West

Carter............................26%
Reagan............................40
Anderson..........................26
Other .... *
Undecided.......................... 7

By Politics
Republicans

Carter............................11%
Reagan............................68
Anderson..........................16
Other 1
Undecided.......................... 4

Democrats

Carter............................62%
Reagan............................18
Anderson..........................16
Other .... *
Undecided.......................... 4

Independents

Carter............................32%
Reagan............................32
Anderson..........................25
Other 2
Undecided.......................... 9

*Less than 1%

Note: In the current test election, Anderson, tested as an independent candidate in a three-way race against Carter and Reagan, wins the support of 18% of registered voters to 41% for Carter and 34% for Reagan. Anderson draws almost as much support from registered Democrats as from registered Republicans, but his greatest popularity is among the college educated and those living in the West.

Further evidence of the president's vulnerability to the stalemated Iranian hostage situation, as well as the deterioration of the nation's economy, is seen in two other key Gallup measurements. First, Carter's once commanding lead over Senator Edward Kennedy among Democrats nationwide as their party's candidate for the 1980 presidential nomination has declined considerably since earlier this year. Carter now receives the vote of 52% of Democrats, compared to 34% for the Massachusetts senator. In a February survey, the president was chosen by 61% of Democrats to 32% for Kennedy.

Second, a similar attrition has been found in public approval of Carter's handling of his presidential duties. Currently, only 40% of Americans give the president a favorable performance rating, compared to 61% recorded shortly after the seizure of the U.S. embassy in Tehran.

APRIL 24
IDEAL FAMILY SIZE

Interviewing Date: 3/7–10/80
Survey #150-G

What is the ideal number of children for a family to have?

One 3%
Two 51
Three 21
Four 12
Five 2
Six or more 2
None 1
Don't know 8

Those Saying Four or More Children
By Sex

Male...............................15%
Female.............................18

By Education

College.............................12%
High school........................16
Grade school.......................25

By Age

18–24 years 21%
25–29 years........................10
30–49 years........................13
50 years and over..................20

By Religion

Protestants 17%
Catholics...........................19

Percent Saying Four or More is Ideal Number of Children

1980.............................16%
1978.............................17
1977.............................13
1974.............................19
1973.............................20
1971.............................23
1968.............................41
1966.............................35
1963.............................42
1960.............................45
1957.............................38
1953.............................41
1947.............................47
1945.............................49
1941.............................41
1936.............................34

Note: During the last twelve years a sharp decline has occurred in the proportion of Americans who favor large families, with the trend far more pronounced among Catholics than Protestants. In 1968, 50% of Catholics believed that the ideal family included four or more children, but only 19% hold this view today. Among Protestants the trend since 1968 has been from 37% to 17% in the 1980 survey, which closely parallels the current figure for Catholics.

Among all American adults, 16% favor larger families, only one percentage point less than that recorded in 1978. Slightly more than half of the public (51%) favors having two children.

The proportion of the public favoring large families, after declining dramatically from 41% in 1968 to 13% in 1977, increased slightly in 1978 and remained at this level in 1980. The 1977 figure was the lowest since the Gallup Poll began this measurement in 1936, when 34% said that four or more children represented the ideal family size. The figure rose sharply, from 41% in 1941 to a high of 49% in 1945, anticipating the postwar baby boom. However, by 1971 the figure had dropped to 23% and continued to decline to the present 16%.

APRIL 27

THE 1980 PRESIDENTIAL ELECTION— A GALLUP SURVEY

The results reported below are based on personal interviews in nationwide surveys conducted during the first four months of 1980. More than 1,500 adults (18 years and older) were interviewed in each survey.

Note: Four Gallup Poll political barometers provide added evidence to what the latest test election figures show—the presidential race in November is likely to be extremely close as it was in 1976.

Events and economic factors, however, can alter the political outlook. At this point (six months before the election) Gallup Poll barometers dealing with the personalities involved, the issues, and two different assessments of basic party strength all point to a tight battle if Carter and Reagan are the major party candidates.

Neither candidate generates much personal enthusiasm at present, with only 26% of the public giving Carter a highly favorable rating compared to 23% for Reagan. These current ratings are almost identical to those recorded at this time in 1976.

Personal enthusiasm for Carter and Reagan is lower in this presidential year than it has been for leading candidates in any other presidential election year since 1952. Generating the most personal appeal in a presidential year was President Dwight Eisenhower in July 1956, when 65% of the public gave him a highly favorable rating.

For nearly four decades the Gallup Poll has asked Americans what they consider to be the most important problems facing the nation and which political party they believe can better deal with these problems. The results have proved to be a good "issue barometer" of the outcome of presidential elections.

In the current survey, 53% of those who choose between the parties think the Democratic party is better able to deal with current problems, while 47% name the Republican party. And 74% of Americans cite the high cost of living as the most important problem facing the nation today.

Three other indicators of basic party strength at the grass-roots level indicate little momentum for the GOP at this time, First, the national support for congressional candidates shows little change in the relative strength of the two parties in the last four years. In the most recent Gallup survey dealing with congressional choices, 59% of registered voters favor Democratic candidates for the House, while 41% support GOP candidates. In summer 1976 the comparable figures were 63% for Democrats and 37% for Republicans.

Second, basic party strength is measured by political affiliation. Here also little change is found since 1976. In six national Gallup surveys since the beginning of 1980, 21% of Americans classify themselves as Republicans, 47% as Democrats, and 32% as independents. In surveys conducted between March and May 1976, 22% identified themselves as Republicans, 46% as Democrats, and 32% as independents.

And third, to measure attitudes toward the political parties and the major personalities involved in the presidential race, the Stapel Scalometer was employed. The scalometer consists of ten squares ranging from +5 for someone or something liked very much all the way down to −5 for someone or something disliked very much. Each respondent is asked to indicate which square best represents his or her feelings about an organization or a particular person.

The Republican and Democratic parties currently receive highly favorable ratings of 17% and 28%. These ratings are similar to those recorded before the 1976 presidential contest. In November 1975 the Republican and Democratic parties had highly favorable ratings of 15% and 31%, respectively.

The following shows the trend in highly favorable ratings for the two leading presidential candidates in the past eight election years:

Highly Favorable Ratings
May 1980
Carter...............................23%
Reagan.............................20

May 1976
Carter...............................25%
Ford.................................22

August 1972
Nixon................................40%
McGovern..........................23

May 1968
Nixon................................28%
Humphrey..........................27

May 1964
Johnson.............................59%
Goldwater..........................15

May 1960
Kennedy............................41%
Nixon...............................41

July 1956
Eisenhower.........................65%
Stevenson 28

Eisenhower 47%
Stevenson 37

For the "issue barometer" the following question was asked first:

What do you think is the most important problem facing this country today?

Inflation; high cost of living 74%
International problems 17
Energy problems 8
Unemployment 4
Dissatisfaction with government 4
Crime 2
Moral decline 2
Other 6
No opinion 1
                                   118%*

*Total adds to more than 100% due to multiple responses.

All persons who named a problem were then asked:

Which political party do you think can do a better job of handling the problem you have just mentioned—the Republican party or the Democratic party?

Republican 28%
Democratic 32
No difference 28
No opinion 12

Excluding those who say there is no difference in each major party's ability to cope with these problems and those who do not express an opinion, this division between the parties is obtained:

Republican 47%
Democratic 53

The following question was asked of registered voters to determine basic congressional strength:

If the elections for Congress were being held today, which party would you like to see win in this congressional district, the Republican party or the Democratic party? [Those who named another party or who were undecided were asked: As of today, do you lean more to the Republican party or the Democratic party?]

Republican 37%
Democratic 53
Other 2
Undecided 8

Taking into account only those who choose one or the other of the major parties, the division of the vote is as follows:

Republican 41%
Democratic 59

Here are the findings from an August 1976 survey, based on registered voters:

Vote for Congress

Republican 34%
Democratic 57
Other 1
Undecided 8

On a two-way basis the 1976 vote divided as follows:

Republican 37%
Democratic 63

To determine political party allegiance, the following question has been asked regularly since 1940:

In politics, as of today, do you consider yourself a Republican, Democrat, or independent?

Following are the latest results and those from early 1976 surveys. (Both sets of figures exclude the 2% or 3% of the electorate who did not classify themselves as belonging to one of these political entities.)

Political Affiliation

	1980	1976
Republicans	21%	22%
Democrats	47	46
Independents	32	32

APRIL 28
PRESIDENTIAL TRIAL HEAT—
IRANIAN SITUATION

Interviewing Date: 4/25–27/80
Special Telephone Survey

Asked of registered voters: Suppose the presidential election were being held today. If Jimmy Carter were the Democratic candidate and Ronald Reagan were the Republican candidate, which would you like to see win? [Those who named another person or who were undecided were asked: As of today, do you lean more to Carter, the Democrat, or to Reagan, the Republican?]

Carter	47%
Reagan	43
Other	3
Undecided	7

Do you feel President Carter was right or not right to try to rescue the hostages by military force?

Right	71%
Not right	18
No opinion	11

Do you feel that President Carter was right or not right in his decision not to consult with congressional leaders before he undertook the recent military mission in Iran?

Right	63%
Not right	27
No opinion	10

Do you approve or disapprove of the way Jimmy Carter is handling the crisis in Iran?

Approve	46%
Disapprove	42
No opinion	12

Do you approve or disapprove of the way Carter is handling his job as president?

Approve	43%
Disapprove	39
No opinion	18

Note: The ill-fated attempt on April 24 to rescue the American hostages in Iran has had little effect on the relative standing of President Jimmy Carter and Ronald Reagan, the current front-runners for the presidential election in November.

In a Gallup Poll trial heat conducted two days after the abortive Iranian mission, Carter was the choice of 47% of registered voters nationwide, compared to 43% for Reagan. These figures are virtually identical to those recorded two weeks earlier, when Carter was preferred by 49% and Reagan by 43%.

An examination of several other aspects of public opinion suggests that President Carter has been the immediate beneficiary of substantial goodwill despite the failure of the Iranian venture.

1. According to a *Newsweek*/Gallup survey conducted on April 25, by an overwhelming 71% to 18% margin the public feels that the president was right in attempting to rescue the hostages by using military force.

2. By a 2-to-1 ratio, Americans give their backing to the president's decision not to consult with congressional leaders prior to undertaking the military operation. In this decision Carter has the support of 63% of the electorate, while 27% believe he was at fault.

3. Approval of the president's handling of the Iranian situation has increased from 40% in a late March Gallup Poll, taken before the rescue attempt, to 46% in the April 25 survey. However, this figure is far below the 76% approval rating for Carter's Iranian policies recorded in December shortly after the takeover of the American embassy.

4. The president's overall performance rating has changed very little within the past two weeks. In a Gallup Poll conducted at that time, 39% of the public approved of Carter's handling of his presidential duties, while in the April 25 survey the president's approval score was 43%.

Perhaps the most significant factor between the two surveys is that the percentage of the public disapproving of Carter's handling of his job declined by 11 points, from 50% in the mid-April poll to 39% at present. In the same interim, those who did not express an opinion on the president's overall effectiveness went from 11% to 18%, suggesting that many people are withholding judgment until more is known about the Iranian venture.

MAY 4
CANDIDATE BEST FOR KEEPING PEACE AND FOR DEALING WITH RUSSIA

Interviewing Date: 4/26–27/80
Special Telephone Survey

Regardless of which man you happen to prefer—Jimmy Carter or Ronald Reagan—please tell me which one you, yourself, feel would do a better job of keeping the United States out of war?

Carter...........................46%
Reagan..........................31
Undecided......................23

By Education
College

Carter...........................41%
Reagan..........................38
Undecided......................21

High School

Carter...........................47%
Reagan..........................29
Undecided......................24

Grade School

Carter...........................56%
Reagan..........................19
Undecided......................25

By Region
East

Carter...........................50%
Reagan..........................26
Undecided......................24

Midwest

Carter...........................41%
Reagan..........................35
Undecided......................24

South

Carter...........................50%
Reagan..........................27
Undecided......................23

West

Carter...........................41%
Reagan..........................38
Undecided......................21

By Age
18–29 Years

Carter...........................54%
Reagan..........................30
Undecided......................16

30–49 Years

Carter...........................48%
Reagan..........................33
Undecided......................19

50 Years and Over

Carter...........................41%
Reagan..........................30
Undecided......................29

Regardless of which man you might happen to prefer—Jimmy Carter or Ronald

Reagan—please tell me which one you, yourself, feel would do a better job of dealing with Russia?

Carter............................ 41%
Reagan............................ 38
Undecided......................... 21

By Education
College

Carter............................ 37%
Reagan............................ 46
Undecided......................... 17

High School

Carter............................ 41%
Reagan............................ 36
Undecided......................... 23

Grade School

Carter............................ 51%
Reagan............................ 19
Undecided......................... 30

By Age
18–29 Years

Carter............................ 47%
Reagan............................ 39
Undecided......................... 14

30–49 Years

Carter............................ 39%
Reagan............................ 42
Undecided......................... 19

50 Years and Over

Carter............................ 40%
Reagan............................ 34
Undecided......................... 26

Note: Despite widespread concern that the recent rescue mission in Iran could have led to military involvement on a broader scale, many Americans feel that President Carter would do a better job than Ronald Reagan of keeping the United States out of war. In a Gallup Poll conducted two days after the abortive Iranian venture, 46% of persons interviewed said they believed Carter would be more likely than Reagan to keep the nation at peace, while 31% credited Reagan in this respect.

While Carter holds a definite edge over Reagan on the issue of keeping the country out of war, the president's advantage is slightly blunted by the fact that he has only a marginal lead over Reagan as the candidate that the public thinks is likely to do a better job of dealing with Russia. The current survey shows 41% favoring Carter in this respect, compared to 38% selecting Reagan.

Sharp differences of opinion on this key voter issue are found on the basis of formal education. While the nation as a whole leans decidedly toward Carter on this issue, persons with a college background are closely divided in their views, with 41% crediting Carter compared to 38% who believe that Reagan would be more capable of keeping us out of war.

The public's views on which man would be better able to deal with the peace issue correspond closely with the vote in the latest test race between Carter and Reagan. For example, Reagan is closest to Carter on this issue in the West, where Reagan also receives his strongest support in trial heat contests against Carter. Similarly, Carter makes a very strong trial showing against Reagan among registered voters under thirty.

MAY 8
PRAYERS IN PUBLIC SCHOOLS—INFLUENCE OF RELIGION ON AMERICAN LIFE

Interviewing Date: 3/28–31/80
Survey #151-G

Do you favor or oppose an amendment to the Constitution that would permit prayers to be said in the public schools?

Favor............................. 76%
Oppose............................ 15
No opinion 9

By Education
College
Favor...............................66%
Oppose............................24
No opinion 10

High School
Favor...............................79%
Oppose............................12
No opinion 9

Grade School
Favor...............................82%
Oppose............................ 9
No opinion 9

By Region
East
Favor...............................73%
Oppose............................20
No opinion 7

Midwest
Favor...............................75%
Oppose............................14
No opinion 11

South
Favor...............................85%
Oppose............................ 9
No opinion 6

West
Favor...............................67%
Oppose............................18
No opinion 15

By Age
18–29 Years
Favor...............................66%
Oppose............................23
No opinion 11

30–49 Years
Favor...............................77%
Oppose............................12
No opinion 11

50 Years and Over
Favor...............................81%
Oppose............................12
No opinion 7

By Income
$25,000 and Over
Favor...............................66%
Oppose............................23
No opinion 11

$20,000–$24,999
Favor...............................80%
Oppose............................17
No opinion 3

$15,000–$19,999
Favor...............................82%
Oppose............................ 9
No opinion 9

$10,000–$14,999
Favor...............................80%
Oppose............................12
No opinion 8

$5,000–$9,999
Favor...............................75%
Oppose............................14
No opinion 11

Under $5,000
Favor...............................77%
Oppose............................11
No opinion 12

By Politics
Republicans

Favor..............................79%
Oppose.............................13
No opinion 8

Democrats

Favor..............................78%
Oppose.............................15
No opinion 7

Independents

Favor..............................70%
Oppose.............................17
No opinion 13

By Religion
Protestants

Favor..............................82%
Oppose.............................10
No opinion 8

Catholics

Favor..............................77%
Oppose.............................16
No opinion 7

Interviewing Date: 4/11–14/80
Survey #153-G

At the present time, do you think religion as a whole is increasing its influence on American life or losing its influence?

Increasing 35%
Losing 46
Same 11
Don't know 8

By Education
College

Increasing 38%
Losing 45
Same 11
Don't know 6

High School

Increasing 36%
Losing 46
Same 11
Don't know 7

Grade School

Increasing 26%
Losing 48
Same 11
Don't know 15

By Region
East

Increasing 31%
Losing 48
Same 16
Don't know 5

Midwest

Increasing 38%
Losing 45
Same 10
Don't know 7

South

Increasing 36%
Losing 47
Same 9
Don't know 8

West

Increasing 35%
Losing 44
Same 8
Don't know 13

By Age
18–29 Years

Increasing 37%
Losing 48
Same 10
Don't know 5

30–49 Years

Increasing 36%
Losing 44
Same 13
Don't know 7

50 Years and Over

Increasing 33%
Losing 47
Same 9
Don't know 11

By Income
$25,000 and Over

Increasing 35%
Losing 47
Same 13
Don't know 5

$20,000–$24,999

Increasing 36%
Losing 49
Same 9
Don't know 6

$15,000–$19,999

Increasing 35%
Losing 47
Same 12
Don't know 6

$10,000–$14,999

Increasing 41%
Losing 43
Same 7
Don't know 9

$5,000–$9,999

Increasing 35%
Losing 46
Same 11
Don't know 8

Under $5,000

Increasing 26%
Losing 49
Same 10
Don't know 15

By Religion
Protestants

Increasing 38%
Losing 46
Same 9
Don't know 7

Catholics

Increasing 34%
Losing 48
Same 11
Don't know 7

Note: Although the courts over the last two decades have consistently struck down efforts to permit Bible reading and prayers in the nation's public schools, the American people just as consistently have voted in favor of allowing religious observances in the schools.

In a nationwide Gallup survey, three persons in four (76%) said they favor an amendment to the Constitution that would permit prayers to be said in the public schools.

The public has not budged on this issue, despite the fact that the courts have opposed any effort to breach the constitutional separation of church and state. For example, when the issue was put to voters in a Gallup Poll in 1974, 77% said they would favor an amendment to the Constitution that would permit public school prayers.

These findings are consistent with still earlier poll results based on comparable questions. In a survey conducted shortly after the U.S. Supreme Court's 1963 ruling that religious exercises in public schools are illegal, 70% of the U.S. public expressed disapproval of the ruling, while 24% approved.

While the public favors prayers in schools,

the prevailing opinion among all groups and faiths in the United States is that the home is more important than either the church or schools in the religious training of children. A 1979 Gallup survey showed 75% naming the home, 16% the church, and only 3% naming the schools as most important to the religious and spiritual development of a child.

Although many religious organizations concur with the Supreme Court, including the National Council of Churches and the U.S. Catholic Conference, various groups and individuals continue to challenge the 1963 ruling.

In an effort to circumvent the Supreme Court decision, Massachusetts passed a law permitting students and teachers voluntarily to offer prayer in public schools, allowing those who did not wish to participate to abstain. The Massachusetts Supreme Court, however, ruled this law unconstitutional.

Almost a dozen states currently have laws that provide for a period of silent meditation in the public schools and these laws have not been challenged.

On a national level, Congress has turned back legislative proposals for school prayer nearly every year since the Supreme Court's 1963 ruling. Most recently Senator Jesse Helms (R-NC) and Representative Philip Crane (R-IL) sponsored a constitutional amendment that would deny the Supreme Court jurisdiction over prayer in schools and leave such decisions to the states.

Analysis of the survey results by demographic groups shows that those most in favor include women, nonwhites, persons with only a grade school education, and older adults.

Interestingly, little difference is found between the views of Protestants (82% favor an amendment) and Catholics (77% do so).

The overwhelming public support found for prayer in the public schools is related to the widespread belief that religion is losing its influence in American society. In a recent survey, 46% feel that religion is losing its influence on life in the United States, while 35% think that religion is increasing its influence. Another 11% see little change.

MAY 11
JOHN ANDERSON—
A GALLUP ANALYSIS

Interviewing Date: 3/28–31; 4/11–14; 4/26–27/80
(Telephone Survey)
Survey #151-G; #153-G

The following combined trial heat results are based on choices of registered voters:

By Age
18–24 Years

Carter............................39%
Reagan............................31
Anderson..........................28
Other; undecided 2

25–29 Years

Carter............................44%
Reagan............................31
Anderson..........................21
Other; undecided 4

30–49 Years

Carter............................40%
Reagan............................34
Anderson..........................21
Other; undecided 5

50 Years and Over

Carter............................40%
Reagan............................36
Anderson..........................17
Other; undecided 7

By Education
College

Carter............................32%
Reagan............................36
Anderson..........................26
Other; undecided 6

High School

Carter.............................	43%
Reagan.............................	35
Anderson...........................	17
Other; undecided	5

Grade School

Carter.............................	52%
Reagan.............................	30
Anderson...........................	12
Other; undecided	6

By Region
East

Carter.............................	40%
Reagan.............................	29
Anderson...........................	24
Other; undecided	7

Midwest

Carter.............................	40%
Reagan.............................	35
Anderson...........................	20
Other; undecided	5

South

Carter.............................	48%
Reagan.............................	36
Anderson...........................	9
Other; undecided	7

West

Carter.............................	28%
Reagan.............................	40
Anderson...........................	26
Other; undecided	6

Note: An analysis of survey results based on interviews with 3,300 registered voters sheds considerable light on some of Representative John Anderson's principal strengths and weaknesses as he begins his campaign as an independent candidate for the presidency.

Anderson's present national support of 19% comes close to matching the highest percentage given a third-party candidate in a presidential election year in the forty-five year history of the Gallup Poll. At one point in the 1968 presidential campaign Governor George Wallace was the choice of 21%.

Support for third-party candidates has tended to decline in the closing days of presidential campaigns. For example, Wallace received 13.5% of the popular vote in 1968. His share of the vote, however, exceeded that of States' Rights candidate Senator J. Strom Thurmond (2.4%) in the 1948 presidential election and that of Progressive party candidate Henry Wallace (2.4%), but it was still less than the vote for Robert M. LaFollette in 1924 (16.6%) or for Theodore Roosevelt in 1912 (27.4%).

While Anderson's chances of winning the presidency look slim at this time, his candidacy could open the way to active discussion of the desirability of a third major party—a center party whose political philosophy would fall between the Republicans on the right and the Democrats on the left.

Gallup surveys have indicated that a center party, similar to that found in many European countries, would have a special appeal to younger voters, the higher educated, and to political independents. While such a party has yet to appear on the American political scene, considerable public support is found for such a political entity, with 37% of American voters holding the view that there is a place for a center party in the United States today.

For a more detailed study of the John Anderson constituency, see Everett Carll Ladd and G. Donald Ferree, Jr., "The Anderson Constituency and the 1980 Presidential Election: Early Soundings," *Public Opinion* (July/August 1980).

MAY 15
SPORTS

Interviewing Date: 4/11–14/80
Survey #153-G

Which of these sports and activities have you, yourself, participated in within the

*last twelve months? [Respondents were
handed a card listing forty-seven sports
and activities.]*

Swimming 37%
Bicycling 27
Bowling 24
Fishing 24
Hiking 21
Camping 19
Basketball 18
Frisbee 17
Softball 16
Tennis 14
Volleyball 13
Ping-Pong 13
Hunting 13
Roller-skating 12
Motorboating 12
Touch/flag football 11
Motorcycling 10
Baseball (hardball) 10
Golf 8
Target shooting 8
Water-skiing 7
Canoeing/rowing 7
Ice-skating 7
Sledding 7
Horseback riding 7
Raquetball 6
Skiing (snow) 6
Badminton 6
Backpacking 5
Paddle/platform tennis 4
Handball 4
Sailing 4
Soccer 4
Skeet/trap shooting 3
Archery 3
Snowmobiling 3
Skate-boarding 2
Snorkeling 2
Distance/marathon running 2
Surfing 2
Scuba-diving 1
Squash 1
None 29
Don't know 1

Sports Participation Trend

	1980	1972	1964	1959
Bicycling	27%	28%	20%	—%
Bowling	24	28	31	18
Fishing	24	24	38	32
Tennis	14	12	10	4
Roller-skating	12	5	8	4
Motorboating	12	20	16	—
Hunting	13	14	16	16
Golf	8	14	10	8
Skiing	6	5	4	3

Note: The latest Gallup Survey of Leisure Activities shows a decline in participation in many
sports and outdoor activities, undoubtedly due
in considerable measure to the energy crunch.

For example, within the last year only 12%
of Americans have gone motorboating compared to 20% in 1972. During the same period
there also has been a decline in other outdoor
activities such as camping and fishing.

Bowling and golf have been on a general
downtrend since 1964, while tennis has shown a
steady increase since 1959. A dramatic growth
is also shown in the popularity of roller-skating.

*Now, which of these sports or activities
would you, yourself, like to participate in
more often?*

Scuba-diving 56%
Sailing 49
Deep-sea fishing 48
Snorkeling 46
Hunting 39
Horseback riding 38
Backpacking 37
Golf 37
Tennis 36
Camping 33
None 29
Don't know 1

*Aside from any work you do, here at home
or at a job, do you do anything regularly—
that is, on a daily basis—that helps you
keep physically fit?*

Yes 46%
No 54

Note: About half of Americans today (46%) exercise on a regular basis. This figure closely matches the 47% recorded in the previous 1977 survey, which represented one of the most dramatic changes in American lifestyles in recent decades. For example, the percentage of Americans who exercised daily was only 24% in 1961 when the question was first asked.

Those most likely to say they exercise daily are the upscale, socioeconomic groups, the college educated, those in the upper- and upper-middle income brackets, and professionals, business people, and others in white-collar positions.

In addition, young people (under thirty years old) are more likely to say they exercise than are their elders, men more likely than women, and people living in the Northeast and Far West are more likely than midwesterners and southerners.

Asked of those who do anything regularly—on a daily basis—that keeps them physically fit: Do you happen to jog, or not?

Yes.................................12%
No.................................34
                                   ———
                                   46%

Note: The form of exercise that has undoubtedly received the most attention during the current exercise boom is jogging, with 12% today as opposed to 11% in 1977 saying they jog on a daily basis.

The demographic picture of the jogger tends to conform to that of the person who regularly exercises; that is, joggers tend to be young, college educated, single, in the upper-middle income brackets and live in the Northeast and Far West. In fact, almost three in ten young adults today say they jog daily.

MAY 18
VOTER REGISTRATION

Interviewing Date: January–April, 1980
Various Surveys

Is your name now recorded in the registration book of the precinct or election district where you now live?

	Yes
National	70%

By Sex

Male	70%
Female	71

By Race

White	71%
Nonwhite	65

By Education

College	77%
High school	67
Grade school	66

By Age

18–24 years	45%
25–29 years	54
30–49 years	73
50 years and over	84

By Politics

Republicans	79%
Democrats	75
Independents	59

Note: Some political observers believe that the relatively high turnout in certain state primaries this spring signals greater voter participation in the presidential election in November. However, voter registration today—70%—is no higher than it was at this time in 1976, when voter turnout sank to a twenty-eight-year low of 54%.

Registration is likely to take on added importance this year since the two leading candidates—President Jimmy Carter and Ronald Reagan—are now closely matched in voter appeal, as determined by Gallup Poll trial heat measurements. The election very well could hinge on the efforts of party workers to see that unregistered Republicans and Democrats get their names on the books so they can vote in November.

Particularly disappointing is the continued low level of registration on the part of young people. About half the potential voters (49%) between the ages of eighteen and twenty-nine are now registered to vote, roughly the same proportion recorded at this time in 1976.

In every presidential contest since 1972, when 18- to 20-year-olds were granted the right to vote in federal elections, far fewer citizens under thirty have cast their ballots than have those thirty and older.

The National Association for the Advancement of Colored People recently announced a voter registration campaign to sign up one-half million young blacks. While the proportion of blacks who are registered continues to lag behind the level of whites, registration efforts in recent years are clearly paying off. Today 65% of blacks are registered compared to 56% in 1976. The registration figure for whites has remained the same at 71%.

A somewhat smaller proportion of Democrats (75%) than Republicans (79%) are now registered to vote, illustrating the importance of registration campaigns by Democratic political strategists. Registration among independents (59%) is far below the level for Republicans and Democrats.

It should be stressed that not all those now registered will actually vote. Past voting patterns indicate that only about eight out of ten persons registered will go to the polls. The percentages of the eligible voter population participating in each of the last five presidential elections are as follows:

Percent of Voting Age
Population Voting for President

1976................................54%
1972................................56
1968................................61
1964................................62
1960................................64

MAY 19
PRESIDENTIAL TRIAL HEATS

Interviewing Date: 5/16–19/80
Survey #155-G

Asked of registered voters: Suppose the presidential election were being held today.

If Jimmy Carter were the Democratic candidate and Ronald Reagan were the Republican candidate, which would you like to see win? [Those who named another person or who were undecided were asked: As of today, do you lean more to Carter, the Democrat, or to Reagan, the Republican?]

Carter...............................49%
Reagan..............................39
Other 4
Undecided..........................8

By Sex
Male

Carter...............................45%
Reagan..............................44
Other 4
Undecided..........................7

Female

Carter...............................53%
Reagan..............................35
Other 4
Undecided..........................8

By Race
White

Carter...............................46%
Reagan..............................43
Other 4
Undecided..........................7

Nonwhite

Carter...............................73%
Reagan..............................11
Other 2
Undecided..........................14

By Education
College

Carter...............................42%
Reagan..............................46
Other 7
Undecided..........................5

High School

Carter............................52%
Reagan...........................38
Other 2
Undecided........................ 8

Grade School

Carter............................58%
Reagan...........................30
Other 1
Undecided........................11

By Region

East

Carter............................47%
Reagan...........................39
Other 4
Undecided........................10

Midwest

Carter............................52%
Reagan...........................38
Other 3
Undecided........................ 7

South

Carter............................53%
Reagan...........................38
Other 3
Undecided........................ 6

West

Carter............................45%
Reagan...........................44
Other 4
Undecided........................ 7

By Age

18–29 Years

Carter............................60%
Reagan...........................29
Other 5
Undecided........................ 6

30–49 Years

Carter............................45%
Reagan...........................45
Other 2
Undecided........................ 8

50 Years and Over

Carter............................49%
Reagan...........................39
Other 4
Undecided........................ 8

By Income

$25,000 and Over

Carter............................38%
Reagan...........................54
Other 4
Undecided........................ 4

$20,000–$24,999

Carter............................50%
Reagan...........................38
Other 4
Undecided........................ 8

$15,000–$19,999

Carter............................55%
Reagan...........................36
Other 2
Undecided........................ 7

$10,000–$14,999

Carter............................50%
Reagan...........................39
Other 3
Undecided........................ 8

$5,000–$9,999

Carter............................56%
Reagan...........................31
Other 4
Undecided........................ 9

Under $5,000

Carter.............................56%
Reagan............................31
Other 3
Undecided.........................10

Asked of Carter supporters: Do you strongly support him or do you only moderately support him?

Strongly...........................38%
Moderately 59
Can't say 3

Democrats Only

Strongly...........................44%
Moderately 54
Can't say 2

Independents Only

Strongly...........................13%
Moderately 81
Can't say 6

Asked of Reagan supporters: Do you strongly support him or do you only moderately support him?

Strongly...........................32%
Moderately 65
Can't say 3

Republicans Only

Strongly...........................45%
Moderately 52
Can't say 3

Independents Only

Strongly...........................22%
Moderately 72
Can't say 6

Asked of Carter supporters: Do you strongly oppose Reagan or do you only moderately oppose him?

Strongly...........................41%
Moderately 50
Can't say 9

Democrats Only

Strongly...........................42%
Moderately 48
Can't say 10

Independents Only

Strongly...........................43%
Moderately 53
Can't say 4

Asked of Reagan supporters: Do you strongly oppose Carter or do you only moderately oppose him?

Strongly...........................44%
Moderately 51
Can't say 5

Republicans Only

Strongly...........................52%
Moderately 45
Can't say 3

Independents Only

Strongly...........................42%
Moderately 53
Can't say 5

Asked of registered voters: If President Jimmy Carter were the Democratic candidate, running against Ronald Reagan, the Republican candidate, and John Anderson, the independent candidate, which would you like to see win? [Those who named another person or who were undecided were asked: As of today, do you lean more to Carter, the Democrat, to Reagan, the Republican, or to Anderson, the independent?]

Carter.............................40%
Reagan............................32
Anderson..........................21
Other 1
Undecided.........................6

By Sex
Male
Carter............................38%
Reagan............................34
Anderson..........................22
Other 1
Undecided........................ 5

Female
Carter............................43%
Reagan............................29
Anderson..........................19
Other 1
Undecided........................ 8

By Race
White
Carter............................36%
Reagan............................35
Anderson..........................22
Other 1
Undecided........................ 6

Nonwhite
Carter............................67%
Reagan............................ 7
Anderson..........................13
Other 2
Undecided........................11

By Education
College
Carter............................30%
Reagan............................36
Anderson..........................28
Other 1
Undecided........................ 5

High School
Carter............................44%
Reagan............................31
Anderson..........................18
Other 1
Undecided........................ 6

Grade School
Carter............................52%
Reagan............................25
Anderson..........................12
Other 1
Undecided........................10

By Region
East
Carter............................38%
Reagan............................30
Anderson..........................25
Other .... *
Undecided........................ 7

Midwest
Carter............................40%
Reagan............................29
Anderson..........................23
Other 1
Undecided........................ 7

South
Carter............................48%
Reagan............................33
Anderson..........................11
Other 1
Undecided........................ 7

West
Carter............................33%
Reagan............................37
Anderson..........................24
Other 2
Undecided........................ 4

By Age
18–24 Years
Carter............................47%
Reagan............................18
Anderson..........................32
Other .... *
Undecided........................ 3

25–29 Years

Carter.............................50%
Reagan.............................22
Anderson..........................21
Other 2
Undecided......................... 5

30–49 Years

Carter.............................36%
Reagan.............................36
Anderson..........................22
Other .... *
Undecided......................... 6

50 Years and Over

Carter.............................41%
Reagan.............................34
Anderson..........................16
Other 1
Undecided......................... 8

By Politics

Republicans

Carter.............................14%
Reagan.............................65
Anderson..........................19
Other .... *
Undecided......................... 2

Democrats

Carter.............................60%
Reagan.............................15
Anderson..........................16
Other 1
Undecided......................... 8

Independents

Carter.............................24%
Reagan.............................37
Anderson..........................34
Other .... *
Undecided......................... 5

*Less than 1%

Note: In order to construct a larger and more stable base for statistical analysis than is found in any single survey, the results from several recent polls have been combined. This composite of three-way trial heats makes it possible to examine patterns in presidential voting preferences and to present more detailed and reliable demographic breakdowns than could be obtained from an individual survey. The analysis of survey results is based on interviews with 3,362 registered voters and sheds considerable light on the principal strengths and weaknesses of the three major candidates.

On a regional basis President Carter is strongest in the Midwest and in the South, where he receives the support of 47% of the public. His weakest region is the West, where he trails Ronald Reagan by 7 percentage points and leads John Anderson by only 4 points. Anderson fares well on the East and West coasts, but his support drops sharply in the Midwest and particularly in the South. On the other hand, Reagan has fairly consistent support (35%) in all the regions except the East (28%).

Educationally, voter sentiment appears to be divided according to traditional lines, with Carter doing well among those with limited formal education and Reagan receiving more support from citizens who have attended college. John Anderson, the independent contestant, is clearly at his strongest among the college-educated segment of the public.

Anderson also has strong appeal (28%) among voters from the youngest age group in the electorate—18- to 24-year-olds. However, his support diminishes to a low of 16% as the age groupings become progressively older. Support for Carter is fairly stable across all age groups, while Reagan receives marginally greater backing from citizens aged thirty and over.

President Carter leads his competition among most traditionally Democratic groups, but his support is not as great as expected for an incumbent president. Carter captures 46% of the union vote, while Reagan receives 27% and Anderson 21%. People living in large cities, families with incomes under $10,000, and blue-collar workers give Carter pluralities of their support, while a clear majority of nonwhite citizens favors Carter over Reagan and Anderson. One group that is normally heavily Democratic—Jewish voters—is generally unwilling to support President Carter. Carter's 27% of the Jewish vote is far behind Anderson's 44% and only slightly ahead of Reagan's 19%.

MAY 20
PRESIDENTIAL TRIAL HEATS

Interviewing Date: 5/16–19/80
Survey #155-G

Asked of registered voters: Suppose the presidential election were being held today. If Walter Mondale were the Democratic candidate and Ronald Reagan were the Republican candidate, which would you like to see win? [Those who named another person or who were undecided were asked: As of today, do you lean more to Mondale, the Democrat, or to Reagan, the Republican?]

Mondale	40%
Reagan	46
Other	3
Undecided	11

By Race
White

Mondale	37%
Reagan	51
Other	3
Undecided	9

Nonwhite

Mondale	58%
Reagan	18
Other	2
Undecided	22

By Education
College

Mondale	38%
Reagan	49
Other	4
Undecided	9

High School

Mondale	41%
Reagan	47
Other	2
Undecided	10

Grade School

Mondale	40%
Reagan	39
Other	2
Undecided	19

By Region
East

Mondale	40%
Reagan	46
Other	2
Undecided	12

Midwest

Mondale	42%
Reagan	44
Other	4
Undecided	10

South

Mondale	34%
Reagan	50
Other	3
Undecided	13

West

Mondale	44%
Reagan	47
Other	2
Undecided	7

By Age
18–24 Years

Mondale 39%
Reagan..............................47
Other 3
Undecided..........................11

25–29 Years

Mondale 41%
Reagan..............................39
Other 5
Undecided..........................15

30–49 Years

Mondale 40%
Reagan..............................49
Other 3
Undecided.......................... 8

50 Years and Over

Mondale 40%
Reagan..............................46
Other 2
Undecided..........................12

Independents Only

Mondale 32%
Reagan..............................56
Other 3
Undecided.......................... 9

Asked of registered voters: Suppose the presidential election were being held today. If Edward Kennedy were the Democratic candidate and Ronald Reagan were the Republican candidate, which would you like to see win? [Those who named another person or who were undecided were asked: As of today, do you lean more to Kennedy, the Democrat, or to Reagan, the Republican?]

Kennedy 38%
Reagan..............................51
Other 4
Undecided.......................... 7

By Race
White

Kennedy 31%
Reagan..............................58
Other 4
Undecided.......................... 7

Nonwhite

Kennedy 83%
Reagan.............................. 5
Other 3
Undecided.......................... 9

By Education
College

Kennedy 30%
Reagan..............................55
Other 8
Undecided.......................... 7

High School

Kennedy 40%
Reagan..............................52
Other 2
Undecided.......................... 6

Grade School

Kennedy 48%
Reagan..............................40
Other .... *
Undecided..........................12

By Region
East

Kennedy 44%
Reagan..............................45
Other 4
Undecided.......................... 7

Midwest

Kennedy	37%
Reagan	52
Other	3
Undecided	8

South

Kennedy	31%
Reagan	58
Other	3
Undecided	8

West

Kennedy	43%
Reagan	48
Other	5
Undecided	4

By Age
18–24 Years

Kennedy	48%
Reagan	45
Other	2
Undecided	5

25–29 Years

Kennedy	51%
Reagan	38
Other	4
Undecided	7

30–49 Years

Kennedy	37%
Reagan	53
Other	4
Undecided	6

50 Years and Over

Kennedy	34%
Reagan	54
Other	3
Undecided	9

Independents Only

Kennedy	30%
Reagan	56
Other	5
Undecided	9

*Less than 1%

Note: Vice-president Walter Mondale, although not a candidate for president, draws a surprising amount of public support when matched against Ronald Reagan. In the latest trial heat, Mondale was the choice of 40% of registered voters to 46% for Reagan, with 14% choosing another candidate or undecided.

The vice-president did almost as well against Reagan as did Senator Edward Kennedy in a test election in the same survey. Kennedy was preferred by 38% of registered voters to 51% for Reagan.

Although most political observers believe it is unlikely that President Carter will withdraw from the race, there has been persistent speculation that the Democratic convention might turn to a compromise candidate if Carter's standing with the electorate deteriorates further. In fact, concern over the strength of Carter's candidacy has caused some leading political figures, including New York Governor Hugh Carey, to urge that both Carter and Kennedy release their delegates and let an "open" convention decide who will be the Democratic nominee.

Both Mondale and Kennedy have less support than Carter against Reagan, with the president continuing to hold a lead over his GOP rival. Carter is the current choice of 49% of registered voters nationwide compared to 39% for Reagan.

President Carter has led Reagan in every test election contest conducted by the Gallup Poll since last fall, with Carter's margin ranging from 6 points in October to nearly 2 to 1 in February. Reagan's best recent showing was recorded in early September 1979, when he received the support of 46% of registered voters to 47% for Carter. In only two of eighteen test elections between the two men—June and July 1979—

has the former California governor led the president.

MAY 23
"DEATH OF A PRINCESS"

Interviewing Date: 5/16–19/80
Survey #155-G

> Many public television stations broadcast a show on May 12 called "Death of a Princess." Did you happen to see, hear, or read anything about this television program?

Yes, saw program.................... 13%
No, didn't see but heard or read
   about............................ 52
Didn't see, hear, or read about......... 35

> Asked of those who saw, heard, or read about the program: Do you think this program should or should not have been shown on television?

Should............................ 51%
Should not.......................... 21
No opinion 28

Note: The U.S. telecast of a British-produced docudrama in May touched off a brief but intense flurry of diplomatic activity. The film was a fictionalized treatment of the execution for adultery committed by a real-life Saudi Arabian princess and her lover. Prior to the U.S. showing of the film, the Saudi government made an official protest to the U.S. State Department, claiming that "the film shows a completely false picture of the life, religion, customs and traditions of Saudi Arabia." The Saudi protest was forwarded to the Public Broadcasting System, which broadcast the program despite the protest.

According to a Gallup Poll conducted shortly after the telecast, four times as many Americans heard or read about "Death of a Princess" as actually saw the show, with viewing substantially higher among the college-educated and upper-income segments of the population.

All those who had seen, heard, or read about the program were asked whether they thought the show should or should not have been shown on television. A bare 51% majority replied affirmatively, with the proportion rising to 66% among younger adults.

MAY 29
IMMIGRATION TO THE UNITED STATES

Interviewing Date: 5/16–19/80
Survey #155-G

> Have you heard or read about the Cubans who are leaving Cuba to come to live in the United States?

Yes............................... 97%
No................................ 3

> Asked of those who replied in the affirmative: Should the U.S. government permit these Cubans to come and live in the United States, or not?

Should............................ 34%
Should not.......................... 57
Don't know 9

By Race
White

Should............................ 35%
Should not.......................... 56
Don't know 9

Nonwhite

Should............................ 24%
Should not.......................... 63
Don't know 13

By Education
College

Should............................ 49%
Should not.......................... 43
Don't know 8

High School

Should	28%
Should not	61
Don't know	11

Grade School

Should	21%
Should not	71
Don't know	8

By Region

East

Should	37%
Should not	56
Don't know	7

Midwest

Should	30%
Should not	62
Don't know	8

South

Should	29%
Should not	58
Don't know	13

West

Should	39%
Should not	51
Don't know	10

By Age

18–24 Years

Should	36%
Should not	58
Don't know	6

25–29 Years

Should	38%
Should not	49
Don't know	13

30–49 Years

Should	38%
Should not	54
Don't know	8

50 Years and Over

Should	27%
Should not	62
Don't know	11

By Income

$25,000 and Over

Should	45%
Should not	47
Don't know	8

$20,000–$24,999

Should	42%
Should not	48
Don't know	10

$15,000–$19,999

Should	38%
Should not	51
Don't know	11

$10,000–$14,999

Should	30%
Should not	62
Don't know	8

$5,000–$9,999

Should	23%
Should not	68
Don't know	9

Under $5,000

Should	18%
Should not	74
Don't know	8

By Religion

Protestants

Should 28%
Should not 62
Don't know 10

Catholics

Should 41%
Should not 54
Don't know 5

Labor Union Families Only

Should 31%
Should not 61
Don't know 8

Non-Labor Union Families Only

Should 34%
Should not 56
Don't know 10

Some people say that the U.S. government should permit persons who leave other countries because of political oppression to come and live in the United States. Others say that the federal government should halt all immigration until the national employment rate falls below 5 percent. Which point of view comes closer to the way you feel—that political refugees should be permitted to immigrate to the United States, or that immigration should be halted until the unemployment rate in the United States drops?

Allow immigration .26%
Halt immigration 66
Not sure 8

By Race

White

Allow immigration .28%
Halt immigration 64
Not sure 8

Nonwhite

Allow immigration .16%
Halt immigration 79
Not sure 5

By Education

College

Allow immigration .44%
Halt immigration 49
Not sure 7

High School

Allow immigration .21%
Halt immigration 71
Not sure 8

Grade School

Allow immigration .10%
Halt immigration 81
Not sure 9

By Region

East

Allow immigration .28%
Halt immigration 65
Not sure 7

Midwest

Allow immigration .25%
Halt immigration 67
Not sure 8

South

Allow immigration .22%
Halt immigration 69
Not sure 9

West

Allow immigration .32%
Halt immigration 61
Not sure 7

By Age
18–24 Years

Allow immigration................... 30%
Halt immigration 64
Not sure........................... 6

25–29 Years

Allow immigration................... 28%
Halt immigration 62
Not sure........................... 10

30–49 Years

Allow immigration................... 31%
Halt immigration 63
Not sure........................... 6

50 Years and Over

Allow immigration................... 20%
Halt immigration 70
Not sure........................... 10

By Income
$25,000 and Over

Allow immigration................... 40%
Halt immigration 52
Not sure........................... 8

$20,000–$24,999

Allow immigration................... 34%
Halt immigration 60
Not sure........................... 6

$15,000–$19,999

Allow immigration................... 33%
Halt immigration 59
Not sure........................... 8

$10,000–$14,999

Allow immigration................... 21%
Halt immigration 72
Not sure........................... 7

$5,000–$9,999

Allow immigration................... 13%
Halt immigration 78
Not sure........................... 9

Under $5,000

Allow immigration................... 13%
Halt immigration 78
Not sure........................... 9

By Religion
Protestants

Allow immigration................... 22%
Halt immigration 70
Not sure........................... 8

Catholics

Allow immigration................... 30%
Halt immigration 63
Not sure........................... 7

By Occupation
Professional and Business

Allow immigration................... 42%
Halt immigration 48
Not sure........................... 10

Clerical and Sales

Allow immigration................... 23%
Halt immigration 68
Not sure........................... 9

Manual Workers

Allow immigration................... 21%
Halt immigration 73
Not sure........................... 6

Non-Labor Force

Allow immigration................... 18%
Halt immigration 74
Not sure........................... 8

Labor Union Families Only

Allow immigration.................... 24%
Halt immigration 70
Not sure............................. 6

Non-Labor Union Families Only

Allow immigration.................... 27%
Halt immigration 64
Not sure............................. 9

Note: Despite the welcome that the American people traditionally have offered immigrants, a majority of Americans (57%) believe that the government should not permit the Cubans now leaving their country to live in the United States, while 34% hold the opposite view.

Further findings reveal that many who oppose the entry of the Cuban refugees are concerned about the unemployment rate in the United States. In fact, two out of three persons believe that the government should halt all immigration until the national unemployment rate—now at 7.8%—falls below 5%.

The importance of the unemployment factor in influencing people's thinking is evident among those who believe that the government should not permit the Cubans to come and live in America. Nine out of ten say that all immigration should be halted until the unemployment rate drops.

On the other hand, among those who believe that the U.S. government should offer a haven to the Cubans, 67% feel that persons who leave their countries because of political oppression to come and live here should be allowed to do so.

More than 100,000 Cubans have entered the United States since the exodus began on April 21. The White House announced they would be treated as applicants for asylum, thus giving the president greater discretionary authority over how many would be permitted to live permanently in the United States.

The American public's attitudes toward the Cuban immigrants closely parallel those recorded in an August 1979 survey on the Indochinese refugees—the so-called boat people—who were then coming to this country.

At that time almost six out of every ten U.S. citizens (57%) said they opposed relaxation of this country's basic immigration policies in order to permit these people to come to live in the United States. Nevertheless, most Americans said that if the Indochinese were to come to their community to live, they would be welcome.

JUNE 1
DEMOCRATIC PRESIDENTIAL CANDIDATES

Interviewing Date: 5/16–19/80
Survey #155-G

Suppose the choice for president in the Democratic convention in 1980 narrows down to Jimmy Carter and Edward Kennedy. Which one would you prefer to have the Democratic convention select?

Choice of Democrats

Carter............................... 58%
Kennedy 31
Undecided........................... 11

Choice of Independents

Carter............................... 53%
Kennedy 28
Undecided........................... 19

Note: As national attention focuses on the important primary elections in California, New Jersey, and Ohio on Tuesday, June 3, President Carter has extended his lead over Senator Edward Kennedy as the choice of Democrats for their party's presidential nomination and now leads by a 2-to-1 margin.

As recently as mid-November Carter trailed Kennedy 36% to 55%. In early December, Carter moved ahead of his rival and continued to gain strength in subsequent surveys. Carter's best showing this year was recorded in a late-February/early-March poll, when he led Kennedy 65% to 27%. The president's advantage then started to decline but has rebounded in the latest survey.

JUNE 2
PRESIDENTIAL TRIAL HEATS

Interviewing Date: 5/30–6/2/80
Survey #156-G

Asked of registered voters: Suppose the presidential election were being held today. If Jimmy Carter were the Democratic candidate and Ronald Reagan were the Republican candidate, which would you like to see win? [Those who named another person or who were undecided were asked: As of today, do you lean more to Carter, the Democrat, or to Reagan, the Republican?]

Carter	49%
Reagan	40
Other	4
Undecided	7

Independents Only

Carter	43%
Reagan	40
Other	8
Undecided	9

Asked of Carter supporters: Do you strongly support him or do you only moderately support him?

Strongly	37%
Moderately	62
Can't say	1

Independents Only

Strongly	22%
Moderately	77
Can't say	1

Asked of Reagan supporters: Do you strongly support him or do you only moderately support him?

Strongly	32%
Moderately	66
Can't say	2

Independents Only

Strongly	22%
Moderately	75
Can't say	3

Asked of Carter supporters: Do you strongly oppose Reagan or do you only moderately oppose him?

Strongly	42%
Moderately	51
Can't say	7

Independents Only

Strongly	46%
Moderately	49
Can't say	5

Asked of Reagan supporters: Do you strongly oppose Carter or do you only moderately oppose him?

Strongly	48%
Moderately	50
Can't say	2

Independents Only

Strongly	47%
Moderately	49
Can't say	4

Asked of registered voters: If President Jimmy Carter were the Democratic candidate, running against Ronald Reagan, the Republican candidate, and John Anderson, the independent candidate, which would you like to see win? [Those who named another person or who were undecided were asked: As of today, do you lean more to Carter, the Democrat, to Reagan, the Republican, or to Anderson, the independent?]

Carter	39%
Reagan	32
Anderson	21
Other	1
Undecided	7

Independents Only

Carter. 26%
Reagan. 29
Anderson. 34
Other 2
Undecided. 9

Note: As the long primary campaign comes to a close, President Jimmy Carter holds a 9 percentage point lead over Ronald Reagan in the 1980 presidential contest.

Responses also indicate that neither Carter nor Reagan can boast of a solid backing, with large majorities saying they only moderately, rather than strongly, support the candidate of their choice. However, there are proportionately more Reagan backers whose choice is based on strong opposition to Carter's candidacy than Carter supporters who firmly oppose Reagan.

When the Carter-Reagan test election is broadened to include independent candidate John Anderson, the latest results are also similar to those found in mid-May. In the current survey Carter is preferred by 39%, Reagan by 32%, and Anderson by 21% of registered voters. As in previous three-way test elections, Anderson draws almost equal support from both Carter and Reagan.

Barring unforeseen circumstances, Ronald Reagan will be the Republican standard-bearer in the presidential election on November 4. Although the political infighting between Senator Edward Kennedy and President Carter continues, according to most observers Carter is now only twenty-four delegates short of the 1,666 needed to assure him a first-ballot majority at the Democratic national convention in August.

JUNE 5
IDEAL LIFE-STYLE FOR WOMEN

Interviewing Date: 3/21–24/80
Special Survey

Asked of women: Let's talk about the ideal life for you personally. Which one of the alternatives on this card do you feel would provide the most interesting and satisfying life for you personally? [Respondents were handed a card listing five alternative life-styles.]

Married with children 74%
  With full-time job 33
  With no full-time job 41
Married with no children. 10
  With full-time job 6
  With no full-time job 4
Unmarried with full-time job 8
Not sure. 8

Note: Despite the growing number of women who are holding jobs outside the home—almost half of all women eighteen years and older now have a full-time or part-time job—they tend to do so within the traditional framework of marriage and parenthood.

The stereotypical career woman's life-style—single, free, and in pursuit of a full-time career—has very little appeal to American women, at least as a permanent way of life. Only 8% say they would prefer this type of existence.

A Gallup survey recently conducted for the White House Conference on Families, which held its opening conference in Baltimore on June 5, shows that the vast majority of American women (74%) view marriage with children as the most interesting and satisfying life for them personally. These latest results almost exactly parallel those recorded in a 1975 study, when 76% said the most interesting and satisfying life-style for them was to be married and have children.

Although 41% of all women interviewed say their ideal life-style would be to be married, have children, and not have a full-time job, 33% of those who prefer marriage and motherhood would like to have a full-time job as well. Presumably, this proportion would be still higher if survey respondents were asked about part-time jobs.

Analysis of the views of women by key population groups shows:

Young women (18- to 29-year-olds) hold almost identical views to those of the total adult female population, with 76% saying the most rewarding life for them would be to be married and have children.

The relatively few women who express a preference for being single with a full-time job are more likely to be under thirty years old, college educated, and living in the West. However, at the same time the vast majority of women, regardless of background characteristics or region of the country, want marriage and children.

The White House Conference on Families was called by President Jimmy Carter to "examine the strengths of American families, the difficulties they face, and the ways in which family life is affected by public policies."

JUNE 8
CONFIDENCE IN U.S. FOREIGN POLICY

Interviewing Date: 5/21–28/80
Special Telephone Survey

How much confidence do you have in the ability of the United States to deal wisely with present world problems—very great, considerable, little, or very little confidence?

Very great 14%
Considerable 39
Little 22
Very little 19
None at all (volunteered) 2
No opinion 4

Has your confidence in the ability of America to deal with world problems tended to go up lately, go down, or remain about the same?

Gone up 10%
Gone down 45
Remained the same 41
No opinion 4

Do you think Carter is or is not proving to be a good president of the United States?

Is 35%
Is not 46
No opinion 19

Has your own opinion of President Carter gone up recently, gone down, or remained the same?

Gone up 12%
Gone down 41
Remained the same 43
No opinion 4

Note: Confidence in the ability of the United States to deal with world problems has declined sharply, according to a recently completed nationwide Gallup survey.

Nearly half of all persons interviewed (45%) say their confidence in our international efforts has gone down lately, while 41% say it has remained the same and only 10% say it has gone up.

In response to another question in the survey series, 53% express very great or considerable confidence in the ability of this country to deal wisely with present world problems. However, as many as four in ten (43%) say they have little or very little confidence or volunteer that they have no confidence.

These findings are recorded after a recent period of confrontations and diplomatic setbacks for the United States in international affairs, including the failure to secure the release of U.S. hostages in Iran, the Russian invasion of Afghanistan, and the breakdown of the SALT II ratification process.

In addition, while more than fifty countries are supporting President Carter's call for a boycott of the Moscow Olympics this summer in order to protest the Soviet invasion of Afghanistan, athletes from at least sixty countries, including most of the major Western European countries, will participate.

In the same survey, 41% of Americans say their opinion of President Carter has gone down recently, 43% say it has remained the same, and 12% say their opinion of the president has gone up.

At present, 35% of survey respondents believe Carter is proving to be a good president, 46% feel he is not, and 19% do not express an opinion.

When the same questions were asked by the British Gallup Poll, a smaller proportion of Britons than Americans said their confidence in the ability of the United States to deal with world problems has declined.

In the United Kingdom, three in ten (31%) say their confidence has gone down, 13% say it has gone up, and 49% say it has remained the same. However, the British have less confidence than Americans in U.S. foreign policy, with 37% saying they have very great or considerable confidence in the ability of the United States to deal wisely with present world problems, as opposed to 53% expressing little, very little, or no confidence.

JUNE 9
IRANIAN SITUATION

Interviewing Date: 5/16–19; 5/21–28/80
(Special Telephone Survey)
Survey #155-G

Do you approve or disapprove of the way Jimmy Carter is handling the crisis in Iran?

Approve.............................42%
Disapprove 48
No opinion 10

Do you approve or disapprove of the recent economic and diplomatic measures the United States has taken against Iran?

United States

Approve.............................58%
Disapprove 29
No opinion 13

United Kingdom

Approve.............................56%
Disapprove 24
No opinion 20

West Germany

Approve.............................72%
Disapprove 21
No opinion 7

Do you think economic and diplomatic sanctions against Iran will or will not secure the release of the American prisoners?

United States

Will 17%
Will not 59
Depends (on who/what) 8
No opinion 16

United Kingdom

Will 14%
Will not 55
Depends (on who/what) 13
No opinion 18

Do you think (name of country) should or should not impose economic and diplomatic sanctions against Iran such as the United States has done?

United Kingdom

Should.............................71%
Should not.........................11
No opinion 18

Canada

Should.............................61%
Should not.........................26
No opinion 13

Netherlands

Should.............................53%
Should not.........................32
No opinion 15

West Germany

Should.............................51%
Should not.........................41
No opinion 8

Switzerland

Should 35%
Should not 48
No opinion 17

Sweden

Should 29%
Should not 55
No opinion 16

Uruguay

Should 16%
Should not 35
No opinion 49

Note: Six Americans out of ten approve of the recent economic and diplomatic sanctions that the United States has taken against Iran, but most express doubts that these actions will secure the release of the American hostages.

A majority of the publics in both Great Britain and West Germany also support the U.S. Iranian moves, and the British share the doubts of Americans that these sanctions will pay off. (The question regarding the release of the hostages was not asked in West Germany.)

A survey of public opinion in seven countries by Gallup-affiliated organizations shows that the citizens of three favor their country imposing sanctions against Iran, three are opposed, and one is evenly divided.

Canadians, West Germans, and Netherlanders lean toward the view that their nation should employ economic and diplomatic sanctions against Iran such as the United States has done. Public opinion, however, is split in Great Britain, and in Sweden, Switzerland, and Uruguay residents oppose their country following the U.S. lead.

Although the nine-member European Economic Community agreed in April to impose stringent sanctions against Iran, the Europeans have implemented only watered-down countermeasures far less strict than those President Carter had requested.

JUNE 12
NEW "CENTER" POLITICAL PARTY

Interviewing Date: 5/2–5/80
Survey #154-G

Asked of registered voters: Suppose there were three major parties—the Republican party, the Democratic party, and a new center party that would appeal to people whose political views are middle of the road, in between those of the Republicans and Democrats, which party would you favor—the Republican party, the Democratic party, or the new center party?

Republican 20%
Democratic 36
Center 31
No opinion 13

By Race
White

Republican 22%
Democratic 31
Center 34
No opinion 14

Nonwhite

Republican 4%
Democratic 73
Center 16
No opinion 7

By Education
College

Republican 18%
Democratic 27
Center 39
No opinion 16

High School

Republican 18%
Democratic 39
Center 32
No opinion 11

Grade School

Republican 30%
Democratic............................ 52
Center 9
No opinion 9

By Region
East

Republican 19%
Democratic............................ 38
Center 30
No opinion 13

Midwest

Republican 21%
Democratic............................ 27
Center 39
No opinion 13

South

Republican 13%
Democratic............................ 48
Center 27
No opinion 12

West

Republican 25%
Democratic............................ 33
Center 28
No opinion 14

By Age
18–24 Years

Republican 14%
Democratic............................ 32
Center 44
No opinion 10

25–29 Years

Republican 11%
Democratic............................ 40
Center 36
No opinion 13

30–49 Years

Republican 17%
Democratic............................ 34
Center 37
No opinion 12

50 Years and Over

Republican 25%
Democratic............................ 39
Center 22
No opinion 14

By Politics
Republicans

Republican 66%
Democratic............................ *
Center 26
No opinion 8

Democrats

Republican 1%
Democratic............................ 71
Center 20
No opinion 8

Independents

Republican 8%
Democratic............................ 10
Center 57
No opinion 25

*Less than 1%

Note: A new "center" political party that would appeal to people whose political views are middle of the road has considerable attraction for American voters, perhaps reflecting disenchantment with the Republican and Democratic presidential candidates as well as with the present two-party political system.

A new party alignment that would include a center party, in addition to the Republican and

Democratic parties, finds surprising support among registered voters nationwide.

Of particular significance is the fact that two bellwether groups in the total adult population—college-educated voters and younger voters (18- to 24-year-olds)—favor a center party over either of the two traditional parties.

While much has been written about the advantages of the present two-party system, critics maintain that the system has not operated effectively during the past fifty years. Party strength is best measured at the grass-roots level and by the number of Democrats and Republicans elected to Congress. The GOP has had a majority in the House during only four of the last fifty years and recent Gallup Poll findings suggest that there is little chance that the Republicans can win a majority in the congressional elections in November.

There is no doubt that our political system has not worked as well as it might in involving citizens in the electoral process. Gallup Poll registration figures indicate that voter turnout this fall may be no higher than it was in 1976, when participation, at 54%, was lower than it had been since 1948.

The survey results suggest that in the Midwest a center party might well become the dominant political entity, appealing to more persons than either the present Republican or Democratic parties.

While a three-party system might make it difficult for any candidate to win a majority of votes in the Electoral College, the public has long favored a constitutional reform that would award the election to the presidential candidate who wins the most popular votes.

Pluralities in favor of a center party over either the Republican or Democratic parties are found among persons with a college background, those under fifty years of age, midwesterners, and persons who classify themselves as political independents.

Conversely, there is far less support for a center party among voters fifty and older, and persons whose education ended at the grade-school level give almost no support to the proposed new party.

JUNE 15
ECONOMIC SITUATION

Interviewing Date: 5/16–19/80
Survey #155-G

During the next twelve months, do you expect prices to go up at about the same rate as in the last twelve months, or will inflation get worse, or will there be less inflation?

Same rate 30%
Worse inflation 39
Less inflation 25
No opinion 6

Now looking ahead—do you expect that this time next year you will be financially better off than now, or worse off than now, or about the same?

Better off 41%
Worse off 28
Same 23
No opinion 8

Thinking of economic conditions in the country as a whole, during the next twelve months do you expect the country will have good times financially, or bad times, or what?

Good times 11%
Bad times 70
Mixed 12
No opinion 7

During the next twelve months, do you expect your income to go up more than prices go up, about the same, or less than prices go up?

More than prices 7%
Same 30
Less than prices 55
No opinion 8

Asked of employed persons: Thinking about the next twelve months, how likely do you think it is that you will lose your job or be laid off—very likely, fairly likely, not too likely, or not at all likely?

Very likely	6%
Fairly likely	8
Not too likely	24
Not at all likely	60
No opinion	2

By Race
White

Very likely	5%
Fairly likely	8
Not too likely	24
Not at all likely	62
No opinion	1

Nonwhite

Very likely	14%
Fairly likely	9
Not too likely	25
Not at all likely	49
No opinion	3

By Education
College

Very likely	3%
Fairly likely	3
Not too likely	20
Not at all likely	73
No opinion	1

High School

Very likely	8%
Fairly likely	10
Not too likely	25
Not at all likely	56
No opinion	1

Grade School

Very likely	9%
Fairly likely	16
Not too likely	33
Not at all likely	37
No opinion	5

By Age
18–24 Years

Very likely	12%
Fairly likely	6
Not too likely	25
Not at all likely	55
No opinion	2

25–29 Years

Very likely	5%
Fairly likely	20
Not too likely	17
Not at all likely	56
No opinion	2

30–49 Years

Very likely	5%
Fairly likely	5
Not too likely	24
Not at all likely	66
No opinion	*

50 Years and Over

Very likely	4%
Fairly likely	8
Not too likely	28
Not at all likely	57
No opinion	3

By Income
$25,000 and Over

Very likely	3%
Fairly likely	4
Not too likely	17
Not at all likely	75
No opinion	1

$20,000–$24,999

Very likely	3%
Fairly likely	7
Not too likely	30
Not at all likely	59
No opinion	1

$15,000–$19,999

Very likely	9%
Fairly likely	5
Not too likely	28
Not at all likely	57
No opinion	1

$10,000–$14,999

Very likely	8%
Fairly likely	10
Not too likely	25
Not at all likely	54
No opinion	3

$5,000–$9,999

Very likely	6%
Fairly likely	19
Not too likely	27
Not at all likely	46
No opinion	2

Under $5,000

Very likely	14%
Fairly likely	7
Not too likely	20
Not at all likely	55
No opinion	4

Labor Union Families Only

Very likely	8%
Fairly likely	9
Not too likely	22
Not at all likely	60
No opinion	1

Non-Labor Union Families Only

Very likely	4%
Fairly likely	7
Not too likely	24
Not at all likely	63
No opinion	2

*Less than 1%

Note: For the first time in almost two years the American public is beginning to be less pessimistic about the prospects for a continuation of the nation's crippling inflation rate.

In a recent Gallup survey not only has there been a sharp increase in the proportion of Americans who expect prices to rise less steeply than they have in the past twelve months but also perceptions about their personal financial situation a year from now show a marked improvement.

Nevertheless, while the public is more optimistic about the future outlook for inflation and for their own financial situation, it remains decidedly gloomy about the present state of the national economy. Most political observers agree that if the nation's faltering economy continues to worsen between now and November, President Jimmy Carter's chances for re-election will be seriously jeopardized.

An assessment of the public's current economic mood brings the following to light:

1. A higher percentage of Americans today than in March believe prices will rise less sharply during the next twelve months. At the same time, almost seven in ten (69%) think there either will be no improvement from current high inflation rates or that inflation will become worse.

2. There is also a positive trend since April in the percentage of the public anticipating an improvement in their personal financial situation.

3. Although the public remains very pessimistic about economic conditions in the country as a whole, a slightly smaller majority today than in April foresees bad economic times during the next twelve months.

4. Americans' perceptions on the bedrock issue of whether their income will outstrip prices continue to be strongly negative, with a majority feeling they will lose ground to inflation within the coming year.

5. The Gallup Poll's latest Job Security Index—the proportion of adult Americans holding either full-time or part-time jobs outside the home who think it is very or fairly likely they will lose their jobs within the next twelve months—is now at 14%, or about the same as the 12%

recorded last November. However, with the official government unemployment figure for May reaching 7.8%, it is significant to note that an additional 14% of Americans feel their jobs are in jeopardy.

JUNE 16
PRESIDENTIAL TRIAL HEATS

Interviewing Date: 6/13–16/80
Survey #157-G

Do you approve or disapprove of the way Carter is handling his job as president?

Approve............................32%
Disapprove 56
No opinion 12

By Politics
Republicans

Approve............................15%
Disapprove 75
No opinion 10

Democrats

Approve............................43%
Disapprove 46
No opinion 11

Independents

Approve............................31%
Disapprove 56
No opinion 13

Asked of registered voters: Suppose the presidential election were being held today. If President Jimmy Carter were the Democratic candidate and Ronald Reagan were the Republican candidate, which would you like to see win? [Those who named another person or who were undecided were asked: As of today, do you lean more to Carter, the Democrat, or to Reagan, the Republican?]

Carter..............................43%
Reagan.............................44
Other 6
Undecided.........................7

By Region
East

Carter..............................40%
Reagan.............................42
Other 9
Undecided.........................9

Midwest

Carter..............................42%
Reagan.............................47
Other 4
Undecided.........................7

South

Carter..............................46%
Reagan.............................45
Other 4
Undecided.........................5

West

Carter..............................42%
Reagan.............................40
Other 11
Undecided.........................7

Asked of registered voters: If President Jimmy Carter were the Democratic candidate, running against Ronald Reagan, the Republican candidate, and John Anderson, the independent candidate, which would you like to see win? [Those who named another person or who were undecided were asked: As of today, do you lean more to Carter, the Democrat, to Reagan, the Republican, or to Anderson, the independent?]

Carter..............................35%
Reagan.............................33
Anderson..........................24
Other 3
Undecided.........................5

By Education
College

Carter................................25%
Reagan................................34
Anderson..............................35
Other 3
Undecided............................. 3

High School

Carter................................38%
Reagan................................33
Anderson..............................21
Other 2
Undecided............................. 6

Grade School

Carter................................48%
Reagan................................30
Anderson.............................. 9
Other 3
Undecided.............................10

By Region
East

Carter................................29%
Reagan................................30
Anderson..............................30
Other 4
Undecided............................. 7

Midwest

Carter................................35%
Reagan................................34
Anderson..............................24
Other 1
Undecided............................. 6

South

Carter................................40%
Reagan................................38
Anderson..............................17
Other 1
Undecided............................. 4

West

Carter................................36%
Reagan................................29
Anderson..............................28
Other 5
Undecided............................. 2

By Age
18–24 Years

Carter................................32%
Reagan................................26
Anderson..............................37
Other .... *
Undecided............................. 5

25–29 Years

Carter................................31%
Reagan................................40
Anderson..............................23
Other 3
Undecided............................. 3

30–49 Years

Carter................................33%
Reagan................................32
Anderson..............................25
Other 3
Undecided............................. 7

50 Years and Over

Carter................................38%
Reagan................................35
Anderson..............................21
Other 2
Undecided............................. 4

By Income
$25,000 and Over

Carter................................29%
Reagan................................38
Anderson..............................30
Other 1
Undecided............................. 2

$20,000–$24,999

Carter............................34%
Reagan............................29
Anderson..........................27
Other 5
Undecided......................... 5

$15,000–$19,999

Carter............................28%
Reagan............................42
Anderson..........................24
Other 1
Undecided......................... 5

$10,000–$14,999

Carter............................37%
Reagan............................28
Anderson..........................25
Other 2
Undecided......................... 8

$5,000–$9,999

Carter............................44%
Reagan............................26
Anderson..........................19
Other 5
Undecided......................... 6

Under $5,000

Carter............................44%
Reagan............................31
Anderson..........................16
Other .... *
Undecided......................... 9

By Politics
Republicans

Carter............................ 9%
Reagan............................68
Anderson..........................19
Other 1
Undecided......................... 3

Democrats

Carter............................53%
Reagan............................16
Anderson..........................22
Other 3
Undecided......................... 6

Independents

Carter............................25%
Reagan............................34
Anderson..........................33
Other 2
Undecided......................... 6

*Less than 1%

Note: According to the latest nationwide Gallup Poll, President Jimmy Carter's approval rating has slipped to 32%. The president's declining popularity also is reflected in the latest test election against the probable Republican nominee, Ronald Reagan, who now holds a 44% to 43% lead over Carter among registered voters. This is the first time since last July that Reagan has headed Carter in these presidential trial heats.

President Carter's margin over Reagan has eroded steadily since January, when Carter led 62% to 33%. In a late-May/early-June test election, Carter had a 49% to 40% advantage over Reagan.

In the same Gallup Poll, Carter's approval rating stood at 38%. The president's popularity has declined by 29 percentage points since early December, shortly after the seizure of the U.S. hostages in Iran—from 61% to the current 32%.

Carter's lowest performance rating since taking office was 28% approval in June-July 1979, while his high point was 75% recorded in March 1977 shortly after his inauguration.

Representative John Anderson continues to show considerable strength as an independent candidate, winning the support of 24% of registered voters in a three-way contest against Carter and Reagan. As has been the case in each of the six earlier surveys, Anderson draws about equal support from both Carter and Reagan.

JUNE 17
PRESIDENTIAL TRIAL HEAT

Interviewing Date: 6/13–16/80
Survey #157-G

Asked of registered voters: Suppose the presidential election were being held today. If Edward Kennedy were the Democratic candidate and Ronald Reagan were the Republican candidate, which would you like to see win? [Those who named another person or were undecided were asked: As of today, do you lean more to Kennedy, the Democrat, or to Reagan, the Republican?]

Kennedy 36%
Reagan 54
Other 4
Undecided 6

Note: Although President Carter now has more than enough delegates for a first-ballot nomination at the Democratic National Convention in August, Senator Edward Kennedy, buoyed by his victories in the California and New Jersey primaries on June 3, apparently is determined to battle for the nomination.

Kennedy was the consistent winner in test elections against Reagan conducted during 1978 and 1979, at times by margins of almost 2 to 1. And as recently as January, prior to the Democratic primaries, Kennedy held a slim 50% to 42% lead over Reagan.

Those opposed to Kennedy's present campaign efforts believe he will split the Democratic party and help Reagan's chances in November. Some Kennedy supporters fear that by staying in the race he will jeopardize any chances he may have of winning the Democratic nomination in 1984.

While some Democrats would like to see Kennedy step aside, others favor his continuing the battle. In the latest *Newsweek* Poll conducted by the Gallup Organization Inc., 56% of registered Democrats and 53% of all voters agree with Kennedy that President Carter should release his convention delegates to vote for whichever candidate they wish in New York City in August.

JUNE 26
CONGRESSIONAL ELECTIONS

Interviewing Date: 6/13–16/80
Survey #157-G

Asked of registered voters: If the elections for Congress were being held today, which party would you like to see win in this congressional district, the Democratic party or the Republican party? [Those who named another party or who were undecided were asked: As of today, do you lean more to the Democratic party or to the Republican party?]

Democratic 54%
Republican 39
Other 1
Undecided 6

By Region
East

Democratic 51%
Republican 43
Other 1
Undecided 5

Midwest

Democratic 48%
Republican 43
Other 1
Undecided 8

South

Democratic 57%
Republican 36
Other 1
Undecided 6

West

Democratic 63%
Republican 31
Other 2
Undecided 4

Note: The claims of some of the more optimistic Republican leaders that the GOP will win control of Congress this fall would appear to be premature.

From the evidence now at hand, the Republicans appear likely to pick up few, if any, seats in the House this fall, leaving the current composition almost the same as it is (275 Democrats and 159 Republicans).

The actual division of the popular vote for candidates for the House of Representatives in the 1978 election was Democrats 55% and Republicans 45%.

JUNE 29
CANDIDATE BEST ABLE TO HANDLE NATION'S PROBLEMS

Interviewing Date: 5/30–6/2/80
Survey #156-G

Regardless of which man you happen to prefer—Carter, Reagan, or Anderson—please tell me which one you, yourself, feel would do a better job of handling each of the following problems:

Keeping the United States out of war?

Carter 48%
Reagan 20
Anderson 10
Undecided 22

Dealing with racial problems?

Carter 44%
Reagan 20
Anderson 12
Undecided 24

Dealing with Russia?

Carter 35%
Reagan 33
Anderson 10
Undecided 22

Handling the Iranian situation?

Carter 34%
Reagan 29
Anderson 10
Undecided 27

Building trust in government?

Carter 33%
Reagan 30
Anderson 16
Undecided 21

Reducing unemployment?

Carter 29%
Reagan 32
Anderson 14
Undecided 25

Reducing government spending?

Carter 28%
Reagan 40
Anderson 12
Undecided 20

Reducing inflation?

Carter 25%
Reagan 38
Anderson 14
Undecided 23

Note: As in the past if issues play a dominant role in the presidential election outcome this year, a continuing high inflation rate would likely impair President Jimmy Carter's chances, while an international crisis almost certainly would hurt GOP challenger Ronald Reagan.

In a recent nationwide Gallup Poll, a cross section of the public was asked to indicate which of the three major presidential contenders—Carter, Reagan, or John Anderson—would do a better job of handling each of eight key domestic and international issues.

Of the two major-party candidates, Reagan leads Carter as the one better able to deal with inflation. Carter, on the other hand, enjoys his greatest advantage over his Republican rival as better able to keep the United States out of war.

The survey shows Carter winning on four issues: keeping the United States out of war, dealing with racial problems, dealing with Russia, and handling the Iranian crisis, while Reagan wins on reducing inflation and cutting government spending. A close division of public opinion regarding the relative ability of the two men is found on the remaining two issues: reducing unemployment and building trust in government.

Anderson, running as an independent candidate, lags behind Carter and Reagan on each of the eight issues tested, with his support ranging from 10% to 16%. It should be borne in mind, however, that voter preference for Anderson in the latest Gallup Poll test election is considerably less than that accorded his two rivals for the presidency.

It is politically significant to note which issues would draw Anderson voters to either Carter or Reagan in the event Anderson's support during the campaign were to decline or if he withdraws from the race. An analysis shows that Anderson backers lean heavily to Reagan on the inflation issue but turn overwhelmingly to Carter on the peace issue.

Although issues tend to play a dominant role in presidential elections, party loyalty, personality factors, and perceptions of leadership ability are also of prime significance. According to a recent *Newsweek* Poll conducted by the Gallup Organization Inc., for example, Reagan enjoys a decisive lead over Carter and Anderson for his perceived leadership qualities, while the president has the edge in personal characteristics.

JULY 1
PRESIDENTIAL TRIAL HEATS

Interviewing Date: 6/27–30/80
Survey #158-G

Do you approve or disapprove of the way Carter is handling his job as president?

Approve 31%
Disapprove 58
No opinion 11

Asked of registered voters: Suppose the presidential election were being held today. If Jimmy Carter were the Democratic candidate and Ronald Reagan were the Republican candidate, which would you like to see win? [Those who named another person or who were undecided were asked: As of today, do you lean more to Carter, the Democrat, or to Reagan, the Republican?]

Carter 41%
Reagan 46
Other 4
Undecided 9

Asked of registered voters who named Carter: Do you strongly support him or do you only moderately support him?

Strongly 31%
Moderately 67
Can't say 2

Asked of registered voters who named Reagan: Do you strongly support him or do you only moderately support him?

Strongly 30%
Moderately 68
Can't say 2

Asked of registered voters: If President Jimmy Carter were the Democratic candidate, running against Ronald Reagan, the Republican candidate, and John Anderson, the independent candidate, which would you like to see win? [Those who named another person or who were undecided were asked: As of today, do you lean more to Carter, the Democrat, to Reagan, the Republican, or to Anderson, the independent?]

Carter................................32%
Reagan...............................39
Anderson............................22
Other................................ 1
Undecided........................... 6

Asked of registered voters who named Carter: Do you strongly support him or do you only moderately support him?

Strongly..............................42%
Moderately 57
Can't say........................... 1

Asked of registered voters who named Reagan: Do you strongly support him or do you only moderately support him?

Strongly..............................35%
Moderately 64
Can't say........................... 1

Asked of registered voters who named Anderson: Do you strongly support him or do you only moderately support him?

Strongly..............................32%
Moderately 64
Can't say........................... 4

Note: Ronald Reagan has stretched his lead over President Jimmy Carter in the most recent Gallup Poll test election and now holds a 46% to 41% advantage among registered voters nationwide. In comparison a Gallup Poll conducted two weeks earlier showed Reagan with a marginal 44% to 43% lead, representing the first time Reagan has led the president since last July.

When the Carter-Reagan test election is broadened to include independent candidate John Anderson, the three-way test results also show a gain for Reagan since the previous survey. Reagan now wins 39% of the support of registered voters to 32% for Carter and 22% for Anderson.

Over a period of three months and in eight national surveys, the vote for Anderson has stayed within a narrow 5-point range, varying from 18% to 23%. As in previous trial heats,

Anderson's support comes almost equally from both Carter and Reagan. In the current survey he draws 9 percentage points from Carter and 7 from Reagan.

Responses to another survey question indicate that none of the three candidates can boast of very solid or enthusiastic backing. Large majorities say they only moderately, rather than strongly, support the candidate of their choice in both the two-way and three-way trial heats.

Economic attitudes are clearly a factor in the downtrend in Carter's rating in recent months, with approval of Carter related in some measure to Americans' assessment of their own financial status. Among persons who say their financial situation is better today than it was a year ago, 40% approve of the president's performance in office. Among those who say their situation is about the same, 31% approve and among those who say they are financially worse off, the figure is 29%.

JULY 2
REPUBLICAN
VICE-PRESIDENTIAL
CANDIDATES

Interviewing Date: 6/13–16/80
Survey #157-G

The following shows the choices of Republicans and independents, with Ford's name included and when his vote is redistributed:

Republicans

	First choices	With Ford's vote redistributed
Gerald Ford	31%	—%
George Bush	20	29
Howard Baker	10	15
John Connally	7	12
Charles Percy	3	4
Robert Dole	2	3
William Cohen	2	2
Philip Crane	*	2
Jesse Helms	*	2
Jack Kemp	*	2

Richard Lugar	*	2
Other	11	8
No opinion	14	19

Independents

	First choices	With Ford's vote redistributed
Gerald Ford	20%	—%
George Bush	20	29
Howard Baker	13	16
John Connally	6	9
Charles Percy	5	5
Nancy Kassebaum	2	2
Jack Kemp	2	2
Anne Armstrong	2	2
Philip Crane	2	2
Robert Dole	2	2
Jesse Helms	*	2
Elliot Richardson	2	*
Richard Thornburgh	2	2
Other	3	4
No opinion	19	21

*Less than 1%

Interviewing Date: 5/30–6/2/80
Survey #156-G

Asked of registered voters: If Ronald Reagan is the Republican candidate this year and he chooses a black to be his running mate, would this make you more likely or less likely to vote for this ticket?

More likely 11%
Less likely 19
No difference (volunteered) 66
No opinion 4

By Politics

Republicans

More likely 9%
Less likely 17
No difference (volunteered) 70
No opinion 4

Democrats

More likely 11%
Less likely 20
No difference (volunteered) 64
No opinion 5

Independents

More likely 11%
Less likely 19
No difference (volunteered) 67
No opinion 3

Nonwhite Only

More likely 25%
Less likely 13
No difference (volunteered) 56
No opinion 6

Asked of registered voters: If Ronald Reagan is the Republican candidate this year and he chooses a woman to be his running mate, would this make you more likely or less likely to vote for this ticket?

More likely 14%
Less likely 20
No difference (volunteered) 62
No opinion 4

By Politics

Republicans

More likely 11%
Less likely 24
No difference (volunteered) 62
No opinion 3

Democrats

More likely 13%
Less likely 21
No difference (volunteered) 61
No opinion 5

Independents

More likely 19%
Less likely 13
No difference (volunteered) 64
No opinion 4

Women Only

More likely 18%
Less likely 18
No difference (volunteered) 61
No opinion 3

Note: With former President Gerald Ford out of the running, George Bush is the overwhelming first choice of both Republican and independent voters nationwide as vice-president on the GOP ticket with Ronald Reagan.

Emerging as the clear winner among the twenty-two persons listed is Gerald Ford, a man who is actually not in the race for the number two spot on the GOP ticket. Ford receives 31% of the support of Republicans to 20% for Bush. When Ford's vote is redistributed to the twenty-one other persons on the list on the basis of second choices, in view of his decision to take himself out of active consideration, Bush comes out far ahead with 29% of the vote of the GOP rank and file. Following Bush is Senator Howard Baker with 15%, John Connally with 12%, and Charles Percy with 4%. All others on the list receive 3% or less of the vote.

The vote of political independents historically has been of crucial importance to Republican presidental tickets in view of the GOP's minority party status. In all presidential elections in recent decades successful Republican candidates have had to rely on significant support from voters who classify themselves as independents.

When the choices of independents in the current survey are examined, with Ford's vote allocated on the basis of second choices, Bush again is the winner with 29% of the independent vote. Next is Baker with 16%, followed by Connally with 9%, Percy with 5%, and all others on the list receive 2% or less of the independent vote.

Although some of the candidates included in the survey make relatively poor showings, it is important to bear in mind that persons who are well known to the public have a built-in advantage.

While some strategists favor the selection of a conservative vice-presidential candidate for the Reagan ticket, others feel that he should choose a political moderate in order to appeal to a broader spectrum of Republicans as well as to independents and dissident Democrats. In the current survey, support for moderate Republicans among the twenty-one men and women included in the test (excluding Ford) clearly outweighs backing for more conservative Republicans.

Findings also reveal that the selection of a woman or of a black would be slightly more of a hindrance than a help in terms of electing a GOP ticket headed by Ronald Reagan. Among registered voters nationwide, 20% say they would be less likely to vote for Reagan if he selected a woman as his running mate, 14% say they would be more likely to do so, and an overwhelming 62% say it would make no difference.

Most inclined to say they would be more likely to vote for the Reagan ticket if he named a woman are young adults, independents, persons with a college background, and women themselves. Almost equal proportions of women report that they are either more likely or less likely, while men lean 2 to 1 on the less likely side.

Nineteen percent of registered voters say they would be less likely to vote for a Reagan-headed ticket if he chose a black, while 11% say they would be more likely. However, a majority (66%) say it would make no difference. The groups most inclined to vote for a Reagan ticket if he named a black as his running mate are blacks, by a 2-to-1 margin, young adults, the college educated, and independents.

JULY 10

PARTY BEST FOR KEEPING PEACE AND PROSPERITY

Interviewing Date: 6/27–30/80
Survey #158-G

Which political party do you think will do a better job of keeping the country prosperous—the Republican party or the Democratic party?

Republican 31%
Democratic 37
No difference 20
No opinion 12

By way of comparison, here are the percentages for each party back to September 1972; the no difference and no opinion figures have been omitted:

	Republican	Democratic
March 1978	23%	41%
August 1976	23	47
September 1974	17	47
March 1974	19	49
September 1972	38	35

Which political party do you think would be more likely to keep the United States out of World War III—the Republican party or the Democratic party?

Republican 28%
Democratic 32
No difference 24
No opinion 16

By way of comparison, here are the percentages for each party back to September 1972; the no difference and no opinion figures have been omitted:

	Republican	Democratic
March 1978	25%	31%
August 1976	29	32
September 1974	21	29
March 1974	24	33
September 1972	32	28

Note: Peace and prosperity have been bread and butter issues in most election campaigns. This is demonstrated by the fact that the party with the lead on both these issues at election time has seen its candidate elected.

JULY 14
PRESIDENT CARTER—
PRESIDENTIAL TRIAL HEAT

Interviewing Date: 7/11–14/80
Survey #159-G

Do you approve or disapprove of the way Carter is handling his job as president?

Approve 33%
Disapprove 55
No opinion 12

Asked of registered voters: Suppose the presidential election were being held today. If President Jimmy Carter were the Democratic candidate, running against Ronald Reagan, the Republican candidate, and John Anderson, the independent candidate, which would you like to see win? [Those who named another person or who were undecided were asked: As of today, do you lean more to Carter, the Democrat, to Reagan, the Republican, or to Anderson, the independent?]

Carter 34%
Reagan 37
Anderson 21
Other 1
Undecided 7

Asked of registered voters who named Carter: Do you strongly support him or do you only moderately support him?

Strongly 44%
Moderately 55
Can't say 1

Asked of registered voters who named Reagan: Do you strongly support him or do you only moderately support him?

Strongly 38%
Moderately 61
Can't say 1

Asked of registered voters who named Anderson: Do you strongly support him or do you only moderately support him?

Strongly. 31%
Moderately 65
Can't say 4

Asked of registered voters: Regardless of how you, yourself, feel, which candidate do you think will win the presidential election this fall—Reagan, Carter, or Anderson?

Reagan. 41%
Carter. 45
Anderson. 2
Undecided. 12

Note: In the latest nationwide Gallup survey, Ronald Reagan maintains his lead over President Jimmy Carter and independent candidate John Anderson. Reagan wins the support of 37% of registered voters to 34% for Carter and 21% for Anderson. These current figures are almost identical to those recorded in a late-June survey that showed Reagan with 39%, Carter with 32%, and Anderson with 22%.

While voters currently prefer Reagan, they give Carter almost an equal chance of winning the presidency. Forty-five percent of registered voters think Carter will win, 41% say Reagan, only 2% say Anderson, and another 12% are undecided.

The vote for Anderson over the period of three and one-half months and in nine national surveys has stayed within a narrow 5-point range, varying from 18% to 23%. As in previous trial heats, Anderson's support comes almost equally from both Carter and Reagan. In the current survey he draws 10 percentage points from Reagan and 9 from Carter. The latest two-way race shows Reagan with 46% of the vote of registered voters, Carter with 43%.

Responses also indicate that none of the three candidates can boast of very solid or enthusiastic backing. Large majorities say they only moderately, rather than strongly, support the candidate of their choice in the latest trial heat.

JULY 17
PRESIDENTIAL TRIAL HEAT

Interviewing Date: 7/11–14/80
Survey #159-G

Asked of registered voters: Suppose the presidential election were being held today. Which of these tickets would you vote for—a Republican ticket of Ronald Reagan and George Bush, a Democratic ticket of Jimmy Carter and Walter Mondale, or an independent ticket headed by John Anderson? [Those who named another person or who were undecided were asked: As of today, would you lean more to a Republican ticket of Reagan and Bush, a Democratic ticket of Carter and Mondale, or to an independent ticket headed by Anderson?]

Reagan-Bush. 41%
Carter-Mondale 37
Anderson. 15
Other 1
Undecided. 6

By Sex
Male

Reagan-Bush. 43%
Carter-Mondale 35
Anderson. 15
Other 1
Undecided. 6

Female

Reagan-Bush. 39%
Carter-Mondale 39
Anderson. 14
Other 1
Undecided. 7

By Race
White

Reagan-Bush. 46%
Carter-Mondale 32
Anderson. 15

Other 1
Undecided.......................... 6

Nonwhite

Reagan-Bush........................ 7%
Carter-Mondale 68
Anderson........................... 10
Other 3
Undecided......................... 12

By Education
College

Reagan-Bush.......................41%
Carter-Mondale 31
Anderson........................... 23
Other 1
Undecided.......................... 4

High School

Reagan-Bush.......................42%
Carter-Mondale 39
Anderson........................... 11
Other 1
Undecided.......................... 7

Grade School

Reagan-Bush.......................36%
Carter-Mondale 45
Anderson........................... 9
Other 1
Undecided.......................... 8

By Region
East

Reagan-Bush.......................37%
Carter-Mondale 39
Anderson........................... 16
Other 1
Undecided.......................... 7

Midwest

Reagan-Bush.......................40%
Carter-Mondale 37
Anderson........................... 17
Other .... *
Undecided.......................... 5

South

Reagan-Bush.......................41%
Carter-Mondale 39
Anderson........................... 11
Other 1
Undecided.......................... 7

West

Reagan-Bush.......................47%
Carter-Mondale 31
Anderson........................... 15
Other 1
Undecided.......................... 6

By Age
18–24 Years

Reagan-Bush.......................28%
Carter-Mondale 42
Anderson........................... 21
Other .... *
Undecided.......................... 9

25–29 Years

Reagan-Bush.......................30%
Carter-Mondale 38
Anderson........................... 19
Other 2
Undecided......................... 11

30–49 Years

Reagan-Bush.......................43%
Carter-Mondale 35
Anderson........................... 16
Other .... *
Undecided.......................... 6

50 Years and Over

Reagan-Bush.......................45%
Carter-Mondale 37
Anderson........................... 11
Other 1
Undecided.......................... 6

By Politics
Republicans

Reagan-Bush.......................81%
Carter-Mondale 6

Anderson........................ 10
Other .... *
Undecided...................... 3

Democrats

Reagan-Bush.................... 19%
Carter-Mondale 62
Anderson........................ 12
Other 1
Undecided...................... 5

Independents

Reagan-Bush.................... 42%
Carter-Mondale 19
Anderson........................ 25
Other 1
Undecided...................... 12

By Religion
Protestants

Reagan-Bush.................... 43%
Carter-Mondale 39
Anderson........................ 11
Other 1
Undecided...................... 6

Catholics

Reagan-Bush.................... 40%
Carter-Mondale 33
Anderson........................ 20
Other 1
Undecided...................... 6

By Occupation
Professional and Business

Reagan-Bush.................... 45%
Carter-Mondale 31
Anderson........................ 19
Other .... *
Undecided...................... 5

Clerical and Sales

Reagan-Bush.................... 39%
Carter-Mondale 36
Anderson........................ 20

Other 1
Undecided...................... 4

Manual Workers

Reagan-Bush.................... 35%
Carter-Mondale 42
Anderson........................ 14
Other 1
Undecided...................... 8

Non-Labor Force

Reagan-Bush.................... 47%
Carter-Mondale 37
Anderson........................ 8
Other 1
Undecided...................... 7

Labor Union Families Only

Reagan-Bush.................... 37%
Carter-Mondale 44
Anderson........................ 12
Other .... *
Undecided...................... 7

Non-Labor Union Families Only

Reagan-Bush.................... 42%
Carter-Mondale 35
Anderson........................ 16
Other 1
Undecided...................... 6

*Less than 1%

Note: The first national test of the major party tickets shows the GOP ticket of Ronald Reagan and George Bush holding a 4-point lead over the Democratic slate of Carter and Mondale.

JULY 20
REGISTRATION AND THE DRAFT

Interviewing Date: 7/11–14/80
Survey #159-G

Do you favor or oppose the registration of the names of all young men so that in the event of an emergency the time needed to call up men for a draft would be reduced?

Favor.............................80%
Oppose............................15
No opinion 5

By Sex
Male

Favor.............................81%
Oppose............................15
No opinion 4

Female

Favor.............................80%
Oppose............................15
No opinion 5

By Race
White

Favor.............................82%
Oppose............................14
No opinion 4

Nonwhite

Favor.............................67%
Oppose............................24
No opinion 9

By Age
18–24 Years

Favor.............................66%
Oppose............................27
No opinion 7

25–29 Years

Favor.............................84%
Oppose............................14
No opinion 2

30–49 Years

Favor.............................82%
Oppose............................13
No opinion 5

50 Years and Over

Favor.............................85%
Oppose............................11
No opinion 4

Do you favor or oppose the registration of the names of all young women under these circumstances?

Favor.............................49%
Oppose............................45
No opinion 6

By Sex
Male

Favor.............................50%
Oppose............................44
No opinion 6

Female

Favor.............................48%
Oppose............................46
No opinion 6

By Race
White

Favor.............................53%
Oppose............................42
No opinion 5

Nonwhite

Favor.............................28%
Oppose............................62
No opinion 10

By Age
18–24 Years

Favor.............................44%
Oppose............................48
No opinion 8

25–29 Years

Favor.............................50%
Oppose............................47
No opinion 3

30–49 Years

Favor.................................52%
Oppose...............................43
No opinion 5

50 Years and Over

Favor.................................49%
Oppose...............................45
No opinion 6

Do you think we should return to the military draft at this time, or not?

Should................................58%
Should not...........................34
No opinion 8

By Sex
Male

Should................................62%
Should not...........................32
No opinion 6

Female

Should................................54%
Should not...........................36
No opinion 10

By Race
White

Should................................61%
Should not...........................32
No opinion 7

Nonwhite

Should................................36%
Should not...........................49
No opinion 15

By Age
18–24 Years

Should................................37%
Should not...........................57
No opinion 6

25–29 Years

Should................................60%
Should not...........................35
No opinion 5

30–49 Years

Should................................64%
Should not...........................30
No opinion 6

50 Years and Over

Should................................62%
Should not...........................27
No opinion 11

If a draft were to become necessary, should young women be required to participate as well as young men, or not?

Should................................49%
Should not...........................47
No opinion 4

By Sex
Male

Should................................55%
Should not...........................42
No opinion 3

Female

Should................................44%
Should not...........................51
No opinion 5

By Race
White

Should................................52%
Should not...........................44
No opinion 4

Nonwhite

Should................................31%
Should not...........................62
No opinion 7

By Age
18–24 Years

Should 45%
Should not 50
No opinion 5

25–29 Years

Should 51%
Should not 45
No opinion 4

30–49 Years

Should 51%
Should not 46
No opinion 3

50 Years and Over

Should 50%
Should not 45
No opinion 5

Asked of those who replied that women should participate in the draft: Should women be eligible for combat roles, or not?

Should 22%
Should not 25
No opinion 2
$\qquad$ 49%*

By Sex
Male

Should 23%
Should not 30
No opinion 2
$\qquad$ 55%*

Female

Should 21%
Should not 22
No opinion 1
$\qquad$ 44%*

By Race
White

Should 23%
Should not 27
No opinion 2
$\qquad$ 52%*

Nonwhite

Should 13%
Should not 14
No opinion 4
$\qquad$ 31%*

By Age
18–24 Years

Should 23%
Should not 20
No opinion 2
$\qquad$ 45%*

25–29 Years

Should 21%
Should not 27
No opinion 3
$\qquad$ 51%*

30–49 Years

Should 24%
Should not 24
No opinion 3
$\qquad$ 51%*

50 Years and Over

Should 19%
Should not 30
No opinion 1
$\qquad$ 50%*

*Percentage of total sample

Note: President Carter has backed Selective Service legislation as a way of showing U.S. resolve in the face of the Soviet Union's military intervention in Afghanistan. And when this nation's approximately two million twenty-year-old men register for the draft they will do so amidst public opinion that not only favors registration but also a return to the military draft.

The plan to reinstate obligatory draft registration for the nation's 19- to 20-year-old males follows a five-year period during which men were not required to register. Under the plan enacted all twenty-year-old men must register the week of July 21 at post offices across the country, with nineteen-year-old males registering the following week. The penalty for any youth who willfully fails to register is a fine of $10,000 and up to five years in prison. Carter also included women in the plan, but Congress restricted the registration to only males.

Although the Carter administration has maintained that the current registration plan is not necessarily a prelude to the military draft, draft protest groups have sprung up across the country. Some social observers predict campus unrest when colleges reopen this fall.

While more than seven in ten in both the 18- to 24-year-old group and those twenty-five years and older favor the registration plan, the young vote 57% to 37% against reviving the draft. On the other hand, older adults vote 64% to 30% in favor of such action at this time.

According to the latest Gallup Youth Survey conducted in May, an overwhelming majority (62%) of American teen-agers (13- to 18-year-olds) also oppose a reinstatement of the draft, while only 38% favor such a move.

Support for drafting women outweighs opposition among the general public, and majorities of men favor both steps. And national opinion is almost evenly divided on whether women should be eligible for combat roles, with little difference found between the views of men and women.

The possibility of a return to the draft has prompted discussion of a national service program. Gallup surveys over the last three decades consistently have shown a large majority of the American people in favor of a proposal to require every young man eighteen years and older to give one year of service to the country, either in military or nonmilitary work. These surveys also show that young people would be more likely to sign up for nonmilitary work under such a plan. However, evidence indicates that enough youths still would opt for military service to more than fill the manpower needs of the armed forces.

JULY 24
STATUS OF BLACKS IN AMERICA

Interviewing Date: 5/30–6/2/80
Survey: #156-G

In your opinion, how well do you think blacks are treated in this community?

Same as whites 66%
Not very well 19
Badly 4
Don't know 11

By Race
White

Same as whites 68%
Not very well 17
Badly 3
Don't know 12

Nonwhite

Same as whites 45%
Not very well 31
Badly 14
Don't know 10

Northern Black

Same as whites 46%
Not very well 26
Badly 16
Don't know 12

Southern Black

Same as whites 41%
Not very well 41
Badly 11
Don't know 7

By Education
College

Same as whites 61%
Not very well 23
Badly 4
Don't know 12

High School

Same as whites 67%
Not very well 18
Badly 4
Don't know 11

Grade School

Same as whites 68%
Not very well 14
Badly 5
Don't know 13

By Region
East

Same as whites 62%
Not very well 20
Badly 7
Don't know 11

Midwest

Same as whites 68%
Not very well 16
Badly 3
Don't know 13

South

Same as whites 64%
Not very well 22
Badly 3
Don't know 11

West

Same as whites 68%
Not very well 18
Badly 4
Don't know 10

By Community Size
One Million and Over

Same as whites 60%
Not very well 22
Badly 8
Don't know 10

500,000–999,999

Same as whites 59%
Not very well 25
Badly 7
Don't know 9

50,000–499,999

Same as whites 67%
Not very well 22
Badly 3
Don't know 8

2,500–49,999

Same as whites 69%
Not very well 16
Badly 3
Don't know 12

Under 2,500; Rural

Same as whites 69%
Not very well 13
Badly 2
Don't know 16

Looking back over the last ten years, do you think the quality of life of blacks in the United States has gotten better, stayed about the same, or gotten worse?

Gotten better 71%
Stayed same 17
Gotten worse 8
No opinion 4

By Race
White

Gotten better 75%
Stayed same 16
Gotten worse 5
No opinion 4

Nonwhite

Gotten better 45%
Stayed same 27
Gotten worse 24
No opinion 4

Northern Black

Gotten better 41%
Stayed same 29
Gotten worse 28
No opinion 2

Southern Black

Gotten better 52%
Stayed same 28
Gotten worse 19
No opinion 1

By Education
College

Gotten better 70%
Stayed same 22
Gotten worse 5
No opinion 3

High School

Gotten better 73%
Stayed same 15
Gotten worse 8
No opinion 4

Grade School

Gotten better 64%
Stayed same 17
Gotten worse 14
No opinion 5

By Region
East

Gotten better 68%
Stayed same 19
Gotten worse 9
No opinion 4

Midwest

Gotten better 74%
Stayed same 17
Gotten worse 6
No opinion 3

South

Gotten better 73%
Stayed same 15
Gotten worse 9
No opinion 3

West

Gotten better 66%
Stayed same 20
Gotten worse 9
No opinion 5

By Community Size
One Million and Over

Gotten better 65%
Stayed same 18
Gotten worse 11
No opinion 6

500,000–999,999

Gotten better 67%
Stayed same 20
Gotten worse 11
No opinion 2

50,000–499,999

Gotten better 74%
Stayed same 17
Gotten worse 6
No opinion 3

2,500–49,999

Gotten better 73%
Stayed same 17
Gotten worse 6
No opinion 4

Gotten better 73%
Stayed same 17
Gotten worse 7
No opinion 3

Have you heard or read about the recent racial troubles in Miami, Florida?

Yes 91%
No 9

Asked of those who replied in the affirmative: In your opinion, what were the main causes of this trouble?

Trial and acquittal of policemen 34%
Lack of communication between races . . . 5
Lack of respect for authority 4
Black leadership problem 1
Racial problem (general) 18
Blacks not given equal opportunity 7
Immigration of Cubans 10
Employment competition between
   blacks and Cubans 5
Economic pressures brought about
   by Cubans 12
Other 4
Don't know 18
                        118%*

By Race
White

Trial and acquittal of policemen 33%
Lack of communication between races . . . 4
Lack of respect for authority 4
Black leadership problem 1
Racial problem (general) 18
Blacks not given equal opportunity 7
Immigration of Cubans 10
Employment competition between
   blacks and Cubans 5
Economic pressures brought about
   by Cubans 13
Other 4
Don't know 19
                        118%*

Nonwhite

Trial and acquittal of policemen 46%
Lack of communication between races . . . 5
Lack of respect for authority 1
Black leadership problem 1
Racial problem (general) 18
Blacks not given equal opportunity 11
Immigration of Cubans 9
Employment competition between
   blacks and Cubans 5
Economic pressures brought about
   by Cubans 6
Other 1
Don't know 12
                        115%*

*Totals add to more than 100% due to multiple responses.

Do you think that racial conflicts are or are not likely to be a serious problem in this community during the next six months?

Are likely 14%
Are not likely 78
Don't know 8

By Race
White

Are likely 13%
Are not likely 80
Don't know 7

Nonwhite

Are likely 19%
Are not likely 63
Don't know 18

By Community Size
One Million and Over

Are likely 14%
Are not likely 76
Don't know 10

500,000–999,999

Are likely 16%
Are not likely 82
Don't know 2

50,000–499,999

Are likely	21%
Are not likely	70
Don't know	9

2,500–49,999

Are likely	14%
Are not likely	78
Don't know	8

Under 2,500; Rural

Are likely	7%
Are not likely	83
Don't know	10

Note: Whites and blacks hold widely divergent views on how well blacks are being treated in the United States today and on whether the quality of life for blacks has improved or gotten worse over the last ten years.

Almost seven in ten whites (68%) say blacks are treated the same as whites in their community, while 17% say not very well, and 3% say they are treated badly. Nonwhites, however, paint a bleaker picture with 45% reporting they are treated the same as whites. An additional survey reveals that three-fourths of whites (75%) hold the view that the quality of life for blacks has improved over the last decade, but only 45% of nonwhites are in agreement.

The recent racial tension in Miami focused attention on the plight of blacks in America. Despite progress, economic conditions in black central cities remain critical, with possible violence just below the surface. New factors accentuate the resentment of the blacks, including increasingly widespread unemployment due to the recession and the recent influx of immigrants who, blacks fear, may cause further competition for jobs.

The racial violence in Miami, which began on May 17 and resulted in the deaths of at least fifteen persons and property damage of $200 million, prompted many people to wonder whether the racial conflict was a precursor of widespread racial troubles elsewhere in the country.

While a 34% plurality cited the acquittal by an all-white jury of four policemen accused of killing a black, others named racial unrest in general (18%) or problems associated with the influx of Cuban refugees (10%).

JULY 27
PRESIDENTIAL CANDIDATES

Interviewing Date: 6/27–30/80
Survey #158-G

Here is a list of terms—shown as pairs of opposites—that have been used to describe Jimmy Carter/Ronald Reagan/John Anderson. [Respondents were handed a card with terms listed.] From each pair of opposites, would you select the term which you feel best describes Carter/Reagan/Anderson?

In order to facilitate direct comparisons between the three candidates, the following shows the percentages of survey respondents ascribing each characteristic to each man, excluding those who did not express an opinion.

Comparative Profiles

	Carter	Reagan	Anderson
A religious person....	88%	31%	44%
A man of high moral principles.........	85	73	74
Takes moderate, middle-of-the-road positions	80	58	56
A likable person	76	73	67
Bright, intelligent	67	76	80
Displays good judgment in a crisis..........	72	79	72
Sympathetic to problems of the poor..........	63	44	57
Says what he believes even if unpopular..	60	53	63
Puts country's interests ahead of politics	53	45	50

Sides with the average citizen	48	49	58
A man you can believe in	38	51	47
Offers imaginative, innovative solutions to national problems	35	56	56
Decisive, sure of himself..........	31	72	67
Has strong leadership qualities	29	67	54
A person of exceptional abilities	27	41	46
You know where he stands on issues ...	26	57	52
Has a well-defined program for moving country ahead...........	24	51	42

Note: A recent Gallup study of the public's perceptions of the personality traits of the three leading presidential candidates shows that President Jimmy Carter is seen as "a religious person" and "a man of high moral principles." Ronald Reagan scores high for his intelligence and decisiveness, while John Anderson is perceived as being "bright, intelligent" and "a man of high moral principles."

It is important to bear in mind that the electorate's image of Anderson is still in the formative stage because of his comparatively recent exposure to public scrutiny. It is therefore not surprising to find many people unable to make judgments at this time about Anderson's personal characteristics.

Despite the fact that President Carter's overall performance rating has declined 28 percentage points since early December, large majorities of Americans not only see him as religious and moral but also continue to ascribe the following terms to him: "a likable person" and a man who is "sympathetic to problems of the poor." While there has been a slight decrease over the last two years in the proportion of voters who attribute these characteristics to Carter, the

trend has been remarkably stable in the five previous studies conducted during this period.

On the other hand, during the same time there has been a marked reduction in the percentage of people who believe that the president is "decisive, sure of himself," "a man you can believe in," one who "offers imaginative, innovative solutions to national problems," "has strong leadership qualities," "sides with the average citizen," and "has a well-defined program for moving country ahead."

Still, Carter now has a comparative advantage over both Reagan and Anderson on a number of personal characteristics. The president also has a wide lead over Reagan as a person who "takes moderate, middle-of-the-road positions" on issues, which is not an insignificant advantage since most presidential elections are won in the middle of the political spectrum.

Although Carter comes across better than Reagan and Anderson, he trails both in certain important respects such as "decisive, sure of himself," "has strong leadership qualities," "you know where he stands on issues," and "has a well-defined program for moving country ahead."

JULY 31
EQUAL RIGHTS AMENDMENT

Interviewing Date: 7/11–14/80
Survey #159-G

Have you heard or read about the Equal Rights Amendment to the United States Constitution which would give women equal rights and equal responsibilities?

Yes..................................	91%
No..................................	9

Asked of those who replied in the affirmative: Do you favor or oppose this amendment?

Favor................................	58%
Oppose..............................	34
No opinion	8

By Sex
Male

Favor......................................61%
Oppose....................................28
No opinion 11

Female

Favor......................................54%
Oppose....................................34
No opinion 12

By Race
White

Favor......................................55%
Oppose....................................34
No opinion 11

Nonwhite

Favor......................................73%
Oppose....................................16
No opinion 11

By Education
College

Favor......................................63%
Oppose....................................27
No opinion 10

High School

Favor......................................57%
Oppose....................................33
No opinion 10

Grade School

Favor......................................48%
Oppose....................................35
No opinion 17

By Region
East

Favor......................................61%
Oppose....................................27
No opinion 12

Midwest

Favor......................................57%
Oppose....................................33
No opinion 10

South

Favor......................................50%
Oppose....................................42
No opinion 8

West

Favor......................................64%
Oppose....................................23
No opinion 13

By Age
18–24 Years

Favor......................................65%
Oppose....................................20
No opinion 15

25–29 Years

Favor......................................60%
Oppose....................................29
No opinion 11

30–49 Years

Favor......................................63%
Oppose....................................30
No opinion 7

50 Years and Over

Favor......................................56%
Oppose....................................34
No opinion 10

By Income
$15,000 and Over

Favor......................................59%
Oppose....................................32
No opinion 9

Under $15,000

Favor 60%
Oppose 29
No opinion 11

By Politics

Republicans

Favor 47%
Oppose 41
No opinion 12

Democrats

Favor 63%
Oppose 28
No opinion 9

Independents

Favor 59%
Oppose 28
No opinion 13

By Occupation

Professional and Business

Favor 63%
Oppose 27
No opinion 10

Clerical and Sales

Favor 67%
Oppose 20
No opinion 13

Manual Workers

Favor 59%
Oppose 31
No opinion 10

Non-Labor Force

Favor 44%
Oppose 42
No opinion 14

Note: Although the U.S. public as a whole continues to support ratification of the Equal Rights Amendment by nearly a 2-to-1 margin, Republican voters have shifted toward opposition since 1976.

Nationally, 58% of Americans who have heard or read about ERA favor ratification, while 34% are opposed. Republicans support ratification but by a much narrower 47% to 41% margin.

On July 9 a heated debate was touched off when the platform committee of the Republican National Convention adopted a women's rights plank that generally pleased party conservatives but alienated the GOP's feminists as well as the party's moderate wing.

The plank that cleared the committee by a 90-to-0 vote endorsed "equal rights and equal opportunities for women," but it added that the fate of the Equal Rights Amendment should be left solely to the states "without federal interference or pressure."

The proposed amendment states: "Equality of rights under the law shall not be denied or abridged by the United States or any state on account of sex." GOP presidential candidate Ronald Reagan says he favors equal rights for women but opposes the ERA because such rights should be a matter of laws, not part of the Constitution.

Three-fourths of the state legislatures (38 states) must ratify the proposed amendment before it becomes law. To date only 35 states have done so, none since January 1977. In Illinois ratification recently was defeated for the seventh time.

Although Republicans are closely divided on whether they favor or oppose the amendment, Democrats are more than 2 to 1 in favor. The views of independents—a crucial bloc of voters—fall between those of Republicans and Democrats. These figures represent a fairly radical departure from those obtained in 1976, when the attitudes of Republicans and Democrats were very similar and those of independents were most supportive of ERA ratification.

Consistent with earlier results, the latest survey reveals that men are somewhat more likely to express support for ratification of the amendment (61%) than are women themselves (54%).

Trend in Public Opinion

	Favor	Oppose	No opinion
1978	58%	31%	11%
1976	57	24	19
1975	58	24	18

AUGUST 1
PRESIDENT CARTER

Interviewing Date: 7/14–25/80
Special Telephone Survey

Do you approve or disapprove of the way Carter is handling his job as president?

Approve............................21%
Disapprove 63
No opinion 16

Note: In a recently completed national telephone survey, President Jimmy Carter's popularity rating is at 21% approval, which is the lowest recorded for any president since the Gallup Poll initiated these measurements in 1938.

The previous all-time low points in popularity were the 23% recorded for Harry Truman in November 1951 at the time of the Korean War, and the 24% for Richard Nixon in August 1974 on the eve of his resignation from the presidency.

The president's current rating is down 7 points from his previous low point, recorded exactly one year ago, and 40 points down from his rating in early December, recorded one month after the Iranian hostage crisis erupted.

The following shows the low points during the tenure of the last eight presidents:

Low Points of Approval

	Percent approval	Principal public concern
Carter	21% July 1980	High cost of living/ unemployment
Ford	37% Jan., Mar. 1975	High cost of living/ unemployment
Nixon	24% Aug. 1974	High cost of living/ unemployment
Johnson	35% Aug. 1968	Vietnam/crime and lawlessness
Kennedy	56% Sept. 1963	Keeping peace/ race relations
Eisenhower	48% Mar., Apr. 1958	Unemployment/ keeping peace
Truman	23% Nov. 1951	Korean war/ economic problems
Roosevelt	54% Nov. 1938	Keeping out of war/ unemployment

Although President Carter's current rating is at a historic low, Gallup Poll history over the last four decades has shown that a president frequently rebounds from a low point in popularity. Gerald Ford eventually regained 15 percentage points in approval after his low point, while Johnson's approval rating went up 14 points, Eisenhower's 18 points, Truman's 8 points, and Roosevelt's 30 points.

Carter's approval ratings have been characterized by considerable volatility, with its sometimes steep downward and upward movements. Foreign policy successes such as the conclusion of the Camp David "framework for peace" in September 1978 and the signing of the Israeli-Egyptian peace treaty in March 1979 gave the president's popularity a substantial lift. Most remarkable was the peak of approval measured in early December 1979, as the country closed ranks behind the president in the wake of the Iranian hostage crisis.

In the interim periods between these foreign policy successes, however, the Carter approval ratings mostly have gone down. This is perhaps not surprising since a chronic economic malaise has persisted for much of the Carter administration. The president's economic policies have had little or no visible effect in curbing inflation and reducing unemployment, nor has Carter been able to offer much in the way of charismatic leadership.

Is there a bedrock level below which presidential popularity is unlikely to sink? Perhaps, notwithstanding any unforeseen catastrophe. Between May and November of 1979, for instance, Carter's popularity never left the narrow range of 28 to 33 percentage points. In spite of dreary economic developments—continued high inflation and gas lines—approval ratings refused to drop below 28%. The July 1980 measurement of 21% approval represents an exceptional downward trend and does not necessarily reflect an even lower level of continuing lack of confidence in the president's handling of his job.

Carter Approval Trend

	Approve	Dis- approve	No opinion
1980			
July 14–25	21%	63%	16%
July 11–14	33	55	12
June 27–30	31	58	11
June 13–16	32	56	12
May 30–June 2	38	52	10
May 16–19	38	51	11
May 2–5	43	47	10

Hostage Rescue Attempt Fails

Apr. 11–14	39%	50%	11%
Mar. 28–31	39	51	10
Mar. 7–10	43	45	12
Feb. 1–4	55	36	9
Jan. 18–21	58	32	10
Jan. 4–7	56	33	11

1979

USSR Invades Afghanistan

Dec. 7–10	54%	35%	11%
Dec. 5–6	61	30	9
Nov. 30–Dec. 3	51	37	12
Nov. 16–19	38	49	13

American Embassy in Tehran Seized

Nov. 2–5	32%	55%	13%
Oct. 12–15	31	55	14
Oct. 5–8	29	58	13
Sept. 28–Oct. 1	33	54	13
Sept. 7–10	30	55	14
Aug. 17–20	32	54	14
Aug. 10–13	33	55	12
Aug. 3–6	32	53	15
July 13–16	29	58	13
June 29–July 2	28	59	13
June 22–25	29	57	14

SALT II Treaty Signed

June 1–4	29%	56%	15%
May 18–21	32	53	15
May 3–7	37	49	14
Apr. 6–9	40	46	14
Mar. 23–26	42	44	14
Mar. 16–19	47	39	14

Sadat and Begin Sign Peace Treaty

Mar. 2–5	39%	48%	13%
Feb. 23–26	37	46	17
Feb. 2–5	42	42	16
Jan. 19–22	43	41	16
Jan. 5–8	50	36	14

1978
U.S. Recognizes People's Republic of China

Dec. 8–11	51%	34%	15%
Dec. 1–4	50	34	16
Nov. 10–13	50	34	16
Oct. 27–30	49	36	15
Sept. 22–25	48	34	18

Camp David Peace Agreements Concluded

Sept. 15–18	45%	40%	15%
Sept. 8–11	42	42	16
Aug. 18–21	43	41	16
Aug. 11–14	40	43	17
Aug. 4–7	39	44	17
July 21–24	39	44	17
July 7–10	40	41	19
June 16–19	42	42	16
June 2–5	44	41	15
May 19–22	43	43	14
May 5–8	41	43	16
April 28–May 1	41	42	17

April 14–17   40%   44%   16%

Production of Neutron Bomb Deferred

Mar. 31–Apr. 3	48%	39	13%
Mar. 10–13	50	35	15
Mar. 3–6	49	33	18
Feb. 24–27	50	33	17
Feb. 10–13	47	34	19
Jan. 20–23	52	28	20
Jan. 6–9	55	27	18

1977

Dec. 9–12	57%	27%	16%
Nov. 18–21	56	30	14
Nov. 4–7	55	30	15
Oct. 28–31	51	31	18
Oct. 21–24	54	30	16
Oct. 14–17	55	29	16
Sept. 30–Oct. 3	59	24	17

Lance Resignation Accepted

Sept. 9–12	54%	29%	17%
Aug. 19–22	66	26	8

U.S. and Panama Agree to Transfer Canal

Aug. 5–8	60%	23%	17%
July 22–25	67	17	16
July 8–11	62	22	16
June 17–20	63	18	19
June 3–6	63	19	18
May 20–23	64	19	17
May 6–9	66	19	15
Apr. 29–May 1	63	18	19
Apr. 15–18	63	18	19

Energy Speech: "Moral Equivalent of War"

Apr. 1–4	67%	14%	19%
Mar. 25–28	72	10	18
Mar. 18–21	75	9	16
Mar. 4–7	70	9	21
Feb. 18–21	71	9	20
Feb. 4–7	66	8	26

AUGUST 3
MOST IMPORTANT PROBLEM

Interviewing Date: 7/11–14/80
Survey #159-G

What do you think is the most important problem facing this country today?

Inflation; high cost of living	56%
Unemployment	15
International problems	12
Dissatisfaction with government	8
Energy problems	6
Moral decline	5
Other	14
No opinion	3
	119%*

*Total adds to more than 100% due to multiple responses.

Asked of those who named a problem: Which political party do you think can do a better job of handling the problem you have just mentioned—the Republican party or the Democratic party?

Republican	30%
Democratic	27
No difference	30
No opinion	13

Note: For almost thirty-five years the Gallup Poll has asked Americans what they consider to be the most important problem facing the nation and which political party they believe can better deal with that problem. In the current survey, 52% of those who choose between the parties think that the Republicans are better able to handle the nation's problems, while 48% name the Democratic party.

In all previous surveys since October 1972 when the GOP was the choice of 57% of the public, the Democratic party has been favored, with the margin as wide as 28 percentage points in the spring of 1975. In sixty Gallup Poll measurements dating back to 1945, the GOP has been named more often than the Democratic party only ten times as being better able to deal with important national problems.

The findings in the current survey represent little change from the previous June study, in which 59% named the high cost of living as the number one problem facing the nation, followed by 16% citing international problems, 14% unemployment, and 5% dissatisfaction with government.

Despite rising unemployment in recent months and widespread concern about joblessness in the months ahead, all groups in the populace name the high cost of living as this country's major problem, including persons hardest hit by unemployment—unskilled workers, persons from lower-income families, and nonwhites.

AUGUST 5
DEMOCRATIC PRESIDENTIAL CANDIDATES

Interviewing Date: 8/1–4/80
Survey #160-G

Asked of Democrats: Suppose the choice for president in the Democratic convention this year narrows down to Jimmy Carter and Edward Kennedy. Which one would you prefer to have the Democratic convention select?

Carter.............................48%
Kennedy 38
Undecided.........................14

Asked of Democrats: Would you like to see the Democratic convention select Jimmy Carter, or select some other person to be the Democratic candidate for president?

Carter.............................39%
Other person......................52
Don't know 9

Asked of those Democrats who replied some other person: What other person would you like to see the Democratic convention select?

Edward Kennedy.....................26%
Walter Mondale..................... 3
Edmund Muskie...................... 3
Henry Jackson 2
Edmund (Jerry) Brown, Jr........... 2
Frank Church 1
Other 4
Don't know 11
                                    ———
                                    52%

Asked of Democrats: President Carter now apparently has enough delegates pledged to him to assure him of the Democratic nomination for president. Some have suggested that President Carter release these delegates to allow them to vote for whomever they wish. Would you like to see him do this, or not?

Yes...............................54%
No................................36
Don't know 10

Note: Never before in the almost fifty years of Gallup Polls has an incumbent president entered a convention with less grass-roots support from his own party than will President Jimmy Carter in this year's Democratic nomination convention in New York City. At the same time, however, he retains more support with the nation's Democratic voters than does his chief rival, Senator Edward Kennedy of Massachusetts.

Only 39% of Democrats in the latest Gallup survey say they would select Carter for their presidential nominee, while 52% say they would prefer some other person. This finding is recorded at a time when Carter's national popularity rating has declined to 21%, which is his own low point as well as the lowest recorded for any president since the Gallup Poll began these measurements more than forty years ago. Among Democrats, Carter's popularity is the lowest (29%) of any of the eight last presidents.

Most significant is Carter's declining voter strength against challengers Ronald Reagan and Representative John Anderson. A recent survey for *Newsweek*, conducted by the Gallup Organization Inc., shows Reagan with the support of 46% to 28% for Carter and 17% for Anderson.

A mid-July survey showed Reagan and Carter virtually in a dead heat.

Kennedy, however, has made considerable gains as the choice of the nation's Democratic voters for their party's nomination. The current survey shows Carter with a 48% to 38% lead, whereas he led by 60% to 34% in mid-July.

In addition, a majority of Democrats (54%) now favors what has been labeled as an "open convention," with the president releasing his delegates to vote for whomever they wish. This course of action is strenuously advanced by the Massachusetts senator.

Although Kennedy clearly has gained some support in recent weeks, he continues to generate little enthusiasm among the nation's Democratic voters. In fact, the senator attracts even less support than the president. While 52% imply they would like anyone but Carter, an even larger proportion clearly wants anybody but Kennedy. In addition, Kennedy currently displays no greater potential for obtaining votes than does the president in national test elections against Reagan and Anderson. The latest figures show Reagan with 48% of the vote, compared to 27% for Kennedy and 18% for Anderson.

Other prominent Democrats do not attract as much support from party members as do potential compromise candidates. In response to an open-end survey asking those who are opposed to Carter whom they would prefer, only 3% mention either Secretary of State Muskie or Vice-president Mondale, and only 2% either Senator Jackson or Governor Brown of California.

Most important, when tested among all registered voters (regardless of political affiliation) all five, including Carter and Kennedy, presently trail front-runner Reagan by 14 to 25 percentage points.

Interviewing Date: 7/30–31/80
Special Telephone Survey

Asked of registered voters: Suppose the presidential election were being held today. If Edmund Muskie were the Democratic candidate, running against Ronald Reagan, the Republican candidate, and John Anderson, the independent candidate, which would you like to see win? [Those who named another person or who were undecided were asked: As of today, do you lean more to Muskie, the Democrat, Reagan, the Republican, or to Anderson, the independent?]

Muskie............................31%
Reagan............................45
Anderson..........................16
Undecided......................... 8

Democrats Only

Muskie............................50%
Reagan............................25
Anderson..........................14
Undecided........................11

Asked of registered voters: Suppose the presidential election were being held today. If Jimmy Carter were the Democratic candidate, running against Ronald Reagan, the Republican candidate, and John Anderson, the independent candidate, which would you like to see win? [Those who named another person or who were undecided were asked: As of today, do you lean more to Carter, the Democrat, Reagan, the Republican, or to Anderson, the independent?]

Carter.............................28%
Reagan............................46
Anderson..........................17
Undecided......................... 9

Democrats Only

Carter.............................48%
Reagan............................25
Anderson..........................17
Undecided........................10

Asked of registered voters: Suppose the presidential election were being held today. If Walter Mondale were the Democratic candidate, running against Ronald

Reagan, the Republican candidate, and John Anderson, the independent candidate, which would you like to see win? [Those who named another person or who were undecided were asked: As of today, do you lean more to Mondale, the Democrat, Reagan, the Republican, or to Anderson, the independent?]

Mondale	27%
Reagan	47
Anderson	18
Undecided	8

Democrats Only

Mondale	45%
Reagan	26
Anderson	18
Undecided	11

Asked of registered voters: Suppose the presidential election were being held today. If Edward Kennedy were the Democratic candidate, running against Ronald Reagan, the Republican candidate, and John Anderson, the independent candidate, which would you like to see win? [Those who named another person or who were undecided were asked: As of today, do you lean more to Kennedy, the Democrat, Reagan, the Republican, or to Anderson, the independent?]

Kennedy	27%
Reagan	48
Anderson	18
Undecided	7

Democrats Only

Kennedy	44%
Reagan	28
Anderson	18
Undecided	10

Asked of registered voters: Suppose the presidential election were being held today. If Henry Jackson were the Democratic candidate, running against Ronald

Reagan, the Republican candidate, and John Anderson, the independent candidate, which would you like to see win? [Those who named another person or who were undecided were asked: As of today, do you lean more to Jackson, the Democrat, Reagan, the Republican, or to Anderson, the independent?]

Jackson	21%
Reagan	46
Anderson	20
Undecided	13

Democrats Only

Jackson	33%
Reagan	27
Anderson	21
Undecided	19

Note: None of the five potential Democratic nominees does significantly better than the others in trial heats against Reagan and Anderson when tested among Democratic voters. Jackson, in fact, has only a 6-point edge over Reagan among his own party's rank and file.

AUGUST 10
PRESIDENTIAL TRIAL HEAT

Interviewing Date: 8/1–4/80
Survey #160-G

Asked of registered voters: Suppose the presidential election were being held today. If President Jimmy Carter were the Democratic candidate, running against Ronald Reagan, the Republican candidate, and John Anderson, the independent candidate, which would you like to see win? [Those who named another person or who were undecided were asked: As of today, do you lean more to Carter, the Democrat, to Reagan, the Republican, or to Anderson, the independent?]

Carter	29%
Reagan	45

Anderson...........................14
Other 3
Undecided......................... 9

Asked of registered voters who named Carter: Do you strongly support him or do you only moderately support him?

Strongly............................36%
Moderately 61
Can't say......................... 3

Asked of registered voters who named Reagan: Do you strongly support him or do you only moderately support him?

Strongly............................36%
Moderately 62
Can't say......................... 2

Asked of registered voters who named Anderson: Do you strongly support him or do you only moderately support him?

Strongly...........................18%
Moderately 80
Can't say......................... 2

Note: In the latest nationwide Gallup Poll, Ronald Reagan has substantially widened his lead over President Jimmy Carter and independent candidate John Anderson. Reagan now wins the support of 45% of registered voters to 29% for Carter and 14% for Anderson. Prior to the current survey, the vote for Anderson had stayed within a narrow 6-point range, varying from 18% to 24%.

Not only has the Anderson vote slipped sharply but also enthusiasm for the Illinois congressman is lower than that recorded for either Reagan or Carter. While about one-third of registered voters who choose either Reagan or Carter in the latest trial heat say they strongly support their candidate, only 18% strongly back Anderson. As in previous test elections, Anderson's support comes almost equally from both Carter and Reagan. In the current survey he draws 8 percentage points from Reagan and 7 from Carter.

At the present time Carter is suffering a serious loss of his own party members, with only about half of Democratic voters choosing him in the latest trial heat. The president's current rate of defection exceeds even that recorded for Senator George McGovern in a test election against Richard Nixon in the summer of 1972.

Among all registered voters, the president scores slightly better in his native South than elsewhere, but even there Reagan holds the lead, with 48% of the vote to 34% for Carter and 7% for Anderson.

AUGUST 10
SHAH'S DEATH

Interviewing Date: 8/1–4/80
Survey #160-G

As you know, the Shah of Iran died on July 27. Do you think the shah's death will or will not mean a speedier release of the American hostages being held captive in Iran?

Will 11%
Will not 79
Don't know 10

By Education
College

Will 11%
Will not 83
Don't know 6

High School

Will 10%
Will not 80
Don't know 10

Grade School

Will 17%
Will not 69
Don't know 14

Note: Shah Mohammed Reza Pahlavi led a peripatetic existence since fleeing Iran early last year. After his death in July there was speculation for a brief time that this might affect the chances for the release of the fifty-two American hostages being held captive in Iran.

AUGUST 14
CONGRESSIONAL ELECTIONS

Interviewing Date: 8/1–4/80
Survey #160-G

Asked of registered voters: If the elections for Congress were being held today, which party would you like to see win in this congressional district, the Democratic party or the Republican party? [Those who named another party or who were undecided were asked: As of today, do you lean more to the Democratic party or to the Republican party?]

Democratic..........................55%
Republican 39
Other 1
Undecided..........................5

By Region
East

Democratic..........................62%
Republican 32
Other 1
Undecided..........................5

Midwest

Democratic..........................50%
Republican 45
Other 1
Undecided..........................4

South

Democratic..........................53%
Republican 40
Other ....*
Undecided..........................7

West

Democratic..........................55%
Republican 38
Other ....*
Undecided..........................6

*Less than 1%

Note: At this point in the 1980 election contests the strong showing of Republican presidential candidate Ronald Reagan is not reflected in comparable support for Republican congressional candidates.

While the most recent Gallup Poll test election shows Reagan far ahead of President Jimmy Carter (as well as other Democrats tested) and independent candidate John Anderson, the Republican party has not picked up any demonstrable strength in terms of the national vote for Congress since surveys conducted earlier this year.

The situation could change in the months ahead, although the current national vote for the House of Representatives, based on the choices of registered voters, shows the Democratic party with a 57% to 43% advantage over the Republican party.** The previous mid-June survey showed the Democratic party with a similar 58% to 42% lead, the exact figures recorded in a survey conducted in late February/early March.

By way of comparison, in the latest presidential trial heat Reagan is the choice of 45% of registered voters to 29% for Carter and 14% for Anderson.

Gallup preelection findings have proved to be remarkably accurate estimates of the popular vote for Congress. For example, in the 1978 congressional elections the final Gallup estimate of the national vote was 55% Democratic and 45% Republican, while the actual division of the popular vote was virtually the same with 54.6% and 45.4% for each of the two parties, respectively.

Although the Gallup national vote for Con-

**These figures are reached by splitting the other and undecided votes evenly between the major parties.

gress cannot be translated directly into House seats, on the basis of the current survey evidence it is difficult to foresee any major changes in the present composition of the House—275 Democrats and 159 Republicans.

AUGUST 17
JOHN ANDERSON

Interviewing Date: 8/1–4/80
Survey #160-G

Asked of registered voters: Would you be more likely to vote for Anderson if he chooses a Democrat for his vice-presidential running mate or more likely to vote for him if he chooses a Republican?

Chooses a Democrat................... 18%
Chooses a Republican................. 11
Makes no difference; not
    planning to vote for him............. 60
No opinion 11

By Politics
Republicans

Chooses a Democrat................... 2%
Chooses a Republican................. 24
Makes no difference; not
    planning to vote for him............. 65
No opinion 9

Democrats

Chooses a Democrat................... 31%
Chooses a Republican................. 2
Makes no difference; not
    planning to vote for him............. 56
No opinion 11

Independents

Chooses a Democrat................... 11%
Chooses a Republican................. 14
Makes no difference; not
    planning to vote for him............. 66
No opinion 9

Those Who Choose Reagan in Two-Way Reagan-Carter Trial Heat

Chooses a Democrat................... 9%
Chooses a Republican................. 19
Makes no difference; not
    planning to vote for him............. 66
No opinion 6

Those Who Choose Carter in Two-Way Reagan-Carter Trial Heat

Chooses a Democrat................... 34%
Chooses a Republican................. 2
Makes no difference; not
    planning to vote for him............. 55
No opinion 9

Those Who Choose Anderson in Three-Way Reagan-Carter-Anderson Trial Heat

Chooses a Democrat................... 42%
Chooses a Republican................. 15
Makes no difference................... 32
No opinion 11

Note: As speculation mounts over John Anderson's selection of a vice-presidential running mate, his supporters, by a 3-to-1 ratio, say they would prefer the independent presidential candidate to choose a Democrat rather than a Republican to round out his ticket.

In a nationwide Gallup Poll completed on August 4, 42% of registered voters who choose Anderson in a test election against Ronald Reagan and Jimmy Carter say they would be more likely to vote for the Illinois congressman if he selects a Democrat for the number two spot on his ticket, while 15% indicate their preference for a Republican. Of the balance, 32% say the political affiliation of Anderson's running mate will not affect their decision, and 11% had no opinion.

Anderson is expected to name his vice-presidential choice in the near future. At least twenty names have been advanced as possibilities. Those mentioned prominently include New York Governor Hugh Carey and Boston Mayor Kevin White, both Democrats.

Anderson's choice of a running mate may be particularly relevant—even crucial—at this time. In the latest test election Anderson receives 14% of the vote to 45% for Ronald Reagan and 29% for Jimmy Carter. This is the first time support for Anderson has fallen below the 20% plateau he has maintained in the eight earlier Gallup trial heats.

While the falloff in the Anderson vote from the previous test election has occurred among all population groups, it is most pronounced among registered voters who identify themselves as political independents, dropping from 33% in a mid-July Gallup Poll to 22% in the current survey.

The Anderson vote not only has dropped sharply in the latest test election but also only 18% of Anderson backers now say they strongly support him compared to 31% who made the same claim in the mid-July survey, a decline of 13 points. The comparable drop in enthusiastic support for Carter is 8 and for Reagan it is 2 percentage points.

Another campaign development that adds urgency to Anderson's need to generate more public support for his candidacy is that in order to qualify for a forthcoming series of televised debates sponsored by the League of Women Voters he must demonstrate substantial public backing at the end of this month.

Some analysts feel that Anderson's sagging political fortunes can be bolstered by the selection of a strong vice-presidential running mate. On the strength of the survey evidence at hand, it would appear that a Democrat would best fill that need.

Among the electorate as a whole, by a 3-to-2 ratio, voters say they would be more likely to support Anderson if he chooses a Democrat rather than a Republican to be his vice presidential nominee.

In the current survey, 18% of registered voters express a preference for a Democrat for the number two spot on Anderson's ticket, compared to 11% who would prefer a Republican. However, six voters in ten (60%) say either that they do not plan to back Anderson or that the political affiliation of his running mate is immaterial to them.

Among college-educated and younger voters, both groups in which Anderson's candidacy has enjoyed its greatest support, opinion is more evenly divided but still favors a Democrat as Anderson's choice. Among independents, who have provided much of the backbone for Anderson's quest for the presidency, a majority leans toward a Republican vice-presidential choice.

AUGUST 18
BILLY CARTER

Interviewing Date: 8/1–4/80
Survey #160-G

Have you heard or read about the president's brother, Billy Carter, dealing with Libyan government officials?

Yes............................... 94%
No................................. 6

Asked of those who replied in the affirmative: As a result of this, do you have a less favorable opinion of President Jimmy Carter than you had before, or hasn't it had any effect on your opinion?

Less favorable 25%
No effect 67
Don't know 2
                                      ――
                                      94%*

By Region
East

Less favorable 30%
No effect 61
Don't know 2
                                      ――
                                      93%*

Midwest

Less favorable 23%
No effect 70
Don't know 4
                                      ――
                                      97%*

South

Less favorable	21%
No effect	70
Don't know	2
	93%*

West

Less favorable	28%
No effect	63
Don't know	1
	92%*

By Politics

Republicans

Less favorable	33%
No effect	63
Don't know	1
	97%*

Democrats

Less favorable	24%
No effect	68
Don't know	3
	95%*

Independents

Less favorable	23%
No effect	69
Don't know	2
	94%*

*Percentage of total sample

Note: Just a few weeks before the Democratic convention in New York City, President Carter unexpectedly found himself confronted with a scandal with the potential for far-reaching political damage. Despite the media's enthusiasm in covering the revelations concerning the dealings of the president's brother Billy with the Libyan government, which culminated in the coining of the word "Billygate," the damage was surprisingly light. Sixty-seven percent of the public said that the affair had had no effect on their opinion of the president.

The Billy Carter affair involved several issues. First, it was discovered that the president's brother had had numerous financial dealings with Libya. He had received $220,000 from the Libyan government, ostensibly as a loan. In addition, he had requested the Florida-based Charter Oil Company to ask Libya to supply the company with oil in exchange for which Charter was willing to pay Billy fees amounting to more than $5 million; the deal eventually fell through.

Second, there were allegations that Libyan officials' financial dealings (apparently private) with Billy were part of an influence-peddling scheme on the part of that country's government. It could not be demonstrated, however, that Billy actually had exerted any significant influence.

Third, despite Billy's apparent lack of influence on White House policy, the president handled the case poorly. Confidential State Department cables regarding Libya had been given to the president's brother before he made his trip to Libya.

Finally and most unusual, the president's wife Rosalynn and National Security Adviser Zbigniew Brzezinski attempted to elicit, through Billy's Libyan connection, the help of that nation's notorious strongman Colonel Muammar Gadaffi in securing the release of the American hostages in Teheran.

Members of the Senate Committee investigating Billygate quickly became entangled in partisan wrangling. The Republicans sought a thorough investigation that was certain to keep the issue alive well into the fall election campaign. With the exception of Edward Kennedy who withdrew from the committee for the duration of the deliberations, the Democratic senators, led by Birch Bayh of Indiana, wanted a speedy investigation in order to keep the matter from impinging on the campaign.

When survey respondents were asked to rate Billy Carter on a ten-point scale called the Stapel Scalometer, the negative opinion was overwhelming; 57% gave him a very unfavorable rating, with only 4% rating him favorably.

PRESIDENT CARTER— DEMOCRATIC CONVENTION— PRESIDENTIAL TRIAL HEAT

Interviewing Date: 8/15–18/80*
Survey #161-G

Do you approve or disapprove of the way Carter is handling his job as president?

Approve..............................32%
Disapprove 55
No opinion 13

By Region
East

Approve..............................28%
Disapprove 64
No opinion 8

Midwest

Approve..............................30%
Disapprove 53
No opinion 17

South

Approve..............................42%
Disapprove 47
No opinion 11

West

Approve..............................25%
Disapprove 56
No opinion 19

By Politics
Republicans

Approve..............................14%
Disapprove 78
No opinion 8

Democrats

Approve..............................48%
Disapprove 40
No opinion 12

Independents

Approve..............................20%
Disapprove 65
No opinion 15

*Post-Democratic convention

Did you happen to watch the Democratic convention on television?

Yes..................................64%
No...................................36

Asked of those who watched the Democratic convention on television: Did watching the convention give you a more favorable or a less favorable impression of the Democratic party?

More favorable.......................18%
Less favorable.......................20
No change............................25
No opinion 1
                                     64%*

By Politics
Republicans

More favorable....................... 6%
Less favorable.......................34
No change............................23
No opinion 1
                                     64%*

Democrats

More favorable.......................28%
Less favorable.......................14
No change............................26
No opinion 2
                                     70%*

Independents

More favorable.......................12%
Less favorable.......................23
No change............................25
No opinion 1
                                     61%*

*Percentage of total sample

Asked of registered voters: If the presidential election were being held today, which candidate would you vote for—Jimmy Carter, the Democrat, Ronald Reagan, the Republican, or John Anderson, the independent? [Those who named another person or who were undecided were asked: As of today, do you lean more to Carter, the Democrat, to Reagan, the Republican, or to Anderson, the independent?]

Carter	39%
Reagan	38
Anderson	13
Other	1
Undecided	9

By Region

East

Carter	34%
Reagan	36
Anderson	15
Other	2
Undecided	13

Midwest

Carter	38%
Reagan	39
Anderson	13
Other	1
Undecided	9

South

Carter	45%
Reagan	39
Anderson	7
Other	1
Undecided	8

West

Carter	38%
Reagan	36
Anderson	19
Other	1
Undecided	6

By Politics
Republicans

Carter	9%
Reagan	79
Anderson	8
Other	1
Undecided	3

Democrats

Carter	65%
Reagan	16
Anderson	11
Other	1
Undecided	7

Independents

Carter	16%
Reagan	42
Anderson	24
Other	2
Undecided	16

Note: President Jimmy Carter and GOP challenger Ronald Reagan are now in a dead heat in the 1980 contest for the presidency, as determined by the latest nationwide Gallup survey. The latest trial heat results, based on the choices of registered voters, show Reagan with 38%, Carter with 39%, and Anderson with 13%.

Carter registered dramatic gains since the previous survey conducted prior to the Democratic convention, when Reagan lead with 45% to 29% for Carter and 14% for Anderson.

The gains for Carter, who before the convention faced a seriously divided party, reflect in large measure the closing of ranks of Democratic voters, many of whom had preferred Senator Edward Kennedy as their party's nominee but who subsequently shifted their support to nominee Carter rather than vote for the Republican challenger, Ronald Reagan.

In the preconvention survey Carter was suffering severe losses among his own party members, with only about half (48%) of Democratic voters choosing the president. The rate of defection suffered by Carter exceeded even that recorded for Senator George McGovern in a test election against President Richard Nixon in the summer of 1972. In the latest survey, however, Carter has a clear majority (65%) of Democratic voters in his camp.

In assessing the president's gains in the latest test run, it should be borne in mind that nominating conventions frequently give the nominee a boost. In 1976, for example, Carter's vote in these trial heats jumped 9 percentage points in a survey conducted immediately after the Democratic convention.

This postconvention test race further shows that Anderson's candidacy is more damaging to Carter than to Reagan. A trial race between just Reagan and Carter conducted at the same time shows Carter leading 45% to 39%. When Anderson is added as an independent candidate, Carter's vote drops 6 percentage points, while Reagan loses only 1 percentage point.

Paralleling his gains in the latest test race, President Carter's popularity rating has shown a sharp rise. The current survey shows 32% approving of his performance in office, up 11 percentage points from a previous telephone survey conducted during the period July 14–25.

AUGUST 28
ABORTION

Interviewing Date: 7/11–14/80
Survey #159-G

Do you think abortions should be legal under any circumstances, legal only under certain circumstances, or illegal in all circumstances?

Legal, any circumstances 25%
Legal, certain circumstances 53
Illegal, all circumstances. 18
No opinion 4

By Sex
Male

Legal, any circumstances 24%
Legal, certain circumstances 51
Illegal, all circumstances. 20
No opinion 5

Female

Legal, any circumstances 26%
Legal, certain circumstances 54
Illegal, all circumstances. 16
No opinion 4

By Race
White

Legal, any circumstances 25%
Legal, certain circumstances 55
Illegal, all circumstances. 17
No opinion 3

Nonwhite

Legal, any circumstances 23%
Legal, certain circumstances 42
Illegal, all circumstances. 25
No opinion 10

By Education
College

Legal, any circumstances 35%
Legal, certain circumstances 53
Illegal, all circumstances. 9
No opinion 3

High School

Legal, any circumstances 23%
Legal, certain circumstances 56
Illegal, all circumstances. 17
No opinion 4

Grade School

Legal, any circumstances 13%
Legal, certain circumstances 42
Illegal, all circumstances. 37
No opinion 8

By Region
East

Legal, any circumstances 25%
Legal, certain circumstances 52
Illegal, all circumstances. 20
No opinion 3

Midwest

Legal, any circumstances 23%
Legal, certain circumstances 53
Illegal, all circumstances. 19
No opinion 5

South

Legal, any circumstances 21%
Legal, certain circumstances 53
Illegal, all circumstances. 23
No opinion 3

West

Legal, any circumstances 32%
Legal, certain circumstances 53
Illegal, all circumstances. 8
No opinion 7

By Age
18–24 Years

Legal, any circumstances 29%
Legal, certain circumstances 51
Illegal, all circumstances. 16
No opinion 4

25–29 Years

Legal, any circumstances 34%
Legal, certain circumstances 49
Illegal, all circumstances. 15
No opinion 2

30–49 Years

Legal, any circumstances 27%
Legal, certain circumstances 54
Illegal, all circumstances. 15
No opinion 4

50 Years and Over

Legal, any circumstances 19%
Legal, certain circumstances 54
Illegal, all circumstances. 22
No opinion 5

By Income
$15,000 and Over

Legal, any circumstances 27%
Legal, certain circumstances 58

Illegal, all circumstances. 13
No opinion 2

Under $15,000

Legal, any circumstances 22%
Legal, certain circumstances 47
Illegal, all circumstances. 24
No opinion 7

By Politics
Republicans

Legal, any circumstances 22%
Legal, certain circumstances 55
Illegal, all circumstances. 21
No opinion 2

Democrats

Legal, any circumstances 25%
Legal, certain circumstances 53
Illegal, all circumstances. 19
No opinion 3

Independents

Legal, any circumstances 28%
Legal, certain circumstances 55
Illegal, all circumstances. 13
No opinion 4

By Religion
Protestants

Legal, any circumstances 23%
Legal, certain circumstances 55
Illegal, all circumstances. 18
No opinion 4

Catholics

Legal, any circumstances 22%
Legal, certain circumstances 55
Illegal, all circumstances. 21
No opinion 2

By Occupation
Professional and Business

Legal, any circumstances 36%
Legal, certain circumstances 54
Illegal, all circumstances. 9
No opinion 1

Clerical and Sales

Legal, any circumstances 29%
Legal, certain circumstances 54
Illegal, all circumstances. 13
No opinion 4

Manual Workers

Legal, any circumstances 20%
Legal, certain circumstances 54
Illegal, all circumstances. 22
No opinion 4

Non-Labor Force

Legal, any circumstances 21%
Legal, certain circumstances 50
Illegal, all circumstances. 24
No opinion 5

By Community Size
One Million and Over

Legal, any circumstances 33%
Legal, certain circumstances 45
Illegal, all circumstances. 16
No opinion 6

500,000–999,999

Legal, any circumstances 28%
Legal, certain circumstances 50
Illegal, all circumstances. 16
No opinion 6

50,000–499,999

Legal, any circumstances 27%
Legal, certain circumstances 51
Illegal, all circumstances. 17
No opinion 5

2,500–49,999

Legal, any circumstances 19%
Legal, certain circumstances 63
Illegal, all circumstances. 15
No opinion 3

Under 2,500; Rural

Legal, any circumstances 19%
Legal, certain circumstances 56
Illegal, all circumstances. 23
No opinion 2

Carter Supporters

Legal, any circumstances 26%
Legal, certain circumstances 52
Illegal, all circumstances. 19
No opinion 3

Reagan Supporters

Legal, any circumstances 25%
Legal, certain circumstances 55
Illegal, all circumstances. 18
No opinion 2

Anderson Supporters

Legal, any circumstances 28%
Legal, certain circumstances 56
Illegal, all circumstances. 12
No opinion 4

Note: Despite the emotional and political turmoil surrounding the issue of abortion, public opinion on this controversial topic has changed remarkably little since the Supreme Court ruled in 1973 that women have the right to have abortions performed. In that year the Supreme Court overruled all state laws that prohibit or restrict a woman's right to obtain an abortion during her first three months of pregnancy.

The following shows that current attitudes closely parallel those recorded in earlier surveys.

Trend on Views on Abortion

	1980	1979	1977	1975
Legal, any circumstances	25%	22%	22%	21%
Legal, certain circumstances	53	54	55	54
Illegal, all circumstances	18	19	19	22
No opinion	4	5	4	3

The Republican and Democratic nominating conventions served to sharpen the focus on the abortion issue. Republican convention delegates insisted on the inclusion of a plank in the

GOP platform that would support a constitutional ban on abortions, while the Democratic platform opposed such an amendment. Interestingly, the views of Republicans and Democrats in the current survey are remarkably similar.

AUGUST 29
RATINGS OF VICE-PRESIDENTIAL CANDIDATES

Interviewing Date: 8/1–4/80
Survey #160-G

You will notice that the ten boxes on this card go from the highest position of +5 for someone you have a very favorable opinion of all the way down to the lowest position of −5 for someone you have a very unfavorable opinion of. How far up the scale or how far down the scale would you rate:

George Bush?

Highly favorable (+5, +4)	16%
Moderately favorable (+3, +2, +1)	55
Moderately unfavorable (−1, −2, −3)	15
Highly unfavorable (−4, −5)	6
Don't know	8

Republicans Only

Highly favorable (+5, +4)	28%
Moderately favorable (+3, +2, +1)	54
Moderately unfavorable (−1, −2, −3)	9
Highly unfavorable (−4, −5)	5
Don't know	4

Walter Mondale?

Highly favorable (+5, +4)	16%
Moderately favorable (+3, +2, +1)	47
Moderately unfavorable (−1, −2, −3)	21
Highly unfavorable (−4, −5)	9
Don't know	7

Democrats Only

Highly favorable (+5, +4)	24%
Moderately favorable (+3, +2, +1)	49

Moderately unfavorable (−1, −2, −3)	15
Highly unfavorable (−4, −5)	6
Don't know	6

Note: Survey findings show that equal proportions of the public give vice-presidential candidates George Bush and Walter Mondale a highly favorable rating. This reflects a positive position based on a ten-point attitude scale called the Stapel Scalometer, which was employed to measure the degree of survey respondents' enthusiasm for each candidate.

Congressman John Anderson's newly selected running mate, former Wisconsin Governor Patrick Lucey, was not included in the survey because the interviewing was completed prior to his selection. However, it is reasonable to assume that the proportion of voters who are familiar enough with Lucey to rate him on this scale would be too small to make a valid comparison with those who rated the major party vice-presidential candidates.

AUGUST 31
VOTER REGISTRATION

Interviewing Date: 8/1–4; 15–18/80
Survey #160-G; #161-G

Is your name now recorded in the voter registration book of the precinct or election district where you now live?

	Yes
National	71%

By Sex

Male	72%
Female	71

By Race

White	72%
Nonwhite	64

By Education

College	78%
High school	69
Grade school	67

By Region

East	73%
Midwest	77
South	68
West	66

By Age

18–29 years	51%
30–49 years	74
50 years and over	84

By Politics

Republicans	77%
Democrats	74
Independents	65

Note: The current low level of voter registration suggests that turnout on November 4 may be no higher than it was for the 1976 election, when only 54% of the eligible population—a twenty-eight-year low—cast their ballots.

In two recent Gallup surveys, only 71% of adults indicated that they were registered to vote, the same percentage recorded at this time in 1976. This current national level of registration is only marginally higher than at the beginning of the year when 69% were registered.

Although Democrats now enjoy more than a 2-to-1 numerical margin over Republicans, more Republicans (77%) than Democrats (74%) say they are registered to vote. Registration among the crucial bloc of independent voters (65%) is below the level for Republicans and Democrats.

The continued low level of registration on the part of young people between 18 and 29 is particularly disappointing, with only 51% now registered to vote. In every presidential contest since 1972, when 18- to 20-year-olds were first able to vote in federal elections, a far smaller proportion of citizens under 30 have cast their ballots than have those 30 years and older.

In most of the United States, citizens who wish to vote are required to register—that is, have their names placed on a list of eligible voters. Designed primarily to prevent fraud, registration also provides a means of ensuring that a voter actually resides in the election district and is thus eligible to vote on local matters. The cutoff date for registration is generally ten to thirty days before an election. In some states, however, it is longer—up to fifty days in Arizona, for example. In Minnesota, Wisconsin, North Dakota, Maine, and Oregon, voters can register as late as election day.

Following is the trend in national registration levels at comparable periods during previous presidential election years:

Registered to Vote

1980	71%
1976	71
1972	75
1968	77

It should be stressed that not all those who are registered will actually vote. Past voting patterns indicate that only about eight out of ten persons registered will go to the polls. The percentages of the eligible voter population participating in each of the last five presidential elections are as follows:

Voter Turnout

1976	54%
1972	56
1968	61
1964	62
1960	64

SEPTEMBER 4
EPILEPSY

Interviewing Date: 8/12–15/79; 1/4–7/80
Survey #136-G; #146-G

Have you ever heard or read about the disease called epilepsy or convulsive seizures (fits)?

Yes	95%
No	5

Asked of those who knew about epilepsy: Did you ever know anyone who had epilepsy?

Yes.................................63%
No..................................32
                                    ———
                                    95%

Asked of those who knew about epilepsy: Have you ever seen anyone who was having a seizure (fit)?

Yes.................................59%
No..................................36
                                    ———
                                    95%

Asked of those who knew about epilepsy: Do you think epileptics should or should not be employed in jobs like other people?

Should..............................79%
Should not.......................... 9
Don't know.......................... 7
                                    ———
                                    95%

Asked of those who knew about epilepsy: Would you object to having any of your children in school, or at play, associate with persons who sometimes had seizures (fits)?

Yes, would 6%
No, would not.......................84
Don't know.......................... 5
                                    ———
                                    95%

Asked of those who knew about epilepsy: Do you think epilepsy is a form of insanity, or not?

Is.................................. 3%
Is not 86
Don't know.......................... 6
                                    ———
                                    95%

Asked of those who knew about epilepsy: What do you think is the cause of epilepsy?

Brain, nervous system disorder 37%
Heredity, birth defect................16

Other diseases, injury 7
Mental or emotional 2
Blood disorder 1
Other 2
Don't know 34
                                    ———
                                    99%*

*Total adds to more than 95% due to multiple responses.

Asked of those who knew about epilepsy: Would you object to having a son or daughter of yours marry a person who sometimes had seizures (fits)?

Would 17%
Would not...........................64
Don't know 14
                                    ———
                                    95%

By Education
College

Would 12%
Would not...........................78
Don't know 8
                                    ———
                                    98%

High School

Would 17%
Would not...........................64
Don't know 14
                                    ———
                                    95%

Grade School

Would 29%
Would not...........................39
Don't know 19
                                    ———
                                    87%

By Age
18–29 Years

Would 9%
Would not...........................74
Don't know 12
                                    ———
                                    95%

30–49 Years

Would 12%
Would not 72
Don't know 12
                                    ——
                                    96%

50 Years and Over

Would 28%
Would not 50
Don't know 16
                                    ——
                                    94%

Note: The public's views on epilepsy have undergone profound changes over the last three decades. In 1949, 45% of American adults believed that epileptics should not be discriminated against in employment, compared to 79% today. Also in that year 24% said they objected to having their children go to school or play with epileptic children, while currently only 6% would object. And 13% of those interviewed in 1949 thought epilepsy was a form of insanity; today the comparable figure is 3%.

In assessing the significance of the survey data, Dr. William F. Caveness, chief of the Laboratory of Experimental Neurology of the National Institute of Neurological and Communicative Disorders and Stroke, cites five major factors that he feels have led to a more favorable public attitude toward epilepsy:

1. More enlightened views of the public toward dread diseases such as cancer, tuberculosis, insanity, syphilis, and epilepsy.
2. Improved medical control of epileptic seizures.
3. Educational efforts on the part of the medical professional and lay associations concerning epilepsy.
4. Reasonable modifications in legal restrictions concerning epileptics in terms of immigration, marriage, and the operation of motor vehicles.
5. Programs for the employment of epileptics in a number of major American industries.

Impressive headway has been made in recent years in research, diagnosis, and treatment of epilepsy, with the result that about half of the nation's 2 million epileptics are free of seizures and an additional 30% have improved control over their seizures.

Epilepsy is a disorder of the nervous system in which certain brain cells are electrically abnormal. These cells sporadically produce electrical impulses that trigger bodily responses that are termed seizures. The main known causes of epilepsy are head injuries, infections, damage to the brain before or during birth, metabolic and nutritional disorders, and brain tumors. For many people epilepsy cannot be traced to a specific cause. Contrary to a widely held notion that epilepsy is often inherited, heredity is thought to play only a modest role.

The stigma of epilepsy, according to Dr. Caveness, "stems from public misconceptions that equate epilepsy with mental illness, mental retardation, violence and even possession by the devil." Since 1949, at the request of Drs. Caveness, William G. Lennox, and Houston Merritt, every five years the Gallup Poll, as a public service, has conducted a national indepth survey of public attitudes toward epilepsy.

SEPTEMBER 5
EDUCATION*

Interviewing Date: 5/1–8/80
Special Survey

What do you think are the biggest problems with which the public schools in this community must deal?

Public-School Parents Only

1. Lack of discipline
2. Use of drugs
3. Lack of proper financial support
4. Poor curriculum/poor standards
5. Integration/busing

*This special survey on education was sponsored by the Charles F. Kettering Foundation, a philanthropic foundation with a primary focus on improving the learning environment of elementary and secondary schools.

Nonpublic-School Parents Only**

1. Lack of discipline
2. Use of drugs
3. Poor curriculum/poor standards
4. Integration/busing
5. Lack of proper financial support

**In this survey nonpublic-school parents include those of students attending private, independent, and parochial schools.

Students are often given the grades A, B, C, D, and Fail to denote the quality of their work. Suppose the public schools themselves, in this community, were graded in the same way. What grade would you give the public schools here—A, B, C, D, or Fail?

A rating............................10%
B rating............................25
C rating............................29
D rating............................12
Fail................................. 6
No opinion 18

Note: Since 1974 when this survey series was first introduced, there has been a decline in the ratings given to the public schools. This decline may be due to changes in the emphasis placed upon the basics in many school districts, or to a better understanding among the general public of just what the schools are achieving. In any event the downward trend, at least for the present, has ended.

An examination of the survey results by major demographic groups indicates that those most dissatisfied with their local public schools are northern blacks, with 33% giving their schools a "D" or a "Fail" rating compared to 13% for southern blacks. Residents living in rural communities with populations under 50,000 give higher ratings than do those living in larger cities. Persons living in the Midwest and South are more satisfied with their schools than inhabitants of the East and West. And young adults are more critical than those in older age brackets.

How much confidence do you, yourself, have in these American institutions to serve the public's needs—a great deal of confidence, a fair amount, or very little:

Churches?

Great deal..........................42%
Fair amount 40
Very little..........................15
None (volunteered) 2
Undecided........................... 1

Public schools?

Great deal..........................28%
Fair amount 46
Very little..........................20
None (volunteered) 3
Undecided........................... 3

Courts?

Great deal..........................19%
Fair amount 45
Very little..........................28
None (volunteered) 5
Undecided........................... 3

Local government?

Great deal..........................19%
Fair amount 51
Very little..........................23
None (volunteered) 4
Undecided........................... 3

State government?

Great deal..........................17%
Fair amount 52
Very little..........................24
None (volunteered) 4
Undecided........................... 3

Federal government?

Great deal..........................14%
Fair amount 47
Very little..........................31
None (volunteered) 5
Undecided........................... 3

Labor unions?

Great deal 17%
Fair amount 38
Very little 30
None (volunteered) 9
Undecided 6

Big business?

Great deal 13%
Fair amount 42
Very little 36
None (volunteered) 5
Undecided 4

How important are schools in one's future success—extremely important, fairly important, or not too important?

Extremely important 82%
Fairly important 15
Not too important 2
No opinion 1

Here are a number of things which may have a good effect on the education students receive in the public schools of this community. Will you choose four (from a list of fourteen suggestions) which you think are particularly important?

Well-educated teachers and principals . . . 50%
Emphasis on basics such as reading,
  writing, and computation 49
Teachers and principals personally
  interested in progress of students 44
Good parent/teacher relationships 40
Careful check on student progress and
  effort 32
Orderly but not rigid atmosphere 27
Useful materials and adequate supplies . . . 25
Small classes 25
Special classes for handicapped
  students 24
High goals and expectations on part
  of students 19
Wide variety of vocational courses 18
Advanced classes for the gifted 12

Extracurricular activities 6
Successful athletic teams 4
Don't know; no answer 6

In your opinion, who should have the greatest influence in deciding what is taught in the public schools here—the federal government, the state government, or the local school board?

Federal government 9%
State government 15
Local school board 68
Don't know 8

Asked of parents: Is it your impression that the local public school system gives enough attention, or not enough attention, to reading, writing, and arithmetic?

Public-School Parents Only

Enough 34%
Not enough 61
Don't know 5

Nonpublic-School Parents Only

Enough 17%
Not enough 72
Don't know 11

In your opinion, should or should not parents be asked to meet with school personnel before each school semester to examine the grades, test scores, and career goals for each child and to work out a program to be followed both in school and at home?

Yes, parents should 84%
No, parents should not 11
Don't know 5

Note: Overwhelming support for this idea comes from every group in the population in every area of the nation. The highest vote in favor of this plan was found among northern blacks who voted 95 to 1.

As you may know, a new federal Department of Education has been established with cabinet status. We would like to know what you think this new department should give special attention to in the next few years. Will you choose five of the areas listed on this card which you think are most important?

Basic education (reading, writing,
  arithmetic) 69%
Vocational training (training students
  for jobs) 56
Improving teacher training and
  education 46
Helping students choose careers 46
Parent training to help parents become
  more fully involved in their
  children's education 45
Helping more students obtain a
  college education 35
Developing individual educational
  plans for every child 33
Providing more opportunities for
  gifted students 25
Preschool education 24
Life-long learning (continuing
  education through adult life) 23
Better educational use of television 20
International education including
  foreign language study 19
Improving opportunities for women
  and minorities 18

Here are some student behavior problems which may occur in school. In your opinion, who should deal with each kind of problem—should it be the parents, the school, or the courts?

Truancy (skipping school)?

Parents 72%
School 45
Courts 9
Don't know 2
                                              128%*

Vandalism of school property?

Parents 44%
School 39
Courts 50
Don't know 2
                                              135%*

Bringing weapons to school?

Parents 41%
School 35
Courts 59
Don't know 3
                                              138%*

Fighting in school?

Parents 42%
School 75
Courts 10
Don't know 3
                                              130%*

Using alcohol or drugs on school property?

Parents 50%
School 57
Courts 35
Don't know 2
                                              144%*

Striking a teacher?

Parents 43%
School 56
Courts 35
Don't know 3
                                              137%*

Stealing money or clothing from other students?

Parents 48%
School 58
Courts 30
Don't know 3
                                              139%*

*Totals add to more than 100% due to multiple responses.

Should a student be able to progress through the school system at his own speed and without regard to the usual grade levels? This would mean that he might study seventh-grade math, but only fifth-grade English. Would you favor or oppose such a plan in the local schools?

Favor.............................62%
Oppose............................30
No opinion 8

Public-School Parents Only

Favor.............................60%
Oppose............................35
No opinion 5

Nonpublic-School Parents Only

Favor.............................60%
Oppose............................37
No opinion 3

Would you favor or oppose instruction in the schools that would deal with morals and moral behavior?

Favor.............................79%
Oppose............................16
No opinion 5

Note: In 1975 an overwhelming 79% voted in favor of instruction within the schools that would deal with morals and moral behavior, 15% opposed, and 6% had no opinion. In the present survey almost identical results were recorded.

Anyone who examines the McGuffey Readers, first published in 1836, will discover that the teaching of morals during the early years of public school education was considered an integral part of the educational program. The *Columbia Encyclopedia* observes that "their influence in shaping the American mind of the mid-19th century can scarcely be exaggerated."

No one has yet found a modern equivalent as effective as these readers to instruct students in morals and moral behavior, but the public is hoping that a way to achieve such instruction will be forthcoming. It is significant that parents of children now attending school are the group that most favor this instruction, although all major groups in the population strongly approve of the idea.

It costs taxpayers about two dollars an hour for each student for each class he or she attends, or about ten dollars for each school day. Are these figures higher, lower, or about the same as what you had thought?

Higher 29%
Lower.............................19
About the same......................34
Don't know 18

Note: The idea has been advanced that if parents and their school-age children knew the amount of money that was being spent to provide an education for them, absenteeism would decline. If absence from school could be correlated with dollars, then the temptation to stay away from school and classes would be reduced.

The costs can be estimated in this way. The average school year consists of 184 days, and the average cost per child per school year is approximately $1,800 to $2,000, or about $10 per day. Since there are usually five class periods per day, the cost per class per student is about $2.

If high-school students can meet academic requirements in three years instead of four, should they, or should they not, be permitted to graduate early?

Should 77%
Should not.........................19
Don't know 4

Public-School Parents Only

Should 73%
Should not.........................24
Don't know 3

Nonpublic-School Parents Only

Should 70%
Should not 26
Don't know 4

Note: Every major group in the population believes that if high-school students can meet academic requirements in three years, instead of four, they should be permitted to graduate early. Those most in favor are recent graduates (18- to 29-year-olds).

It can be argued that in an era of increasing specialization, with students requiring more and more years of college and postcollege training, an earlier start on college work would permit a student to engage in his or her chosen career that much sooner. Many parents, however, are reluctant to see their children go off to college at the age of seventeen or younger.

In your opinion, should or should not the public schools add personnel to help students and recent graduates get jobs?

Should 64%
Should not 30
Don't know 6

Note: The most perplexing problem that modern industrial societies face is how best to deal with student transition from school to job. The very high unemployment rate in the United States among high-school graduates and dropouts has yet to be solved. Some European nations have found that a combination of postsecondary schooling and job apprenticeship helps bridge the transition. In the United States, judging from the high unemployment rate of youth, we have still to find a solution. This perhaps accounts for the highly favorable vote for the proposal to add personnel to the school staff in order to help students and recent graduates obtain jobs. Every group in the population favors this idea, especially the nonwhites who have the highest youth unemployment rate.

The number of one-parent families in the United States is growing each year due to the high divorce rate, and it is predicted that nearly half of the children born in 1980 will live, for a considerable period of time, with only one parent. Because of this, some people believe that the schools must find new ways to deal with the children from these broken homes. Of course, this will cost more money. Now, here are three proposals. For each one tell me whether you think it would be a good idea or a poor idea for the schools here to:

Make school personnel available for evening counseling with single parents who are working if their children are having trouble at school?

Good idea 86%
Poor idea 10
Don't know 4

Give teachers training to help them deal with special problems of children from one-parent families?

Good idea 83%
Poor idea 12
Don't know 5

Provide activities so children can spend more time at school rather than going home to an empty house?

Good idea 76%
Poor idea 18
Don't know 6

Many families who come from other countries have children who cannot speak English. Should or should not these children be required to learn English in special classes before they are enrolled in the public schools?

Should 82%
Should not 13
Don't know 5

Note: Bilingual education continues to be a controversial program. Should students be taught in the language of their parents, or should they be able to learn some of their subjects in their native language while they are learning English? An alternative would be to require students to learn English in special classes before they are enrolled in the public schools. This alternative appeals to more than eight out of every ten persons included in the present survey, and it receives overwhelming approval of all major groups.

Asked of parents: Should students spend more time than they now do learning about other nations of the world and the way people live there, or do you think they spend enough time now?

Public-School Parents Only

More time 45%
Enough time 46
Don't know 9

Nonpublic-School Parents Only

More time 46%
Enough time 47
Don't know 7

Are you now taking, or have you ever taken, any courses in an adult education program?

Yes 29%
No 70
Don't know 1

Note: Approximately 45 million Americans, 18 years and older, say that they have taken courses in an adult education program or are presently engaged in such a program. And a total of 13 million say they have taken such a course during the last year. The greatest enrollment comes from the 18- to 29-age group and from those who have attended college.

Teachers now receive certificates to teach upon completion of their college course work. Some people believe that teachers should be required to spend one year as

interns in the schools at half pay before they are given a certificate to teach. Do you think this is a good idea or a poor idea?

Good idea 56%
Poor idea 36
Don't know 8

Note: In the twelve years that this survey series has been conducted, many of those interviewed complained about the difficulty of getting good teachers to place this problem among the top ten most important problems facing the local schools. This may explain, in part, why the public favors the idea of an internship of one year at half pay for those who wish to enter the teaching profession. On the other hand, this idea may discourage many young persons from entering this profession, which is already losing some of its appeal.

Should public-school teachers be permitted to strike or not?

Should 40%
Should not 52
Don't know 8

Public-School Parents Only

Should 43%
Should not 49
Don't know 8

Nonpublic-School Parents Only

Should 41%
Should not 51
Don't know 8

Note: As evidenced by survey findings, the conservative trend in most areas of American life apparently accounts for the increasing number of citizens who oppose strikes by public-school teachers. Compared to the present survey, in 1975 only a slight majority (48%) opposed strikes, 45% were in favor, and 7% had no opinion.

The greatest changes are found among the college educated, who five years ago favored strikes by a 52% to 44% margin but now are opposed 51% to 43%.

Regionally, the eastern states were equally divided in 1975, with 46% both favoring and opposing strikes; today the comparable figures are 34% in favor and 58% opposed.

Interestingly, parents of children attending public schools have less objection to strikes than do those who have no school-age children.

In schools where there are teachers' unions, should those teachers who do not belong to the union be required to pay union dues since they share the benefits of union bargaining?

Should	47%
Should not	44
Don't know	9

Note: Survey results indicate that southern states oppose this issue by 54% to 37%; that sentiment is evenly divided in the small cities and rural communities; and that the college educated, who are found largely in the upper-income levels, vote against this requirement by 58% to 35%.

Would you like to have a child of yours take up teaching in the public schools as a career?

Yes	48%
No	40
Don't know	12

Note: When this question was first asked in 1969, 75% of all respondents said they would like to have a child of theirs take up teaching, compared to 67% in the 1972 survey.

SEPTEMBER 7
POLITICAL IMPACT OF EVANGELICALS, I

Interviewing Date: 8/1–4; 15–18/80
Survey #160-G; #161-G

Asked of registered voters: If the presidential election were being held today, which candidate would you vote for, Carter, the Democrat, Reagan, the Republican, or Anderson, the independent? [Those who named another person or who were undecided were asked: As of today, do you lean more to Carter, the Democrat, to Reagan, the Republican, or to Anderson, the independent?]

Carter	39%
Reagan	38
Anderson	13
Other; undecided	10

Evangelicals Only*

Carter	52%
Reagan	31
Anderson	6
Other; undecided	11

Non-Evangelicals Only

Carter	36%
Reagan	39
Anderson	15
Other; undecided	10

*This survey defines Evangelicals as those with three basic characteristics: (1) they describe themselves as born-again Christians, or say they have had a born-again experience; (2) they have encouraged other people to believe in Jesus Christ; and (3) they believe in a literal interpretation of the Bible, or accept the absolute authority of the Bible.

Note: Approximately one-fifth (19%) of the total national sample (30 million adults) answered in the affirmative to all three questions. This proportion closely parallels the percentage found in a major study entitled "Evangelical Christianity in the United States," which was conducted for *Christianity Today* magazine.

Do you approve or disapprove of the way Carter is handling his job as president?

Approve	32%
Disapprove	55
No opinion	13

Evangelicals Only

Approve	46%
Disapprove	42
No opinion	12

Non-Evangelicals Only

Approve	29%
Disapprove	58
No opinion	13

Aside from how you feel about a presidential candidate in other respects, would you be more likely to vote for a candidate who considers himself a born-again evangelical Christian, less likely to do so, or wouldn't it make any difference either way?

More likely	19%
Less likely	9
No difference	66
No opinion	6

Evangelicals Only

More likely	55%
Less likely	2
No difference	38
No opinion	5

Non-Evangelicals Only

More likely	11%
Less likely	11
No difference	72
No opinion	6

Is your name now recorded in the registration book of the precinct or election district where you now live?

Yes	70%
No	30

Evangelicals Only

Yes	73%
No	27

Non-Evangelicals Only

Yes	69%
No	31

Asked of registered voters: If the elections for Congress were being held today, which party would you like to see win in this congressional district, the Democratic party or the Republican party? [Those who were undecided or named another party were asked: As of today, do you lean more to the Democratic party or to the Republican party?]

Democratic	55%
Republican	39
Other; undecided	6

Evangelicals Only

Democratic	63%
Republican	29
Other; undecided	8

Non-Evangelicals Only

Democratic	56%
Republican	35
Other; undecided	9

In politics, as of today, do you consider yourself a Democrat, a Republican, or an independent?

Democrat	49%
Republican	24
Independent	27

Evangelicals Only

Democrat	57%
Republican	23
Independent	20

Non-Evangelicals Only

Democrat	47%
Republican	24
Independent	29

People who are conservative in their political views are referred to as being right of center and people who are liberal in their political views are referred to as being left of center. Which of these categories best describes your own political position? [Respondents were handed a card listing eight categories.]

Left of center 22%
Middle of the road (volunteered) 37
Right of center 31
Don't know 10

Evangelicals Only

Left of center 20%
Middle of the road (volunteered) 31
Right of center 37
Don't know 12

Non-Evangelicals Only

Left of center 23%
Middle of the road (volunteered) 38
Right of center 29
Don't know 10

Do you happen to know whether or not these men consider themselves to be born-again evangelical Christians:

Carter?

Yes, does............................ 51%
No, does not 12
Don't know 37

Evangelicals Only

Yes, does............................ 72%
No, does not 7
Don't know 21

Non-Evangelicals Only

Yes, does............................ 47%
No, does not 13
Don't know 40

Reagan?

Yes, does............................ 14%
No, does not 26
Don't know 60

Evangelicals Only

Yes, does............................ 21%
No, does not 18
Don't know 61

Non-Evangelicals Only

Yes, does............................ 12%
No, does not 28
Don't know 60

Anderson?

Yes, does............................ 11%
No, does not 20
Don't know 69

Evangelicals Only

Yes, does............................ 11%
No, does not 13
Don't know 76

Non-Evangelicals Only

Yes, does............................ 11%
No, does not 22
Don't know 67

Which of these statements comes closest to describing your feelings about the Bible? [Respondents were handed a card listing the following statements]: (A) the Bible is the actual word of God and is to be taken literally, word for word; (B) the Bible is the inspired word of God but not everything in it should be taken literally, word for word; or (C) the Bible is an ancient book of fables, legends, history, and moral precepts recorded by men.

Actual word of God.................. 40%
Inspired word of God 45
Ancient book of fables............... 9
Other .... *
None 2
Can't say.......................... 4

By Sex
Male

Actual word of God.................. 36%
Inspired word of God 45

Ancient book of fables. 12
Other . . . . *
None 3
Can't say 4

Female

Actual word of God. 43%
Inspired word of God 44
Ancient book of fables. 7
Other . . . . *
None 2
Can't say 4

By Race
White

Actual word of God. 37%
Inspired word of God 47
Ancient book of fables. 10
Other . . . . *
None 2
Can't say 4

Nonwhite

Actual word of God. 56%
Inspired word of God 26
Ancient book of fables. 6
Other . . . . *
None 4
Can't say 8

By Education
College

Actual word of God. 25%
Inspired word of God 57
Ancient book of fables. 15
Other . . . . *
None 2
Can't say 1

High School

Actual word of God. 42%
Inspired word of God 43
Ancient book of fables. 8
Other . . . . *

None 2
Can't say 5

Grade School

Actual word of God. 60%
Inspired word of God 22
Ancient book of fables. 5
Other . . . . *
None 4
Can't say 9

By Region
East

Actual word of God. 36%
Inspired word of God 48
Ancient book of fables. 11
Other . . . . *
None 2
Can't say 3

Midwest

Actual word of God. 37%
Inspired word of God 48
Ancient book of fables. 9
Other . . . . *
None 2
Can't say 4

South

Actual word of God. 52%
Inspired word of God 36
Ancient book of fables. 6
Other . . . . *
None 2
Can't say 4

West

Actual word of God. 31%
Inspired word of God 46
Ancient book of fables. 12
Other . . . . *
None 4
Can't say 7

By Age

18–29 Years

Actual word of God...................34%
Inspired word of God 51
Ancient book of fables................ 8
Other .... *
None 3
Can't say........................... 4

30–49 Years

Actual word of God...................38%
Inspired word of God 43
Ancient book of fables................12
Other .... *
None 3
Can't say........................... 4

50 Years and Over

Actual word of God...................46%
Inspired word of God 40
Ancient book of fables................ 8
Other .... *
None 2
Can't say........................... 4

*Less than 1%

Have you ever tried to encourage someone to believe in Jesus Christ or to accept Him as his or her Savior?

                                    Yes
National 44%

By Sex

Male...............................38%
Female.............................50

By Race

White..............................42%
Nonwhite...........................61

By Education

College............................42%
High school........................43
Grade school.......................54

By Region

East 32%
Midwest............................ 43
South 61
West............................... 40

By Age

18–29 years 39%
30–49 years........................ 45
50 years and over.................. 48

Would you say that you have been born again or have had a born-again experience—that is, a turning point in your life when you committed yourself to Christ?

                                    Yes
National 38%

By Sex

Male...............................32%
Female.............................43

By Race

White..............................35%
Nonwhite...........................58

By Education

College............................31%
High school........................38
Grade school.......................49

By Region

East 23%
Midwest............................36
South 57
West...............................33

By Age

18–29 years 34%
30–49 years........................37
50 years and over..................42

The following shows a demographic profile of Evangelicals:

National 19%

By Sex

Male............................. 15%
Female........................... 22

By Race

White............................ 16%
Nonwhite......................... 36

By Education

College.......................... 12%
High school...................... 19
Grade school..................... 30

By Region

East 10%
Midwest.......................... 16
South 33
West............................. 13

By Age

18–29 years 28%
30–49 years...................... 19
50 years and over................ 22

By Politics

Republicans 22%
Northern Democrats 15
Southern Democrats 39
Independents..................... 14

By Religion

Protestants 28%
   Episcopalians..................... 4
   Presbyterian group of churches....... 10
   Lutheran group of churches......... 16
   Methodist group of churches........ 18
   Baptist group of churches.......... 42
Catholics........................ 6

By Occupation

Professional and business............. 11%
Clerical and sales................... 25

Manual workers 21
Non-labor force 21

By Community Size

One million and over................ 14%
500,000–999,999 14
50,000–499,999.................... 17
2,500–49,999...................... 20
Under 2,500; rural................. 26

Note: Although the presidential race is currently neck and neck between President Jimmy Carter and Ronald Reagan, Carter is clearly the favorite among the one-fifth of the electorate who can be described as Evangelicals, a group whose vote could be decisive in a close election. Among this group 46% approve of the president's performance in office, compared to only 29% of non-Evangelicals.

One of the unique aspects of the 1980 presidential race is the fact that all three of the leading contenders—Carter, Reagan, and Anderson—consider themselves born-again evangelical Christians, which is more a political asset than a liability.

A large majority of non-Evangelicals (78%) indicate that their preference is not influenced by whether a presidential candidate is an Evangelical or they have no opinion. Those preferring an Evangelical are equal in number (11%) to those who say they are less likely to vote for such a candidate.

In contrast, the views of the nation's Evangelicals are decidedly pro-Evangelical, with 55% saying they would be more likely to vote for a candidate with Evangelical beliefs, 43% say it would make no difference or have no opinion, and only 2% are against.

Nationally, almost twice as many (19%) say they would be more likely to vote for an Evangelical presidential nominee, compared to 9% who would be less likely.
a candidate with Evangelical beliefs, 43% say it would make no difference or have no opinion, and only 2% are against.

Nationally, almost twice as many (19%) say they would be more likely to vote for an Evangelical presidential nominee, compared to 9% who would be less likely.

A demographic profile of Evangelicals shows that women, nonwhites, those with less than a college education, southerners, older adults, Protestants, rural residents, and the less affluent are overrepresented.

Despite the fact that Evangelicals tend to a greater degree than non-Evangelicals to be among those who have a poor record of voter participation, the percentage currently registered and who indicate a likelihood of voting closely parallel the figures for non-Evangelicals. Politically, Evangelicals are inclined to be more Democratic (57%) than non-Evangelicals (47%).

In addition, the fact that many more voters (51%) are aware that the president considers himself a born-again Christian is also contributing to boost Carter's standing. Those who know that Reagan and Anderson are evangelical Christians are only 14% and 11%, respectively.

SEPTEMBER 8
POLITICAL IMPACT OF EVANGELICALS, II

Interviewing Date: 8/1–4; 15–18/80
Survey #160-G; #161-G

This card lists various proposals being discussed in this country today. Would you tell me whether you generally favor or generally oppose each of these proposals?

	Evangelicals	Non-Evangelicals
Registration of all firearms	57%	58%
Death penalty for murder	51	53
More nuclear power plants	41	42
Government social programs	54	52
The ERA..........	53	66
Ban on all abortions..	41	29
Increased defense spending........	78	68
Prayer in public schools	81	54

Homosexuals
allowed to teach 15   31

Note: A presidential candidate who seeks to win the support of Evangelicals, who account for one-fifth of the electorate, will discover that their opinions are similar to those of non-Evangelicals on such key voter issues as registration of firearms, building more nuclear power plants, the death penalty for murder, and government social programs.

Furthermore, the differences on other key issues are not as substantial as might be expected. For example, 66% of non-Evangelicals favor the ERA and 68% support increased defense spending, while comparison figures for Evangelicals are 53% and 78%, respectively.

Major differences, however, are found between these two groups on issues relating to personal morality and religion. Half as many Evangelicals as non-Evangelicals favor allowing homosexuals to teach in public schools, and 41% of Evangelicals express support for banning abortions compared to only 29% of non-Evangelicals.

The sharpest divergence is found in regard to requiring prayer in the schools (the Supreme Court ruled that public schools may not sponsor prayers), with the vast majority of Evangelicals (81%) voting in support and 54% of non-Evangelicals in favor of such action.

SEPTEMBER 10
CAMPAIGN ISSUES

Interviewing Date: 8/15–18/80
Survey #161-G

Asked of registered voters: This card lists various proposals being discussed in this country today. [Respondents were handed a card listing nine issues.] Would you tell me whether you generally favor or generally oppose each of these proposals:

Registration of firearms?*

Carter supporters 68%
Reagan supporters 45
Anderson supporters 63

Ban on all abortions?*

Carter supporters 33%
Reagan supporters 32
Anderson supporters 22

More nuclear power plants?*

Carter supporters 40%
Reagan supporters 56
Anderson supporters 33

Homosexuals allowed to teach?*

Carter supporters 27%
Reagan supporters 19
Anderson supporters 46

Death penalty for murder?*

Carter supporters 49%
Reagan supporters 61
Anderson supporters 49

The ERA?*

Carter supporters 72%
Reagan supporters 52
Anderson supporters 69

Prayer in public schools?*

Carter supporters 66%
Reagan supporters 59
Anderson supporters 45

Increased defense spending?*

Carter supporters 74%
Reagan supporters 78
Anderson supporters 60

Government social programs?*

Carter supporters 59%
Reagan supporters 31
Anderson supporters 54

*Results given are for those in favor of the proposal.

Asked of registered voters: People who are conservative in their political views are referred to as being right of center and people who are liberal in their political views are referred to as being left of center. Which one of these categories best describes your own political position?

Carter Supporters

Left of center 26%
Middle of the road (volunteered) 38
Right of center 28
Don't know 8

Reagan Suporters

Left of center 11%
Middle of the road (volunteered) 39
Right of center 46
Don't know 4

Anderson Supporters

Left of center 32%
Middle of the road (volunteered) 43
Right of center 20
Don't know 5

Note: President Jimmy Carter's assumption that independent candidate John Anderson would draw substantially more votes from his own candidacy than from GOP challenger Ronald Reagan, which has led to the president's reluctance to debate Anderson, is supported by the latest Gallup Poll test elections.

Contrary to the views of many political observers, who see Anderson as a centrist or middle-of-the-road candidate, his followers take more liberal positions on five of the nine issues than do Carter supporters. On the other four issues only slight differences exist between the opinions of Anderson and Carter backers.

SEPTEMBER 14
MARIJUANA

Interviewing Date: 6/27–30/80
Survey #158-G

Do you think the use of marijuana should be made legal, or not?

Should 25%
Should not 70
No opinion 5

By Sex
Male

Should 31%
Should not 63
No opinion 6

Female

Should 19%
Should not 76
No opinion 5

By Race
White

Should 25%
Should not 71
No opinion 4

Nonwhite

Should 24%
Should not 65
No opinion 11

By Education
College

Should 35%
Should not 60
No opinion 5

High School

Should 24%
Should not 71
No opinion 5

Grade School

Should 11%
Should not 83
No opinion 6

By Region
East

Should 27%
Should not 68
No opinion 5

Midwest

Should 24%
Should not 72
No opinion 4

South

Should 21%
Should not 73
No opinion 6

West

Should 29%
Should not 63
No opinion 8

By Age
18–24 Years

Should 40%
Should not 54
No opinion 6

25–29 Years

Should 47%
Should not 46
No opinion 7

30–49 Years

Should 22%
Should not 73
No opinion 5

50 Years and Over

Should 13%
Should not 82
No opinion 5

By Income
$15,000 and Over

Should 27%
Should not 68
No opinion 5

Under $15,000

Should 23%
Should not 71
No opinion 6

By Politics
Republicans

Should 16%
Should not 79
No opinion 5

Democrats

Should 23%
Should not 72
No opinion 5

Independents

Should 36%
Should not 61
No opinion 2

By Occupation
Professional and Business

Should 32%
Should not 64
No opinion 4

Clerical and Sales

Should 21%
Should not 75
No opinion 4

Manual Workers

Should 27%
Should not 67
No opinion 6

Non-Labor Force

Should 14%
Should not 80
No opinion 6

By Community Size
One Million and Over

Should 32%
Should not 64
No opinion 4

500,000–999,999

Should 27%
Should not 62
No opinion 11

50,000–499,999

Should 28%
Should not 65
No opinion 7

2,500–49,999

Should 20%
Should not 76
No opinion 4

Under 2,500; Rural

Should 18%
Should not 79
No opinion 3

Do you think the possession of small amounts of marijuana should or should not be treated as a criminal offense?

Should 43%
Should not 52
No opinion 5

By Sex
Male

Should 42%
Should not 53
No opinion 5

Female

Should 44%
Should not 51
No opinion 5

By Race
White
Should 43%
Should not 52
No opinion 5

Nonwhite
Should 40%
Should not 52
No opinion 8

By Education
College
Should 30%
Should not 67
No opinion 3

High School
Should 45%
Should not 50
No opinion 5

Grade School
Should 58%
Should not 33
No opinion 9

By Region
East
Should 43%
Should not 52
No opinion 5

Midwest
Should 40%
Should not 54
No opinion 6

South
Should 51%
Should not 45
No opinion 4

West
Should 33%
Should not 60
No opinion 7

By Age
18–24 Years
Should 27%
Should not 67
No opinion 6

25–29 Years
Should 26%
Should not 70
No opinion 4

30–49 Years
Should 45%
Should not 52
No opinion 3

50 Years and Over
Should 54%
Should not 39
No opinion 7

By Income
$15,000 and Over
Should 40%
Should not 56
No opinion 4

Under $15,000
Should 45%
Should not 48
No opinion 7

By Politics
Republicans
Should 49%
Should not 46
No opinion 5

Democrats

Should 47%
Should not 49
No opinion 4

Independents

Should 33%
Should not 63
No opinion 4

By Occupation
Professional and Business

Should 39%
Should not 59
No opinion 2

Clerical and Sales

Should 37%
Should not 55
No opinion 8

Manual Workers

Should 40%
Should not 56
No opinion 4

Non-Labor Force

Should 55%
Should not 39
No opinion 6

By Community Size
One Million and Over

Should 35%
Should not 60
No opinion 5

500,000–999,999

Should 26%
Should not 64
No opinion 10

50,000–499,999

Should 44%
Should not 50
No opinion 6

2,500–49,999

Should 49%
Should not 48
No opinion 3

Under 2,500; Rural

Should 52%
Should not 44
No opinion 4

Note: On the issue of legalizing the use of marijuana, the findings in the latest Gallup survey exactly reflect those percentages recorded two years ago. A majority (70%) voted against legalization, while 25% were in favor. In 1969, when this measurement was first initiated, support for legalization was only 12%.

Although the views of adults as a whole are closely divided with 51% opposed and 43% in favor, opposition to legalizing marijuana is greatest among women, teen-agers, persons with less formal education, and residents of the Midwest and South. On the other hand, Gallup surveys have shown that college students are most in favor of the legalization of marijuana—at times by a 2-to-1 margin.

However, while a majority of the public is opposed to legalization, they are ready to decriminalize marijuana. Fifty-two percent feel that possession of small amounts of the substance should not be treated as a criminal offense, while 43% would retain criminal penalties. Public opinion on this issue has shown little change since three years ago when a survey recorded 53% in favor of decriminalization and 41% opposed.

Presently, only a few states have decriminalized "pot," that is, made possession of small amounts (generally an ounce or less) a civil offense. Of the states that have changed their laws, four are in the West. Thus, it is no surprise that people living in this region are most likely to favor removing criminal penalties for possessing small quantities of marijuana. Southerners are closely divided but lean slightly toward opposition. Opinion in the East and Midwest, however, closely follows the national trend.

Support for decriminalization is found in all major population groups, especially among the young and the college educated. The few exceptions are southerners, those over fifty, and people whose education ended at the grade-school level.

Teen-agers hold views on decriminalization that closely match those of adults. The latest Gallup Youth Survey (conducted in May) shows 52% of teens believe that possession of small amounts of marijuana should not be treated as a crime, while 46% hold the opposite view. The same survey also shows that 40% of teen-agers say they have tried marijuana. Among college students the figure is 66%, compared to only 5% in 1957.

SEPTEMBER 16
PRESIDENTIAL TRIAL HEAT

Interviewing Date: 9/12–15/80
Survey #162-G

Asked of registered voters: If the presidential election were being held today, which would you vote for—the Republican candidates Reagan and Bush, the Democratic candidates Carter and Mondale, or the independent candidates Anderson and Lucey? [Those who named other persons or who were undecided were asked: As of today, do you lean more to Reagan and Bush, more to Carter and Mondale, or more to Anderson and Lucey?]

Reagan-Bush...........................39%
Carter-Mondale 39
Anderson-Lucey......................14
Other; undecided 6
Refused; will not vote 2

By Region
East

Reagan-Bush...........................37%
Carter-Mondale 35

Anderson-Lucey......................18
Other; undecided 9
Refused; will not vote 1

Midwest

Reagan-Bush...........................37%
Carter-Mondale 41
Anderson-Lucey......................13
Other; undecided 6
Refused; will not vote 3

South

Reagan-Bush...........................45%
Carter-Mondale 42
Anderson-Lucey......................7
Other; undecided 5
Refused; will not vote 1

West

Reagan-Bush...........................35%
Carter-Mondale 37
Anderson-Lucey......................21
Other; undecided 6
Refused; will not vote 1

Note: Voter support for President Jimmy Carter, after rising sharply following the Democratic convention, has leveled off in the latest test election. The survey on which these figures are based was conducted between September 12–15, during a period of widespread discussion of the president's refusal to join Ronald Reagan and John Anderson in the presidential debate scheduled for September 21 in Baltimore.

SEPTEMBER 21
SPEED LIMIT

Interviewing Date: 9/12–15/80
Survey #162-G

Do you favor or oppose keeping the present 55-mile-per-hour speed limit on the highways of the nation?

Favor................................81%
Oppose..............................17
No opinion 2

By Community Size

One Million and Over

Favor..............................83%
Oppose.............................13
No opinion 4

500,000–999,999

Favor..............................80%
Oppose.............................18
No opinion 2

50,000–499,999

Favor..............................82%
Oppose.............................17
No opinion 1

2,500–49,999

Favor..............................82%
Oppose.............................18
No opinion.........................*

Under 2,500; Rural

Favor..............................78%
Oppose.............................19
No opinion 3

*Less than 1%

Note: GOP challenger Ronald Reagan will have a difficult time winning votes on at least one of the planks in the Republican platform—that which calls for abolishing the 55-mile-per-hour maximum speed limit, which was imposed as a national law in 1974 primarily because of the energy situation. Public support for retaining this law is at a record high, with an overwhelming 81% of adults in favor.

Even among Reagan's own supporters, 77% say the law should remain on the books. Heavy majorities of Republicans (76%), as well as Democrats (85%) and independents (78%), express approval of the present law.

Solid majorities in each geographical region, including the West where sharpest criticism of the present law is heard, vote in favor of retaining the 55-mile-per-hour limit. Also, young adults (18 to 29) are just as likely to favor this national law as are persons thirty and over.

Proponents favor retaining the present speed limit for three reasons: 1) a substantial reduction in auto fatalities; 2) savings in petroleum (it has been estimated that consumption would increase by one-quarter million barrels a day if the speed limit were removed); and 3) it costs drivers less money to run cars at a lower speed.

SEPTEMBER 21
CAMPAIGN DEBATES

Interviewing Date: 9/12–16/80
Special Telephone Survey

Asked of registered voters: As you may know, the first of the debates by the presidential candidates will be on television on Sunday, September 21. How likely are you to watch this debate? Would you say you are very likely, fairly likely, not very likely, or not at all likely to watch it?

Very likely.........................41%
Fairly likely.......................29
Not very likely 17
Not at all likely; don't know.......13

Asked of registered voters: Do you happen to know which of the presidential candidates will be participating in this debate?

Carter (incorrect)..................25%
Reagan (correct)*...................78
Anderson (correct)*.................60
Others; don't know..................22

*Fifty percent named both Reagan and Anderson.

Asked of registered voters: President Carter has said that he will not take part in the first debate. Do you think he should or should not have made this decision?

Should..............................25%
Should not..........................61
No opinion 14

Asked of registered voters: What issues would you most like to have the candidates debate?

High cost of living; inflation 51%
Foreign affairs 17
Unemployment 15
Tax cut 12
Energy matters 10
Conservation and the environment 3
Race relations; minority rights 2
Abortion 2
Women's rights; ERA 2
Other 31
Don't know 22
167%*

*Total adds to more than 100% due to multiple responses.

Note: By a 2-to-1 margin (61% to 25%), Americans disapprove of President Jimmy Carter's decision not to participate in the television debate with Republican Ronald Reagan and independent John Anderson.

Large majorities of registered Republicans and independents are critical of the president's decision. While opinion is more evenly divided among Carter's fellow Democrats, 48% disapprove of his decision and 38% approve.

Despite the extensive media coverage given to Carter's decision, only half the public was correctly able to name Reagan and Anderson as the two debaters. It is also surprising that while one-fourth of the voters (26%) thought the president would take part in the forum, another 21% did not know who the participants would be.

At least four persons in ten (41%) say they are very likely to watch the debate and 29% say they are fairly likely. A similar degree of interest is voiced in all major population groups with the exception of those over fifty and Republicans.

SEPTEMBER 25
WAGE-PRICE CONTROLS

Interviewing Date: 9/12–15/80
Survey #162-G

Would you favor or oppose having the government bring back wage and price controls?

Favor 52%
Oppose 39
No opinion 9

By Income
$15,000 and Over

Favor 43%
Oppose 50
No opinion 7

Under $15,000

Favor 61%
Oppose 26
No opinion 13

Carter Supporters

Favor 58%
Oppose 34
No opinion 8

Reagan Supporters

Favor 47%
Oppose 46
No opinion 7

Anderson Supporters

Favor 52%
Oppose 38
No opinion 10

Note: In all the discussion about inflation in the presidential campaign since Labor Day, none of the candidates has suggested that we adopt a plan that is supported by a majority of Americans—the reimposition of mandatory wage-price controls.

Although the latest figure (52%) represents a decline in support from a February survey when 57% expressed approval, the public consistently has been in favor of controls, particularly in periods of severe inflation. Just after President Nixon froze wages and prices in 1971, a Gallup Poll showed Americans supported the move by a margin of 6 to 1. Furthermore, surveys conducted at regular intervals during the three phases of Nixon's economic program repeatedly showed that the public favored stricter controls as opposed to relaxing those then in force.

Although President Jimmy Carter continually has rejected wage-price controls, it recently was reported that the Carter administration plans to abandon the present voluntary wage-price program in the next few weeks. This program has been heavily criticized in certain quarters as being ineffective.

SEPTEMBER 28
PARTY BEST FOR KEEPING PEACE AND PROSPERITY

Interviewing Date: 9/12–15/80
Survey #162-G

Which political party do you think would be more likely to keep the United States out of World War III—the Republican party or the Democratic party?

Republican 25%
Democratic 42
No difference 21
No opinion 12

Which political party—the Republican party or the Democratic party—do you think will do the better job of keeping the country prosperous?

Republican 35%
Democratic 36
No difference 19
No opinion 10

Note: With the presidential election only five weeks away, the Democratic party has gained the widest lead (42% to 25%) over the Republicans since 1964 as the party perceived as better able to keep the United States out of war.

The peace issue gained major prominence in this year's election when President Jimmy Carter, criticizing his GOP opponent Ronald Reagan, told a Los Angeles audience that in this election "you will determine what kind of life you and your families will have, whether this nation will make progress or go backward and whether we have peace or war."

The Democrats' 2-to-1 advantage on this issue, based on a survey conducted prior to the recent intensification of hostilities between Iraq and Iran, is an important one since the twin issues of peace and prosperity have been dominant in virtually every presidential election in this century.

The impact that international events and concern over war can have on a presidential election was revealed dramatically in the 1956 presidential contest. Throughout two months of intensive campaigning that year by Dwight Eisenhower and Adlai Stevenson, there was very little change in their standing. Then, in the closing days of the race, the Hungarian revolution and the Suez Canal crisis caused a sharp upswing in the Eisenhower vote. An estimated 3 to 4 million votes swung to the GOP ticket in the last ten days of the campaign.

The Democratic advantage on the peace issue is at least partially offset by the fact that equal proportions of the public now name the Republican as well as the Democratic party as better able to keep the nation prosperous. In the June survey, 32% cited the GOP and 37% the Democrats. This is the first time that the Republicans have enjoyed parity with the Democrats on this issue since the fall of 1972, shortly before Richard Nixon's landslide reelection victory.

OCTOBER 2
MOST IMPORTANT PROBLEM

Interviewing Date: 9/12–15/80
Survey #162-G

What do you think is the most important problem facing this country today?

High cost of living; inflation 60%
Unemployment 16
International problems 15
Dissatisfaction with government 6
Energy problems 4
Moral decline 3

Others 14
No opinion 2
                                                    120%*

*Total adds to more than 100% due to multiple responses.

Asked of those who named a problem: Which political party do you think can do a better job of handling the problem you have just mentioned—the Republican party or the Democratic party?

Republican 36%
Democratic 34
No difference 21
No opinion 9

Eliminating those who say there is no difference between the parties or who do not express an opinion, this division between the parties is obtained:

Republican 51%
Democratic 49

Which do you think the federal government should give greater attention to—trying to curb inflation or trying to reduce unemployment?

Curb inflation 61%
Reduce unemployment 33
No opinion 6

By Race
White

Curb inflation 65%
Reduce unemployment 30
No opinion 5

Nonwhite

Curb inflation 38%
Reduce unemployment 51
No opinion 11

By Income
$15,000 and Over

Curb inflation 67%
Reduce unemployment 29
No opinion 4

Under $15,000

Curb inflation 55%
Reduce unemployment 36
No opinion 9

By Occupation
Professional and Business

Curb inflation 67%
Reduce unemployment 30
No opinion 3

Clerical and Sales

Curb inflation 65%
Reduce unemployment 28
No opinion 10

Manual Workers

Curb inflation 58%
Reduce unemployment 37
No opinion 5

Non-Labor Force

Curb inflation 60%
Reduce unemployment 30
No opinion 10

Labor Union Members Only

Curb inflation 59%
Reduce unemployment 35
No opinion 6

Non-Labor Union Members Only

Curb inflation 62%
Reduce unemployment 32
No opinion 6

Note: Over the last thirty-five years the Gallup

Poll issue barometer has been a successful measurement for closely reflecting the actual outcome in both presidential and congressional elections.

Results of this latest measurement indicate that domestic issues, particularly those relating to the economy, far overshadow international issues in the minds of voters. In the latest survey, 60% of the public views the high cost of living as the most important problem facing the nation, followed by unemployment (16%), and international problems (15%). In comparison, a July survey showed 56% naming the high cost of living, 15% unemployment, and 12% international problems.

Events in the final weeks of this year's campaign can change the picture, but presently 51% of those who choose between the parties believe that the Republicans are better able to deal with the problems they consider to be most important, while 49% name the Democratic party. These findings closely parallel those recorded in the July survey when the GOP had a 52% to 48% advantage, and therefore they represent the best showing for the Republican party since the 1972 presidential campaign.

The current results on the issue barometer are reflective of the status of the presidential contest at this time. The latest *Newsweek* test election measurement, based on telephone interviews with 1,045 registered voters and conducted on September 24–25, shows Ronald Reagan with a slight lead over President Jimmy Carter (39% to 35%), with 14% for John Anderson.

OCTOBER 5
PRESIDENTIAL TRIAL HEAT

Interviewing Date: 8/15–18; 9/12–15/80
Survey #161-G; #162-G

Asked of registered voters: If the presidential election were being held today, which would you vote for—the Republican candidates Reagan and Bush, the Democratic candidates Carter and Mondale, or

the independent candidates Anderson and Lucey? [Those who named other persons or who were undecided were asked: As of today, do you lean more to Reagan and Bush, more to Carter and Mondale, or more to Anderson and Lucey?]

Reagan-Bush........................40%
Carter-Mondale 38
Anderson-Lucey.....................15
Other; undecided 7

Asked of those who named a candidate: Do you strongly support (candidates of choice), or do you only moderately support them? Do you strongly oppose (names of other candidates), or do you only moderately oppose them?

Soft* Carter Voters

Moderately support Carter;
moderately oppose Reagan/Anderson ... 14%

Soft Reagan Voters

Moderately support Reagan;
moderately oppose Carter/Anderson 11

Soft Anderson Voters

Moderately support Anderson;
moderately oppose Carter/Reagan 4

Undecided voters 11
                                    ——
                                    40%**

*"Soft" voters are those who qualify their presidential choice by indicating that they only moderately support their candidate and at the same time are only moderately opposed to his opponents.
**Total soft voters

Note: In a presidential election campaign characterized by unusual volatility, Gallup surveys through mid-September have shown that as many as one-third of all registered voters might change their candidate preference during the final seven weeks of the campaign.

Gallup test elections show 11% of registered voters undecided or unwilling to express a preference for President Jimmy Carter, Ronald Reagan, or John Anderson—about the same level of indecision among the electorate as recorded at this time in 1976. The undecided, however, represent only a fraction of the total number of voters who were not strongly committed to one of the three major contenders as of late summer. Although more than nine out of ten (89%) stated a candidate preference, approximately one-third of these can be considered soft in their preferences.

Soft voters represent the battleground on which a close contest such as the 1980 election may be won. It is here that the candidates will have to concentrate their efforts during the remainder of the campaign. The soft vote undoubtedly has accounted for much of the volatility in preference that has been apparent so far. While candidate preferences have shifted from time to time during the campaign—Reagan was ahead in early August, for instance, but neck and neck with Carter later that month—there has been remarkably little change in the relative proportions of each candidate's soft vote.

The incidence of soft voters is particularly high among certain groups of voters. The following is an overview of the least committed groups and how they differ from the total electorate on key campaign issues:

1. In the East and Midwest about 40% of registered voters are not strongly committed, compared to approximately one-third in the South and West—the home regions of Carter and Reagan, respectively. The industrial East and Midwest have felt the most impact of the recession. In the East the 14% undecided vote is twice the national average, and in the Midwest the Carter vote is particularly soft.

2. Throughout the campaign Reagan and Carter have divided the normally Democratic blue-collar vote almost evenly and continue to do so, but 44% of manual workers are only moderately committed to their choices or are still undecided, 16% are soft Carter voters, and 13% are soft Reagan voters. The economy is obviously a critical issue to this bloc.

3. The vote of young people has been especially changeable, and John Anderson has made a strong showing with this group. Currently, 40% of voters under thirty years of age are uncommitted. Young Reagan voters are softer than young supporters of incumbent Carter. Social issues and nuclear power differentiate young voters the most from their elders. Young people are more supportive of the ERA and abortion and are most opposed to nuclear power. They also tend to take a more liberal position on homosexual rights.

4. Although Catholics continue to favor Carter by a slight margin, 40% of this total vote remains soft. A particularly large percentage of the Carter Catholic vote is only moderately committed.

As the campaign moves into its final month, the trends in preferences of uncommitted voters will be critical. Each candidate's soft vote represents a prime target for his opponent. It is likely that much of the current soft vote will firm up as the election draws near, but in this campaign, which already has experienced several major shifts in sentiment, it may be that many voters will remain soft in their preferences right up to election day.

OCTOBER 9
PERCEPTION OF
PRESIDENTIAL CANDIDATES

Interviewing Date: 9/12–15/80
Survey #162-G

People who are conservative in their political views are referred to as being right of center and people who are liberal in their political views are referred to as being left of center. [Respondents were handed a card with eight categories listed.] Which one of these categories best describes Ronald Reagan's political position, Jimmy Carter's, John Anderson's, your own?

	Reagan	Carter	Anderson	Public
Left of center	16%	29%	25%	17%
Middle of the road (volunteered)	24	35	26	44
Right of center	46	21	15	28
Don't know	14	15	34	11

Note: In past presidential elections the political philosophies of the candidates as perceived by the voters have proven to be good indicators of potential support. Historically, presidential candidates who have veered too far to the left or to the right of the political ideology of the electorate as a whole have failed to win elections. Two examples are Senator George McGovern in 1972, who was perceived as too far left, and Senator Barry Goldwater in 1964, who was perceived as too far right.

A mid-September survey shows that 44% feel at home in the political center, and they consider themselves either slightly left or slightly right of center, or volunteered the response middle of the road. The public's self-reported political tendencies have not changed significantly since an earlier Gallup survey, conducted in May, when 40% of Americans placed themselves in the political center.

The political philosophy of the electorate is remarkably stable. In August 1976 a similar percentage (39%) of respondents in a Gallup survey placed themselves squarely in the middle of the political spectrum. In contrast to this relative stability of the public's perception of itself, perceptions of the candidates' political positions have moved considerably since May.

President Jimmy Carter has moved to the left according to the voters. The percentage placing the president to the left of the political center has risen from 21% to 29%. Conversely, the proportions perceiving incumbent Carter as middle of the road and right of center have decreased to 35% and 21%, respectively. Nonetheless, Carter is still seen as primarily a centrist candidate, albeit with strong leftward leanings.

In the 1976 presidential race then candidate Jimmy Carter also was viewed by an increasing number of voters as veering toward the left as the campaign progressed. This trend helped to explain why Carter was unable to maintain his earlier wide lead over President Ford. The chemistry of the 1980 race is not comparable to that of the 1976 contest. Ford in 1976 was a centrist candidate able to contest the middle-of-the-road segment of the electorate with Carter.

Ronald Reagan's perceived political philosophy, on the other hand, could spell electoral trouble. He is not seen as a centrist candidate with rightward leanings, which would put him in the most advantageous position to fight for middle-of-the-road voters, who, by virtue of their sheer numbers (44% of all adults today), are crucial in any election. Instead, 46% of Americans see the former California governor as decidedly to the right of center; only 28% of voters feel at home there themselves.

To some extent perceptions of Carter and Reagan are influenced probably by the party labels that they carry. Independent candidate John Anderson, although a Republican when he represented Illinois's 16th District in the House, is running without a party. This makes voters' perceptions of his political philosophy especially critical, since they are the only guideline for potential supporters besides his stands on individual issues. Party attachments and coattails mean little for an independent presidential candidate.

The development of the public's views of Anderson does not augur well for him. In May, 38% placed him in the center; by September that proportion had dropped to 26%. Especially interesting is where the decrease went. Over the course of the summer the percentage of people saying they simply did not know where Anderson fits into the political spectrum rose 10 percentage points.

For a candidate whose foremost problem, aside from his uphill fight against the two major party candidates, is simply to become better known, this is bad news. But there is a hopeful sign. Of those who recognize him, Anderson is considered a centrist candidate with leftward leanings and thus in a position to fight for the middle-of-the-road vote. However, factors other than ideology—most notably, simple public awareness of who Anderson is—probably will be the most important in determining how successful his challenge will be.

OCTOBER 12
CONGRESSIONAL ELECTIONS

Interviewing Date: 9/12–15/80
Survey #162-G

Asked of likely voters: If the elections for Congress were being held today, which party would you like to see win in this congressional district—the Democratic party or the Republican party? [Those who name another party or who were undecided were asked: As of today, do you lean more to the Democratic party or to the Republican party?]

Democratic 51%
Republican 42
Other 2
Undecided 5

Dividing the other and undecided vote evenly between the major parties, the division of the vote is:

Democratic 55%
Republican 45

Note: With election day only three weeks away, the Democratic party holds a wide lead (55% to 45%) over the Republicans in the race for the House of Representatives. These percentages are the same as those recorded in the Gallup Poll's final estimate of the national vote in the 1978 congressional election. The actual division of the vote in that election was 54.6% and 45.4% for Democrats and Republicans, respectively.

Although the national vote for Congress in the latest survey cannot be translated directly into House seats, according to these survey results, it appears highly unlikely that the GOP will win a majority of the seats in the House on November 4.

Republicans appear to be more loyal to their party than are Democrats. As many as three out of ten persons (31%) who would vote for a

Democrat in their local congressional district say they will not vote for President Carter.

Reagan is more successful in winning over voters who choose Republicans at the local level. About one-fourth of voters (23%) choosing Republican congressional candidates do not pick Reagan, as shown below:

Vote for Congress*
Democrats

Vote for president
   Carter 69%
   Reagan 13
   Anderson 12
Other; undecided 6

Republicans

Vote for president
   Carter 8%
   Reagan 77
   Anderson 11
Other; undecided 4

Independents

Vote for president
   Carter 17%
   Reagan 26
   Anderson 24
Other; undecided 33

*Based on likely voters

OCTOBER 14
PRESIDENTIAL TRIAL HEAT

Interviewing Date: 10/10–13/80
Survey #163-G

Asked of likely voters: If the presidential election were being held today, which would you vote for—the Republican candidates Reagan and Bush, the Democratic candidates Carter and Mondale, or the independent candidates Anderson and Lucey? [Those who named other persons or who were undecided were asked: As of today, do you lean more to Reagan and

Bush, more to Carter and Mondale, or more to Anderson and Lucey?]

Reagan-Bush.........................44%
Carter-Mondale 41
Anderson-Lucey..................... 9
Other; undecided 6

By Sex
Male

Reagan-Bush.........................51%
Carter-Mondale 34
Anderson-Lucey..................... 8
Other; undecided 7

Female

Reagan-Bush.........................37%
Carter-Mondale 47
Anderson-Lucey..................... 9
Other; undecided 7

By Race
White

Reagan-Bush.........................48%
Carter-Mondale 35
Anderson-Lucey..................... 9
Other; undecided 8

Nonwhite

Reagan-Bush......................... 8%
Carter-Mondale 81
Anderson-Lucey..................... 4
Other; undecided 7

By Education
College

Reagan-Bush.........................49%
Carter-Mondale 32
Anderson-Lucey.....................13
Other; undecided 6

High School

Reagan-Bush.........................41%
Carter-Mondale 44
Anderson-Lucey..................... 7
Other; undecided 8

Grade School

Reagan-Bush.........................39%
Carter-Mondale 49
Anderson-Lucey..................... 1
Other; undecided 11

By Region
East

Reagan-Bush.........................38%
Carter-Mondale 42
Anderson-Lucey.....................11
Other; undecided 9

Midwest

Reagan-Bush.........................46%
Carter-Mondale 36
Anderson-Lucey..................... 8
Other; undecided 10

South

Reagan-Bush.........................43%
Carter-Mondale 50
Anderson-Lucey..................... 4
Other; undecided 7

West

Reagan-Bush.........................49%
Carter-Mondale 32
Anderson-Lucey.....................14
Other; undecided 5

By Age
18–24 Years

Reagan-Bush.........................46%
Carter-Mondale 45
Anderson-Lucey..................... 9
Other; undecided .... *

25–29 Years

Reagan-Bush.........................35%
Carter-Mondale 45
Anderson-Lucey.....................14
Other; undecided 6

30–49 Years

Reagan-Bush........................47%
Carter-Mondale 37
Anderson-Lucey.....................11
Other; undecided 5

50 Years and Over

Reagan-Bush........................42%
Carter-Mondale 42
Anderson-Lucey..................... 5
Other; undecided 11

By Income
$25,000 and Over

Reagan-Bush........................53%
Carter-Mondale 31
Anderson-Lucey.....................10
Other; undecided 6

$20,000–$24,999

Reagan-Bush........................52%
Carter-Mondale 30
Anderson-Lucey.....................12
Other; undecided 6

$15,000–$19,999

Reagan-Bush........................43%
Carter-Mondale 42
Anderson-Lucey..................... 9
Other; undecided 6

$10,000–$14,999

Reagan-Bush........................36%
Carter-Mondale 48
Anderson-Lucey..................... 8
Other; undecided 8

$5,000–$9,999

Reagan-Bush........................43%
Carter-Mondale 44
Anderson-Lucey..................... 4
Other; undecided 9

Under $5,000

Reagan-Bush........................29%
Carter-Mondale 54
Anderson-Lucey..................... 8
Other; undecided 9

By Politics
Republicans

Reagan-Bush........................81%
Carter-Mondale 8
Anderson-Lucey..................... 6
Other; undecided 5

Democrats

Reagan-Bush........................17%
Carter-Mondale 71
Anderson-Lucey..................... 6
Other; undecided 6

Independents

Reagan-Bush........................48%
Carter-Mondale 20
Anderson-Lucey.....................19
Other; undecided 13

By Religion
Protestants

Reagan-Bush........................45%
Carter-Mondale 41
Anderson-Lucey..................... 7
Other; undecided 7

Catholics

Reagan-Bush........................42%
Carter-Mondale 40
Anderson-Lucey.....................10
Other; undecided 8

By Occupation
Professional and Business

Reagan-Bush........................55%
Carter-Mondale 26
Anderson-Lucey.....................12
Other; undecided 7

Clerical and Sales

Reagan-Bush........................38%
Carter-Mondale 50
Anderson-Lucey..................... 6
Other; undecided 6

Manual Workers

Reagan-Bush........................40%
Carter-Mondale 44
Anderson-Lucey.....................10
Other; undecided 6

Non-Labor Force

Reagan-Bush........................40%
Carter-Mondale 44
Anderson-Lucey..................... 7
Other; undecided 9

By Community Size
One Million and Over

Reagan-Bush........................39%
Carter-Mondale 42
Anderson-Lucey.....................11
Other; undecided 8

500,000–999,999

Reagan-Bush........................42%
Carter-Mondale 34
Anderson-Lucey.....................15
Other; undecided 9

50,000–499,999

Reagan-Bush........................44%
Carter-Mondale 43
Anderson-Lucey..................... 8
Other; undecided 5

2,500–49,999

Reagan-Bush........................42%
Carter-Mondale 43
Anderson-Lucey..................... 8
Other; undecided 7

Under 2,500; Rural

Reagan-Bush........................48%
Carter-Mondale 40
Anderson-Lucey..................... 5
Other; undecided 7

Labor Union Families Only

Reagan-Bush........................38%
Carter-Mondale 47
Anderson-Lucey..................... 7
Other; undecided 8

Non-Labor Union Families Only

Reagan-Bush........................45%
Carter-Mondale 39
Anderson-Lucey..................... 9
Other; undecided 7

*Less than 1%

Note: As the presidential campaign enters its final stage, among likely voters the GOP ticket of Ronald Reagan and George Bush holds a slight 44% to 41% edge over the Democratic ticket of Jimmy Carter and Walter Mondale, with the independent slate of John Anderson and Patrick Lucey winning the support of 9%.

The current results represent gains for both the Democratic and Republican tickets since mid-September, when the Reagan-Bush ticket was the choice of 41% of likely voters compared to 37% for Carter and Mondale. The vote for the independent ticket has declined 6 points over this same period, from 15% in September to 9% today.

A comparison of the two most recent surveys indicates that the Republican slate has gained 4 percentage points and the Democratic ticket 5 points as a result of the decline in support for the Anderson ticket, as well as a downtrend in the number of voters who remain undecided.

The turnout on November 4 can be crucial in the event of a close election, which now appears possible. Historically, only slightly more than half of eligible voters bother to cast their ballots on election day. To identify these voters the Gallup Poll has developed a scale of voting intention that has been used during the last seven presidential elections. When the sample is broadened to include all registered voters, the race is a virtual dead heat, with the Democrats winning 43% and the Republicans 42%. The Anderson-Lucey ticket receives 10% of the support of registered voters.

Anderson's support among registered voters had been as high as 24% in mid-June. Following the nominating conventions of the two major parties in July and August, his support stood at 14% in mid-September; today he is the choice of only 10% of registered voters. Although Anderson's backing has slipped in recent weeks, a majority (56%) say he should not withdraw from the race; in September the comparable figure was 63%.

One of the key questions now being asked is: How are Democrats, including former Kennedy supporters, lining up in the current presidential battle? Prior to the Democratic convention in July, Carter suffered a record rate of defection among Democrats, many of whom were Kennedy backers at that time. Only about half of Democrats chose Carter over Reagan and Anderson. Following the convention, however, many Democrats rallied behind Carter, giving him a boost in the race against Reagan and Anderson. Nevertheless, in the latest survey 17% of Democrats defect to Reagan and 6% to Anderson.

The following percentages, based on the choices of registered voters, show that the GOP ticket is suffering less defection than the Carter-Mondale slate. It is also interesting to note the strength of Anderson among independents.

By Politics
Republicans

Reagan-Bush.	80%
Carter-Mondale	10
Anderson-Lucey.	5
Other; undecided	5

Democrats

Reagan-Bush.	14%
Carter-Mondale	73
Anderson-Lucey.	6
Other; undecided	7

Independents

Reagan-Bush.	40%
Carter-Mondale	27
Anderson-Lucey.	21
Other; undecided	12

Although many Kennedy supporters shifted over to the Carter-Mondale ticket following the Democratic convention rather than back Reagan and Bush, as many as three in ten Kennedy Democrats are still holdouts, with 16% of this group currently choosing the Republican candidates and another 10% backing Anderson and Lucey.

The following question was asked of registered Democrats:

At the time of the Democratic convention in August, who did you want to see win the Democratic nomination for president— Jimmy Carter or Edward Kennedy?

Carter.	58%
Kennedy	34
Neither.	4
Can't say	4

Current Preference of Kennedy Democrats

Reagan-Bush.	16%
Carter-Mondale	64
Anderson-Lucey.	10
Other; undecided	10

Given the closeness of the current race a number of factors, including international events, could tip the balance to either major party candidate. For example, in the 1956 presidential contest the Hungarian revolution and the Suez Canal crisis caused a sharp upswing in the Eisenhower vote. An estimated 3 to 4 million votes shifted to the incumbent in the last ten days of the campaign.

It is important to bear in mind that the current survey findings refer to the popular, not the electoral vote. To report the electoral vote it would be necessary to conduct separate full-scale surveys in each of the fifty states.

OCTOBER 19
PRESIDENTIAL CANDIDATES—
ELECTION

Interviewing Date: 9/12–15/80
Survey #162-G

Here is a list of terms—shown as pairs of opposites—that have been used to describe Jimmy Carter/Ronald Reagan/John Anderson. From each pair of opposites, would you select the term which you feel best describes Carter/Reagan/Anderson?

Positive Terms*	Carter	Reagan	Anderson
A religious person	87%	40%	46%
A man of high moral principles	83	70	73
Takes moderate, middle-of-the-road positions	82	48	57
Bright, intelligent	73	73	82
Sympathetic to problems of the poor	68	41	58
Says what he believes even if unpopular	57	54	64
Sides with the average citizen	56	43	60
Displays good judgment in a crisis	55	55	55
Decisive, sure of himself	37	69	70
Offers imaginative, innovative solutions to national problems	37	52	56
You know where he stands on issues	33	54	50
Has strong leadership qualities	31	65	52
Has a well-defined program for moving country ahead	27	53	40
Has a clear understanding of issues facing country	50	55	53
Has well thought out, carefully considered solutions for national problems	36	45	42
Has colorful, interesting personality	50	70	59
Has modern, up-to-date solutions to national problems	39	51	53
A person who can get the job done	39	56	48

*For the purpose of brevity only the positive terms have been included.

Note: In order to facilitate direct comparisons between the three candidates, the above figures show the percentages of survey respondents ascribing each characteristic to each man, excluding those who did not express an opinion.

Asked of registered voters: This card lists various problems with which the man elected president this November will have to deal. Regardless of which man you happen to prefer—Carter, Reagan, or Anderson—please tell me which one you, yourself, feel would do a better job of handling each of the following problems:

Foreign relations?

Carter	43%
Reagan	37
Anderson	11
Don't know	9

By Sex
Male

Carter	42%
Reagan	38
Anderson	13
Don't know	7

Female

Carter	44%
Reagan	35
Anderson	9
Don't know	12

By Race
White

Carter.............................39%
Reagan.............................40
Anderson...........................11
Don't know.........................10

Nonwhite

Carter.............................72%
Reagan.............................12
Anderson........................... 8
Don't know......................... 8

By Education
College

Carter.............................39%
Reagan.............................41
Anderson...........................16
Don't know......................... 4

High School

Carter.............................43%
Reagan.............................37
Anderson........................... 9
Don't know.........................11

Grade School

Carter.............................54%
Reagan.............................24
Anderson........................... 6
Don't know.........................16

By Region
East

Carter.............................41%
Reagan.............................34
Anderson...........................14
Don't know.........................11

Midwest

Carter.............................45%
Reagan.............................33
Anderson...........................12
Don't know.........................10

South

Carter.............................45%
Reagan.............................40
Anderson........................... 6
Don't know......................... 9

West

Carter.............................41%
Reagan.............................41
Anderson...........................10
Don't know......................... 8

By Age
18–29 Years

Carter.............................41%
Reagan.............................36
Anderson...........................17
Don't know......................... 6

30–49 Years

Carter.............................43%
Reagan.............................38
Anderson...........................12
Don't know......................... 7

50 Years and Over

Carter.............................45%
Reagan.............................35
Anderson........................... 7
Don't know.........................13

Domestic affairs?

Carter.............................36%
Reagan.............................42
Anderson...........................14
Don't know......................... 8

By Sex
Male

Carter.............................36%
Reagan.............................42
Anderson...........................15
Don't know......................... 7

Female

Carter......................................37%
Reagan....................................41
Anderson.................................13
Don't know 9

By Race
White

Carter......................................32%
Reagan....................................45
Anderson.................................15
Don't know 8

Nonwhite

Carter......................................66%
Reagan....................................16
Anderson................................. 7
Don't know 11

By Education
College

Carter......................................32%
Reagan....................................43
Anderson.................................21
Don't know 4

High School

Carter......................................37%
Reagan....................................43
Anderson.................................11
Don't know 9

Grade School

Carter......................................49%
Reagan....................................32
Anderson................................. 8
Don't know 11

By Region
East

Carter......................................33%
Reagan....................................39
Anderson.................................17
Don't know 11

Midwest

Carter......................................37%
Reagan....................................43
Anderson.................................12
Don't know 8

South

Carter......................................42%
Reagan....................................46
Anderson................................. 7
Don't know 5

West

Carter......................................33%
Reagan....................................38
Anderson.................................22
Don't know 7

By Age
18–29 Years

Carter......................................31%
Reagan....................................38
Anderson.................................24
Don't know 7

30–49 Years

Carter......................................37%
Reagan....................................43
Anderson.................................16
Don't know 4

50 Years and Over

Carter......................................39%
Reagan....................................43
Anderson................................. 8
Don't know 10

Reducing inflation?

Carter......................................29%
Reagan....................................44
Anderson.................................13
Don't know 14

By Sex
Male

Carter	28%
Reagan	45
Anderson	15
Don't know	12

Female

Carter	29%
Reagan	43
Anderson	12
Don't know	16

By Race
White

Carter	24%
Reagan	48
Anderson	14
Don't know	14

Nonwhite

Carter	59%
Reagan	18
Anderson	10
Don't know	13

By Education
College

Carter	22%
Reagan	48
Anderson	19
Don't know	11

High School

Carter	29%
Reagan	45
Anderson	11
Don't know	15

Grade School

Carter	41%
Reagan	34
Anderson	7
Don't know	18

By Region
East

Carter	27%
Reagan	40
Anderson	15
Don't know	18

Midwest

Carter	27%
Reagan	44
Anderson	14
Don't know	15

South

Carter	31%
Reagan	51
Anderson	7
Don't know	11

West

Carter	28%
Reagan	42
Anderson	18
Don't know	12

By Age
18–29 Years

Carter	23%
Reagan	44
Anderson	23
Don't know	10

30–49 Years

Carter	27%
Reagan	47
Anderson	17
Don't know	9

50 Years and Over

Carter	32%
Reagan	42
Anderson	7
Don't know	19

Keeping the United States out of war?

Carter.............................50%
Reagan............................25
Anderson..........................12
Don't know 13

By Sex
Male

Carter.............................50%
Reagan............................26
Anderson..........................13
Don't know 11

Female

Carter.............................49%
Reagan............................25
Anderson..........................11
Don't know 15

By Race
White

Carter.............................46%
Reagan............................28
Anderson..........................13
Don't know 13

Nonwhite

Carter.............................69%
Reagan............................ 8
Anderson..........................10
Don't know 13

By Education
College

Carter.............................48%
Reagan............................26
Anderson..........................16
Don't know 10

High School

Carter.............................50%
Reagan............................26
Anderson..........................11
Don't know 13

Grade School

Carter.............................51%
Reagan............................24
Anderson.......................... 5
Don't know 20

By Region
East

Carter.............................45%
Reagan............................25
Anderson..........................15
Don't know 15

Midwest

Carter.............................51%
Reagan............................24
Anderson..........................12
Don't know 13

South

Carter.............................50%
Reagan............................28
Anderson.......................... 9
Don't know 13

West

Carter.............................52%
Reagan............................25
Anderson..........................13
Don't know 10

By Age
18–29 Years

Carter.............................49%
Reagan............................17
Anderson..........................25
Don't know 9

30–49 Years

Carter.............................55%
Reagan............................23
Anderson..........................11
Don't know 11

50 Years and Over

Carter...............................46%
Reagan.............................30
Anderson...........................7
Don't know........................17

Reducing unemployment?

Carter...............................32%
Reagan.............................41
Anderson..........................14
Don't know........................13

By Sex
Male

Carter...............................34%
Reagan.............................40
Anderson..........................16
Don't know........................10

Female

Carter...............................30%
Reagan.............................42
Anderson..........................12
Don't know........................16

By Race
White

Carter...............................28%
Reagan.............................45
Anderson..........................14
Don't know........................13

Nonwhite

Carter...............................60%
Reagan.............................15
Anderson..........................12
Don't know........................13

By Education
College

Carter...............................27%
Reagan.............................42
Anderson..........................21
Don't know........................10

High School

Carter...............................31%
Reagan.............................43
Anderson..........................12
Don't know........................14

Grade School

Carter...............................43%
Reagan.............................35
Anderson...........................6
Don't know........................16

By Region
East

Carter...............................27%
Reagan.............................40
Anderson..........................15
Don't know........................18

Midwest

Carter...............................32%
Reagan.............................40
Anderson..........................16
Don't know........................12

South

Carter...............................37%
Reagan.............................45
Anderson...........................7
Don't know........................11

West

Carter...............................30%
Reagan.............................39
Anderson..........................22
Don't know.........................9

By Age
18–29 Years

Carter...............................27%
Reagan.............................41
Anderson..........................23
Don't know.........................9

30–49 Years

Carter............................32%
Reagan...........................41
Anderson.........................18
Don't know 9

50 Years and Over

Carter............................33%
Reagan...........................42
Anderson......................... 8
Don't know 17

Handling the Iranian situation?

Carter............................33%
Reagan...........................39
Anderson.........................11
Don't know 17

By Sex
Male

Carter............................33%
Reagan...........................40
Anderson.........................12
Don't know 15

Female

Carter............................34%
Reagan...........................38
Anderson.........................10
Don't know 18

By Race
White

Carter............................30%
Reagan...........................42
Anderson.........................11
Don't know 17

Nonwhite

Carter............................56%
Reagan...........................19
Anderson......................... 9
Don't know 16

By Education
College

Carter............................28%
Reagan...........................43
Anderson.........................15
Don't know 14

High School

Carter............................34%
Reagan...........................40
Anderson......................... 9
Don't know 17

Grade School

Carter............................44%
Reagan...........................28
Anderson......................... 5
Don't know 23

By Region
East

Carter............................33%
Reagan...........................36
Anderson.........................11
Don't know 20

Midwest

Carter............................30%
Reagan...........................38
Anderson.........................15
Don't know 17

South

Carter............................37%
Reagan...........................41
Anderson......................... 6
Don't know 16

West

Carter............................34%
Reagan...........................43
Anderson.........................11
Don't know 12

By Age
18–29 Years

Carter........................29%
Reagan........................38
Anderson........................20
Don't know........................13

30–49 Years

Carter........................31%
Reagan........................44
Anderson........................11
Don't know........................14

50 Years and Over

Carter........................37%
Reagan........................36
Anderson........................7
Don't know........................20

Strengthening national defense?

Carter........................28%
Reagan........................55
Anderson........................7
Don't know........................10

By Sex
Male

Carter........................26%
Reagan........................59
Anderson........................7
Don't know........................8

Female

Carter........................31%
Reagan........................51
Anderson........................7
Don't know........................11

By Race
White

Carter........................24%
Reagan........................60
Anderson........................7
Don't know........................9

Nonwhite

Carter........................59%
Reagan........................22
Anderson........................6
Don't know........................13

By Education
College

Carter........................18%
Reagan........................68
Anderson........................7
Don't know........................7

High School

Carter........................32%
Reagan........................50
Anderson........................7
Don't know........................11

Grade School

Carter........................42%
Reagan........................41
Anderson........................5
Don't know........................12

By Region
East

Carter........................29%
Reagan........................50
Anderson........................9
Don't know........................12

Midwest

Carter........................26%
Reagan........................56
Anderson........................8
Don't know........................10

South

Carter........................32%
Reagan........................55
Anderson........................3
Don't know........................10

West

Carter............................26%
Reagan............................60
Anderson.........................7
Don't know.......................7

By Age
18–29 Years

Carter............................22%
Reagan............................62
Anderson.........................8
Don't know.......................8

30–49 Years

Carter............................25%
Reagan............................59
Anderson.........................7
Don't know.......................9

50 Years and Over

Carter............................34%
Reagan............................49
Anderson.........................6
Don't know.......................11

Women's rights?

Carter............................48%
Reagan............................23
Anderson.........................17
Don't know.......................12

By Sex
Male

Carter............................51%
Reagan............................20
Anderson.........................18
Don't know.......................11

Female

Carter............................45%
Reagan............................25
Anderson.........................16
Don't know.......................14

By Race
White

Carter............................44%
Reagan............................25
Anderson.........................19
Don't know.......................12

Nonwhite

Carter............................72%
Reagan............................7
Anderson.........................9
Don't know.......................12

By Education
College

Carter............................47%
Reagan............................20
Anderson.........................24
Don't know.......................9

High School

Carter............................47%
Reagan............................24
Anderson.........................16
Don't know.......................13

Grade School

Carter............................54%
Reagan............................24
Anderson.........................5
Don't know.......................17

By Region
East

Carter............................49%
Reagan............................22
Anderson.........................16
Don't know.......................13

Midwest

Carter............................47%
Reagan............................21
Anderson.........................18
Don't know.......................14

South

Carter..............................49%
Reagan.............................25
Anderson..........................15
Don't know........................11

West

Carter..............................46%
Reagan.............................21
Anderson..........................20
Don't know........................13

By Age
18–29 Years

Carter..............................43%
Reagan.............................18
Anderson..........................28
Don't know........................11

30–49 Years

Carter..............................50%
Reagan.............................20
Anderson..........................22
Don't know.........................8

50 Years and Over

Carter..............................49%
Reagan.............................26
Anderson...........................9
Don't know........................16

Improving the economy?

Carter..............................30%
Reagan.............................44
Anderson..........................12
Don't know........................14

By Sex
Male

Carter..............................29%
Reagan.............................44
Anderson..........................15
Don't know........................12

Female

Carter..............................31%
Reagan.............................43
Anderson..........................10
Don't know........................16

By Race
White

Carter..............................26%
Reagan.............................48
Anderson..........................13
Don't know........................13

Nonwhite

Carter..............................60%
Reagan.............................16
Anderson...........................7
Don't know........................17

By Education
College

Carter..............................24%
Reagan.............................47
Anderson..........................18
Don't know........................11

High School

Carter..............................29%
Reagan.............................45
Anderson..........................11
Don't know........................15

Grade School

Carter..............................46%
Reagan.............................30
Anderson...........................6
Don't know........................18

By Region
East

Carter..............................25%
Reagan.............................40
Anderson..........................16
Don't know........................19

Midwest

Carter.............................30%
Reagan............................45
Anderson..........................14
Don't know........................11

South

Carter.............................34%
Reagan............................47
Anderson.......................... 7
Don't know........................12

West

Carter.............................30%
Reagan............................43
Anderson..........................14
Don't know........................13

By Age
18–29 Years

Carter.............................24%
Reagan............................43
Anderson..........................24
Don't know........................ 9

30–49 Years

Carter.............................28%
Reagan............................47
Anderson..........................14
Don't know........................11

50 Years and Over

Carter.............................34%
Reagan............................41
Anderson.......................... 7
Don't know........................18

Improving conditions for minorities including blacks and Hispanics?

Carter.............................49%
Reagan............................22
Anderson..........................13
Don't know........................16

By Sex
Male

Carter.............................50%
Reagan............................23
Anderson..........................13
Don't know........................14

Female

Carter.............................47%
Reagan............................22
Anderson..........................13
Don't know........................18

By Race
White

Carter.............................46%
Reagan............................25
Anderson..........................14
Don't know........................15

Nonwhite

Carter.............................67%
Reagan............................ 6
Anderson.......................... 7
Don't know........................20

By Education
College

Carter.............................48%
Reagan............................22
Anderson..........................18
Don't know........................12

High School

Carter.............................48%
Reagan............................22
Anderson..........................12
Don't know........................18

Grade School

Carter.............................51%
Reagan............................25
Anderson.......................... 4
Don't know........................20

By Region

East

Carter..............................47%
Reagan..............................21
Anderson............................16
Don't know..........................16

Midwest

Carter..............................49%
Reagan..............................25
Anderson............................10
Don't know..........................16

South

Carter..............................50%
Reagan..............................23
Anderson............................12
Don't know..........................15

West

Carter..............................50%
Reagan..............................19
Anderson............................13
Don't know..........................18

By Age

18–29 Years

Carter..............................50%
Reagan..............................18
Anderson............................19
Don't know..........................13

30–49 Years

Carter..............................48%
Reagan..............................22
Anderson............................16
Don't know..........................14

50 Years and Over

Carter..............................49%
Reagan..............................25
Anderson............................ 8
Don't know..........................18

Dealing with Russia?

Carter..............................40%
Reagan..............................37
Anderson............................11
Don't know..........................12

By Sex

Male

Carter..............................39%
Reagan..............................39
Anderson............................12
Don't know..........................10

Female

Carter..............................42%
Reagan..............................36
Anderson............................ 9
Don't know..........................13

By Race

White

Carter..............................38%
Reagan..............................40
Anderson............................10
Don't know..........................12

Nonwhite

Carter..............................58%
Reagan..............................19
Anderson............................10
Don't know..........................13

By Education

College

Carter..............................35%
Reagan..............................44
Anderson............................15
Don't know.......................... 6

High School

Carter..............................42%
Reagan..............................36
Anderson............................ 9
Don't know..........................13

Grade School

Carter......................................47%
Reagan..................................27
Anderson................................ 5
Don't know............................21

By Region
East

Carter......................................41%
Reagan..................................33
Anderson..............................12
Don't know............................14

Midwest

Carter......................................43%
Reagan..................................34
Anderson..............................11
Don't know............................12

South

Carter......................................42%
Reagan..................................40
Anderson................................ 6
Don't know............................12

West

Carter......................................34%
Reagan..................................44
Anderson..............................14
Don't know............................ 8

By Age
18–29 Years

Carter......................................39%
Reagan..................................39
Anderson..............................14
Don't know............................ 8

30–49 Years

Carter......................................41%
Reagan..................................39
Anderson..............................11
Don't know............................ 9

50 Years and Over

Carter......................................41%
Reagan..................................35
Anderson................................ 8
Don't know............................16

Dealing with racial problems?

Carter......................................47%
Reagan..................................26
Anderson..............................15
Don't know............................12

By Sex
Male

Carter......................................45%
Reagan..................................26
Anderson..............................18
Don't know............................11

Female

Carter......................................49%
Reagan..................................26
Anderson..............................12
Don't know............................13

By Race
White

Carter......................................44%
Reagan..................................28
Anderson..............................16
Don't know............................12

Nonwhite

Carter......................................68%
Reagan..................................11
Anderson................................ 7
Don't know............................14

By Education
College

Carter......................................45%
Reagan..................................25
Anderson..............................21
Don't know............................ 9

High School

Carter............................47%
Reagan............................27
Anderson..........................13
Don't know........................13

Grade School

Carter............................52%
Reagan............................24
Anderson...........................6
Don't know........................18

By Region
East

Carter............................42%
Reagan............................25
Anderson..........................18
Don't know........................15

Midwest

Carter............................49%
Reagan............................27
Anderson..........................11
Don't know........................13

South

Carter............................51%
Reagan............................28
Anderson..........................13
Don't know.........................8

West

Carter............................49%
Reagan............................22
Anderson..........................18
Don't know........................11

By Age
18–29 Years

Carter............................48%
Reagan............................23
Anderson..........................22
Don't know.........................7

30–49 Years

Carter............................44%
Reagan............................26
Anderson..........................19
Don't know........................11

50 Years and Over

Carter............................49%
Reagan............................27
Anderson...........................9
Don't know........................15

Building trust in government?

Carter............................32%
Reagan............................37
Anderson..........................18
Don't know........................13

By Sex
Male

Carter............................30%
Reagan............................36
Anderson..........................23
Don't know........................11

Female

Carter............................34%
Reagan............................38
Anderson..........................13
Don't know........................15

By Race
White

Carter............................27%
Reagan............................40
Anderson..........................19
Don't know........................14

Nonwhite

Carter............................64%
Reagan............................14
Anderson..........................10
Don't know........................12

By Education
College

Carter...............................24%
Reagan..............................38
Anderson...........................29
Don't know......................... 9

High School

Carter...............................34%
Reagan..............................38
Anderson...........................14
Don't know.........................14

Grade School

Carter...............................42%
Reagan..............................30
Anderson........................... 8
Don't know.........................20

By Region
East

Carter...............................29%
Reagan..............................36
Anderson...........................19
Don't know.........................16

Midwest

Carter...............................35%
Reagan..............................35
Anderson...........................15
Don't know.........................15

South

Carter...............................33%
Reagan..............................40
Anderson...........................15
Don't know.........................12

West

Carter...............................31%
Reagan..............................35
Anderson...........................25
Don't know......................... 9

By Age
18–29 Years

Carter...............................30%
Reagan..............................32
Anderson...........................31
Don't know......................... 7

30–49 Years

Carter...............................30%
Reagan..............................39
Anderson...........................21
Don't know.........................10

50 Years and Over

Carter...............................34%
Reagan..............................38
Anderson...........................10
Don't know.........................18

Improving the energy situation?

Carter...............................34%
Reagan..............................40
Anderson...........................14
Don't know.........................12

By Sex
Male

Carter...............................33%
Reagan..............................41
Anderson...........................15
Don't know.........................11

Female

Carter...............................35%
Reagan..............................38
Anderson...........................13
Don't know.........................14

By Race
White

Carter...............................29%
Reagan..............................44
Anderson...........................15
Don't know.........................12

Nonwhite

Carter................................62%
Reagan................................11
Anderson.............................. 9
Don't know 18

By Education
College

Carter................................30%
Reagan................................43
Anderson..............................18
Don't know 9

High School

Carter................................34%
Reagan................................39
Anderson..............................13
Don't know 14

Grade School

Carter................................43%
Reagan................................33
Anderson.............................. 9
Don't know 15

By Region
East

Carter................................29%
Reagan................................36
Anderson..............................19
Don't know 16

Midwest

Carter................................35%
Reagan................................35
Anderson..............................15
Don't know 15

South

Carter................................33%
Reagan................................40
Anderson..............................15
Don't know 12

West

Carter................................31%
Reagan................................35
Anderson..............................25
Don't know 9

By Age
18–29 Years

Carter................................32%
Reagan................................36
Anderson..............................24
Don't know 8

30–49 Years

Carter................................33%
Reagan................................41
Anderson..............................15
Don't know 11

50 Years and Over

Carter................................36%
Reagan................................40
Anderson.............................. 9
Don't know 15

Improving and dealing with environmental issues?

Carter................................37%
Reagan................................32
Anderson..............................17
Don't know 14

By Sex
Male

Carter................................38%
Reagan................................30
Anderson..............................19
Don't know 13

Female

Carter................................36%
Reagan................................34
Anderson..............................15
Don't know 15

By Race
White
Carter.............................35%
Reagan............................34
Anderson..........................18
Don't know........................13

Nonwhite
Carter.............................57%
Reagan............................14
Anderson.......................... 9
Don't know........................20

By Education
College
Carter.............................35%
Reagan............................27
Anderson..........................27
Don't know........................11

High School
Carter.............................36%
Reagan............................35
Anderson..........................13
Don't know........................16

Grade School
Carter.............................49%
Reagan............................27
Anderson.......................... 8
Don't know........................16

By Region
East
Carter.............................32%
Reagan............................33
Anderson..........................19
Don't know........................16

Midwest
Carter.............................39%
Reagan............................30
Anderson..........................16
Don't know........................15

South
Carter.............................41%
Reagan............................33
Anderson..........................13
Don't know........................13

West
Carter.............................37%
Reagan............................29
Anderson..........................23
Don't know........................11

By Age
18–29 Years
Carter.............................41%
Reagan............................27
Anderson..........................23
Don't know........................ 9

30–49 Years
Carter.............................34%
Reagan............................32
Anderson..........................21
Don't know........................13

50 Years and Over
Carter.............................38%
Reagan............................33
Anderson..........................12
Don't know........................17

Spending taxpayers' money wisely?
Carter.............................29%
Reagan............................42
Anderson..........................16
Don't know........................13

By Sex
Male
Carter.............................27%
Reagan............................43
Anderson..........................18
Don't know........................12

Female

Carter............................31%
Reagan............................41
Anderson..........................13
Don't know........................15

By Race
White

Carter............................24%
Reagan............................47
Anderson..........................16
Don't know........................13

Nonwhite

Carter............................64%
Reagan.............................9
Anderson..........................12
Don't know........................15

By Education
College

Carter............................23%
Reagan............................48
Anderson..........................19
Don't know........................10

High School

Carter............................30%
Reagan............................40
Anderson..........................16
Don't know........................14

Grade School

Carter............................40%
Reagan............................33
Anderson...........................8
Don't know........................19

By Region
East

Carter............................25%
Reagan............................40
Anderson..........................19
Don't know........................16

Midwest

Carter............................30%
Reagan............................42
Anderson..........................18
Don't know........................10

South

Carter............................33%
Reagan............................45
Anderson...........................9
Don't know........................13

West

Carter............................28%
Reagan............................39
Anderson..........................18
Don't know........................15

By Age
18–29 Years

Carter............................27%
Reagan............................39
Anderson..........................23
Don't know........................11

30–49 Years

Carter............................26%
Reagan............................43
Anderson..........................20
Don't know........................11

50 Years and Over

Carter............................33%
Reagan............................43
Anderson...........................9
Don't know........................15

Helping the poor and needy?

Carter............................49%
Reagan............................24
Anderson..........................14
Don't know........................13

By Sex
Male
Carter.............................49%
Reagan............................23
Anderson..........................15
Don't know........................13

Female
Carter.............................49%
Reagan............................24
Anderson..........................13
Don't know........................14

By Race
White
Carter.............................46%
Reagan............................26
Anderson..........................15
Don't know........................13

Nonwhite
Carter.............................69%
Reagan............................ 5
Anderson..........................10
Don't know........................16

By Education
College
Carter.............................51%
Reagan............................22
Anderson..........................17
Don't know........................10

High School
Carter.............................47%
Reagan............................25
Anderson..........................14
Don't know........................14

Grade School
Carter.............................52%
Reagan............................22
Anderson.......................... 8
Don't know........................18

By Region
East
Carter.............................45%
Reagan............................23
Anderson..........................18
Don't know........................14

Midwest
Carter.............................47%
Reagan............................24
Anderson..........................15
Don't know........................14

South
Carter.............................54%
Reagan............................25
Anderson.......................... 9
Don't know........................12

West
Carter.............................51%
Reagan............................24
Anderson..........................14
Don't know........................11

By Age
18–29 Years
Carter.............................52%
Reagan............................19
Anderson..........................19
Don't know........................10

30–49 Years
Carter.............................50%
Reagan............................22
Anderson..........................16
Don't know........................12

50 Years and Over
Carter.............................48%
Reagan............................26
Anderson..........................10
Don't know........................16

Dealing with the Arab-Israeli situation?

Carter..............................47%
Reagan.............................30
Anderson...........................9
Don't know.........................14

By Sex
Male

Carter..............................47%
Reagan.............................30
Anderson...........................12
Don't know.........................11

Female

Carter..............................46%
Reagan.............................29
Anderson...........................8
Don't know.........................17

By Race
White

Carter..............................44%
Reagan.............................32
Anderson...........................10
Don't know.........................14

Nonwhite

Carter..............................69%
Reagan.............................12
Anderson...........................7
Don't know.........................12

By Education
College

Carter..............................45%
Reagan.............................31
Anderson...........................13
Don't know.........................11

High School

Carter..............................45%
Reagan.............................32
Anderson...........................9
Don't know.........................14

Grade School

Carter..............................58%
Reagan.............................19
Anderson...........................6
Don't know.........................17

By Region
East

Carter..............................47%
Reagan.............................28
Anderson...........................11
Don't know.........................14

Midwest

Carter..............................46%
Reagan.............................29
Anderson...........................11
Don't know.........................14

South

Carter..............................48%
Reagan.............................32
Anderson...........................6
Don't know.........................14

West

Carter..............................46%
Reagan.............................30
Anderson...........................11
Don't know.........................13

By Age
18–29 Years

Carter..............................42%
Reagan.............................30
Anderson...........................17
Don't know.........................11

30–49 Years

Carter..............................46%
Reagan.............................32
Anderson...........................11
Don't know.........................11

50 Years and Over

Carter. 50%
Reagan. 28
Anderson. 6
Don't know 16

Increasing respect for the United States overseas?

Carter. 31%
Reagan. 42
Anderson. 13
Don't know 14

By Sex
Male

Carter. 29%
Reagan. 44
Anderson. 15
Don't know 12

Female

Carter. 33%
Reagan. 40
Anderson. 11
Don't know 16

By Race
White

Carter. 27%
Reagan. 46
Anderson. 13
Don't know 14

Nonwhite

Carter. 58%
Reagan. 15
Anderson. 11
Don't know 16

By Education
College

Carter. 23%
Reagan. 49
Anderson. 15
Don't know 13

High School

Carter. 33%
Reagan. 40
Anderson. 13
Don't know 14

Grade School

Carter. 45%
Reagan. 32
Anderson. 6
Don't know 17

By Region
East

Carter. 28%
Reagan. 39
Anderson. 17
Don't know 16

Midwest

Carter. 32%
Reagan. 39
Anderson. 15
Don't know 14

South

Carter. 35%
Reagan. 44
Anderson. 8
Don't know 13

West

Carter. 30%
Reagan. 48
Anderson. 12
Don't know 10

By Age
18–29 Years

Carter. 28%
Reagan. 41
Anderson. 23
Don't know 8

30–49 Years

Carter.............................29%
Reagan............................44
Anderson..........................14
Don't know 13

50 Years and Over

Carter.............................34%
Reagan............................41
Anderson.......................... 8
Don't know 17

Note: The public's, and more specifically registered voters', perceptions of the candidates' abilities closely parallel the reputations that the parties have developed in this election year. In a mid-September Gallup survey, President Jimmy Carter was considered best able to handle foreign relations by 43% of registered voters, against 37% who believe Ronald Reagan to be the most capable. Anderson received only 11%. The former California governor, representing a Republican party perceived as best for prosperity is considered better able to handle domestic affairs (42%) than is Carter (36%), with Anderson once again trailing (14%).

Whether it is the perceptions of the candidates that have shaped those of the parties or vice versa is not clear. Whatever the case may be, the peace-prosperity dichotomy between the two major parties and their standard-bearers is plainly apparent throughout the whole array of issues presented to respondents by the Gallup Poll.

This comes as no surprise in view of the campaigns that the two opposing camps have been waging since Labor Day. Carter has gone to great pains to remind the voters of Reagan's "warmonger" tendencies. Reagan's attacks on the incumbent have concentrated on the areas of unemployment and inflation.

Carter is significantly ahead on two other counts related to peace: keeping the United States out of war (50%) and dealing with the Arab-Israeli situation (47%). In contrast, Reagan's fortes are found on economic issues: reducing inflation (44%), reducing unemployment (41%), improving the energy situation (40%), spending taxpayers' money wisely (42%), and improving the economy in general (44%).

On all issues included in the survey, independent candidate John Anderson is a distant third. This fact is, to a large extent, a reflection of the public's lack of knowledge about the independent challenger. Anderson is severely handicapped by not having available to him the resources of one of the two major parties. This not only robs him of quick recognition (by association) but also makes it difficult for him to get on the ballot in many states and to finance a viable presidential campaign, including the media spots so vital to increasing public awareness of his candidacy.

Interviewing Date: 10/10–13/80
Survey #163-G

You will notice that the ten boxes on this scale go from the highest position of +5 for someone you have a very favorable opinion of all the way down to the lowest position of −5 for someone you have a very unfavorable opinion of. How far up the scale or how far down the scale would you rate:

Jimmy Carter?

Highly favorable (+5, +4).............30%
Mildly favorable (+3, +2, +1).........36
Mildly unfavorable (−1, −2, −3).......15
Highly unfavorable (−4, −5)...........16
No opinion 3

Ronald Reagan?

Highly favorable (+5, +4).............25%
Mildly favorable (+3, +2, +1).........36
Mildly unfavorable (−1, −2, −3).......20
Highly unfavorable (−4, −5)...........15
No opinion 4

John Anderson?

Highly favorable (+5, +4).............10%
Mildly favorable (+3, +2, +1).........53
Mildly unfavorable (−1, −2, −3).......17
Highly unfavorable (−4, −5)...........14
No opinion 6

Note: In the latest survey President Carter receives a larger proportion of highly favorable ratings than does Ronald Reagan. The rating is derived from a ten-point scale designed to measure the personality factor, or enthusiasm for the candidate himself. Thirty percent of Americans view Carter as highly favorable, compared to 25% for Reagan. Just two months ago the standings were reversed: Reagan, 31% highly favorable; Carter, 20%.

When a comparison is made with previous presidential years, it is found that personal enthusiasm for the two major party candidates is currently lower than it has been in nearly all campaigns over the last three decades:

Highly Favorable Ratings
Late September 1976

Carter.............................41%
Ford...............................28

October 1972

McGovern..........................21%
Nixon..............................41

Early September 1968

Humphrey..........................25%
Nixon..............................38

Mid-October 1964

Johnson............................49%
Goldwater..........................16

Mid-September 1960

Kennedy...........................42%
Nixon..............................40

Mid-October 1956

Stevenson.........................33%
Eisenhower.........................59

August 1952

Stevenson.........................37%
Eisenhower.........................47

In politics, as of today, do you consider yourself a Republican, a Democrat, or an independent?

Republican 25%
Democrat............................48
Independent 27

Note: These figures exclude the 2% to 3% of the electorate who do not classify themselves as belonging to one of these political groups.

In 1980 the number of Americans who consider themselves Democrats is greater than the number of Republicans by a 2-to-1 margin; this is virtually the same as in 1976. However, this is offset somewhat by the fact that the Democrats are less likely to have registered to vote and less likely to actually cast their ballots on election day.

What is especially noteworthy this year is the finding that the Democratic ticket is currently suffering a higher defection rate than is the Republican ticket. As many as three in ten Democrats who preferred Kennedy prior to the Democratic convention currently say they would vote for either Reagan or Anderson.

Interviewing Date: 9/12–15/80
Survey #162-G

What do you think is the most important problem facing this country today? Asked of those who named a problem: Which political party do you think can do a better job of handling the problem you have just mentioned—the Republican party or the Democratic party?

Republican 35%
Democratic..........................32
No difference (volunteered) 22
No opinion 11

Dividing equally those who say there is no difference between the parties or who do not express an opinion, the results are:

Republican 51%
Democratic..........................49

Note: Since July the Republicans have maintained a slight edge over the Democrats. This is quite significant since the last time that voters felt the Republicans could better handle the nation's problems was in October 1972, during Richard Nixon's reelection bid.

Interviewing Date: 10/10–13/80
Survey #163-G

Is your name now recorded in the registration book of the precinct or election district where you now live?

	Yes
National	72%

By Politics

Republicans	82%
Democrats	76
Independents	64

Note: The current voter registration falls below the 77% recorded at this time in 1976.

Asked of registered voters: How much thought have you given to the coming November election—quite a lot, or only a little?

Quite a lot	60%
Some (volunteered)	22
A little	16
None (volunteered)	2

By Politics
Republicans

Quite a lot	66%
Some (volunteered)	21
A little	11
None (volunteered)	2

Democrats

Quite a lot	58%
Some (volunteered)	23
A little	16
None (volunteered)	3

Independents

Quite a lot	55%
Some (volunteered)	23
A little	21
None (volunteered)	1

Note: In addition to the course of events between now and November 4, the outcome of the current close contest between the Democratic ticket of Jimmy Carter and Walter Mondale and the GOP ticket of Ronald Reagan and George Bush will depend to a great extent on four key factors: 1) enthusiasm for the candidates; 2) party loyalty; 3) perceptions of the candidates' ability to deal with key problems; and 4) voter turnout.

OCTOBER 23
PRESIDENTIAL ELECTION: THE NONWHITE VOTE— A GALLUP ANALYSIS

Interviewing Date: 9/12–15; 10/10–13/80
Survey #162-G; #163-G

Note: In the latest test elections, President Jimmy Carter continues to hold a commanding lead among nonwhite voters. His support among this group is as strong as it was in 1976 and comparable to the levels of nonwhite support enjoyed by Democratic candidates George McGovern in 1972 and Hubert Humphrey in 1968.

Results of the two latest national Gallup surveys show 75% of likely nonwhite voters supporting Carter, 13% for Ronald Reagan, 4% for John Anderson, and 8% undecided. Allocating the undecided vote proportionately, to facilitate comparison with past elections, Carter receives 82% of the support of nonwhites, compared to 14% for Reagan and 4% for Anderson. In the 1976 election, in which their vote was crucial to Carter's victory, 85% voted for Carter to 15% for Gerald Ford.

The last time the nonwhite vote for the Democratic presidential candidate was significantly lower than it is today was in the 1960 election, when 68% voted for John Kennedy and 32% for Richard Nixon. The following compares the levels of nonwhite support for Carter and for the Democratic candidates in previous presidential elections:

Vote for Democratic Candidates

By Nonwhite

1980	82%*
1976	85
1972	87
1968	85
1964	94
1960	68
1956	61
1952	79

Comparison on Key Voter Issues

Percent favoring

	Nonwhite	White
Government social programs	74%	43
Equal Rights Amendment	74	62
Prayer in public schools	74	52
Registration of all firearms	71	55
Increased defense spending	64	72
Death penalty for murder	51	53
More nuclear power plants	48	51
Homosexual teachers	40	31
Ban on all abortions	36	32

Although the president still has not quite attracted his former level of support with this group, his greatest strength is nevertheless found among nonwhites, even higher than among such traditionally Democratic groups as Catholics, Jews, and manual workers.

Despite the lower likelihood of voting among nonwhites, they are a key voting bloc because they represent a disproportionately large part of the electorate in those areas of the nation generally conceded to be the prime election battleground—the large industrial states of the Northeast and Midwest. Furthermore, given the closeness of the race in the South, the vote of nonwhites there could be decisive in the outcome on November 4.

Although Carter leads Reagan by an overwhelming margin among nonwhites, this preference reflects an almost institutionalized one for the Democratic party and candidates, rather than a particularly positive feeling about Carter himself.

Much of Carter's support is party based instead of candidate based. When nonwhites are asked to rate Carter separately, without matching him against other candidates in test races, only 50% give him a highly favorable rating. Even fewer (14%) however, give Reagan this rating.

Further evidence of the Democratic sympathies of nonwhites is seen in the relatively high proportion of this group who call themselves Democrats (78% compared to 48% of the total electorate) and in their positions on key issues, as seen in the following table:

*Figure is based on the two most recent surveys.

Insight into the "whys" behind the stated presidential choices of nonwhites can be seen from an examination of their perceptions regarding: 1) the comparative ability of each candidate to deal with national problems, particularly those of greatest concern; 2) perceptions of the personal attributes and characteristics of the candidates; and 3) what they say worries or bothers them most about each candidate.

Among nonwhites domestic concerns far overshadow international issues. Although inflation is their primary concern, as it is among whites, unemployment is rated much higher among nonwhites. Accenting these worries is the fear among 23% of nonwhites, who hold jobs outside the home, that it is very or fairly likely they will lose them within the next twelve months. With the government unemployment figure for September at 14% for this group, it is significant to note that an additional 23% feel their jobs are in jeopardy. The comparable figure for employed whites fearful of being laid off is 13%.

On the issue of unemployment, 59% of nonwhites say Carter is best able to reduce unemployment, while 15% name Reagan, and 12% Anderson. The views of whites are in sharp contrast, with 27% saying Carter is best able to reduce unemployment, 45% Reagan, and 14% Anderson.

When nonwhites are asked which candidate can best deal with inflation, 59% say Carter, 18% Reagan, and 10% Anderson, compared to whites who credit Carter 24%, Reagan 48%, and Anderson 14%. Although the margins among nonwhites in favor of Carter on both these vital economic issues are impressive, as many as three in ten name Reagan or Anderson rather than Carter as better able to cope with unemployment and inflation.

On the key issue of which candidate is perceived as best able to deal with racial issues, 68% of nonwhites name Carter, 11% Reagan, and 7% Anderson. Whites also lean toward Carter (44%), while 28% say Reagan, and 16% Anderson. And on the issue of which candidate can best improve conditions for minorities, similar results are found. Sixty-seven percent of nonwhites say Carter, only 6% Reagan, and 7% Anderson. Among whites the comparable figures are 46%, 25%, and 14%, respectively.

In regard to the perceived personal qualities and attributes of the candidates, nonwhites follow national opinion and give President Carter high marks for being "a religious person"; "a man of high moral principles"; and one who is "sympathetic to problems of the poor." At the same time, however, a significant proportion (four in ten) ascribe the following negative attributes to the president: "uncertain, indecisive, unsure"; "hard to know where he stands on issues"; "has no clear-cut program for moving the country ahead"; and "lacks strong leadership qualities."

Basic to an understanding of candidate preferences among nonwhites is their persistent worries about each of the men involved. Survey results reveal that half feel that Reagan is not sympathetic to the problems of blacks and other minority groups, while 17% express this view about Carter. And one-third of this group also shares a concern of many whites that Reagan might lead the nation into a "shooting war," while half (and four in ten voters nationally) feel that Reagan is too old for the presidency.

While one-fifth of nonwhites now vote for Reagan or Anderson, a strong trend for Carter in the closing days of the campaign is a distinct possibility in view of the traditionally Democratic voting behavior of this group. In this respect, the efforts of Senator Edward Kennedy— the top choice of nonwhites for the Democratic nomination prior to the convention—to win back Democratic voters who have strayed to Reagan or Anderson, or who are uncommitted, will be of considerable importance.

OCTOBER 26
PRESIDENTIAL ELECTION:
THE MALE AND FEMALE VOTE—
A GALLUP ANALYSIS

Interviewing Date: 9/12–15; 10/10–13/80
Survey #162-G; #163-G

Note: Results of the two latest Gallup test elections show male likely voters choosing Reagan over Carter by a wide 43% to 36% margin. Women, who have been consistently more inclined toward Carter than have men since these trial heat measurements began in March, are closely divided—42% for Reagan and 40% for Carter. These survey findings represent a reversal from 1976, when men voted for Carter 53% to 45% and women voted for Ford 51% to 48%. Independent candidate John Anderson receives the vote of 14% and 10% of male and female likely voters, respectively.

In most presidential elections the vote of women has not been crucial in determining the winner. This was true in the landslide election of 1972 when Richard Nixon defeated George McGovern and the 1964 contest when Lyndon Johnson beat Barry Goldwater. If women alone had the vote, however, Nixon would have been elected over John Kennedy in 1960; Hubert Humphrey over Nixon in 1968; and Gerald Ford over Carter in 1976.

As shown below, a somewhat higher proportion of women than men now claim affiliation with the Democratic party and proportionately fewer women say they are political independents. This may partially account for Carter's better test election showing with women than with men. However, in five of the last seven presidential elections, women have voted Republican.

Political Affiliation

	Women	Men
Democrats	51%	47%
Republicans	26	25
Independents	23	27

Voter turnout on November 4 can be crucial in case of a close election, which now appears likely. Historically, only slightly more than half of eligible voters bother to cast their ballots on election day. The importance of women voters in the coming election is especially accentuated by the fact that although the same percentage of men and women are considered very likely to vote, there are approximately 9 million more women than men in the total eligible voter population.

President Carter enjoys substantially more support from women voters than from men, but when asked which of the three major candidates could best deal with each of nineteen problems or issues, regardless of which man they planned to vote for, the proportion of both sexes citing Carter, Reagan, and Anderson is about the same.

A somewhat greater disparty is found on which of the candidates could best deal with women's rights, with 51% of men and 45% of women saying Carter, while 20% of men and 26% of women cite Reagan.

The following survey findings show the percentages of men and women as to which candidate they feel is better able to handle three key issues:

Peace and Prosperity Issues

	Women	Men
Keeping United States out of war		
Carter	49%	50%
Reagan	25	26
Anderson	11	13
Don't know	15	11
Reducing inflation		
Carter	28%	28%
Reagan	43	45
Anderson	12	15
Don't know	17	12

Reducing unemployment		
Carter	30%	34%
Reagan	42	40
Anderson	12	16
Don't know	16	10

When survey respondents were asked if there were one single issue so important that a candidate's stand on it would determine their voting behavior, about half of men and women responded affirmatively. The issues and the percentages of men and women citing each are shown below:

Bullet Issues

	Women	Men
Defense spending	36%	22%
Abortion	21	10
Homosexual teachers	20	16
Government social programs	15	21
Nuclear power generation	15	12
Equal Rights Amendment	15	7
Capital punishment	12	10
Prayer in schools	11	10
Gun registration	5	10

The candidates' stands on abortion and the Equal Rights Amendment are of considerable more importance to women than to men, but even among women neither issue ranks much above prayer in schools and nuclear power generation. Respondents were also asked whether they favored or opposed each of nine issues. The results indicate that similar proportions of men (33%) and women (30%) favor a ban on abortions, and 66% of men and 61% of women favor ERA.

When the candidates are measured on which man generates more enthusiasm or personal appeal, aside from their positions on the issues, men hold Reagan in substantially higher regard than Carter. However, the reverse is found for women, who rate Carter more highly favorable, as the following percentages show:

Personal Appeal of Candidates

	Highly favorable	
	Women	Men
Carter	32%	23%
Reagan	27	34
Anderson	10	9

OCTOBER 27
PRESIDENTIAL TRIAL HEAT—
SEMI-FINAL SURVEY*

Interviewing Date: 10/24–27/80
Survey #GO-80135

Asked of likely voters: If the presidential election were being held today, which would you vote for—the Republican candidates Reagan and Bush, the Democratic candidates Carter and Mondale, or the independent candidates Anderson and Lucey? [Those who named other persons or who were undecided were asked: As of today, do you lean more to Reagan and Bush, more to Carter and Mondale, or more to Anderson and Lucey?]

and

*Asked of likely voters: Suppose you were voting today for president and vice-president of the United States. Here is a Gallup Poll Secret Ballot listing the candidates for these offices. Will you please mark that secret ballot for the candidate you favor today and then drop the folded ballot into the box.** [Respondents who said they were undecided or refused to mark the ballot were asked: Would you please mark the ballot for the candidates toward whom you lean as of today.]*

Reagan-Bush.	39%
Carter-Mondale	45
Anderson-Lucey.	9
Other; undecided	7

By Sex
Male

Reagan-Bush.	43%
Carter-Mondale	42
Anderson-Lucey.	8
Other; undecided	7

Female

Reagan-Bush.	36%
Carter-Mondale	49
Anderson-Lucey.	9
Other; undecided	6

By Race
White

Reagan-Bush.	43%
Carter-Mondale	41
Anderson-Lucey.	9
Other; undecided	7

Nonwhite

Reagan-Bush.	5%
Carter-Mondale	83
Anderson-Lucey.	2
Other; undecided	10

By Education
College

Reagan-Bush.	47%
Carter-Mondale	38
Anderson-Lucey.	11
Other; undecided	4

High School

Reagan-Bush.	38%
Carter-Mondale	46
Anderson-Lucey.	8
Other; undecided	8

Grade School

Reagan-Bush.	23%
Carter-Mondale	63
Anderson-Lucey.	4
Other; undecided	10

By Region

East

Reagan-Bush. 36%
Carter-Mondale 47
Anderson-Lucey. 10
Other; undecided 7

Midwest

Reagan-Bush. 41%
Carter-Mondale 38
Anderson-Lucey. 10
Other; undecided 11

South

Reagan-Bush. 38%
Carter-Mondale 56
Anderson-Lucey. 2
Other; undecided 4

West

Reagan-Bush. 46%
Carter-Mondale 40
Anderson-Lucey. 11
Other; undecided 3

By Age

18–29 Years

Reagan-Bush. 44%
Carter-Mondale 39
Anderson-Lucey. 15
Other; undecided 2

30–49 Years

Reagan-Bush. 38%
Carter-Mondale 45
Anderson-Lucey. 11
Other; undecided 6

50 Years and Over

Reagan-Bush. 38%
Carter-Mondale 48
Anderson-Lucey. 5
Other; undecided 9

By Politics

Republicans

Reagan-Bush. 79%
Carter-Mondale 12
Anderson-Lucey. 5
Other; undecided 4

Democrats

Reagan-Bush. 14%
Carter-Mondale 73
Anderson-Lucey. 5
Other; undecided 8

Independents

Reagan-Bush. 44%
Carter-Mondale 28
Anderson-Lucey. 21
Other; undecided 7

Those Who Voted for Carter in 1976

Reagan-Bush. 19%
Carter-Mondale 66
Anderson-Lucey. 7
Other; undecided 8

Those Who Voted for Ford in 1976

Reagan-Bush. 70%
Carter-Mondale 16
Anderson-Lucey. 10
Other; undecided 4

*The semi-final survey had a split ballot.
**The ballot listed the names of this year's three major pairs of candidates under headings corresponding to the name of the party or political affiliation each pair represents. Each voter marked and folded his ballot and placed it in a ballot box.

Note: In the latest nationwide in-person survey the Democratic ticket of Jimmy Carter and Walter Mondale has moved ahead of the Republican ticket of Ronald Reagan and George Bush, 45% to 39%, with the independent slate of John Anderson and Patrick Lucey winning 9% of the likely vote.

In the previous mid-October survey the GOP ticket held a 45% to 42% lead over the Democratic ticket, with the independent ticket the choice of 8%. Thus, in the short interval between the two surveys the Carter slate has gained 3 percentage points and the Reagan ticket has declined by 6 points.

Factors helping to explain Carter's gains in recent weeks may be found in a recent *Newsweek* survey in which the president was seen by 52% of voters as the candidate best able to keep the nation out of a third world war, compared to 23% who named Reagan. In mid-September the results were 38% and 23%, respectively.

Also, despite continuing double-figure inflation, which the government reported was running at an annual rate of 12%, 48% of respondents in the *Newsweek* survey said they had a great deal or a fair amount of confidence in President Carter's ability to deal with the economy, against 54% with similar confidence in challenger Reagan. Since June, however, confidence in Carter's ability to handle the economy has increased by 5 percentage points, while Reagan's has slipped 9 points.

The low undecided vote in the latest Gallup trial heat is due to two principal factors: 1) the use of in-person as opposed to telephone interviews; and 2) the secret ballot technique, which approximates an actual voting situation.

It is important to bear in mind that the current survey findings refer to the popular, not the electoral vote. To report the electoral vote, it would be necessary to conduct separate full-scale surveys in each of the fifty states.

NOVEMBER 2
POLITICS AND RELIGION

Interviewing Date: 10/10–13/80
Survey #163-G

> Certain religious groups are actively working for the defeat of political candidates who do not agree with their position on certain issues. Do you think they are right or wrong to do this?

Right 28%
Wrong 60
Undecided........................... 12

By Religion
Protestants
Right 28%
Wrong 62
Undecided........................... 10

Catholics
Right 32%
Wrong 57
Undecided........................... 11

Church Members
Right 31%
Wrong 58
Undecided........................... 11

Nonchurch Members
Right 21%
Wrong 64
Undecided........................... 15

Attend Church Regularly
Right 33%
Wrong 54
Undecided........................... 13

Do Not Attend Church Regularly
Right 23%
Wrong 65
Undecided........................... 12

By Politics
Reagan-Bush Supporters
Right 30%
Wrong 59
Undecided........................... 11

Carter-Mondale Supporters
Right 26%
Wrong 62
Undecided........................... 12

Anderson-Lucey Supporters

Right 30%
Wrong 61
Undecided. 9

A Catholic cardinal recently said that it was a sin to vote for political candidates who favor abortion. Do you think the cardinal was right or wrong to make this statement?

Right 27%
Wrong 59
Undecided. 14

By Religion
Protestants

Right 26%
Wrong 61
Undecided. 13

Catholics

Right 33%
Wrong 55
Undecided. 12

Church Members

Right 30%
Wrong 57
Undecided. 13

Nonchurch Members

Right 20%
Wrong 64
Undecided. 16

Attend Church Regularly

Right 34%
Wrong 52
Undecided. 14

Do Not Attend Church Regularly

Right 22%
Wrong 64
Undecided. 14

By Politics
Reagan-Bush Supporters

Right 26%
Wrong 63
Undecided. 11

Carter-Mondale Supporters

Right 30%
Wrong 57
Undecided. 13

Anderson-Lucey Supporters

Right 20%
Wrong 74
Undecided. 6

Note: Efforts of religious leaders to tell voters which presidential candidate they should or should not vote for was not well received by a majority of American voters. Survey evidence showed that by a 2-to-1 margin voters say it is wrong for religious groups to actively work for the defeat of candidates who do not agree with their position on certain issues.

By a similar margin voters expressed their opinion that it was wrong for a Roman Catholic cardinal to tell his parishioners not to vote for candidates who favor abortion. Recently, the archbishop of Boston, Cardinal Humberto Medeiros, had a pastoral letter read in the churches of his diocese, saying it was sinful to vote for political candidates favoring abortion. In the survey Catholics disagree with the cardinal's statement to almost the same extent as does the total population.

Analysis of the survey results also shows that supporters of the leading presidential candidates lean heavily toward the view that religious groups should not work to defeat candidates who oppose their position on key issues.

Church members and regular churchgoers are more inclined than are nonchurch members and nonchurchgoers to say it is right for religious groups to follow this practice. However, majorities of the more religiously active public oppose the interference of religious groups in political activities.

NOVEMBER 3

PRESIDENTIAL TRIAL HEAT—FINAL SURVEY

Interviewing Date: 10/30–11/1/80
Special Survey

Asked of likely voters: Suppose you were voting today for president and vice-president of the United States. Here is a Gallup Poll Secret Ballot listing the candidates for these offices. Will you please mark that secret ballot for the candidates you favor today and then drop the folded ballot into the box.

Reagan-Bush......................... 47%
Carter-Mondale 44
Anderson-Lucey...................... 8
Other; undecided 1

Note: For the Gallup Poll's final preelection analysis, about 3,500 persons were interviewed in more than 300 scientifically selected election precincts across the nation. The survey results reflect the division of presidential preferences at the time the in-person interviews were conducted and do not constitute a prediction of which candidate will win the election. Events subsequent to the completion of interviewing on November 1 obviously could affect the actual vote on election day if, for example, either party gets a higher proportion of its followers to the polls than does the opposition. The winning party generally has been found to put forth more strenuous efforts at the grass-roots level on or before election day.

Following is the trend among likely voters prior to the final survey:

Choices of Likely Voters

October 24–27

Reagan-Bush......................... 39%
Carter-Mondale 45
Anderson-Lucey...................... 9
Other; undecided 7

October 10–13

Reagan-Bush......................... 44%
Carter-Mondale 41
Anderson-Lucey...................... 9
Other; undecided 6

September 12–15

Reagan-Bush......................... 41%
Carter-Mondale 37
Anderson-Lucey...................... 15
Other; undecided 7

It is important to bear in mind that the current survey findings refer to the popular vote, not the electoral vote. To report the electoral vote, it would be necessary to conduct separate full-scale surveys in each of the fifty states.

Some error is inherent in all sample surveys; no measuring instrument dealing with human behavior is perfect. Although the problems that arise in every election seem to be similar to those that have been faced in previous elections, each contest involves unique variables and problems of measurement. A margin of error of plus or minus 3 percentage points either way in the vote for each candidate should be taken into account.

The interviewing areas used in this survey constitute a probability sample of election precincts throughout the United States. Selection of households and respondents within households is not left to the discretion of interviewers but is controlled by a procedure designed to provide an objective, systematic choice of respondents.

One of the continuing problems in election polling in this country is that of voter turnout. If every adult in the nation voted, one of the most serious sources of possible polling error would be eliminated. In practice, however, far fewer eligible voters bother to cast their ballots. Actually, in 1976 only 54% of the electorate voted in the presidential election.

The Gallup Poll uses a battery of screening questions in order to identify those voters most likely to go to the polls. These questions are designed to measure such factors as interest in politics, amount of thought given to the upcoming election, and whether or not the person is registered to vote. The final results are based on those individuals among the approximately 3,500 interviewed who were judged, on the basis of their replies to these screening questions, to be most likely to vote—approximately 1,900 persons.

Another major problem is the undecided vote. In the voting booth a choice has to be made, but in survey situations some respondents are reluctant to actually choose and prefer to call themselves undecided. The final figures reported by the Gallup Poll always reflect an allocation of the undecided vote to the major candidates. If this step were not taken there would be no clear way to judge how close a particular poll has come in estimating the vote.

The average deviation, that is, the amount by which final Gallup Poll figures have differed from the actual election results, has been 2.4 percentage points in surveys beginning in 1936. For fifteen national elections (presidential and congressional) beginning in 1950, the Gallup Poll's accuracy has improved to 1.4 percentage points. The largest deviation occurred in 1936, when the Gallup Poll missed by 6.8 percentage points. The smallest came in the 1972 presidential race, with a deviation of only 0.2 of 1%.

NOVEMBER 5
PRESIDENTIAL ELECTION—
A GALLUP ANALYSIS

Note: President-elect Ronald Reagan's sweeping victory in Tuesday's November 4 election reflects one of the most dramatic shifts ever recorded in voter preferences in the last week of a presidential campaign. Based on unofficial returns, Reagan received 50.75% of the popular vote to 41.02% for Carter.

Just prior to the presidential debate on October 28, President Jimmy Carter led Reagan 45% to 39%. Immediately following the debate the race narrowed to Reagan 44% and Carter 43%. In the final Gallup survey, conducted

Thursday, October 30 through Saturday, November 1, Reagan held an edge over Carter, 47% to 44%.

The following is the trend in Gallup surveys during the last days of the campaign:

Final Eleven Days of Campaign

Saturday, October 25–
Sunday, October 26

Reagan-Bush	42%
Carter-Mondale	45
Anderson-Lucey	9
Other; undecided	4

Wednesday, October 29–
Thursday, October 30
(Debate held Tuesday, October 28)

Reagan-Bush	44%
Carter-Mondale	43
Anderson-Lucey	8
Other; undecided	5

Thursday, October 30–
Saturday, November 1
(Hostage demands set by Iran on
Friday, October 31)

Reagan-Bush	47%
Carter-Mondale	44
Anderson-Lucey	8
Other*	1

*Unofficial Election Results***

Reagan-Bush	50.75%
Carter-Mondale	41.02
Anderson-Lucey	6.61
Other	1.62

*Undecided vote allocated in final survey figures.
**Reported by state election boards and compiled by the Federal Election Commission. The commission also reported that 53.95% of the eligible voters cast ballots, the lowest since the 1948 election.

As evidenced by these findings, for the third time in twenty years presidential debates have played an important role in the election outcome. During the closing days of the campaign the trend shows that while Carter's momentum was stalled as a result of the debate and that he never regained his previous level of support, popular backing for Reagan accelerated, undoubtedly aided by the public's discouragement and frustration over the dramatic developments in the Iranian hostage situation.

In 1976 the second Ford-Carter debate—on foreign policy—appeared to have dealt a fatal blow to President Gerald Ford's comeback in that race. In early September of that year, Ford trailed Carter by 18 points. Ford then moved into a virtual tie with Carter on the eve of the second debate, which the public felt was won by Carter. That contest brought Ford's momentum to a halt and the Democratic challenger began to recoup some of his earlier losses. The election in 1976 was one of the closest in history, with Carter winning 51.1% of the popular vote for the major-party candidates, compared to 48.9% for Ford.

And in 1960, Vice-president Richard Nixon led Senator John Kennedy prior to the first televised debate. Following this forum, which the public by a 2-to-1 margin thought was won by Kennedy, Nixon lost the lead and never regained it. His loss to Kennedy was even closer than the 1976 election; Kennedy won 50.1% of the popular vote for the major-party candidates and Nixon 49.9%.

Demographic characteristics such as age, sex, and occupation of voters are not recorded on election ballots. It is only through survey methods of proven accuracy that such information can be collected and analyzed in presidential elections. The following shows the vote by demographic breakdowns, which were prepared by the Gallup Poll and are tailored to actual results:

Reagan-Bush..........................51%
Carter-Mondale 41
Anderson-Lucey...................... 7
Other 1

By Sex
Male

Reagan-Bush..........................53%
Carter-Mondale 38
Anderson-Lucey...................... 7
Other 2

Female

Reagan-Bush..........................49%
Carter-Mondale 44
Anderson-Lucey...................... 6
Other 1

By Race
White

Reagan-Bush..........................56%
Carter-Mondale 36
Anderson-Lucey...................... 7
Other 1

Nonwhite

Reagan-Bush..........................10%
Carter-Mondale 86
Anderson-Lucey...................... 2
Other 2

By Education
College

Reagan-Bush..........................53%
Carter-Mondale 35
Anderson-Lucey......................10
Other 2

High School

Reagan-Bush..........................51%
Carter-Mondale 43
Anderson-Lucey...................... 5
Other 1

Grade School

Reagan-Bush..........................42%
Carter-Mondale 54
Anderson-Lucey...................... 3
Other 1

By Age

18–29 Years

Reagan-Bush........................41%
Carter-Mondale 47
Anderson-Lucey......................11
Other 1

30–49 Years

Reagan-Bush........................52%
Carter-Mondale 38
Anderson-Lucey..................... 8
Other 2

50 Years and Over

Reagan-Bush........................54%
Carter-Mondale 41
Anderson-Lucey..................... 4
Other 1

By Religion

Protestants

Reagan-Bush........................54%
Carter-Mondale 39
Anderson-Lucey..................... 6
Other 1

Catholics

Reagan-Bush........................47%
Carter-Mondale 46
Anderson-Lucey..................... 6
Other 1

Jews

Reagan-Bush........................38%
Carter-Mondale 52
Anderson-Lucey..................... 7
Other 3

By Politics

Republicans

Reagan-Bush........................86%
Carter-Mondale 8
Anderson-Lucey..................... 5
Other 1

Democrats

Reagan-Bush........................26%
Carter-Mondale 69
Anderson-Lucey..................... 4
Other 1

Independents

Reagan-Bush........................55%
Carter-Mondale 29
Anderson-Lucey......................14
Other 2

By Occupation

Professional and Business

Reagan-Bush........................55%
Carter-Mondale 33
Anderson-Lucey......................10
Other 2

Clerical and Sales

Reagan-Bush........................51%
Carter-Mondale 40
Anderson-Lucey..................... 9
Other ....***

Manual Workers

Reagan-Bush........................46%
Carter-Mondale 48
Anderson-Lucey..................... 5
Other 1

Farmers

Reagan-Bush........................61%
Carter-Mondale 31
Anderson-Lucey..................... 7
Other 1

Non-Labor Force

Reagan-Bush........................50%
Carter-Mondale 46
Anderson-Lucey..................... 3
Other 1

Labor Union Families Only

Reagan-Bush 43%
Carter-Mondale 50
Anderson-Lucey 5
Other 2

***Less than 1%

These findings are based on in-person interviews with 1,975 adults (eighteen years and older) who were considered to be likely voters. The interviews were conducted in more than 300 scientifically selected localities across the nation between October 30 and November 1. For results on the total sample of likely voters, one can say with 95% confidence that the error attributable to sampling and other random effects could be 3 percentage points in either direction.

In comparison with the above figures, the following is a breakdown for the 1976 election:

Carter-Mondale 50%
Ford-Dole 48
Other 2

By Sex
Male

Carter-Mondale 53%
Ford-Dole 45
Other 2

Female

Carter-Mondale 48%
Ford-Dole 51
Other 1

By Race
White

Carter-Mondale 46%
Ford-Dole 52
Other 2

Nonwhite

Carter-Mondale 85%
Ford-Dole 15
Other . . . . ***

By Education
College

Carter-Mondale 42%
Ford-Dole 55
Other 3

High School

Carter-Mondale 54%
Ford-Dole 46
Other . . . . ***

Grade School

Carter-Mondale 58%
Ford-Dole 41
Other 1

By Age
18–29 Years

Carter-Mondale 53%
Ford-Dole 45
Other 2

30–49 Years

Carter-Mondale 48%
Ford-Dole 49
Other 3

50 Years and Over

Carter-Mondale 52%
Ford-Dole 48
Other . . . . ***

By Religion
Protestants

Carter-Mondale 46%
Ford-Dole 53
Other 1

Catholics

Carter-Mondale 57%
Ford-Dole 42
Other . . . . ***

By Politics

Republicans

Carter-Mondale 9%
Ford-Dole 91
Other. . . . . ***

Democrats

Carter-Mondale 82%
Ford-Dole 18
Other. . . . . ***

Independents

Carter-Mondale 38%
Ford-Dole 57
Other 5

By Occupation

Professional and Business

Carter-Mondale 42%
Ford-Dole 56
Other 2

Clerical and Sales

Carter-Mondale 50%
Ford-Dole 48
Other 2

Manual Workers

Carter-Mondale 58%
Ford-Dole 41
Other . . . . ***

Labor Union Families Only

Carter-Mondale 63%
Ford-Dole 36
Other . . . . ***

***Less than 1%

NOVEMBER 6
CONFIDENCE IN INSTITUTIONS

Interviewing Date: 10/10–13/80
Survey #163-G

I am going to read you a list of institutions in American society. Would you tell me how much confidence you, yourself, have in each one—a great deal, quite a lot, some, or very little:

The church or organized religion?

	Great deal or quite a lot
National	66%

By Sex

Male. 65%
Female. 69

By Race

White. 65%
Nonwhite. 71

By Education

College. 63%
High school. 67
Grade school. 68

By Region

East 63%
Midwest. 73
South 69
West. 54

By Age

18–29 years 59%
30–49 years. 62
50 years and over. 75

Banks and banking?

National 60%

By Sex

Male. 58%
Female. 62

By Race

White. 61%
Nonwhite. 56

By Education

College	64%
High school	60
Grade school	55

By Region

East	59%
Midwest	65
South	63
West	51

By Age

18–29 years	53%
30–49 years	58
50 years and over	68

The military?

National	52%

By Sex

Male	53%
Female	51

By Race

White	53%
Nonwhite	47

By Education

College	47%
High school	54
Grade school	54

By Region

East	50%
Midwest	52
South	58
West	46

By Age

18–29 years	48%
30–49 years	51
50 years and over	56

The public schools?

National	51%

By Sex

Male	51%
Female	52

By Race

White	51%
Nonwhite	55

By Education

College	47%
High school	52
Grade school	55

By Region

East	50%
Midwest	53
South	55
West	44

By Age

18–29 years	52%
30–49 years	51
50 years and over	51

The United States Supreme Court?

National	47%

By Sex

Male	48%
Female	47

By Race

White	48%
Nonwhite	46

By Education

College	56%
High school	44
Grade school	46

By Region

East	51%
Midwest	49
South	45
West	44

By Age

18–29 years	51%
30–49 years	46
50 years and over	46

Newspapers?

National	42%

By Sex

Male	43%
Female	41

By Race

White	41%
Nonwhite	47

By Education

College	41%
High school	43
Grade school	40

By Region

East	44%
Midwest	44
South	42
West	37

By Age

18–29 years	48%
30–49 years	37
50 years and over	42

Organized labor?

National	35%

By Sex

Male	36%
Female	34

By Race

White	33%
Nonwhite	48

By Education

College	24%
High school	40
Grade school	40

By Region

East	38%
Midwest	34
South	34
West	35

By Age

18–29 years	39%
30–49 years	34
50 years and over	34

By Union Membership

Labor union members	53%
Non-labor union members	30

Congress?

National	34%

By Sex

Male	34%
Female	34

By Race

White	34%
Nonwhite	34

By Education

College	35%
High school	33
Grade school	38

By Region

East	38%
Midwest	34
South	34
West	30

By Age

18–29 years	34%
30–49 years	31
50 years and over	37

Television?

National	33%

By Sex

Male	33%
Female	33

By Race

White	32%
Nonwhite	42

By Education

College	23%
High school	35
Grade school	46

By Region

East	37%
Midwest	29
South	34
West	32

By Age

18–29 years	33%
30–49 years	28
50 years and over	38

Big business?

National	29%

By Sex

Male	33%
Female	25

By Race

White	28%
Nonwhite	34

By Education

College	32%
High school	28
Grade school	23

By Region

East	32%
Midwest	28
South	29
West	25

By Age

18–29 years	31%
30–49 years	27
50 years and over	29

By Union Membership

Labor union members	25%
Non-labor union members	30

Note: As a whole the public's confidence in key institutions in our society is no higher today than in the days of Watergate in the early 1970s. In fact, for none of the institutions tested has there been more than a marginal gain in confidence from earlier surveys, and in the case of certain institutions it is actually lower.

The proportion of Americans who now say they have a great deal or quite a lot of confidence in most of the ten institutions tested shows little or no change from earlier surveys, while declines are recorded for others. For example, fewer today (34%) than in 1973 (42%) state that they have this confidence level in the U.S. Congress. Confidence in the public schools is down from 58% in 1973 to 51% today, and a 6-point decline has occurred since 1975 in the case of the military, with 52% expressing a comparable opinion. Confidence in newspapers also has fallen sharply since 1979, but the current level (42%) continues to be higher than that recorded for television (33%).

The church or organized religion receives the highest ratings for confidence, as it has in each of the four previous surveys. Two out of three Americans (66%) hold this institution in high regard. The remaining institutions are banks and banking, with a rating of 60%, followed by the U.S. Supreme Court (47%), and big business (29%), which has experienced a steady downtrend since 1975.

The current views of young adults (18- to 29-year-olds) offer little cause for optimism for the immediate future. The proportion of this group who express a high degree of confidence is no more than that of persons 30 and older in the case of each institution tested, and in some cases it is lower.

NOVEMBER 13
PRESIDENTIAL ELECTION—
A GALLUP ANALYSIS

Various Surveys*

Note: An examination of political indicators and the views of voters on key issues shows that the Reagan landslide was not so much the result of an ideological shift to the right among the electorate as dissatisfaction with the leadership of the nation and a desire for change.

Gallup Poll measurements of both the ideological stance of the electorate and public opinion on certain key issues reveal surprisingly little change since the presidential election four years ago. For example, when Americans are asked to place themselves on a left-right continuum, the proportion who are right of center is virtually the same today as it was in the presidential election year of 1976. The following percentages are based on those who indicated a position:

*In each of the surveys conducted in scientifically selected localities throughout the nation, a minimum of 1,500 adults (eighteen and over) were interviewed. For results based on samples of this size, one can say with 95% confidence that the error attributable to sampling and other random effects could be 3 percentage points in either direction.

Political Ideology

	1980	1976
Right of center	32%	31%
Middle of the road (volunteered)	49	45
Left of center	19	24

During this year's campaign Reagan was perceived by voters to be not only to the right of President Carter but also to the right of where voters place themselves on the left-right scale. Gallup Polls in previous election years have shown that the candidate whose perceived ideological stance more closely matches that of the electorate has fared better in the election. However, this clearly was not the case this year, strongly suggesting that factors other than those related to political philosophy were crucial to Reagan's victory.

Paralleling the findings on political ideology are those on political affiliation, which likewise show little change in the party affiliation of the electorate since 1976:

Political Affiliation

	1980	1976
Republicans	26%	23%
Democrats	48	48
Independents	26	29

Not only is there little evidence of a swing to the right in terms of voter self-perceptions but also little change has been found on those issues on which the views of conservatives and liberals frequently diverge: abortion, the death penalty, the Equal Rights Amendment, gun control, and a balanced federal budget. The trend in attitudes of Americans toward these four issues are shown below:

Abortion

	1980	1979	1977	1975
Legal, any circumstances	25%	22%	22%	21%
Legal, certain circumstances	53	54	55	54
Illegal, all circumstances	18	19	19	22
No opinion	4	5	4	3

Death Penalty for Murder

(Based on those expressing an opinion)

	1980	1974
Favor	56%	64%
Oppose	44	36

Equal Rights Amendment

(Based on those aware of ERA)

	1978	1976	1975
Favor	58%	57%	58%
Oppose	31	24	24
No opinion	11	19	18

Registration of Firearms

(Based on those expressing an opinion)

	1980	1974
Favor	62%	72%
Oppose	38	28

Balanced Federal Budget

	1979	1978	1976
Favor	78%	81%	78%
Oppose	12	11	13
No opinion	10	8	9

The prime reason for Carter's defeat was growing dissatisfaction with his leadership rather than any apparent conservative tide among the electorate. In a series of surveys of the public's perceptions of the personality traits of the three leading presidential candidates, the proportion of the public saying Carter "has strong leadership qualities," already low in January at 34%, sunk yet further in the latest survey.

Parallel declines in the proportions of voters crediting Carter with possessing other traits related to leadership likewise have been in evidence:

Carter Leadership Traits

September 1980

Has strong leadership qualities 29%
Has a well-defined program for
   moving the country ahead 24
Decisive, sure of himself............... 35
Offers imaginative, innovative
   solutions to national problems........ 34

January 1980

Has strong leadership qualities 34%
Has a well-defined program for
   moving the country ahead 31
Decisive, sure of himself............... 39
Offers imaginative, innovative
   solutions to national problems........ 41

Further widespread lack of confidence in President Carter's leadership is seen in the decline in his job performance rating. In early December 1979, four weeks after the American hostages were seized in Iran, as many as 61% of Americans voiced approval of his performance in office; in mid-September 1980 only 37% approved.

NOVEMBER 16
KEY ELECTION ISSUES

Interviewing Date: 9/12–15/80
Survey #162-G

This card lists various proposals being discussed in this country today. [Respondents were handed a card listing various issues.] Would you tell me whether you generally favor or generally oppose each of these proposals:

Increased defense spending?

Favor............................... 69%
Oppose............................ 27
Don't know 4

Equal Rights Amendment?

Favor............................... 64%
Oppose............................ 33
Don't know 3

Registration of all firearms?

Favor............................... 60%
Oppose............................ 37
Don't know 3

Prayer in public schools?

Favor 55%
Oppose 42
Don't know 3

Death penalty for murder?

Favor 54%
Oppose 43
Don't know 3

More nuclear power plants?

Favor 45%
Oppose 51
Don't know 4

Ban on all abortions?

Favor 31%
Oppose 65
Don't know 4

Note: Recent Gallup survey evidence indicates that President-elect Ronald Reagan and the U.S. public do not see eye to eye on two key issues that figured prominently in this year's presidential election campaign—the Equal Rights Amendment and a ban on abortion.

While Reagan opposes the ERA, the public endorses it by an overwhelming 2-to-1 margin, and while the president-elect favors a ban on all abortions, except when the life of the mother is at stake, the public opposes such a measure by 65%. On the other hand, the American people overwhelmingly side with Reagan on other issues, most notably increased defense spending.

A national sample of adults was asked to vote on seven key issues in a survey conducted during the just completed presidential campaign. Those surveyed voted heavily in favor of the registration of all firearms, the ERA, and increased outlays for defense. They leaned toward support of requiring prayer in the public schools, and of a mandatory death penalty for anyone convicted of murder, while the construction of more nuclear power plants was opposed by a narrow margin. The strongest opposition is expressed on the issue of banning all abortions.

It is interesting to note that the views of Republicans and Democrats differ little on each of the seven issues, with the notable exception of the ERA. Slightly more than half of Republicans (54%) favor this amendment, compared to 69% of Democrats.

NOVEMBER 20
UNITED NATIONS

Interviewing Date: 9/12–15/80
Survey #162-G

In general, do you feel the United Nations is doing a good job or a poor job in trying to solve the problems it has had to face?

Good job 31%
Poor job 53
No opinion 16

By Sex
Male

Good job 30%
Poor job 58
No opinion 12

Female

Good job 31%
Poor job 49
No opinion 20

By Education
College

Good job 34%
Poor job 56
No opinion 10

High School

Good job 30%
Poor job 54
No opinion 16

Grade School

Good job 28%
Poor job 45
No opinion 27

By Region

East

Good job 33%
Poor job 54
No opinion 13

Midwest

Good job 30%
Poor job 53
No opinion 17

South

Good job 32%
Poor job 50
No opinion 18

West

Good job 25%
Poor job 59
No opinion 16

By Age

18–29 Years

Good job 34%
Poor job 49
No opinion 17

30–49 Years

Good job 34%
Poor job 53
No opinion 13

50 Years and Over

Good job 26%
Poor job 57
No opinion 17

By Politics

Republicans

Good job 24%
Poor job 60
No opinion 16

Democrats

Good job 36%
Poor job 48
No opinion 16

Independents

Good job 32%
Poor job 54
No opinion 14

Reagan Supporters

Good job 24%
Poor job 61
No opinion 15

Carter Supporters

Good job 39%
Poor job 44
No opinion 17

Anderson Supporters

Good job 32%
Poor job 58
No opinion 10

Note: The Gallup Poll has measured the public's attitude toward the United Nations since its formation in 1945, using questions appropriate to the international situation at the time. At no point since then has satisfaction with the overall performance of the world organization been as low as it is today. Currently, only three Americans in ten (31%) feel that the United Nations is doing a good job in trying to solve the problem it has had to face, while 53% say it is doing a poor job.

Although these latest findings are not significantly lower than those recorded in 1975, when the Gallup Poll's last assessment of the world body was taken, they are far below the ratings obtained in both 1956 and 1967, when about half the public said the United Nations was doing a good job.

The sharp decline since 1967 in approval of UN performance has occurred in every population group but has been most pronounced among Republicans, who in that year gave the United Nations a 50% positive rating compared to 35% in 1975 and 24% in 1980. By comparison, in the same year a similar appraisal (53%) was given by the Democrats. This figure dropped abruptly to 29% approval in 1975 but climbed to 36% in the latest survey.

Backers of President-elect Ronald Reagan are most critical of this world body, and their rating of 24% mirrors that of all Republicans. Thirty-nine percent of Jimmy Carter's supporters say that the United Nations is doing a good job, not significantly different from the 36% of all Democrats who express this opinion. And the 32% of independent candidate John Anderson's backers who say the United Nations is doing a good job is identical to that given by all independents.

Women have been somewhat more favorably disposed toward the United Nations than have men, at least until the 1980 survey that shows no meaningful differences between the sexes—31% of women and 30% of men approve of the way the United Nations is carrying out its responsibilities. However, in 1967, 52% of women and 47% of men expressed this view, while in 1975 the female and male approval ratings were 36% and 28%, respectively.

Older persons consistently have been less sanguine about the United Nations than have those under fifty years of age. Forty-five percent of this group had a positive impression in 1967, compared to 25% in 1975 and 26% in 1980. In contrast, 53% of those under fifty gave this organization a positive performance in 1967, 37% in 1975, and 34% today.

Here is the trend since 1956, showing a steady decline in the proportion saying the United Nations is doing a good job:

	Good job	Poor job	No opinion
1975	33%	51%	16%
1971	35	43	22
1970	44	40	16
1967	49	35	16
1956	51	37	12

NOVEMBER 23
CAMPAIGN CHANGES

Interviewing Date: 11/7–10/80
Survey #164-G

Would you like to see any changes in the way political campaigns are conducted?

Yes, would 53%
No, would not........................ 30
Don't know 17

Asked of those who replied in the affirmative: In what ways?

Cut expense; too expensive and costly ... 26%
Shorten campaign; too long; starts
  too early 24
Clean up campaign; dignify campaigns;
  more truthful campaigns............. 20
Select candidates by popular vote 12
Less media coverage 6
Prevent television from reporting
  results until polls close............. 5
More television debates............... 5
More definition and discussion
  of the issues 4
More attention given to third parties..... 3
Equal funds for candidates 3
Other 7
Don't know 9
                                       124%*

*Total adds to more than 100% due to multiple responses.

Note: The current survey indicates that the American public wants to put even tighter limits on campaign spending than those already in effect. Ingrained in their thinking is the belief that every person should have an equal opportunity to run for office and that money should not be a deciding factor.

The public also believes the federal government should provide a fixed amount of money for the election campaigns of candidates for Congress and at the same time prohibit all other contributions. In the latest survey on this issue, 57% favor public financing for congressional candidates; 30% are opposed.

NOVEMBER 27
IRANIAN SITUATION

Interviewing Date: 11/7–10/80
Survey #164-G

Have you heard or read about the Iranian situation?

Yes................................. 97%
No................................. 3

Asked of those who replied in the affirmative: Do you happen to recall any of the demands the Iranian government has made in exchange for the release of the hostages?

Could name one or more of the
   demands........................... 74%
Could not name any of the demands..... 26

Asked of those who named a demand (the "informed public"): What, if anything, do you think the United States should do about the situation?

Continue negotiations; wait it out 30%
Apply more (nonmilitary) pressure...... 14
Use military force 13
Meet Iran's demands; return assets...... 12
Don't compromise national honor....... 12
Deport Iranians in United States;
   swap for hostages 2
Miscellaneous........................ 4
Don't know 21
                                         108%*

*Total adds to more than 100% due to multiple responses.

Also asked of the "informed public": In the war between Iraq and Iran, are your sympathies more with Iraq or more with Iran?

More with Iraq....................... 27%
More with Iran 6
Neither country (volunteered) 49
No opinion 18

Note: The dominant mood of the American people as the Iranian hostage situation enters its second year is one of impotence and frustration that our government is powerless to do anything more than it has done already to effect the release of the hostages. Yet, relatively few (13%) advocate the use of military force.

No broad public consensus is found on what steps the U.S. government should now take to obtain the release of the fifty-two Americans held hostage in Iran since November 4, 1979. About one in three (30%) of the "informed public" feels that our government should continue to negotiate or wait it out until the Iranians release the hostages. Other measures suggested include putting more pressure on Iran, short of military intervention (14%); meeting Iran's demands (12%); and not giving in to the demands if it means compromising our national honor (12%).

On November 2 the Iranian Parliament set forth four demands for the hostages' release: a pledge that the United States will not interfere in Iranian affairs; cancellation of financial claims against Iran; return of the late shah's property; and release of Iranian assets held in this country. Although the U.S. government has agreed to Iran's demands "as a basis for resolution of the crisis," the details have yet to be ironed out. At this writing, Prime Minister Mohammed Ali Rajai of Iran has asked the United States for either a positive or a negative response to Tehran's conditions.

The dramatic announcement of the Iranian demands, coming as it did two days before the U.S. general election was seen by many observers to have clearly worked in GOP candidate Ronald Reagan's favor. Public discouragement and frustration rose after it became obvious that these demands would be difficult to meet.

NOVEMBER 30
ILLEGAL ALIENS

Interviewing Date: 11/7–10/80
Survey #164-G

Do you think it should or should not be against the law to employ a person who has come into the United States without proper papers?

Should 76%
Should not 18
No opinion 6

By Race
White

Should 77%
Should not 18
No opinion 5

Nonwhite

Should 67%
Should not 21
No opinion 12

By Education
College

Should 80%
Should not 16
No opinion 4

High School

Should 77%
Should not 18
No opinion 5

Grade School

Should 64%
Should not 22
No opinion 14

By Region
East

Should 74%
Should not 19
No opinion 7

Midwest

Should 79%
Should not 14
No opinion 7

South

Should 75%
Should not 19
No opinion 6

West

Should 73%
Should not 23
No opinion 4

By Occupation
White Collar

Should 77%
Should not 19
No opinion 4

Blue Collar

Should 76%
Should not 17
No opinion 7

Blue Collar—Skilled

Should 79%
Should not 16
No opinion 5

Blue Collar—Unskilled

Should 74%
Should not 18
No opinion 8

Do you believe everyone in the United States should be required to carry an identification card such as a Social Security card, or not?

Should 62%
Should not 33
No opinion 5

By Race
White

Should 61%
Should not 34
No opinion 5

Nonwhite

Should 66%
Should not 21
No opinion 13

By Education
College

Should 44%
Should not 52
No opinion 4

High School

Should 68%
Should not 27
No opinion 5

Grade School

Should 75%
Should not 15
No opinion 10

By Region
East

Should 56%
Should not 39
No opinion 5

Midwest

Should 63%
Should not 30
No opinion 7

South

Should 69%
Should not 26
No opinion 5

West

Should 58%
Should not 37
No opinion 5

By Occupation
White Collar

Should 47%
Should not 50
No opinion 3

Blue Collar

Should 71%
Should not 25
No opinion 4

Blue Collar—Skilled

Should 66%
Should not 32
No opinion 2

Blue Collar—Unskilled

Should 75%
Should not 18
No opinion 7

It has been proposed that illegal aliens who have been in the United States for seven years be allowed to remain in the United States. Do you favor or oppose this proposal?

Favor 37%
Oppose 52
No opinion 11

By Race
White

Favor 36%
Oppose 54
No opinion 10

Nonwhite

Favor 45%
Oppose 37
No opinion 18

By Education
College

Favor 38%
Oppose 53
No opinion 9

High School

Favor...............................35%
Oppose...........................56
No opinion 9

Grade School

Favor...............................42%
Oppose...........................37
No opinion 21

By Region
East

Favor...............................41%
Oppose...........................47
No opinion 12

Midwest

Favor...............................31%
Oppose...........................58
No opinion 11

South

Favor...............................37%
Oppose...........................51
No opinion 12

West

Favor...............................42%
Oppose...........................51
No opinion 7

By Occupation
White Collar

Favor...............................39%
Oppose...........................54
No opinion 7

Blue Collar

Favor...............................37%
Oppose...........................52
No opinion 11

Blue Collar—Skilled

Favor...............................36%
Oppose...........................55
No opinion 9

Blue Collar—Unskilled

Favor...............................38%
Oppose...........................49
No opinion 13

Note: U.S. citizens take a hard line toward illegal aliens, with three out of four adults (76%) favoring a law that would make it illegal to employ a person who has entered the United States without proper papers. Majorities in each region of the country favor such a law. These results closely parallel those recorded in October 1977, when 72% favored such a law.

In addition, the public strongly supports a proposal requiring all U.S. citizens and permanent resident aliens to carry an identification card. This would make it possible for perspective employers to distinguish illegal aliens from legal job seekers.

The public's views also were sought regarding a proposal made by President Carter to grant permanent resident status to all aliens who entered this country illegally and have been in the country for seven years. Survey respondents vote against this proposal 52% to 37%. Almost identical survey results were recorded in 1977.

The hard-line attitude of the public stems in considerable measure from concern over the state of the economy and fear that illegal aliens will take jobs from U.S. citizens. For example, persons engaged in manual work, particularly those in unskilled jobs, are more likely to favor an identification card than are those in white-collar jobs.

Mexican nationals are by far the largest group of illegal immigrants in the United States, with estimates of their numbers ranging from 500,000 to as many as 4 million. Social scientists predict that demand for Mexican workers will increase by 5 to 15 million over the next two decades as fewer young Americans enter the labor market, and as women and resident minority workers move out of unskilled jobs.

However, about one-third of all immigrants to the United States eventually leave and either return to their home countries or to go to third countries, according to estimates prepared for the Select Commission on Migration and Refugee Policy.

President-elect Ronald Reagan's advisers are reportedly working on a program to issue temporary visas to large numbers of Mexicans who, like a majority of undocumented workers, do not intend to remain permanently but seek to earn money that they can take back to Mexico.

DECEMBER 4
ELECTORAL COLLEGE

Interviewing Date: 11/7–10/80
Survey #164-G

Would you approve or disapprove of an amendment to the Constitution which would do away with the Electoral College and base the election of a president on the total vote cast throughout the nation?

Approve............................67%
Disapprove 19
No opinion 14

By Sex
Male

Approve........................... 70%
Disapprove 21
No opinion 9

Female

Approve............................64%
Disapprove 17
No opinion 19

By Education
College

Approve............................69%
Disapprove 23
No opinion 8

High School

Approve............................69%
Disapprove 17
No opinion 14

Grade School

Approve............................56%
Disapprove 16
No opinion 28

By Region
East

Approve............................64%
Disapprove 22
No opinion 14

Midwest

Approve............................65%
Disapprove 18
No opinion 17

South

Approve............................65%
Disapprove 18
No opinion 17

West

Approve............................77%
Disapprove 14
No opinion 9

By Age
18–29 Years

Approve............................69%
Disapprove 21
No opinion 10

30–49 Years

Approve............................69%
Disapprove 17
No opinion 14

50 Years and Over

Approve. 63%
Disapprove 19
No opinion 18

By Politics

Republicans

Approve. 62%
Disapprove 28
No opinion 10

Democrats

Approve. 66%
Disapprove 16
No opinion 18

Independents

Approve. 73%
Disapprove 15
No opinion 12

Note: If a nationwide referendum were being held today, a large majority of the electorate would vote in favor of a proposed constitutional amendment that would base the election of presidents on direct popular vote, abolishing the Electoral College that was written into the Constitution in 1787.

In a Gallup Poll conducted shortly after this year's election, two persons in three (67%) approved of such an amendment. Similar majorities have backed this plan in five surveys dating back to 1966. The greatest support was recorded after the 1968 election, when Richard Nixon defeated Hubert Humphrey in one of the closest elections in history. In that survey eight persons in ten called for the elimination of the Electoral College. Today, 19% oppose such a change and 14% are undecided.

Although Ronald Reagan's decisive victory on November 4 made elimination of the Electoral College seem less urgent for some people, John Anderson's independent candidacy and the closeness of the race between President Jimmy Carter and GOP candidate Reagan earlier in the campaign made it a distinct possibility that neither of the two major party contenders would receive an electoral vote majority, in which case the House of Representatives would have decided the winner. However, Reagan won 51% of the popular vote to 41% for Carter and 7% for Anderson. This translated into a lop-sided electoral vote of 489 for Reagan to 49 for Carter.

Heavy support for a constitutional amendment to replace the Electoral College with direct popular elections is found in every major population group, including Republicans, Democrats, and political independents. However, substantially more Republicans (28%) than Democrats (16%) oppose elimination of the Electoral College, perhaps reflecting GOP satisfaction with a system that delivered such a resounding victory to their candidate.

The present system of voting for electors, who in turn vote for their preferred candidate, is the result of a compromise reached at the Constitutional convention in 1787. The direct election of presidents was opposed by those who believed that the people were not well enough informed to make an intelligent judgment and by those who feared the public would vote disproportionately for favorite-son candidates. Election by the Congress was rejected because it was felt such a procedure would compromise presidential independence from congressional pressure. Similarly, election by the state legislatures was opposed because it was felt an indebted president would be unable to resist state usurpation of federal authority. The Electoral College, which gives each state one electoral vote for each member in Congress, was finally adopted to accommodate all factions, but since 1787 hardly a year has passed without a plan to change this system.

Those who favor changing the present election system do so for many reasons, but primarily because a candidate can now become president while receiving fewer popular votes than his opponent. This has occurred three times in the nation's history and almost happened in 1968 and 1976.

Other arguments in favor of eliminating the Electoral College include: apportioning votes among the states gives a disproportionate influence to the smaller states; not all electors are bound to the wishes of their constituents and may choose to disregard the popular vote results; and the present "unit rule," which generally awards the total electoral vote to a state's popular vote winner, disenfranchises all those who voted for the loser.

The following compares the national trend since 1966 regarding attitudes toward eliminating the Electoral College:

	Approve	Disapprove	No opinion
1977	73%	15%	12%
1968	81	12	7
Oct. 1967	65	22	13
Jan. 1967	58	22	20
1966	63	20	17

DECEMBER 7
PRESIDENTIAL ELECTION

Interviewing Date: 11/7–10/80
Survey #164-G

Asked of those who did not vote: What was it that kept you from voting?

Not registered	42%
Did not like candidates	17
Illness	8
Not interested in politics	5
Not an American citizen	5
New resident	4
Traveling; out of town	3
Working	3
No way to get to polls	1
Did not get absentee ballot	*
No particular reason	10
Other	2

*Less than 1%

Asked of those who voted for Reagan: What was the main reason why you voted for Reagan—that is, why do you think he was the best man?

Anti-Carter

Dissatisfied with Carter	22%
Time for a change	21
Reagan would make a better leader	12
Carter has not accomplished anything	6

Pro-Reagan

Like Reagan's economic policies	17
Like Reagan's policies (general)	14
Other; no opinion	8

Asked of those who voted: When did you make up your mind definitely to vote for Carter/Reagan/Anderson?

Prior to debate and final week of campaign	60%
After watching debate	18
On last two or three days prior to election	7
Election day/last minute	10
Don't remember	5

Asked of those Reagan voters who decided on election day: What were your reasons for voting for Reagan?

The following are listed in order of frequency of mention:

Like Reagan's policies (general)
Like Reagan's foreign policy ⎫
Dislike Carter's handling of   ⎬ tied
  hostage problem   ⎭
Dissatisfied with Carter
Like Reagan's economic policies ⎫
Need a change   ⎬ tied
Because of the debate   ⎭

Asked of those who voted: At any time did you intend to vote for another candidate?

Yes	27%
No; no answer	73

Asked of those who voted: For the various political offices, did you vote for all the candidates of one party—that is, a straight ticket, or did you vote for the candidates of different parties?

Straight ticket 37%
Different parties 60
Don't know 3

Note: The 1980 presidential election was one of the most unusual in recent political history, judging from the Gallup Poll's postelection analysis, which dealt with such key aspects of voting behavior as: How many voters made up their minds in the final days of the campaign? What were the primary reasons for finally choosing the candidate they selected? How many voters shifted their allegiance during the campaign? How many split their tickets on election day? Why did so many refrain from voting?

Following are the key findings from the survey:

1. The vote for President-elect Ronald Reagan was more a vote against President Carter than for Reagan. A far greater number of Reagan voters cited general dissatisfaction and a perceived lack of leadership on Carter's part as a reason for choosing Reagan than offered pro-Reagan reasons—for example, stating a preference for Reagan's economic policies and his policies in general.

2. Support for both major-party candidates was even less enthusiastic than in earlier presidential elections. The percentage of persons who did not vote because they did not like the candidates was higher this year than in the past two presidential contests. In 1972, 10% of nonvoters gave this reason for not casting a ballot for president; in 1976, 14%; and in 1980, 17%.

Analysis of nonvoting also shows an uptrend in the proportion of nonvoters who indicate they did not even take the trouble to register to vote—from 28% in 1972 and 38% in 1976 to 42% in the current survey. However, the proportion unable to vote because they were new to an area has declined as the states have relaxed their residency requirements. Only 52.9% of eligible voters cast a ballot, the lowest turnout since 1948.

Another reason for political apathy may be the disenchantment with the electoral system. A recent Gallup Poll shows that 53% favor changes in the conduct of political campaigns. Leading the list of complaints this year are the length of campaigns and the amount of name calling, followed by the lack of discussion of the issues and the cost of financing political campaigns.

3. About one-sixth of voters did not make up their minds about which candidate to vote for until the last two or three days before the November 4 election, while a total of 35% made up their minds in the final weeks between the debate and the election.

4. The Gallup Poll's postelection analysis confirms the fact that many of the nation's voters in this year's presidential campaign were so-called "soft" or "wavering" voters. As many as one-third of persons said that at one point during the campaign they had intended to vote for another candidate.

5. Ticket splitting this year—that is, voting for candidates of different parties—was more prevalent than in either 1972 or 1976. In the latest survey, 60% of voters said they split their vote in choosing candidates for the various political offices, while 37% voted a straight party ticket.

DECEMBER 11
EXPECTATIONS FOR REAGAN PRESIDENCY

Interviewing Date: 11/21–24/80
Survey #165-G

Do you think the Reagan administration will or will not be able to:

Increase respect for the United States overseas?

Will 62%
Will not 24
Don't know 14

Reagan Voters Only

Will 83%
Will not 8
Don't know 9

Carter Voters Only

Will	46%
Will not	36
Don't know	18

Reduce the size of the federal government?

Yes	52%
No	32
Don't know	16

Reagan Voters Only

Yes	76%
No	14
Don't know	10

Carter Voters Only

Yes	44%
No	40
Don't know	16

Reduce unemployment?

Yes	47%
No	37
Don't know	16

Reagan Voters Only

Yes	71%
No	18
Don't know	11

Carter Voters Only

Yes	27%
No	59
Don't know	14

Reduce inflation?

Yes	46%
No	38
Don't know	16

Reagan Voters Only

Yes	74%
No	14
Don't know	12

Carter Voters Only

Yes	23%
No	61
Don't know	16

Balance the budget?

Yes	30%
No	55
Don't know	15

Reagan Voters Only

Yes	45%
No	42
Don't know	13

Carter Voters Only

Yes	19%
No	67
Don't know	14

Note: The success of President-elect Ronald Reagan in the early months of his administration will depend in considerable measure on how well he lives up to the expectations of the U.S. public.

To discover these expectations, the Gallup Poll posed questions dealing with five key issues, the results of which are as follows:

1. Three in five Americans (62%) think that the Reagan administration will be able to increase respect for the United States overseas, while a smaller majority (52%) believes the new administration will be able to reduce the size of the federal government.

2. On the two issues on which the Reagan campaign focused—unemployment and inflation—less than half of the public expects the new administration to meet with success.

3. A total of 47% of voters thinks that the Reagan administration will be able to reduce unemployment, but 37% hold the opposite view. Similarly, 46% believe the new team in Washington will be able to reduce inflation, while 38% disagree.

A majority of 55% says the Reagan team will not be able to bring expenses into line with expenditures, while 30% think that balancing the budget is possible.

There is agreement among both supporters of Reagan and President Jimmy Carter that the new president will be able to increase respect for the United States and reduce the size of the federal government. But those who voted for Reagan are much more likely to subscribe to these beliefs than are people who voted for Carter.

Disagreement between the two groups of voters is much wider, however, on the questions of reducing unemployment and inflation; Carter supporters are far less likely than Reagan voters to think that the incoming administration will be able to achieve these goals.

DECEMBER 14
MORAL MAJORITY

Interviewing Date: 11/21–24/80
Survey #165-G

Have you heard or read about an organization called the Moral Majority?

Yes.................................40%
No.................................60

Asked of those who replied in the affirmative: From what you know about it, how would you describe the Moral Majority? For example, what are its objectives and what does it stand for?

Note: Judging from their responses to the above question, 26% of the public can be considered "informed" about the Moral Majority.

Asked of the "informed" group: In general, would you say that you mostly approve or mostly disapprove of the Moral Majority?

Approve............................ 8%
Disapprove 13
No opinion 15
           26%*

By Sex
Male

Approve............................ 9%
Disapprove 14
No opinion 5
           28%*

Female

Approve............................ 6%
Disapprove 13
No opinion 5
           24%*

By Education
College

Approve............................11%
Disapprove 28
No opinion 10
           49%*

High School or Less

Approve............................ 6%
Disapprove 7
No opinion 3
           16%*

By Region
East

Approve............................ 5%
Disapprove 14
No opinion 4
           23%*

Midwest

Approve............................ 7%
Disapprove 12
No opinion 4
           23%*

South

Approve............................10%
Disapprove 11
No opinion 6
           27%*

West

Approve	10%
Disapprove	18
No opinion	5
	33%*

By Age
18–29 Years

Approve	4%
Disapprove	11
No opinion	4
	19%*

30–49 Years

Approve	10%
Disapprove	14
No opinion	7
	31%*

50 Years and Over

Approve	9%
Disapprove	15
No opinion	3
	27%*

By Politics
Republicans

Approve	13%
Disapprove	12
No opinion	7
	32%*

Democrats

Approve	4%
Disapprove	14
No opinion	2
	20%*

Independents

Approve	9%
Disapprove	16
No opinion	6
	31%*

Those Who Voted for Reagan

Approve	15%
Disapprove	12
No opinion	8
	35%*

Those Who Voted for Carter

Approve	6%
Disapprove	20
No opinion	3
	29%*

By Religion
Protestants

Approve	9%
Disapprove	13
No opinion	5
	27%*

Catholics

Approve	5%
Disapprove	11
No opinion	4
	20%*

Attend Church Regularly

Approve	12%
Disapprove	12
No opinion	6
	30%*

Do Not Attend Church Regularly

Approve	5%
Disapprove	14
No opinion	4
	23%*

Church Members

Approve	9%
Disapprove	12
No opinion	5
	26%*

Nonchurch Members

Approve.............................. 4%
Disapprove 16
No opinion 4
                                24%*

Those Who Say Religion is Very Important in Their Lives

Approve..............................10%
Disapprove 11
No opinion 6
                                27%*

Those Who Say Religion is Fairly Important in Their Lives

Approve.............................. 6%
Disapprove 11
No opinion 3
                                20%*

Those Who Say Religion is Not Very Important in Their Lives

Approve.............................. 3%
Disapprove 30
No opinion 5
                                38%*

Those Who Watched Religious Television Programs in Last Twelve Months

Approve..............................10%
Disapprove 13
No opinion 4
                                27%*

Those Who Have Not Watched Religious Television Programs in Last Twelve Months

Approve.............................. 6%
Disapprove 14
No opinion 5
                                25%*

*Percentage who have read or heard about the Moral Majority.

Note: "We've got to make sure our political candidates uphold biblical principles. Otherwise we can kiss goodby to our Christian heritage." This was a middle-aged storeowner from New York speaking.

Said a young housewife from Missouri: "I don't mind religious leaders taking a stand on the issues, but I don't go along with these morality indexes of political candidates on issues."

These two comments reflect the controversy surrounding the Moral Majority, the fundamentalist political movement started by the Reverend Jerry Falwell.

The latest Gallup Poll sought to find out the level of public awareness of and attitudes toward the controversial movement that some political observers believe was largely responsible for the defeat of certain key members of Congress in the November elections. The Moral Majority, which claimed in October that it had registered 4 million new fundamentalist voters nationally, gave candidates "morality ratings" according to their stand on issues ranging from abortion to SALT II.

The efforts of the Moral Majority and other conservative Christian groups to mobilize a Christian vote in the recent presidential campaign have drawn sharp criticism from various quarters. The most serious charge made against these religious activists is that they violate the constitutional principle of separation of church and state.

Less than half the total sample (40%) have heard or read about the Moral Majority, while even fewer (26%) are familiar with the objectives and goals of this organization. Among the latter "informed" group, disapproval outweighs approval 13% to 8%, with 15% expressing no opinion.

While a relatively small proportion of the public is supportive of the Moral Majority, it should be noted that the 8% in favor projects to 12 or 13 million adults nationally, a number large enough when distributed among the states to be decisive in close congressional races.

Earlier surveys have indicated that efforts of religious leaders to tell voters which presidential candidates they should or should not vote for do not sit well with most Americans. For example, by a 2-to-1 margin, the public believes it is wrong for religious groups to work actively for the defeat of candidates who do not agree with their position on certain issues.

At the same time, however, the view of at least half the U.S. public, as determined by a survey conducted for *Christianity Today* by the Gallup Organization Inc., is that it is very or fairly important for religious organizations to make public statements on political and economic matters about what they feel would be consonant with the will of God.

Republicans and those who voted for Ronald Reagan are far more likely to hold favorable opinions of the Moral Majority than are Democrats and those who voted for President Jimmy Carter.

Church members, regular churchgoers, those who watch religious television programs, and persons who say religion plays an important role in their lives are more favorably disposed toward the Moral Majority than are their opposite numbers. Southerners are found to be more receptive to the Moral Majority than are persons living in other regions.

DECEMBER 21
PRESIDENTIAL ELECTION—
A GALLUP ANALYSIS

Interviewing Date: 10/30–11/1/80
Special Survey

Note: A comparison of President Jimmy Carter's vote in this year's election with his showing in the 1976 presidential contest reveals the following significant changes in the voting pattern, as measured by the Gallup Poll's postelection analysis of in-person interviews with 1,975 voters:

1. Carter won a hefty 57% of the vote of Catholics in 1976 to 42% for Gerald Ford, but in the recent election he shared the Catholic vote almost equally with his Republican opponent, Ronald Reagan. Carter won the vote of 46% of Catholics to 47% for Reagan, while 6% of

Catholics chose independent candidate John Anderson.

2. The president had the support of nearly six in ten (58%) manual workers in the 1976 election but won only 48% of this group's vote in the 1980 election, barely edging Reagan who garnered 46%. Anderson won 5%.

3. Carter's support from labor union members declined from 63% in 1976 to 50% in this year's election. Although the president did succeed in winning this group from his Republican challenger, Reagan received 43% and Anderson 5%.

4. Reflecting his losses among these three traditionally Democratic groups, Carter's hold on the vote of Democrats slipped from 82% in 1976 to 69% in 1980, nearly matching the record low of 67% of the Democratic vote received by Senator George McGovern in the 1972 election.

5. Carter's vote among men in the 1980 election was far below his showing in the previous election—a full 15 points lower. In the recent election the president lost to Reagan among men 38% to 53%, with 7% for Anderson. Among women the contest was much closer, with Carter winning 44% to 49% for Reagan and 6% for Anderson.

6. In 1976, Carter scored a breakthrough with traditionally Republican groups—the college educated and persons in the professions and in business. In fact, the only Democrat in the last three decades who did better with these groups was Lyndon Johnson in 1964. But in the 1980 election, these groups returned to their normal Republican voting behavior.

7. While Carter lost considerable support between elections among certain key groups, he largely held his ground with nonwhites and young voters. Nonwhites voted as overwhelmingly for Carter in the recent election as they did in 1976, with 86% pulling the Democratic lever. Reagan received 10% and Anderson 2% of this group's vote. In 1976, 85% of black voters cast their ballots for the former George governor.

Support for Carter among young adults (18- to 29-year-olds) was down slightly from 1976, but Carter nevertheless prevailed with the nation's young voters, winning 47% of their votes compared to 41% for Reagan and 11% for Anderson.

While both nonwhites and young adults preferred Carter to his opponents in this year's election, much of the potential impact of their votes undoubtedly was offset by the low turnout in these two groups.

DECEMBER 25
MOST ADMIRED WOMAN

Interviewing Date: 12/5–8/80
Survey #166-G

What woman that you have heard or read about, living today in any part of the world, do you admire the most? Who is your second choice?

Following are the results, based on first and second choices combined:

Rosalynn Carter ⎫
Mother Teresa of Calcutta ⎬ tied
Margaret Thatcher
Betty Ford
Ella Grasso
Barbara Jordan
Barbara Walters
Indira Gandhi
Nancy Reagan
Jacqueline Onassis
Jane Fonda

Note: In 1979 the leading personalities were Rosalynn Carter; Betty Ford; Mother Teresa; Margaret Thatcher; Barbara Walters; Lillian Carter, the president's mother; former First Lady Pat Nixon; singer Anita Bryant; Coretta King, civil rights activist; and Jacqueline Onassis.

Receiving frequent mention but not included in this year's top ten are the following (in alphabetical order); Anita Bryant; Shirley Chisholm, New York representative; Queen Elizabeth II; Lady Bird Johnson, former First Lady; Coretta King; and Pat Nixon.

The top three choices (in order) among men in the current survey are Margaret Thatcher,

Mother Teresa, and Rosalynn Carter. Women picked Rosalynn Carter first, Mother Teresa second, and Margaret Thatcher third.

The differences in choices by religion are also noteworthy. Protestants give first place to Rosalynn Carter, while Margaret Thatcher and Betty Ford take second and third, respectively. Among Catholics, Mother Teresa is the most popular, followed by Rosalynn Carter and Margaret Thatcher.

Survey respondents in these studies, which the Gallup Poll has conducted for more than three decades, are asked to give their choices without the aid of a prearranged list of names. This procedure, while opening the field to all possible choices, tends to favor those who currently or recently have been in the news.

DECEMBER 28
MOST ADMIRED MAN

Interviewing Date: 12/5–8/80
Survey #166-G

What man that you have heard or read about, living today in any part of the world, do you admire the most? Who is your second choice?

The following are listed in order of frequency of mention with first and second choices combined:

Pope John Paul II
Jimmy Carter
Anwar Sadat
Billy Graham
Ronald Reagan
Henry Kissinger
Richard Nixon
Gerald Ford
Edward Kennedy
Menachem Begin

Note: Receiving frequent mention but not included in the top ten are the following (in alphabetical order): Bob Hope, entertainer; the Reverend Jesse Jackson, civil rights leader; and

Helmut Schmidt, chancellor of West Germany.

The top three choices in 1979 were President Jimmy Carter, Pope John Paul II, and Senator Edward Kennedy.

Interesting differences are found between the choices of men and women and between Protestants and Catholics. Among both men and women the pope is the first choice. Egyptian President Anwar Sadat and Jimmy Carter are chosen second and third, respectively, among men, while women select Billy Graham and Carter.

Pope John Paul II is the favorite choice of Catholics as the man they most admire, followed by Presidents Carter and Sadat. Protestants pick Graham first, while Carter and Reagan are second and third, respectively.

Among young adults (18- to 29-year-olds) it is President Carter who wins the greatest number of votes, followed by Pope John Paul II and Anwar Sadat. Further evidence of Carter's relatively high level of popularity among young adults was apparent in the election results. As reported by the Gallup Poll in its special post-election analysis, this group was one of only a few that the president carried on November 4.

Index

A

Abortion
  ban on
    favor or oppose, 251
    nonwhite and white voters favoring, 233
    registered Carter, Reagan, and Anderson supporters favoring, 191
  Catholic cardinal right or wrong to make statement that it was sin to vote for candidate favoring, 239
  as issue you want candidates to debate, 198
  legal under any, certain, or no circumstances, 171-73
    trends from 1975 to 1980 on, 249
  as single issue that would determine female and male voting behavior on, 235
  trend of views since 1975, 173
Adult education
  as choice for special attention of Department of Education, 180
  taking or ever have taken any courses in an adult education program, 183
Afghanistan crisis
  approval of Carter's handling of, 17, 159
  favor or oppose moving 1980 summer Olympics to another nation as protest to, 17
  favor sending troops to Afghans fighting Soviets, sending arms, or putting only economic and diplomatic pressure on Soviet Union, 17
  heard or read about Soviet intervention in Afghanistan, 17
  Soviet intervention caused by U.S. foreign policy not being tough enough, or they would have intervened no matter what U.S. policy was, 17-18
Alcohol, use on school property, parents, school, or courts should deal with, 180
Anderson, John
  best able to handle nation's problems vs. Reagan and Carter, 138
  best for keeping United States out of war vs. Carter and Reagan
    female vs. male voters on, 235

best for reducing inflation vs. Carter and Reagan,
    female vs. male voters on, 235
  best for reducing unemployment vs. Carter and Reagan
    female vs. male voters on, 235
  characteristics rated vs. Carter and Reagan, 154-55, 209
  does or does not consider himself to be a born-again evangelical Christian, Evangelicals on, 186
  as expected winner of presidential election, 144
  heard about, 2
  knowledge of whether or not he is appearing in television debate, 197
  moderate supporters of, 201
  opinion ratings, 230-31
  perceived self-rated political views on, 202-3
  personal appeal compared with Carter and Reagan
    female vs. male voters on, 236
  in presidential trial heats of registered Evangelicals and non-Evangelicals vs. Carter and Reagan, 184
  in presidential trial heats of registered voters
    vs. Carter and Reagan, 80-83, 97-98, 108-9, 114-16, 125-26, 134-36, 139-40, 143, 163-71, 184
    vs. Jackson and Reagan, 163
    vs. Kennedy and Reagan, 163
    vs. Mondale and Reagan, 162-63
    vs. Muskie and Reagan, 162
    vs. Reagan-Bush and Carter-Mondale, 144-46
  supporters
    attitude toward United Nations, 253
    favor or oppose wage-price control reinstatement, 198
    intensity of support for, 140, 144, 164
    vs. Reagan and Carter supporters, likelihood of voting for with Democrat or Republican as running mate, 166
  support and opposition on campaign issues, 190-91
  would do better job of building trust in government
    vs. Carter and Reagan, 222-23
  would do better job of dealing with Arab-Israeli situation
    vs. Carter and Reagan, 228-29
  would do better job of dealing with racial problems
    vs. Carter and Reagan, 221-22
  would do better job of dealing with Russia
    vs. Carter and Reagan, 220-21
  would do better job of handling domestic affairs
    vs. Reagan and Carter, 210-11
  would do better job of handling foreign relations
    vs. Carter and Reagan, 209-10
  would do better job of handling Iranian situation
    vs. Carter and Reagan, 215-16
  would do better job of handling women's rights
    vs. Carter and Reagan, 217-18
  would do better job of helping the poor and needy
    vs. Carter and Reagan, 226-27
  would do better job of improving and dealing with

Anderson, John (*continued*)
    environmental issues
        vs. Carter and Reagan, 224-25
    would do better job of improving economy
        vs. Carter and Reagan, 218-19
    would do better job of improving energy situation
        vs. Carter and Reagan, 223-24
    would do better job of increasing respect for United
        States overseas
        vs. Carter and Reagan, 229-30
    would do better job of keeping United States out of
        war
        vs. Carter and Reagan, 213-14
    would do better job of reducing inflation
        vs. Carter and Reagan, 211-12
    would do better job of reducing unemployment
        vs. Carter and Reagan, 214-15
    would do better job of spending taxpayers' money
        wisely
        vs. Carter and Reagan, 225-26
    would do better job of strengthening national
        defense
        vs. Carter and Reagan, 216-17
Anderson-Lucey ticket
    election results by demographic breakdown, 242-
        44
    in presidential trial heat of former Kennedy Demo-
        crats, 208
    in presidential trial heats during last days of
        campaign
        vs. Carter-Mondale and Reagan-Bush, 241
    in presidential trial heats of likely voters
        vs. Carter-Mondale and Reagan-Bush, 236-37
    in presidential trial heats of registered voters
        vs. Reagan-Bush and Carter-Mondale, 196, 201,
        204-8
    supporters
        right or wrong for Catholic cardinal to make state-
            ment that it was sin to vote for candidates who
            favor abortion, 239
        right or wrong for religious groups to work for
            defeat of candidates disagreeing with their
            positions, 239
    unofficial election results for, 241
Arab-Israeli situation, Carter vs. Reagan vs. Ander-
    son would do better job of dealing with, 228-29
Armstrong, Anne, as choice for Republican vice-presi-
    dential candidate in 1980 with and without
    Ford's vote redistributed, 141

B

Baker, Howard
    as choice for Republican presidential candidate in
        1980, 3
    as choice for Republican vice-presidential candidate
        in 1980 with and without Ford's vote redis-

tributed, 140-41
    heard about, 2
Banks and banking, confidence in, 245-46
Begin, Menachem, as most admired man, 267
Bible, as actual word of God, inspired word of God, or
    ancient book of fables, 186-88
Big business, confidence in, 179, 248
Black people
    quality of life in United States gotten better, stayed
        about the same, or gotten worse in last ten
        years, 151-53
    treatment in this community, 150-51
    see also Minorities; Nonwhite voters; Race; Racial
        problems
Brown, Edmund (Jerry), Jr., as choice for Democratic
    presidential candidate in 1980, 161
Bush, George
    as choice for Republican presidential candidate in
        1980, 3
        vs. Ford, 33-34
        vs. Reagan, 32-33
    as choice for Republican vice-presidential candi-
        date in 1980 with and without Ford's vote
        redistributed, 140-41
    heard about, 2
    in presidential trial heats of registered voters
        vs. Carter, 38-39, 62
        vs. Kennedy, 42-43
    ratings for, 174
    see also Reagan-Bush ticket
Busing/integration, as biggest problem of public
    schools in this community, 177-78

C

Canada, should or should not impose economic and
    diplomatic sanctions against Iran, 128
Capital punishment
    Carter, Reagan, and Anderson supporters on, 191
    Evangelicals and non-Evangelicals on, 190
    favor or oppose in 1974 and 1980, 250
    nonwhite and white voters favoring, 233
    as single issue that would determine female and male
        voting behavior on, 235
Carter, Billy
    dealings with Libyan government officials
        effect on opinion of Jimmy Carter, 167-68
    heard or read about dealings with Libyan govern-
        ment officials, 167
Carter, Jimmy
    approval of handling of Afghanistan situation by, 17
    approval of handling of domestic policy by, 51-52
    approval of handling of foreign policy by, 50-51
    approval of handling of Iranian crisis by, 11-12,
        83-84, 96, 128
    approval of handling of presidency by, 3-5, 49-50,
        60, 64, 96, 102, 134, 139, 143, 158, 169, 184

Carter, Jimmy (*continued*)
vs. Reagan and Anderson, 218-19
would do better job of improving energy situation
vs. Reagan and Anderson, 223-24
would do better job of increasing respect for United States overseas
vs. Reagan and Anderson, 229-30
would do better job of keeping United States out of war
vs. Reagan, 103
vs. Reagan and Anderson, 213-14
would do better job of reducing inflation
vs. Reagan and Anderson, 211-12
would do better job of reducing unemployment
vs. Reagan and Anderson, 214-15
would do better job of spending taxpayers' money wisely
vs. Reagan and Anderson, 225-26
would do better job of strengthening national defense
vs. Reagan and Anderson, 216-17
Carter-Mondale ticket
election results by demographic breakdown, 242-44
in 1976, 244-45
in presidential trial heat of former Kennedy Democrats, 208
in presidential trial heats during last days of campaign
vs. Reagan-Bush and Anderson-Lucey, 241
in presidential trial heats of likely voters
vs. Reagan-Bush and Anderson-Lucey, 236-37
in presidential trial heats of registered voters
vs. Reagan and Anderson, 80-83, 108-9
vs. Reagan-Bush and Anderson, 144-46
vs. Reagan-Bush and Anderson-Lucey, 196, 201, 204-8
reasons for defeat of, 249
supporters
right or wrong for Catholic cardinal to make statement that it was sin to vote for candidates who favor abortion, 239
right or wrong for religious groups to work for defeat of candidates disagreeing with their positions, 238
unofficial election results for, 241
Carter, Rosalynn, as most admired woman, 267
Catholic church, cardinal was right or wrong to make statement that it was sin to vote for candidates favoring abortion, 239
"Center party," hypothetical, support for vs. Republicans and Democrats, 129-30
Children
ideal number for family to have, 98-99
from one-parent families, ratings for proposals for, 182
would or would not like to have yours take up teaching in public schools, 184
would or would not object to son or daughter marrying person who had epileptic seizures, 176-77

would or would not object to yours associated with persons who had epileptic seizures, 176
see also Education; Family budget; Family life; Family size
China
ratings for, 48
U.S. recognition of, approval trends for Carter and, 159
Church, Frank, as choice for Democratic presidential candidate in 1980, 161
Church attendance and membership
approval of Moral Majority by, 264-65
attitude toward Catholic cardinal making statement that it was sin to vote for candidates favoring abortion by, 239
attitude toward religious groups working to defeat candidates who do not agree with their positions by, 238
Churches, confidence in, 178
Cohen, William, as choice for Republican vice-presidential candidate in 1980 with and without Ford's vote redistributed, 140
Congress, Carter right or not right in not consulting on recent military mission in Iran, 102
Congressional elections, hypothetical, choice of Democratic or Republican party as winner in this congressional district, 101, 137-38, 165, 185, 204
Connally, John
as choice for Republican presidential candidate in 1980, 3
as choice for Republican vice-presidential candidate in 1980 with and without Ford's vote redistributed, 140-41
heard about, 2
Conservation *see* Environmental issues
Constitutional amendments
eliminating Electoral College and basing election of president on total vote cast throughout nation, 258-60
permitting prayers to be said in public schools, 104-6
requiring federal government to balance budget each year
arguments for and against, 79
expected effect on government programs for people with low incomes or on welfare, 76-77
expected effect on inflation, 73-74
expected effect on number of government employees, 74-76
expected effect on taxes, 77-78
favor or oppose, 72-73
heard or read about, 72
see also Equal Rights Amendment
Cost of living *see* Inflation; Living costs
Courts
as choice for dealing with student behavior problems
vs. parents and school, 180

confidence in, 178

Crane, Philip
　as choice for Republican vice-presidential candidate in 1980 with and without Ford's vote redistributed, 140-41
　heard about, 2

Credit purchases, good or poor idea to make it more difficult, 94-95

Crime
　as most important national problem, 47, 101
　possession of marijuana should or should not be treated as, 193-96

Cuba, ratings for, 48-49

Cubans
　as cause of recent racial problems in Miami, 153
　leaving Cuba to come and live in United States
　　government should or should not permit, 120-22
　　heard or read about, 120

Curriculum
　favor or oppose instruction in schools dealing with morals, 181
　favor or oppose students progressing at own speed without regard to grade levels, 181
　poor, as biggest problem of public schools in this community, 177-78
　students should spend more time or are spending enough time learning about other nations of the world, 183
　see also Education

D

"Death of a Princess"
　seen, heard, or read about, 120
　should or should not have been shown on television, 120

Defense spending
　favor or oppose
　　Evangelicals and non-Evangelicals on, 190
　　increased, 250
　　　Carter, Reagan, and Anderson supporters on, 191
　　nonwhite and white voters favoring, 233
　as single issue that would determine female and male voting behavior on, 235
　too little, too much, or right amount, 46-47

Democratic party
　national convention
　　gave more or less favorable impression of Democratic party, 169
　　watched on television, 169

Democratic presidential candidates
　Carter should or should not release delegates to allow them to vote for whomever they wish, 161
　choice of Carter vs. Kennedy, 5, 79, 95-96, 124, 161
　choice of Carter vs. some other person, 161
　choice of other than Carter, 161

nonwhite support for, 233
supported Carter or Kennedy at time of Democratic convention, 208
see also Presidential elections

Department of Education, choice of most important areas for special attention of, 180

Discipline, lack of, as biggest problem of public schools in this community, 177-78

Dole, Robert
　as choice for Republican presidential candidate in 1980, 3
　as choice for Republican vice-presidential candidate in 1980 with and without Ford's vote redistributed, 140-41
　heard about, 2

Domestic policy
　approval of Carter's handling of, 51-52
　Carter vs. Reagan vs. Anderson would do better job of handling, 210-11

Draft
　favor or oppose registration of all young men, 58, 146-48
　favor or oppose registration of all young women, 58-59, 148-49
　should or should not reinstitute, 54-55, 148
　women should or should not be required to participate in, 55-56, 148-49

Drug use
　as biggest problem of public schools in this community, 177-78
　on school property, parents, school, or courts should deal with, 180
　see also Marijuana

E

Economy
　Carter vs. Reagan vs. Anderson would do better job of improving, 218-19
　expectations for next twelve months, 131
　expectations for 1980 as year of prosperity or economic difficulty, 1-2
　expectations for prices and income for next twelve months, 131
　government should give greater attention to curbing inflation or reducing unemployment, 200
　likelihood of losing your job in next twelve months, 131-33
　　comparisons from 1972 to 1978, 143
　political party best for keeping country prosperous, 142-43
　wage-price control reinstatement wanted, 44-45, 198
　see also Prices; Taxation; Unemployment

Education
　biggest problem of public schools in this community
　　public-school and nonpublic-school parents on, 177-78

Education (*continued*)

choice of most important areas for special attention of new federal Department of Education, 180

cost of ten dollars per student for each school day higher, lower, or about the same as you had thought, 181

favor or oppose instruction in schools dealing with morals, 181

favor or oppose student progressing at own speed without regard to usual grade levels, 181

federal government, state government, or local school board should have greatest influence in deciding curriculum of public schools in this community, 179

good or poor idea for teachers to spend one year as interns at half pay, 183

grade you would give public schools in this community, 178

high-school students should or should not be permitted to graduate early if they meet academic requirements, 181-82

importance of schools in one's future success, 179

local public school system gives enough or not enough attention to reading, writing, and arithmetic, 179

parents, school, or courts should deal with student behavior problems, 180

parents should or should not be asked to meet with school personnel before each school semester, 179

preschool, as choice for special attention of Department of Education, 180

public schools should or should not add personnel to help students and recent graduates get jobs, 182

public-school teachers should or should not be permitted to strike, 183-84

schools should or should not require children who cannot speak English to learn in special classes, 182

students should spend more time or are spending enough time learning about other nations of the world, 183

things having good effect on public school education in this community, 179

see also Schools; Teachers

Egypt, ratings for, 48

Eisenhower, Dwight

highly favorable ratings for in 1952 vs. Stevenson, 101, 231

highly favorable ratings for in 1956 vs. Stevenson, 100

low points of approval for related to principal public concerns, 158

Election campaigns

believe there are senators and representatives in Congress who won election by using unethical and illegal methods, 65

number of present members of Congress who got there by using unethical and illegal campaign

methods, 65-67

would or would not like changes in way they are conducted, 253

Electoral College, approve or disapprove constitutional amendment eliminating and basing presidential election on total vote throughout country, 258-60

Employment

ideal life-style for women with or without marriage, with or without children, and with or without full-time job, 126-27

of illegal aliens, should or should not be against the law, 254-55

public schools should or should not add personnel to help students and recent graduates get jobs, 182

Energy situation

Carter vs. Reagan vs. Anderson would do better job of improving, 223-24

Carter's speech on, approval trends for Carter and, 160

favor law requiring gasoline rationing, 45-46

as issue you want candidates to debate, 198

as most important national problem, 47, 101, 160, 199

see also Nuclear power plants

Environmental issues

Carter vs. Reagan vs. Anderson would do better job of improving and dealing with, 224-25

as issue you want candidates to debate, 198

Epilepsy

believed cause of, 176

heard or read about, 175

is or is not form of insanity, 176

know anyone who had, 176

seen anyone having seizure, 176

would or would not object to having a son or daughter marry a person who had epileptic seizures, 176-77

would or would not object to your children associating with persons who had seizures, 176

Equal Rights Amendment

Carter, Reagan, and Anderson supporters on, 191

favor or oppose, 155-57, 250

Evangelicals and non-Evangelicals on, 190

in 1975, 1976, and 1978 compared, 250

heard or read about, 155

as issue you want candidates to debate, 198

nonwhite and white voters favoring, 233

as single issue that would determine female and male voting behavior on, 235

Ethics

believe there are senators and representatives now serving in Congress who won election using unethical and illegal methods, 65

number of present members of Congress who got there by using unethical or illegal campaign methods, 65-67

Evangelicals
Anderson does or does not consider himself to be a born-again evangelical Christian, 186
approval of Carter's handling of presidency, 185
Carter does or does not consider himself to be a born-again evangelical Christian, 186
choice of Democrat or Republican in hypothetical congressional elections, 185
consider yourself a Democrat, Republican, or independent, 185
demographic profile, 189
ever had born-again experience, 188-89
favor or oppose ban on all abortions, 190
favor or oppose death penalty for murder, 190
favor or oppose Equal Rights Amendment, 190
favor or oppose government social programs, 190
favor or oppose homosexuals being allowed to teach, 190
favor or oppose increased defense spending, 190
favor or oppose more nuclear power plants, 190
favor or oppose prayer in public schools, 190
favor or oppose registration of all firearms, 190
likelihood of voting for presidential candidate who considers himself a born-again evangelical Christian, 185
presidential trial heats of registered voters among Carter vs. Reagan vs. Anderson, 184
Reagan does or does not consider himself to be a born-again evangelical Christian, 186
registered voters, 185
self-ratings of political views, 186
Expectations for 1980
will be better or worse than 1979, 1
will be year of economic prosperity or economic difficulty, 1-2
for Reagan presidency, 261-63

F

Falwell, Jerry see Moral Majority
Family budget
amount needed for family of four from 1937 to 1980, 71-72
smallest amount needed to get along in this community, 69-70
weekly expenditures on food, 70-72
Family life, ideal life-style for women as married or unmarried, with or without children, and with or without full-time job, 126-27
Family size, ideal, 98-99
Federal budget
constitutional amendment requiring federal government to balance each year
arguments for and against, 79
expected effect on government programs for people with low incomes or on welfare, 76-77
expected effect on inflation, 73-74

expected effect on number of government employees, 74-76
expected effect on taxes, 77-78
favor or oppose balance of in 1976, 1978, and 1979, 250
favor or oppose proposed constitutional amendment requiring balanced, 72-73
heard or read about proposed constitutional amendment requiring balanced, 72
Reagan administration will or will not be able to balance, 262
Female voters
choice of presidential candidate best for keeping United States out of war
compared with male voters, 235
choice of presidential candidate best for reducing inflation
compared with male voters, 235
choice of presidential candidate best for reducing unemployment
compared with male voters, 235
political affiliation compared with male voters, 235
ratings for personal appeal of Carter, Reagan, and Anderson
compared with male voters, 236
on single issue that would determine voting behavior compared with male voters, 235
Fernandez, Benjamin, heard about, 3
Finances
cost of ten dollars per student per day in public schools is higher, lower, or about the same as what you had thought, 181
of election campaigns, changes wanted in, 253
lack of, as biggest problem of public schools in this community, 177-78
see also Family budget; Federal budget
Firearms registration
Evangelicals and non-Evangelicals on, 190
favor or oppose, 250
in 1974 and 1980 compared, 250
nonwhite and white voters on, 233
registered Carter, Reagan, and Anderson supporters on, 190
as single issue that would determine female and male voting behavior on, 235
see also Gun control
Fonda, Jane, as most admired woman, 267
Food, weekly family expenditures on, 70-72
Ford, Betty, as most admired woman, 267
Ford, Gerald
as choice for Republican presidential candidate in 1980, 3, 60-61
vs. Bush, 33-34
vs. Reagan, 31-32
as choice for Republican vice-presidential candidate in 1980, 140-41
heard about, 2
highly favorable ratings for vs. Carter, 100, 231

Ford, Gerald (*continued*)
  low points of approval for related to principal public
    concerns, 158
  as most admired man, 267
  in presidential trial heats of registered voters
    vs. Carter, 6-8, 36-38
    vs. Kennedy, 9-11, 41-42
  supporters in 1976, presidential election choices of,
    237
Ford-Dole ticket, in 1976, results by demographic
    breakdown, 244-45
Foreign policy
  approval of Carter's handling of, 50-51
  approval of Carter's handling of Iranian crisis, 11-12
  confidence in ability of United States to deal wisely
    with world problems, 127
  as issue you want candidates to debate, 198
  as most important national problem, 47
  see also Afghanistan crisis; International relations;
    Iranian situation

G

Gandhi, Indira, as most admired woman, 267
Gasoline rationing, favor or oppose law requiring, 45-
  46
Goldwater, Barry, highly favorable ratings for in 1964
  vs. Johnson, 100, 231
Government
  believe there are senators and representatives in
    Congress who won election by using unethical
    and illegal methods, 65
  Carter vs. Reagan vs. Anderson would do better job of
    building trust in, 222-23
  confidence in, 178
  dissatisfaction with, as most important national prob-
    lem, 47, 101, 160, 199
  employees, expected effect of balanced federal bud-
    get on number of, 74-76
  local, confidence in, 178
  number of present members of Congress who got
    there by using unethical and illegal campaign
    methods, 65-67
  presidential candidate best able to build trust in
    Carter vs. Reagan vs. Anderson, 138
  reinstatement of wage-price controls wanted by, 44-
    45
  should allow immigration because of political oppres-
    sion to halt all immigration until unemployment
    rate drops, 122-24
  should give greater attention to inflation or unem-
    ployment, 200
  should or should not allow Cubans leaving Cuba to
    live here, 120-22
  should or should not have greatest influence in de-
    ciding curriculum of public schools in this com-
    munity, 179

size of, Reagan administration will or will not be able
  to reduce, 262
social programs
  Carter, Reagan, and Anderson supporters on, 191
  Evangelicals and non-Evangelicals on, 190
  nonwhite and white voters on, 233
  as single issue that would determine male and
    female voter behavior on, 235
wage-price control reinstatement by, 198
see also Federal budget
Government spending
  Carter vs. Reagan vs. Anderson would do better job of
    spending taxpayers' money wisely, 225-26
  for national defense and military purposes, too little,
    too much, or about right, 46-47
  presidential candidate best able to reduce
    Carter vs. Reagan vs. Anderson, 138
  see also Defense spending; Federal budget
Graham, Billy, as most admired man, 267
Grasso, Ella, as most admired woman, 267
Great Britain, should or should not impose economic
  and diplomatic sanctions against Iran, 128
Greece, permanent Olympic site, good or bad idea, 63-
  64
Gun control
  approval of law requiring license for person carrying
    gun outside his home, 27-28
  approval of mandatory one-year jail sentence for
    anyone convicted of carrying a gun outside his
    home without license, 28-30
  laws covering sale of handguns should be more strict,
    less strict, or remain the same, 25-27
  should or should not be law forbidding possession of
    pistols and revolvers except by police and other
    authorized persons, 24-25

H

Health *see* Epilepsy; Physical fitness
Helms, Jesse
  as choice for Republican vice-presidential candidate
    in 1980 with and without Ford's vote redis-
    tributed, 140-41
  heard about, 2
Hispanics *see* Minorities; Nonwhite voters; Racial
  problems
Homosexuals
  allowed or not allowed to teach
    Carter, Reagan, and Anderson supporters on, 191
    Evangelicals and non-Evangelicals on, 190
    nonwhite and white voters favoring, 233
    as single issue that would determine male and
      female voting behavior on, 235
Hostage crisis *see* Iranian crisis
Humphrey, Hubert, highly favorable ratings for in 1968
  vs. Nixon, 100, 231

I

Identification cards, everyone in United States should or should not be required to carry, 255-56

Illegal aliens
  everyone in United States should or should not be required to carry an identification card, 255-56
  favor or oppose allowing them to remain in United States if they have been here for seven years, 256-57
  should or should not be against the law to employ, 254-55

Immigration
  of Cubans to United States as cause of racial problems in Miami, 153
  heard or read about Cubans leaving Cuba to come to United States, 120
  U.S. government should allow immigration because of political oppression or halt all immigration until unemployment rate drops, 122-24
  U.S. government should or should not permit Cubans to come and live in United States, 120-22

Independents, choices for Democratic and Republican presidential candidates *see* Democratic presidential candidates; Republican presidential candidates

Inflation
  balanced federal budget would cause increase or decrease in, 73-74
  Carter vs. Reagan vs. Anderson would do better job of reducing, 211-12
    female vs. male voters on, 235
  Carter's economic policies will increase, decrease, or have no effect on, 90–92
  expectations for next twelve months for income and prices, 131
  as issue you want candidates to debate, 198
  as most important national problem, 47, 101, 160, 199
  presidential candidate best able to reduce
    Carter vs. Reagan vs. Anderson, 138
  Reagan administration will or will not be able to reduce, 262
  vs. unemployment for greater government attention, 200

Institutions, confidence in, 178-79

International relations
  Carter vs. Reagan vs. Anderson would do better job of handling, 209-10
  Carter vs. Reagan vs. Anderson would do better job of increasing respect for United States overseas, 229-30
  Carter's handling of relations with Soviet Union, 52-53
  as most important national problem, 47, 101, 160, 199
  ratings of nations, 47-49
  Reagan administration will or will not be able to

increase respect for United States overseas, 261-62
United Nations doing good or poor job in trying to solve problems it has had to face, 251-52

Iran, ratings for, 48

Iranian situation
  actions wanted by United States, 254
  approval of Carter's handling of, 11-12, 83-84, 96, 128
  approval trends for Carter and, 159
  approve or disapprove of recent economic and diplomatic measures United States has taken against Iran, 128
  can or cannot recall any demands made by Iranian government in exchange for release of hostages, 254
  Carter right or not right in not consulting congressional leaders before recent military mission in Iran, 102
  Carter right or not right to try to rescue hostages by military force, 102
  Carter vs. Reagan vs. Anderson would do better job of handling, 215-16
  death of Shah of Iran will or will not mean speedier release of American hostages in Iran, 164
  heard or read about, 254
  presidential candidate best able to handle
    Carter vs. Reagan vs. Anderson, 138
  think economic and diplomatic sanctions against Iran will or will not secure release of American prisoners, 128
  think hostages will or will not be released, 15-17, 87-89
  think other countries should or should not impose economic and diplomatic sanctions against Iran, 128-29
  think United States should punish Iran diplomatically and economically or use military force if hostages are released unharmed, 12-15, 84-85

Iranians, in United States, want deported and swapped for hostages, 254

Iraq-Iran conflict, sympathies more with Iraq or more with Iran, 254

Israel, ratings for, 48

Israeli-Arab peace treaty, approval trends for Carter and, 159

J

Jackson, Henry
  as choice for Democratic presidential candidate in 1980, 161
  in presidential trial heats of registered voters vs. Reagan and Anderson, 163

Jail sentences, mandatory one year for conviction for carrying gun outside home without license, approval of, 28-30

Jogging, 111
John Paul II, Pope, as most admired man, 267
Johnson, Lyndon
    highly favorable ratings for in 1964 vs. Goldwater,
        100, 231
    low points of approval for related to principal public
        concerns, 158
Jordan, Barbara, as most admired woman, 267

K

Kassebaum, Nancy, as choice for Republican vice-
    presidential candidate in 1980 with and without
    Ford's vote redistributed, 141
Kemp, Jack
    as choice for Republican vice-presidential candidate
        in 1980 with and without Ford's vote redis-
        tributed, 140-41
    heard about, 2
Kennedy, Edward
    characteristics of vs. Carter, 22-23
    as choice for Democratic presidential candidate in
        1980, 161
        vs. Carter, 5, 79, 95-96, 124, 161, 208
    as most admired man, 267
    in presidential trial heats of registered voters
        vs. Bush, 42-43
        vs. Ford, 9-11, 41-42
        vs. Reagan, 8-9, 39-41, 118-19, 137
        vs. Reagan and Anderson, 163
    supporters
        choices for president of Reagan, Carter, or Ander-
            son, 208
Kennedy, John F.
    highly favorable ratings for in 1960 vs. Nixon, 100,
        231
    low points of approval for related to principal public
        concerns, 158
Kissinger, Henry, as most admired man, 267

L

Labor unions
    confidence in, 179, 247
    schools with, teachers should or should not be re-
        quired to pay union dues if they do not belong to,
        184
Lance, Bert, resignation accepted, approval trends for
    Carter and, 160
Laws
    wanted or not wanted against employing illegal aliens,
        254-55
    see also Abortion; Capital punishment; Gun control;
        Marijuana
Leisure activities
    do anything on daily basis that helps keep you phys-
        ically fit, 110-11

sports you have participated in during last twelve
    months, 110
sports you would like to participate in more often, 103
Libya, read or heard about Billy Carter's dealings with
    government officials of, 167
Life-style, ideal for women as married or unmarried,
    with or without children, and with or without full-
    time job, 126-27
Living costs
    as most important national problem, 47
    smallest amount needed by family of four to get along
        in this community, 69-70
        comparisons from 1937 to 1980, 71-72
    weekly family expenditures on food, 70-72
    see also Inflation
Lucey, Patrick see Anderson-Lucey ticket
Lugar, Richard, as choice for Republican vice-presiden-
    tial candidate in 1980 with and without Ford's
    vote redistributed, 141

M

McGovern, George, highly favorable ratings for in
    1972 vs. Nixon, 100, 231
Marijuana
    possession of small amounts should or should not be
        treated as criminal offense, 193-96
    should or should not be made legal, 191-93
Marriage see Family life
Military
    Carter right or not right in not consulting congres-
        sional leaders before recent military mission in
        Iran, 102
    Carter right or not right to try to rescue hostages in
        Iran with, 102
    confidence in, 246
    favor sending troops to Afghans fighting Soviets,
        sending arms, or putting only economic and dip-
        lomatic pressure on Soviet Union, 17
    force, wanted against Iran, 254
    registration see Draft
    service, women should or should not be eligible for
        combat roles, 56-58
    United States should punish Iran diplomatically and
        economically or use military force if hostages are
        released unharmed, 12-14, 84-85
    United States should punish Iran diplomatically and
        economically or use military force if one or more
        of hostages is harmed, 14-15
    see also Defense spending
Minorities
    Carter vs. Reagan vs. Anderson would do better job of
        improving conditions for, 219-20
    improving opportunities for, as choice for special
        attention of Department of Education, 180
    rights of, as issue you want candidates to debate,
        198

Mondale, Walter
    as choice for Democratic presidential candidate in 1980, 161
    in presidential trial heats of registered voters
        vs. Reagan, 117-18
        vs. Reagan and Anderson, 162-63
    ratings for, 174
    see also Carter-Mondale ticket
Moral Majority
    approve or disapprove of, 263-66
    heard or read about, 263
Morality
    decline of, as most important national problem, 47, 101, 160, 199
    favor or oppose instruction in schools dealing with, 181
Most admired man, 267-68
Most admired woman, 267
Muskie, Edmund
    as choice for Democratic presidential candidate in 1980, 161
    in presidential trial heats of registered voters vs. Reagan and Anderson, 162

N

National defense
    Carter vs. Reagan vs. Anderson would do better job of strengthening, 216-17
    see also Defense spending
National problems
    government should give greater attention to curbing inflation or reducing unemployment, 200
    most important, 47, 101, 160, 199-200
    political party best for handling, 101, 200, 231
    presidential candidate best able to handle
        Carter vs. Reagan vs. Anderson, 138
    related to low points of approval of presidents, 158
Netherlands, should or should not impose economic and diplomatic sanctions against Iran, 128-29
Neutron bomb, deferral of production of, approval trends for Carter and, 160
Newspapers, confidence in, 247
Nixon, Richard
    highly favorable ratings for in 1960 vs. Kennedy, 100, 231
    highly favorable ratings for in 1968 vs. Humphrey, 100, 231
    highly favorable ratings for in 1972 vs. McGovern, 100, 231
    low points of approval for related to principal public concerns, 158
    as most admired man, 267
Nonwhite voters
    on key voter issues compared with whites, 233-34
    support for Carter compared with other Democratic candidates, 233

    see also Black people
Nuclear power plants
    favor or oppose, 251
        Carter, Reagan, and Anderson supporters on, 191
        Evangelicals and non-Evangelicals on, 190
        nonwhite and white voters on, 233
    safe enough with present regulations or operations should be cut back, 20-21
    as single issue that would determine female and male voting behavior on, 235

O

Olympics
    favor or oppose moving 1980 summer Olympics from Moscow to another nation to protest Soviet intervention in Afghanistan, 17
    good or poor idea to establish permanent site in Greece for, 63-64
    United States should or should not participate in Moscow this summer, 62-63
Onassis, Jacqueline, as most admired woman, 267
Organized religion, confidence in, 245

P

Panama Canal treaty, ratification of, approval trends for Carter and, 160
Parents
    as choice for dealing with student behavior problems vs. school and courts, 180
    ratings on proposals for actions of schools by, 182
    should or should not be asked to meet with school personnel before each school semester, 179
    see also Education
Peace
    Carter vs. Reagan vs. Anderson would do better job of keeping United States out of war, 103, 138, 213-14
        female vs. male voters on, 235
    Carter vs. Reagan would do better job of keeping United States out of war, 103
    political party more likely to keep United States out of World War III, 199
    comparisons from 1972 to 1978, 143
Percy, Charles
    as choice for Republican presidential candidate in 1980, 3
    as choice for Republican vice-presidential candidate in 1980 with and without Ford's vote redistributed, 140-41
    heard about, 2
Physical fitness *see* Sports
Police, trial and acquittal of in Miami, as cause of racial problems, 153

Reagan-Bush vs. Carter-Mondale vs. Anderson, 144-46
Reagan-Bush vs. Carter-Mondale vs. Anderson-Lucey, 196, 201, 204-8
trends in last days of campaign, 241
unofficial election results, 241
Pressler, Larry, heard about, 3
Prices
expectations for next twelve months vs. income, 131
will go up at about same rate as in last twelve months or there will be less or more inflation, 131
see also Inflation
Problems *see* National problems; World problems
Public schools
confidence in, 178, 246
good or poor idea to give teachers training for dealing with special problems of children from one-parent families, 182
good or poor idea to make school personnel available for evening counseling with single parents, 182
good or poor idea to provide activities for children from one-parent families, 182
prayers in *see* Prayers in public schools
teachers should or should not be required to pay union dues if they do not belong to union, 184

Q

Quality of life
gotten better, stayed same, or gotten worse for blacks in United States in past ten years, 151-53
see also Black people

R

Race, likelihood of voting for Reagan if black is running mate, 141
Racial problems
Carter vs. Reagan vs. Anderson would do better job of dealing with, 221-22
issue you want candidates to debate, 198
likelihood of being serious problem in this community during next six months, 153-54
in Miami
cause of, 153
heard or read about, 153
presidential candidate best able to deal with
Carter vs. Reagan vs. Anderson, 138
Rationing, of gasoline, favor or oppose law requiring, 45-46
Ray, Robert, heard about, 3
Reagan, Nancy, as most admired woman, 267
Reagan, Ronald
best able to handle nation's problems vs. Carter and Anderson, 138
best for keeping United States out of war vs. Carter

and Anderson
female vs. male voters on, 235
best for reducing inflation vs. Carter and Anderson
female vs. male voters on, 235
best for reducing unemployment vs. Carter and Anderson
female vs. male voters on, 235
characteristics rated, 209
vs. Carter and Anderson, 154-55
as choice for Republican presidential candidate in 1980, 3
vs. Bush, 32-33
vs. Ford, 31-32
does or does not consider himself to be a born-again evangelical Christian, Evangelicals on, 186
as expected winner of presidential election, 144
heard about, 2
highly favorable ratings for vs. Carter, 100
intensity of opposition to, 80
Carter supporters on, 114
knowledge of whether or not he is appearing in television debate, 197
likelihood of voting for if black is running mate, 141
likelihood of voting for if woman is running mate, 141-42
moderate supporters of, 201
as most admired man, 267
opinion ratings, 230-31
perceived self-rated political views on, 202-3
personal appeal compared with Carter and Anderson
female and male voters on, 236
in presidential trial heats of registered Evangelicals and non-Evangelicals vs. Carter and Anderson, 184
in presidential trial heats of registered voters
vs. Carter, 5-6, 35-36, 61, 79-80, 96-97, 102, 112-14, 125, 134, 139
vs. Carter and Anderson, 80-83, 97-98, 108-9, 114-16, 125-26, 134-36, 139-40, 143, 163-64, 170-71, 184
vs. Jackson and Anderson, 163
vs. Kennedy, 8-9, 39-41, 118-19, 137
vs. Kennedy and Anderson, 163
vs. Mondale, 117-18
vs. Mondale and Anderson, 162-63
vs. Muskie and Anderson, 162
reasons for victory of, 266-67
support because of kind of man he is or positions he takes on issues, 80
supporters
attitude toward United Nations, 253
favor or oppose wage-price control reinstatement, 198
intensity of opposition to Carter, 114
intensity of support for, 80, 114, 139-40, 143, 164
likelihood of voting for Anderson with Democrat or Republican running mate, 166
support and opposition on campaign issues, 190-91

Reagan, Ronald (*continued*)
  voters for
    approval of Moral Majority, 264
    on expectations for Reagan administration, 261-62
    reasons for, 260
  would do better job of building trust in government
    vs. Carter and Anderson, 222-23
  would do better job of dealing with Arab-Israeli
    situation
    vs. Carter and Anderson, 228-29
  would do better job of dealing with racial problems
    vs. Carter and Anderson, 221-22
  would do better job of dealing with Russia
    vs. Carter, 104
    vs. Carter and Anderson, 220-21
  would do better job of handling domestic affairs
    vs. Carter and Anderson, 210-11
  would do better job of handling foreign relations
    vs. Carter and Anderson, 209-10
  would do better job of handling Iranian situation
    vs. Carter and Anderson, 215-16
  would do better job of handling women's rights
    vs. Carter and Anderson, 217-18
  would do better job of helping the poor and needy
    vs. Carter and Anderson, 226-27
  would do better job of improving and dealing with
    environmental issues
    vs. Carter and Anderson, 224-25
  would do better job of improving economy
    vs. Carter and Anderson, 218-19
  would do better job of improving energy situation
    vs. Carter and Anderson, 223-24
  would do better job of increasing respect for United
    States overseas
    vs. Carter and Anderson, 229-30
  would do better job of keeping United States out of
    war
    vs. Carter, 103
    vs. Carter and Anderson, 213-14
  would do better job of reducing inflation
    vs. Carter and Anderson, 211-12
  would do better job of reducing unemployment
    vs. Carter and Anderson, 214-15
  would do better job of spending taxpayers' money
    wisely
    vs. Carter and Anderson, 225-26
  would do better job of strengthening national defense
    vs. Carter and Anderson, 216-17
Reagan administration
  will or will not be able to balance the budget, 262
  will or will not be able to increase respect for United
    States overseas, 261-62
  will or will not be able to reduce inflation, 262
  will or will not be able to reduce the size of the federal
    government, 262
  will or will not be able to reduce unemployment, 261
Reagan-Bush ticket
  election results by demographic breakdown, 242-44

in presidential trial heats during last days of campaign
  vs. Carter-Mondale and Anderson-Lucey, 241
in presidential trial heat of former Kennedy Democrats, 208
in presidential trial heats of likely voters
  vs. Carter-Mondale and Anderson-Lucey, 236-37
in presidential trial heat of registered voters
  vs. Carter-Mondale and Anderson, 144-46
  vs. Carter-Mondale and Anderson-Lucey, 196,
    201, 204-8
reasons for election of, 249
supporters, right or wrong for Catholic cardinal to
  make statement that it was sin to vote for
  candidates who favor abortion, 239
unofficial election results for, 241
Religion
  attitude toward Bible, 186-88
  ever been born again or had a born-again experience,
    188-89
  ever tried to encourage someone to believe in Jesus
    Christ, 188
  favor or oppose constitutional amendment permitting
    prayers in public schools, 104-6
  importance of, and approval of Moral Majority, 265
  increasing or losing its influence on American life,
    106-7
  lack of commitment to, as most important national
    problem, 47
  see also Church attendance and membership; Evan-
    gelicals; Prayers in public schools
Republican presidential candidates
  choice of Ford vs. Bush, 33-34
  choice of Ford vs. Reagan, 31-32
  choice of Reagan vs. Bush, 32-33
  choices for 1980, 3
  Ford wanted as, 60-61
  heard about, 2-3
  see also Presidential elections
Republican vice-presidential candidates
  choice of by Republicans and independents, 140-41
  likelihood of voting for Reagan if black is running
    mate, 141
  likelihood of voting for Reagan if woman is running
    mate, 141-42
Richardson, Elliot
  as choice for Republican vice-presidential candidate
    in 1980 with and without Ford's vote redistrib-
    uted, 141
  heard about, 2
Roosevelt, Franklin Delano, low points of approval for
  related to principal public concerns, 158

S

Sadat, Anwar, as most admired man, 267
Salt II treaty
  heard or read about, 67

signing of, related to approval trends for Carter, 159
support for Senate ratification of, 67-68
trends in, 69
Saudi Arabia *see* "Death of a Princess"
School boards (local), should or should not have greatest influence in deciding curriculum of public schools in this community, 179
Schools *see* Education; Prayers in public schools; Public schools; Teachers
Shah of Iran, death of, will or will not mean speedier release of American hostages in Iran, 164
Simon, William, heard about, 2
Soviet Union
Carter vs. Reagan would do better job of dealing with, 103-4
Carter vs. Reagan vs. Anderson would do better job of dealing with, 138, 220-21
Carter's handling of relations with, 52-53
invasion of Afghanistan by *see* Afghanistan crisis
ratings for, 48
United States should or should not participate in Olympic games in Moscow this summer, 62-63
Speed limits, favor or oppose keeping present 55-mile-per-hour speed limit on highways, 196-97
Sports
joggers, 111
you have participated in within last twelve months, 109-10
you would like to participate in more often, 110
see also Olympics
Stassen, Harold, heard about, 2
State government
confidence in, 178
should or should not have greatest influence in deciding curriculum of public schools in this community, 179
Stevenson, Adlai
highly favorable ratings for
vs. Eisenhower in 1952, 101
vs. Eisenhower in 1956, 100, 231
Strikes, should or should not be allowed for teachers, 183-84
Sweden, should or should not impose economic and diplomatic sanctions against Iran, 129
Switzerland, should or should not impose economic and diplomatic sanctions against Iran, 129

T

Taiwan, ratings for, 48
Taxation
cut in, as issue you want candidates to debate, 198
effect of balanced federal budget on, 77-78
Teachers
good or poor idea to give special training for dealing with children from one-parent families, 182

homosexuals as
Carter, Reagan, and Anderson supporters on, 191
Evangelicals and non-Evangelicals on, 190
nonwhite and white voters favoring, 233
as single issue that would determine female and male voting behavior on, 235
nonmembers of teachers' union in school with union, should or should not be required to pay dues, 184
should or should not be permitted to strike, 183-84
should or should not spend one year as interns at half pay before certification, 183
student striking
parents, school, or courts should deal with, 180
training of, as choice for special attention of Department of Health, 180
would or would not like your child to become, 184
Television
better educational use of, as choice for special attention of Department of Education, 180
campaign debate
knowledge of participants in, 197
likelihood of watching, 197
Carter should or should not have made decision not to take part in first debate on, 197
confidence in, 248
coverage of election campaigns, changes wanted in, 253
"Death of a Princess"
seen, heard, or read about, 120
should or should not have been shown, 120
Democratic convention on
gave more or less favorable impression of Democratic party, 169
watched, 169
watchers of religious programs on
approval of Moral Majority and, 265
Teresa of Calcutta, Mother, as most admired woman, 267
Thatcher, Margaret, as most admired woman, 267
Theft, of money or clothing from other students, parents, school, or courts should deal with, 180
Thompson, Jack, heard about, 2
Thornburgh, Richard, as choice for Republican vice-presidential candidate in 1980 with and without Ford's vote redistributed, 141
Truancy, parents, school, or courts should deal with, 180
Truman, Harry, low points of approval for related to principal public concerns, 158

U

Unemployment
Carter vs. Reagan vs. Anderson would do better job of reducing, 138, 214-15
female vs. male voters on, 235
Carter's economic policies will increase, decrease, or

Unemployment (*continued*)
    have no effect on, 92-94
  vs. inflation for greater government attention, 200
  as issue you want candidates to debate, 198
  likelihood of losing your job in next twelve months, 131-33
  as most important national problem, 47, 101, 160, 199
  Reagan administration will or will not be able to reduce, 262
  U.S. government should allow immigration because of political oppression or halt all immigration until unemployment rate drops, 122-24
United Nations
  approval ratings, female vs. male on, 253
  doing good or poor job in trying to solve problems it has had to face, 251-52
    trend since 1956, 253
United States
  Carter vs. Reagan vs. Anderson would do better job of increasing overseas respect for, 229-30
  Carter vs. Reagan would do better job of keeping out of war, 103
  confidence in ability to deal wisely with world problems, 127
  confidence in institutions in, 178-79
  heard or read about Cubans leaving Cuba to come to live in, 120
  illegal immigration to *see* Illegal aliens
  ratings for, 49
  Reagan administration will or will not be able to increase respect overseas for, 261-62
  religion increasing or losing its influence on American life, 106-7
  should or should not allow Cubans leaving Cuba to live here, 120-22
  should or should not participate in Olympic games in Moscow this summer, 62-63
  status of blacks in *see* Black people
United States Congress *see* Congress
United States Supreme Court, confidence in, 246-47
Uruguay, should or should not impose economic and military sanctions against Iran, 128-29

V

Vandalism, of school property, parents, school, or courts should deal with, 180
Vice-presidential candidates
  likelihood of voting for Anderson with Democrat or Republican as running mate, 166
  ratings for Bush and Mondale, 174
  see also Democratic vice-presidential candidates; Republican vice-presidential candidates
Vocational training, as choice for special attention of Department of Education, 180

Voter participation, reasons for not voting in presidential election, 260
Voter registration
  current, 53-54, 111-12, 174-75, 185, 232
  of Evangelicals and non-Evangelicals, 185
  trends since 1968 in, 175
Voting behavior
  approval of Moral Majority and, 264
  expectations for Reagan administration and, 261-62
  intended to vote for another candidate at any time, 260
  likelihood of voting for Anderson if he chooses Democrat or Republican as running mate, 166
  likelihood of voting for presidential candidate who considers himself a born-again evangelical Christian
    Evangelicals and non-Evangelicals on, 185
  likelihood of voting for Reagan if black is running mate, 141
  likelihood of voting for Reagan if woman is running mate, 141-42
  of nonwhites *see* Nonwhite voters
  reasons for voting for Reagan, 260
  Republicans, Democrats, or hypothetical new "center" party and, 129-30
  single issue that would determine female and male voting behavior on, 235
  timing of decision between Carter, Reagan, and Anderson, 260
  voted for straight ticket or candidates of different parties, 260-61
  see also Congressional elections; Presidential trial heats

W

Wage-price controls, reinstatement wanted, 44-45, 198
Walters, Barbara, as most admired woman, 267
Weapons *see* Gun control; Firearms registration
Welfare recipients, effects of balanced federal budget on government programs for, 76-77
West Germany, should or should not impose economic sanctions against Iran, 118
Women
  approval of United Nations compared with men, 253
  favor or oppose draft registration for, 58-59, 148-49
  ideal life-style as married or unmarried, with or without children, and with or without full-time job, 126-27
  improving opportunities for, as choice for special attention of Department of Education, 180
  likelihood of voting for Reagan if woman is running mate, 141-42
  most admired *see* Most admired woman
  required or not required to participate in draft, 55-56, 148-49